WAYS OF WISDOM

WAYS OF
WISDOM

Moral Education
in the
Early National Period

JEAN E. FRIEDMAN

Including the Diary of
Rachel Mordecai Lazarus

Transcribed and edited
with the assistance of
Glenna Schroeder-Lein

The University of Georgia Press

ATHENS & LONDON

© 2001 by the University of Georgia Press
Athens, Georgia 30602
All rights reserved
Designed by Louise OFarrell
Set in 10.7/13 Adobe Garamond by G & S Typesetters, Inc.
Printed and bound by McNaughton & Gunn
The paper in this book meets the guidelines for
permanence and durability of the Committee on
Production Guidelines for Book Longevity of the
Council on Library Resources.

Printed in the United States of America

04   03   02   01   00   C   5   4   3   2   1

Library of Congress Cataloging-in-Publication Data
Friedman, Jean E.
Ways of wisdom : moral education in the early national period / Jean E. Friedman ; including The diary of Rachel Mordecai Lazarus transcribed and edited with the assistance of
Glenna Schroeder-Lein.
p. cm.
Includes bibliographical references and index.
ISBN 0-8203-2252-0 (alk. paper)
1. Moral education—United States—History.   2. Education, Humanistic—United States—History.   3. Jews—Education—United States—History—19th century.   4. Lazarus,
Rachel Mordecai, 1788–1838.   5. Edgeworth, Richard Lovell,
1744–1817.   I. Title: Moral education in the early national
period.   II. Lazarus, Rachel Mordecai, 1788–1838. Diary of
Rachel Mordecai Lazarus.   III. Schroeder-Lein, Glenna R.,
1951–   IV. Title: Diary of Rachel Mordecai Lazarus.
V. Title.
LC311 .F75 2001
370.11′4′0973—dc21   00-032541

British Library Cataloging-in-Publication Data available

To Vilmos Friedmann and his son Edward,
Anna Friedman and her sister Betty

CONTENTS

PREFACE

Ways of Wisdom is the result of my pursuit of a mystery at the center of a rational educational model that formed and directed generations of early republican women. Why did enlightened pedagogy, which proffered critical method, democratic institutional structure, and secular values, produce so many women who valued religion, honored the patriarchy, and adopted nonrational modes of inquiry? Current scholars debate the meanings of republicanism, but most authors attest to both its secular liberal and its Protestant religious ideological dimensions. Discussions of virtue, masculine courage, and female piety reveal the gendered understanding of republican moral models and the relegation of more sentimental, "benevolent" religious feelings to women. Such evidence of virtue, however, generated female political influence in the training of sons for republican citizenship. In the catalog of republican female virtues, however, one character trait remains unexamined: wisdom. Such is the power of that elusive quality that following its course led to the transformation of knowledge; wise and discerning ways adapted enlightened method to more profound ends.

This case study suggests that ethnoreligious family culture offers the subtext, the way of reading the transmutation of enlightened instruction with its secular assumptions. Two families are closely observed, the Orthodox Jewish Jacob Mordecai family as it received the enlightened method and the celebrated Anglo-Irish family of Maria Edgeworth and her father, Richard Lovell Edgeworth, who together devised the practical pedagogical model. Within the Edgeworthian method, however, is an ambivalent message of women's independence circumscribed by domesticity. Rachel Mordecai's diary, printed entirely in this book, clearly illustrates the dilemma: how to bridge the divide between enlightened critical thinking and the benevolent enlightened Jewish patriarchal family order. The rebellion of Eliza Mordecai, Rachel's pupil, demonstrates the limits of the enlightened system and stringent discipline. Instead, the dialogic process shaped the young women's synergistic identity, their inclination to cooperate with the divine will in the transformation of their lives. Providence offered hard choices, however, as the family split over religious loyalty.

The final evolution of the Edgeworthian method did not end with Rachel and Eliza's experiment. "Past Days," an Evangelical tract, relates Rachel Mordecai's biography, including her teaching experience, but eliminates all reference to the family's Jewish background. The Evangelical didacticism of "Past Days"

ix

appropriates Maria Edgeworth's enlightened teaching and fictional mode. The transition from a rational to a wholly religious educational method in the first few decades of the nineteenth century represents the often contentious ethno-religious generational split within families, a split that displaced any general understanding of the moral instruction of "republican motherhood."

There is another mystery that propelled this study: the search for my Jewish grandfather's origins. The dapper and opportunistic Vilmos Friedmann fled an Eastern European ghetto and immigrated to Bethlehem, Pennsylvania, in the late nineteenth century. He emerged as William "Billy" Friedman, a gambler who hedged his bets by opening a meat market and, later, joining the city police department. Well known as a linguist, he provided leadership for and aided the diverse immigrant population attracted to the Bethlehem Steel mills. But his marriage to my Roman Catholic grandmother, Theresa Stengel, cut him off from his Jewish family. His conversion to Roman Catholicism further embedded him in Bethlehem's predominantly Christian population. The loss of family connections and lack of understanding of my grandfather's shrouded Jewish past is a cause of grief to me. My sincere yet imperfect attempt to reconstruct historic Judaism and comprehend Jewish conversion underlies this narrative.

A word about style: In most cases I preserved the spelling, punctuation, and grammar of Rachel Mordecai Lazarus's original diary. Fortunately, Rachel wrote clearly and exercised great care about grammar. Nonetheless, as a nineteenth-century diarist she tended to overuse dashes and underuse commas; thus I replaced most dashes with commas, semicolons, or question marks as the context required. Since dialogic exchange rather than rote recitation is the mark of enlightened pedagogy, I reformatted the diary in order to highlight the dialogue between Rachel and her pupil, Eliza.

I am indebted to the many scholars and friends who aided me in the development of this study. My first acknowledgment must be of Nelson D. Lankford, editor of the *Virginia Magazine of History and Biography*. After my excited discovery of the Rachel Mordecai Lazarus diary, it was he who first approached me at the Virginia Historical Society with the idea of adding the source to the society's Document Series. When the work in progress enlarged beyond the scope of the Document Series, Nelson then kindly encouraged me to develop the study as a research project.

Francis Pollard, chief reference librarian at the Virginia Historical Society, not only provided initial direction for my research but asked astute questions that prompted further research and development of my work. Over the years I have come to value her advice and treasure her friendship.

The library staff at the Southern Historical Collection, University of North Carolina, welcomed me back to conduct research at their splendid facility. The staff's unfailing courtesy and friendly helpfulness make research there virtually painless. The Duke University Library staff enthusiastically pursued leads about the Mordecai family that contributed greatly to my research. The staff at the National Archives in Washington, D.C., offered attention to my every research problem and request despite the heavy volume of demand they manage. The Jewish Archives at Hebrew Union College in Cincinnati provided warm hospitality along with encouragement for my research. I am especially grateful to Abraham J. Peck for his kind attentions.

This project entailed an interdisciplinary understanding of educational psychology, theology, literary criticism, and family history. The study of these disparate disciplines took some time to master. Therefore, I was very grateful to the University of Georgia's Humanities Center for the grant that afforded me the time to complete the study. Lester Stephens, John Morrow, and David Roberts as successive heads of the Department of History consistently supported my work with travel grants and very constructive advice.

It has been my good fortune to count among my friends perceptive individuals whose criticism opened new levels of inquiry for me. My long and rich friendship with Nancy Felson enabled her to manage sharp criticism with deft encouragement. Her wise and generous contributions to my work and her loyal support sustain me. Carol Berkin, ever the clear-eyed critic, always tempered her comments with great humor. Judith M. McWillie reviewed my early work with great honesty and thoughtfulness. Her insights formed some of the moral understanding of this work. Laura Mason's judicious, careful analysis of my early drafts conveyed all the intensity of a tennis champion. She never let go. I am the beneficiary of her great tenacity and, I might add, of her limitless kindness. Grace Elizabeth Hale's enthusiasm and her addition of pointed comments in the body of the text have helped shape the work. I am especially grateful to my friend and colleague Joseph R. Berrigan, who entered his busy retirement with this manuscript and offered such sage advice and counsel that the work is much stronger for his expert touch. Ellen Harris patiently copyedited some of the chapters and offered valuable editorial advice. Marlene Allen of the University of Georgia Press and Mary M. Hill took charge of the manuscript and improved it; their editorial decisions enhanced the work. Among the literary critics and educators who advised me on the direction of the work I must include Tricia Lootens, Marjanne Gooze, Roxanne Eberle, and Marilyn Gootman.

Parts of chapter 3 appeared in a different version as "The Politics of Pedagogy and Judaism in the Early Republican South: The Case of Rachel and Eliza Mordecai," in *Women of the American South: A Multicultural Reader,* ed. Christie Ann Farnham (New York: New York University Press, 1997), 58–73.

INTRODUCTION

THIS IS A BOOK about wisdom, the animating principle that moved enlightened educators to reform educational practice in the post-Revolutionary period. The ways in which enlightened education fostered virtue, shaped character, and sought to teach justice and charity proved expansive as methods changed according to context and location in the transatlantic cultural community. *Ways of Wisdom* traces an Anglo-Irish enlightened pedagogical system devised by Richard Lovell Edgeworth and his daughter Maria Edgeworth and outlined in their book, *Practical Education,* as it was adopted by the Orthodox Jewish, German American Jacob Mordecai family. Edgeworthian pedagogy advanced the "education of the heart" or the method of "inducing useful and agreeable habits, well regulated sympathy and benevolent affections."[1] Lockean principles of self-control as the basis of both moral judgment and child development informed Edgeworthian pedagogy. The American pedagogy transformed the scientific, secular, critical mode into a self-critical method that created a profound religious inner dialogue of doubt and faith, order and disorder.

Recent scholarship attests to the crucial role of religion, that is, Protestantism, as an agent of change in the enlightened era that extended into the early years of the nineteenth century.[2] However, this study shows the great diversity of the post-Revolutionary period and how ethnicity and Jewish Orthodoxy prompted changes in domestic and social relations as well, initiating a generational conflict that resulted in a more expressive Romantic ethos.

Jacob Mordecai, who founded the renowned Warrenton Female Academy in 1808, and his daughter Rachel Mordecai, who experimented with the Edgeworthian method in exercises with her half sister Eliza, actively promoted critical, dialogic, scientific education, yet they also instilled ways of wisdom, the paths to holiness and intimacy with the divine. Such efforts breathed life into ordinary experience that evinced the presence of God. For "fear of the Lord" the Mordecais instilled virtue and inscribed the law or ethical principles in the hearts of their students. The pursuit of wisdom had difficult and even tragic consequences for the Mordecais because it changed their religious attitudes and identities. Yet one theme persisted: dependence upon divine initiative allied to the use of human reason.[3]

Liberal and republican ideology has provided the traditional intellectual framework for an understanding of the post-Revolutionary period. The term *liberal* refers to an emphasis upon individual rights over the republican concern with civic-mindedness that insisted upon individual sacrifice for the good of the polity. Currently, however, few historians give the terms universal application and instead insist upon their usage only if it is rooted in an historical and/or regional context. Thus, *Ways of Wisdom* views early American educational and religious changes in the lived experience of the Edgeworth and Mordecai families who disciplined, cajoled, and reasoned with an increasingly resistant and rebellious youthful generation.[4]

The Mordecai family inherited a liberal tradition from their German enlightened lineage. English-speaking, cosmopolitan, educated, this family of Jewish merchants broke the European bondage of ghettoization and immigrated to the American colonies, where they promptly joined in the cause of liberty and equality, the American Revolution. Following the Revolution, the Mordecais, the only family of Jews in the provincial town of Warrenton, North Carolina, benefited from the liberal-mindedness of their neighbors, who enthusiastically supported the Warrenton Female Academy and elected Jacob Mordecai justice of the peace. Jacob's election in the late eighteenth century took place at a time when Jews had been excluded from public office in most states. Moreover, Rachel Mordecai, in a letter to Maria Edgeworth, remarked upon the townspeople's lack of prejudice against Jews.

The liberalism of the eighteenth century increasingly gave way in the middle decades of the nineteenth century to the growth of slavery and the defense of the institution in the South. The Mordecais owned slaves and therefore cannot be placed wholly in the liberal tradition. The conundrum of equal rights and slavery confronted Rachel Mordecai during the Nat Turner rebellion, when her own slaves allied themselves to the conspiracy, yet she abstained from embracing abolition. Thus only an historic and regional understanding of liberalism can make sense of the Mordecais' enlightened ideology.

Jewish orthodoxy framed the liberal tradition in the Mordecai household. The reverence for the name of God, the awareness of the workings of Providence, the celebration of the holy days instilled a sense of the presence of God. Members of the Mordecai family, disciplined in religious orthodoxy yet exposed to enlightened critical thinking, developed a special religious integrity. At once dependent upon and confident of the divine Providence of God, Mordecai family members such as Rachel, Eliza, and Ellen pursued their personal paths to holiness. Mordecai women exhibited independence most especially in the pursuit of holiness. Eliza remained an Orthodox Jew, although Rachel and Ellen converted to Christianity. Religious choice involved a conflicted path of self-criticism.

Classical republicans defined their interest in terms of the common good, the ideal community protected by individuals who practiced civic virtue. Republicans promoted virtue as a bulwark against monarchical and executive corruption. Households, too, delegated responsibility for the training of virtue to fathers and mothers, but especially mothers, in the late eighteenth century. The "republican mother" accepted the charge to nurture independent male citizens, not dependent subjects. The early republic then mandated a social mission to inculcate virtue and foster wisdom in men and in the women who reared them.[5] Enlightened sages believed that wisdom, implanted by nature, improved the faculties, offered useful employment for human abilities, and determined good judgment. The source of wisdom lay in the rational capacity to perceive, extend, and order knowledge and experience. Since the extension of knowledge fostered virtue, and virtue promoted happiness, the republican concept of wisdom advanced optimism and progress.[6]

Orthodox Jewish training involved discipline in obedience to the Commandments. The Mosaic Covenant that established the Law instituted a patriarchy responsible for observance of the Commandments. The Orthodox tradition, then, constituted an American republican paradox: the teaching of virtue within a highly stratified family order. Traditional covenanted family order restrained the spirit of freedom upheld by the practice of republican virtue. Republican pursuit of the common good as interpreted in an Orthodox Jewish household meant family unity as well as political participation by white males.

The introduction of wisdom, secular and biblical, into the discussion of early national education reveals the contested nature of moral formation in the first years of the nineteenth century. Republican mothers, assigned to their children's and especially their sons' moral development, adopted, expanded, modified, and challenged received enlightened educational theory according to their family experience and religious wisdom. As female pupils and mentors contested and revised the discipline and rigor of the method, they implanted conflict at the heart of post-Revolutionary character training. The conflict reveals enlightened pedagogy at the intersection of the gender, ethnic, religious, and moral issues that formed the independent yet deferential female identity associated with the political stability of the republic. Moreover, enlightened pedagogy retained its ability to create new female identities out of generational conflict well into the early decades of the nineteenth century. Wisdom, then, represented a way of seeing in scientific, dichotomous terms or, more ambiguously, beyond contradictions or paradoxes to faith in new patterns.[7]

Rachel Mordecai, a Jewish schoolteacher, kept a diary from 1816 (when she was twenty-seven years old) to 1822 that records the moral instruction of her half sister Eliza. Her diary retains the traditional character of wisdom literature, that is, the didactic books of the Bible: Psalms, Proverbs, Job, and Ecclesiastes. It offers a didactic narrative that assumed training was a family matter and determined the boundaries of order according to the Torah. Divine Providence, present at all times in traditional wisdom books, suffused Rachel's chronicle as she sought divine will through prayer in ordinary, concrete circumstances. With the aid of Providence she willingly faced the difficult contradictions of good and evil present in herself and in her charge. With her reason and will allied to Providence, Rachel Mordecai sought knowledge and meaning in both secular and Orthodox Jewish terms.[8]

This case study bears particular importance for scholars as it qualifies and enriches our understanding of the American Enlightenment as an amalgam of religious and ethnic assumptions and reinterprets "republican motherhood" as a culturally diverse and politically complicated domestic paradigm. The Anglo-Irish Edgeworthian pedagogy adapted by Rachel played out across Atlantic boundaries of cultural space and time. Rachel Mordecai's diary describes private educational practices that raise questions about the consequences for the public order: How was social order imposed in the early republic? How were British educational ideas represented to Americans? And how were enlightened texts received in ethnic and religious communities? Why did subsequent generations reject received educational principles? How did enlightened pedagogy change with the development of teacher and pupil?

Chapter 1 examines the evolution of the Mordecai family from an intellectually enlightened to a culturally assimilated family. The practice of the Edgeworthian method never remained discrete in the Mordecai household as family structure, values, and domestic education adapted to an enlightened model and family members negotiated new boundaries of identity, power, and authority in the early republic. Yet in correspondence with the Edgeworths, Rachel Mordecai challenged Maria Edgeworth's preconceptions about Jews. The evolutionary process, never consistent or complete, nonetheless disputed traditional religious values and patriarchal authority. That challenge to patriarchal power, however, remained ambivalent because of the mixed messages of enlightened Edgeworthian pedagogy and experience.

Chapter 2 analyzes the Edgeworth family ideology as imbricated in family structure and form. Although the Edgeworth method enlarged upon Lockean principles of democratic family structure and character formation, reciprocal dependence distinguished Edgeworth family organization.[9] Although forms of property underwent change in early-nineteenth-century Britain, land was still considered the embodiment of virtue and status. Thus the Edgeworths could embrace economic individualism without seeing individuals themselves as autonomous.[10] Through their publications the Edgeworths represented themselves as a model rational family. Nonetheless, although Richard Lovell Edgeworth mentored each of his children, few achieved independent status apart from their father. Lovell Edgeworth, in rivalry with his father, undermined his own career as an educator. Francis attempted an independent literary and teaching career; however, after becoming involved in a scandal, he moved back to Edgeworthstown, Ireland, the family home. Contrary to enlightened gender order, the Edgeworth women provided the rational, stable environment for the volatile and irrational Edgeworth men. Thus, Edgeworthstown imbued Maria Edgeworth with her contradictory sense of women's domestic mission as allied to both benevolent patriarchy and independent rational thought. This internal inconsistency within Edgeworthian fiction and pedagogy shaped an American and Continental "textual community" of educators.[11]

An analysis of Rachel Mordecai's experiment is the focus of chapter 3. In an attempt to understand the breakdown of Edgeworthian method in the face of its inherent contradiction, an examination of contemporary developmental theory informs this study. An explication of each stage of growth and its possibilities gives some depth to the struggles of the child, Eliza, in a text written entirely from the teacher's point of view. The young tutor embraced *Practical Education* and created an objective, abstract world of strict "model relations" for her half sister.[12] When Eliza refused to conform to enlightened patterns of behavior but instead reacted against them with temper tantrums, indifference, and defiance, she challenged the Edgeworthian contradiction: critical thinking subservient to patriarchal family order. Rachel then began to question her own disciplinary practices and adopted a more democratic model of authority. Her wisdom to adapt emanated from Orthodox Judaism and her sensitivity to Eliza's stages of development.

Chapter 4 accounts for the disparate effects of method on the two sisters. Rachel's ethical model, Edgeworthian pedagogy, encouraged children's individuation, but Rachel herself initially held to strict Jewish patriarchal modes of discipline. Nonetheless, she directed Eliza toward imagination, wonder, and longing in the appreciation of nature and literature. Eliza's education grounded her in faith; she displayed confidence in her own value judgments, in knowing where authentic good lay. Although Rachel communicated critical thinking and a malleable structure of discipline, Eliza learned in an Orthodox household threatened by forces of assimilation. Subsequently, Eliza chose the traditional bonds of family and religion over a rigorous intellectual life. Nevertheless, Eliza's moral education propelled her in new directions toward social activism, works of charity, and, eventually, a hallowed death. Dialogue with Maria Edgeworth on many subjects, most important, slavery, heightened Rachel's critical powers. Furthermore, Rachel's intellectual questioning coincided with reform movements within Judaism that challenged traditional authority. Her Jewishness had identified Rachel with her father's strict discipline and intellectuality. When she later chose to copy her mother's model of righteousness, she followed a spiritual path that eventually led to a circle of devout Christian women in Wilmington, North Carolina. Converting to Christianity on her deathbed, Rachel sacrificed family ties and chose instead Evangelical holiness.

Chapter 5 presents an Evangelical literary perception of the Mordecai teaching lessons. The author of "Past Days," the pseudonymous L.N., reinterprets Rachel's life and uses the dialogic method to conform to Evangelical moral principles. This chapter demonstrates the malleability of method and the resultant transformation of individuals within the Mordecai family. The Mordecai family history is portrayed as Evangelical, not Jewish, in this story; self-creation, not assimilation, remains a central narrative element. The rational, open-ended means to a virtuous, harmonious, secular society of autonomous individuals is transformed by the Evangelical narrative into consideration of a nonrational, spirit-directed performance of duties that conform to a spiritual purpose, salvation, and the establishment of religious community.

Ways of Wisdom suggests that the historical construction of self and community in the early nineteenth century included a moral and spiritual process accomplished in different generations through the transformation of intellectual method. The European enlightened experiment operated within a geographically and culturally diverse American environment where educational method did not exist apart from family values or structure. Indeed, wisdom often filled the space between theory and the lived experience of mothers and teachers. Wisdom's handiwork, according to the Psalmist, is the renewal of life;[13] wisdom, then, had its ways of translating republican domestic precept into new forms of Victorian cultural values and social principles.

WAYS OF WISDOM

CHAPTER I

MORDECAI FAMILY WISDOM

Rachel Mordecai
and Family Pedagogy

ɪɔɑɪɔɑɪɔɑɪɔɑɪɔɑɪɔɑɪɔɑɪɔɑɪɔɑɪɔɑɪɔɑɪɔɑɪɔɑɪɔɑɪɔɑɪɔɑ

Enlightened Education

IN 1808, WHEN Jacob Mordecai, a scholarly ex-merchant and an Orthodox Jew of German descent, decided to open the Warrenton Female Academy and offer one of the finest educations for women in the South, he stressed in his advertising handbill, "My object [is] not merely to impart words and exhibit things, but chiefly to form the mind to the labour of thinking upon and understanding what is taught."[1] Clearly, Jacob Mordecai intended the formation of critical thinking, the mark of enlightened education, in young female minds. His daughter Rachel Mordecai, who taught in her father's academy, inherited an enthusiasm for enlightened method and initiated an experiment: she tutored her seven-year-old half sister Eliza according to *Practical Education,* Richard Lovell Edgeworth and his daughter Maria Edgeworth's guide to enlightened, dialogic education. However, the fact that the Mordecais' progressive pedagogy developed in the context of an Orthodox Jewish household makes all the difference in understanding enlightened education as liberal, ethnic, and religious. That distinction proves important in the history of American education because it demonstrates the strains involved in the transition to enlightened pedagogy. In addition, the new consciousness concerning the developmental stages of children, including females, advanced the ethnic and religious adaptation of republican maternal values.

Post-Revolutionary scholars split in their interpretation of republican pedagogy, of how to adapt utilitarian education to the demands of a growing commercial society. The Jeffersonian school encouraged home education as a means of undirected open discourse conducive to a marketplace of ideas. Other educational promoters such as Benjamin Rush and Noah Webster preferred an institutional approach that provided a more systematic, even centralized education that instilled republican values. Whether home-bound or institutional, education in the late eighteenth and early nineteenth centuries proved family-centered. For instance, the new approach to women's education, an insistence upon the use of reason instead of ornamental skill, set domestic parameters for republican women, namely, service to the family.[2]

The Warrenton Female Academy, an illustrious school in Warrenton, North Carolina, offered a curriculum comparable to that of men's schools and exemplified the new republican institution. It was a "nursery of virtue" and hard discipline that prepared even a class-bound young white woman for a variety of casual public roles, as a moral or religious leader or as a defender of her family during a civil crisis.[3] In contrast, Rachel, although a seasoned teacher at the academy, undertook the home education of her half sister Eliza because she did not want her contaminated by the manners and habits of other schoolchildren. She viewed moral education as apt teaching only in the household. Rachel's attitude, remarkable in light of the prestige of her family's academy, reflects both class bias toward tutors and an ideological predilection toward the Jeffersonian or progressive pedagogy. Home education appealed to Rachel because she could openly inculcate Jewish Orthodox precepts in her half sister while instructing her in enlightened subjects such as science, language, history, and grammar.

Religious and Republican Wisdom

Republican educational ideologies did not divide along religious lines. Home education did not offer the sole means of teaching religious principles. Noah Webster, in his enthusiasm for a dominant national culture, equated civic virtue with Protestant Christian morality. A good citizen lived the Christian life.[4] Benjamin Rush, more tolerant of all religious contributions to education, nonetheless believed that "a Christian cannot fail of being a Republican."[5] As Jews the Mordecais offered their own contribution to enlightened education by combining it with Orthodox discipline. In doing so they preserved a religious and cultural wisdom.

At the Warrenton Female Academy, renowned for its discipline and enlightened education, young women read the classics, studied science and mathematics, and thus learned critical thinking. Family members taught and supervised the young women, and in a real sense the academy operated as an extension of the Mordecai household. The school bridged the distance between enlightened ideology and Jewish Orthodoxy, since the Warrenton Female Academy offered the enlightened method while the Mordecais kept an Orthodox household.

The European Enlightenment, disposed toward experiment, reform, and progress, inspired a largely middle-class but ethnically and religiously varied educational movement in the early American republic. Since enlightened education implied the inculcation of moral precepts at various stages of maturation, the nature of enlightened education adapted itself to different ethnic and religious perceptions of morality and development. John Locke noted that "through education human progress, including moral progress, might be promoted."[6] Thomas Jefferson, "a pioneer in this new era of education," according to one historian, promoted the teaching of the classics because "they furnish ethical writings highly and justly esteemed."[7] Enlightened human development instilled a habit of curiosity and criticism that often took the form of a "dialectical interplay" between religion and secular philosophies.[8] Thus the adaptation of the enlightened method did not obscure ethnic and religious considerations of moral wisdom.

Religious wisdom interprets order and meaning in raw experience as the revelation of Providence. According to Jewish tradition, what human experience reveals is often ambiguous and chaotic; love and fear of the Lord, however, lead to an openness, a willingness to accept on faith inevitable consequences or new patterns.[9] Christian thinkers absorbed Jewish concepts and considered wisdom a gift endowed by God and enhanced by reading the Bible. Religious believers insisted that human reason has its limitations, as demonstrated in the Book of Job when God asks, "Where were you when I laid the earth's foundations?"[10] American author Edward Wilkinson expressed the limits of reason in his work "Wisdom—a Poem": "Reason ever wanders wide, / Unless she walks with Wisdom by her side."[11]

The mysterious ways of Providence could be understood only by the pure of heart, those of unquestionable character. Ministers asserted that the character of magistrates determined prosperity, and children learned that good behavior shone as an ornament of wisdom. An implicit faith in wisdom's secret Providence assumed that evil subserved good. The secret Providence or wisdom promoted the highest good, the true interest of society at large, the law by which humankind lived. Providence upheld unselfishness or benevolence as the chief judicial principle.[12]

Education offered the principal means of obtaining enlightened moral wisdom. In 1798 Samuel Harrison Smith, in his prize-winning essay "Remarks on Education: Illustrating the Close Connection between Virtue and Wisdom . . . ," observed the centrality of wisdom in education. He defined wisdom as "that intelligent principle which improves our faculties, affords them the means of useful exertion, and determines the objects on which they are exercised."[13] Smith implied that moral reason, as opposed to contemplative wisdom, or Sophia, ought to steer American educational reform. Education, then, mea-

sured by utility, had pragmatic rather than theoretical consequences. Early republican enlightened and religious scholars may have differed on the source of
wisdom, natural or divine, but both factions accepted the limits of human reason and recognized experience as an enhancement to understanding.

Some southern plantation households eagerly embraced those enlightened
approaches to schooling that discouraged ignorant offspring and instead encouraged thrifty, industrious, self-restrained, and self-reliant children.[14] The
Mordecai academy, influenced by Orthodox Jewish discipline, enlightened Ger-
manic culture, and scholarly endeavor, reinforced the progressive method. The
critical method, which held matters of social and private concern, religion, family, and government to rational standards of consent and scientific scrutiny, also
offered a tolerant exchange of views and freedom of expression, conditions conducive to egalitarian social relations. For Jews the Enlightenment offered another opportunity for salvation or projection into the world.[15] In this way the
enlightened method, whatever its inducements to assimilation, did not open a
singular path but a crossroads toward diverse and complex definitions of gender
and religious self in the early republic.

Gender Roles in the Republic

Rachel Mordecai adapted her father's enlightened methods and Orthodox discipline to her educational experiment in Edgeworthian pedagogy, tested on her
beloved Eliza. *Practical Education,* or "education of the heart," offered the in-
ducement of "useful and agreeable habits, well regulated sympathy and benevolent affections," in short, a warm yet disciplined heart devoted to the practice of
virtue.[16] The experiment, carried out in an Orthodox Jewish household, however, subtly transformed the sisters. Stubborn, vital, intelligent, and clever, the
child Eliza not only challenged her sister's authority and ultimately worked out
a more cooperative method of teaching but created her own romantic Victorian
sensibility. For Rachel, whose strict and rational method constrained a vulnerable and generous nature, the experiment shattered her conventional notions of
teaching and exposed her to the deeper wisdom of trust in divine Providence.
In sum, the sisters made their own way through gendered development cast in
enlightened and religious terms.

The new republic's claim of egalitarian, contractual notions of family obligation obscured the reality of paternal hegemony, a "Republic of Men," a nation
constructed to protect the liberty, equality, and citizenship of males to the exclu-
sion of female rights and citizenship.[17] Historian Mark E. Kann argues that,
nonetheless, within the rhetorical gap complex definitions of male self emerged.
The traditional patriarch's powers destabilized between 1750 and 1800 with the

expansion of economic opportunity, population increase, and commercial development. A companionate ideal motivated by the notion of marital contract emerged with Whig ideology. Moreover, the "self-made manhood" engendered by an entrepreneurial spirit gave rise to an ethic of sobriety and thrift. Alternative male ideals contributed to an acknowledgment of republican women as independent, educated, efficient managers of households and, in some cases, businesses. Tension arose as female independence, perceived as "disorderly," threatened male hierarchy. Defensively, men educated women to cultural and moral standards that valued female subordination, according to Kann.[18]

Kann's observations involve a process in which relationships change, adapt, and resist. It is within this process of liberalizing paternalism that women shaped their own lives in a way as complex as men's lives. The post-Revolutionary period contained at least four different typologies of womanhood: the conservative model, which prescribed a wholly subordinate domestic role for women; the liberal model, which insisted upon equality between the sexes; the radical notion, which recognized individual rights; and the romantic ideal, which followed the inclinations of the heart. The most consistent ideal expressed in middle-class white marriages was the companionate, and it initiated tension between the sexes in definition and purpose. Women simply aspired to greater reciprocity in marriage than men did.[19]

Certainly, the demands of hierarchy and obedience proved less commanding than they had before the American Revolution. Enlightened ideology, with its attack on fixed social orders, addressed rational individuals who nonetheless acted for the common good. Individual integrity, then, proved the measure of the republic, as new demands were placed upon its members, especially women. According to enlightened practice, mothers fostered virtue and wisdom in their children and accepted responsibility for the nurturance of independent male citizens. However, because the republic existed as a mix of peoples, diverse in folkways, the definition of virtue and its instruction proved an amalgam, a repository of ethnic and religious wisdom as well as secular ideology. The republic's special mission to inculcate virtue and foster wisdom, then, resulted in increased attention to women's education.[20]

The education of women as "republican mothers," trained to nurture their sons to become independent citizens, entailed a perilous venture, one with no fixed path. Experimentation in women's education proved to be an exciting experience but produced unexpected results. The younger generation preserved tradition while expanding definitions of domestic boundaries. Republican mentors questioned patriarchal bonds and experienced both confusion and a more mature sense of female independence. As academies and schools offered women advances in education, women themselves struggled to balance new forms of knowledge with traditional ideas of order and hierarchy. Enlightened education, however, began in the home, where women faced the tensions of a changing family structure.

The Mordecai Family

For Orthodox Jews, education contained within it all the contradictions and rewards of dialogue with enlightened secular culture. As German Jews the Mordecais maintained a connection to enlightened social and intellectual currents that gave them a predilection toward secular education. The family also engaged in trade and business.

The beginnings of Mordecai family history can be traced to Moses Mordecai, father of Jacob, who was born in 1707 in Bonn, Germany, a trading center on the banks of the Rhine. The Mordecais, who were of German Jewish descent, inherited notions of enlightened Continental reform, namely, a progressive dialogic educational system that included women. German scholar Moses Mendelssohn established the link between enlightened and Orthodox thought. He studied Locke, Leibniz, and Wolff and then discovered that natural religion was most compatible with his own religion. Only later did he return to his Jewish identity. His work opened German Jews to the educational possibilities of enlightened culture, namely, status and mobility.[21]

Moses Mordecai's trading ventures exposed him to larger possibilities of prosperity and status as well as a desire for learning. He immigrated to England, attracted by its commercial opportunities and liberalized culture. There he married a Jewish convert, Elizabeth Whitlock, who subsequently changed her name to Esther. For the most part heterogeneous and tolerant, the Jewish community in London nonetheless enforced Sephardic proscriptions against marriage to converts. In addition, resident Jewish aliens in England suffered the disabilities of second-class citizenship. Foreign-born Jews could not own land, invest in British shipping, or enter the colonial trade. Perhaps the limited commercial benefits allotted to Jews and the social strictures against converts, although not immediately relevant to Ashkenazic Jews, strengthened Moses' decision to immigrate to America.[22]

Before the Revolution, the couple migrated to Philadelphia, where Moses, a broker, engaged in business, established a reputation for strict integrity, and lived a righteous life. In addition, he pursued learning. Moses Mordecai's library contained many books, among them the classics and a history of the Bible. Moses' ownership of secular books of classical learning indicates his predisposition toward the enlightened German and Continental tradition. The oldest of Moses' three sons, Jacob, born in 1762, absorbed the German Jewish enlightened dilemma in his passion for the classics and his study of Bible history. Later,

Jacob devoted himself to Jewish scholarship when secular culture provoked his own doubts about Judaism. But during the Revolution educated patriots mined the classical tradition for justification for their rebellion. Jacob lived in a patriot family; in 1765 his father signed the Non-Importation Agreement, the protest of a "trading people" that included Jewish merchants such as Michael and Barnard Gratz, and Esther Mordecai upheld the boycott within her household. These parental actions radicalized the young Jacob.[23]

Jacob enthusiastically supported the Revolution and embraced the cause of American nationalism. His devotion to liberty, however, was tempered by educational discipline. In 1774, at the age of twelve, he was sent to a large school run by Capt. Joseph Stiles, a former officer in the British navy who taught mathematics and navigation and enforced a very rigid discipline. Early in the Revolution Captain Stiles was appointed commissary of military stores. The schoolboys then joined town and country military associations. Later, in a letter to his grandson, Jacob remembered that "their uniform generally was a hunting shirt dyed as fancy pointed, and the youths of the schools and colleges in Philadelphia formed themselves in companies distinguished by different colors, armed with guns and trained to military exercise."[24] Young Jacob Mordecai marched with schoolboy companies from Frankfort, Pennsylvania, to Philadelphia in order to escort the First American Congress into the City of Brotherly Love.[25]

After his service Jacob was apprenticed to David Franks, a Jewish trader whose business extended along the western frontier. Early in Jacob's career Moses died in 1781 at the age of seventy-four. Later Esther remarried; she and her new husband, Jacob I. Cohen, a businessman from Philadelphia, settled in Richmond, Virginia. Jacob lived in Richmond for a few years as a junior partner of Cohen and Isaacs but then moved to New York, where he joined Haym Solomon's brokerage firm.

Judith Mordecai: The Maternal Sage

While in New York Jacob transacted business with the Myers family, a connection that may have led him to his future wife.[26] Judith Myers was the daughter of Elkaleh Cohen and Myer Myers, a renowned New York silversmith. During the British invasion of New York the Myerses had fled to Norwalk, Connecticut. After the Revolution Judith lived in Philadelphia with her beloved brother Samuel and her friends. There Jacob, also staying in Philadelphia during this period, encountered Judith, and a "union of hearts commenced."[27] Jacob remembered the "soft and lively expression" of her hazel eyes. "Her whole nature expressed animation and energy yet she remained discrete," Jacob recalled.[28] Discretion only deepened Judith's longing. She wrote, "My inclination to converse with you is so great I cannot refrain [from] telling you how much I wish to see [and] to hear you and to express the tender affection which so unites me to the most deserving and kindest of partners." [29]

After their marriage Jacob had difficulty in setting up an independent commercial venture. In Virginia he tried Goochland County, Richmond, and Petersburg. Finally, the loyal Judith followed him to Warrenton, North Carolina, a trading center that grew prosperous from cotton and tobacco.[30] Their third child and eldest daughter, Rachel, was born there on 1 July 1788. The couple had six children. The family kept the laws of kashrut and observed the High Holidays. As his family grew, Jacob's connections to Richmond never weakened; he was among those who in 1789 founded the first Jewish congregation in Richmond, Beth Shalome. Later, Jacob presided as president of the congregation.[31]

Judith was a devoted wife and mother. When illness necessitated sending Moses to her parents, she coveted every word about him. She assured her parents: "The account you give me of my dear Moses is a cordial to my heart. Do tell him that I love him tenderly." [32] The children flourished under the affectionate care of their mother. Judith mentioned in a letter to her mother that Rachel, Ellen, and Solomon were dancing a reel. "They are old hands at it," she remarked. Judith was a gifted teacher, much admired for her training of the children in reading and spelling. She believed in positive reinforcement. Her daughters developed expert sewing skills because she consistently complimented the girls on their progress.[33] True to Jewish tradition, however, Judith did not believe in "pecuniary rewards," which corrupted children's motivation.[34] Virtue needed no reward. A loving context, not harsh discipline, favored the children's development. Rachel, Moses, Samuel, Ellen, Solomon, and Caroline venerated their mother for her insistence upon virtue and her kindly, patient teaching. Judith Mordecai bound her children to her wisdom; she represented the maternal sage whose authority rested in her household.[35]

Judith's health, always delicate, declined with her seventh pregnancy, and she died on 9 January 1796.[36] She left behind her young family, among them the seven-year-old Rachel, to grieve her loss. Jacob, the afflicted husband, attempted composure in grief. He admitted to his fellow Masonic lodge members, "I find there is no reasoning down our feelings when the heart is corroded by affliction. I will endeavor to 'resist the shock' with becoming fortitude, and to bear this affliction with a rational composure." [37] Privately, Jacob poured out his grief in an anguished letter to his children, whose care had been entrusted to relatives. Their father's letter must have caused them to feel even more keenly the loss of their mother. In his narrative he preserved for his children the memory of Judith as a model of virtue. Although forced to flee several times during the Revolution, Jacob maintained, Judith "always persevered in improving in virtue no matter what the circumstances." In addition, Judith remained "attentive to knowledge."[38] Jacob admonished the children to "bear in remembrance the Virtues of your Mother and venerate her memory."[39] He sent the children their mother's letters and directed them to see "the soundness of her Judgment, the Purity of her Ideas, & the Perspicuity of her State in which Virtue, Truth, & Candour is displayed in language Natural, easy & unaffected."[40]

Judith preserved the order of righteousness and of wisdom: she directed the children "in the path of virtue . . . to lisp praise and adoration to the Father of Mercy." Judith instilled in her children the traditions of holiness, faithfulness to God, and generosity to others: she determined that character training took place always in the presence of God. Jacob recalled that at the moment of her death Judith prayed that "God would keep her children in the path of virtue."[41] Judith inspired her children to "let virtue and prudence ever be your guide."[42]

On her deathbed Judith implored Jacob to "bring [the children] up in the paths of Virtue." She admonished him with explicit instructions carefully drawn to cover his failings and elicit his best efforts. She said, "In correcting their faults never let passion govern you but on all occasions Reprehend them with coolness but with Firmness . . . let them consider you as their best friend . . . be to them the kind endearing Father as you have been the tender, affectionate husband to me."[43] In an effort to impress the virtuous life upon his children, Jacob wrote down and systematized the virtues Judith taught: "Avoid pride . . . Let affability and good Humor be your constant study . . . Avoid being censorious . . . Endeavor to keep on good terms with all the world but place confidence in few . . . Let Virtue and Prudence ever be your guide."[44] Singular in virtue, Judith willed her family a legacy of righteousness.

Unable to manage a large family on his own, Jacob sent the children to relatives willing to care for them. Rachel and her sister Ellen stayed with their mother's brother, Samuel Myers. Moses, Samuel, and Solomon remained with their father in Warrenton.[45] Her mother's death, followed by the breakup of the family, must have had a traumatic effect on Rachel. There is evidence that she presented discipline problems for the Myers family. Rachel's behavior, interpreted as ingratitude by Jacob, masked her grief. He advised her to heed his counsel and to observe strictly the advice of her uncle and aunt:

> Inattention to the counsel of our friends who are zealous to promote our welfare is at all times and in every situation inexcusable. It is a species of ingratitude that will tend to alienate their affections, for when their well meant endeavors to form the mind, cultivate the manners, and improve the person are either obstinately opposed or carelessly attended to their attempts ceasing to be a pleasure, disgust ensues, and we become almost indifferent to the welfare of any one capable of making an unkind, improper, and painful return for our good intentions.[46]

Jacob considered discipline essential to character formation. He admonished Rachel, "Rise early, pay adorations to the Father of Mercy . . . be obedient to the advice you receive . . . and be particularly attentive to cleanliness and avoid every species of sullenness."[47] He admonished Rachel to examine her conduct and correct her errors. "Difficulties always decrease when we encounter them with firmness," he said, "and what at first view appears very difficult, soon becomes familiar, easy, and agreeable."[48] Halakhah, the law of the consciousness of God in all things, required obedience and self-control; upon such discipline rested emergence of the godly element, the distinguishing character of Jewish righteousness.[49]

Jacob expected his daughter to follow his model of grief—self-composure. Alone, abandoned by her family, Rachel learned the price of emotional indulgence—the threat of further loss. But Jacob's tact balanced threat with assurance. Jacob's assertion that "the goodness of your heart will ensure you success and secure the esteem of your kind patrons" places his confidence in her. His reasoning follows Orthodox tradition, which emphasizes moral responsibility in individual choice: a Jew must do good consciously. That same advice conveys a rational moral sense: reasonable practice leads to virtue.[50] Perhaps Rachel, the lonely child, believed that she could earn her father's love as she earned virtue. Preoccupation with her father's acceptance marks her early development. Jacob tied his encouragement of Rachel's intellectual ability to her love for him. He wrote: "Nature has been very bountiful to you, and it is only requisite to use your gifts in order to attain a competent share of knowledge . . . Direct your mind to perfect itself in acquiring an ample share of useful instruction, Reading, Writing and a tolerable knowledge of Arithmetic . . . in short my dearest Rachel I entreat you by the tender affection I know you have for me to improve."[51]

Jacob sent Rachel books and wanted to know her opinion of them. His early solicitude cemented an intellectual relationship between father and daughter.[52] His expectations for her suggest only a conventional level of attainment, however. "I wish to see you an amiable woman, esteemed by your acquaintances and beloved by your relatives & friends for the gentleness of your manners, affability of disposition & adherence to Truth & Candour," he wrote.[53] Obviously, the father upheld Judith as the role model. As a young woman, Rachel valued her intellectual ability, which engaged her father, and carefully constrained any emotional response that might distance him.

Separation from her father and family most certainly did not prepare her for adjustment to her father's second marriage. Jacob acceded to Orthodox custom and married Judith's half-sister, Rebecca Myers. That union produced seven more children. Rebecca Mordecai proved to be a loving and affectionate wife and mother. However, Judith's daughters resented their stepmother's lack of management skills and chafed under the routine of caring for the younger siblings. The eldest daughter complained, "Scarcely have the first years of infancy passed before the entire charge devolves on us, of forming the dispositions, improving the mind, even taking care of the apparel of each child in the family— this we must do, or see all neglected." [54]

From their early teens the older daughters carried a large share of responsibility for the raising of their younger siblings. Nonetheless, Rachel's heavy household responsibilities gave her experience in tending to and educating young children. Rachel described to her brother Samuel her involvement with the care and training of the children: "Caroline and Judy are very well at home. George (age 4) begins to spell. He comes very regularly to me everyday with his book to say his lesson." [55] The young tutor also commented to Sam on the progress of the other siblings, who are reading Maria Edgeworth's works: "Eliza thanks you and so do I for copies of Early Lessons. She can understand a good deal of them now." Alfred "peruses them," and Augustine "divides his researches between Little Frank & Gulliver's Travels," writes Rachel. [56] Not surprisingly, enlightened education marked Rachel's instruction of her younger brothers and sisters. She wrote enthusiastically, "Everything from the pen of Miss Edgeworth, contains so much good sense, so much instruction, & so many useful hints on the subject of Education, that to those earnestly engaged in that pursuit they are invaluable." [57] Satisfaction but also weariness characterized Rachel's domestic teaching experience. In the bone-numbing round of domestic duties, the emotional needs of an eldest daughter carried little importance. Nonetheless, the management of children became increasingly the business of the Mordecai household.

Warrenton Female Academy

In 1807 a financial crisis turned Jacob Mordecai's career toward scholarship and teaching. The tension between the United States and Great Britain placed increased pressure upon the business community and made speculation risky. The Embargo Act effectively stopped both imports and exports. Jacob's investments in tobacco exports ruined him. He sacrificed business and home to pay for his business reverses. [58] Like his father, Jacob had been regarded as an honest businessman, and he endeavored to pay his debts. The impoverished former businessman accepted his lot cheerfully, since the commercial life did not particularly suit him. [59]

Jacob Mordecai preferred the life of a Jewish layman-scholar. One historian compared him to a medieval Jewish sage who demonstrated not only scholarly ability but was useful as a leader in the community. [60] Jacob served both the Jewish and non-Jewish members of his community. Because he acquired an excellent knowledge of Hebrew, he presided at weddings and read at funerals. The men of Warrenton valued Jacob's counsel since he served for twenty years as a justice of the peace. As counselor and leader in his community, Jacob appeared to be the model of a wise man.

Jacob's associates prevailed on him to consider teaching. At first, Jacob supervised the young men's academy in Warrenton. He then considered opening a boarding school for young women. As a sage creates order and propriety, Jacob Mordecai set the foundational principles for such a school.[61] Familiar with progressive pedagogy, he advertised that his school would use the critical method adapted to the stages of growth of his pupils. The notice that circulated on handbills in the summer of 1808 stated that Jacob Mordecai's course of instruction was "the result of observation and some experience and will be adopted to the varied dispositions of the genius of my pupils, not losing sight of systematic Arrangement and Progression. My object not merely to impart words and exhibit things, but chiefly to form the mind to the labour of thinking upon and understanding what is taught."[62] Edgeworthian pedagogy, based on Lockean principles, advanced education as an "experimental science" and adopted observation and experiment as its tools. Enlightened educational theory also recognized stages in childhood learning and development and thus tailored teaching to the individual student. Dialogue, crucial to traditional Jewish and enlightened method, established a critical method of inquiry.

Jacob's vision was exceptional: the new school was the first in the South to offer a curriculum for young women roughly comparable to young men's education. Unlike boys' schools, the Warrenton Female Academy did not offer programmatic courses in the classics, science, and higher mathematics, but students read in those subjects. So enthusiastic were his business associates that a Mr. Miller, who first proposed the idea to Jacob, supported him consistently, delivering the first wagonload of girls, remodeling a store as a schoolroom, and even teaching music.[63] The young pupils represented a southern elite, daughters of planters, professionals, and businessmen. Their education added to their status and hence their chances for marriage.[64]

The Warrenton Female Academy emerged as an innovative school that advanced beyond the mid-eighteenth-century French boarding schools operating in American cities. The French schools emphasized the ornamental arts, needlework, dancing, and penmanship and only gradually added more basic courses such as arithmetic and reading. Such schools appealed to members of the rising American middle class, who used genteel education to solidify their status among the cultural elite. Ornamental education did not make wives the equal of husbands but garnered women some influence in elite social circles.

The Revolution challenged aristocratic education just as the post-Revolutionary period recognized the independence and ability of women to contribute to public life as mothers and teachers. Benjamin Rush encouraged a rigorous curriculum for women that included mathematics, classics, and natural philosophy on the assumption that such ambitious study would make them better wives. Their education would also include a political role, giving them the ability to instill civic culture into their children, especially their sons. The education of women improved dramatically after 1800 as academies offered classical languages and introduced new courses in the sciences and mathematics. Young women benefited from substantive curricula that raised academic subjects to core courses and relegated the ornamental arts to electives. Proprietors of academies also carefully emphasized the extended-family atmosphere of their academies.[65]

Enlightened pedagogy paralleled the critical teaching and scholarly tradition of Orthodox Judaism. Jewish Orthodoxy, grounded in the Torah, is founded upon a teaching tradition; the word *Torah* means "the teaching," of doctrine and practice, religion and morals. The teachings of the Torah emanated from the Mosaic Covenant with its implications for holiness and the "priestly mission" of the Ten Commandments. Holiness is bound up in the ethic of service and the avoidance of idolatry. Religious laws form an educational purpose—"to train the Israelite in self-control" is the first step in the attainment of holiness.[66] The ethical system teaches and trains both individual and society the way to holiness. It is essential, then, that the moral and religious strictures emanate from the heart—an intuitive response to God and other human beings. The Torah then concerns itself with attitude, disposition, intent—that which would predispose the individual toward God, with an enlivened generosity and love.[67] Orthodox Judaism and Edgeworthian pedagogy both recognized that the teaching of knowledge and virtue had to originate in the heart. The Edgeworths believed that habits sensibly taught with love and restraint built character. A child with estimable character recognized larger concerns of self-government, such as charity and benevolence, according to Edgeworthian theory.

Within the traditional household, the natural development of children created tension between absolute authority and the necessary demands of growing children. Traditional rabbinical literature recognized latency stages in children: ages five through seven were appropriate for the memorization of religious stories, followed by a legal age of religious responsibility such as fasting and an age of reasoning by association and abstraction, and finally, adulthood, marriage, and family.[68] Lockean educational theory identified stages in childhood development in which the habits of virtue, wisdom, courtesy, and learning were taught, adapted to age and temperament.[69] Enlightened theory identified maturity with growing independence from parental authority.

The Warrenton Female Academy opened in 1809 with a faculty of family members and three hired teachers.[70] Rachel Mordecai, nineteen years old, anxiously faced her first year of teaching. She wrote to her brother Samuel: "I only wish this week were over; I do not like to acknowledge even to myself, how much I dread it—I endeavor by constant employment to prevent my mind from dwelling on it, but believe me . . . when I reflect on my too conspicuous situation, I sometimes feel awfully agitated, and turn almost sick—a thousand faults hitherto unobserved will be [magnified?]." [71] Rachel suffered the agitation typical of a novice teacher. Her circumstances, however, were not typical. Only a minority of women taught school in the early republic; the feminization of primary education would take place in the middle decades of the nineteenth century.

Rachel preserved her equilibrium with the knowledge that she supported her father. She reflected: "Yet again when I think I now have it in my power, to oblige the best of fathers, to prove my affection for him, to assist and relieve him of part of his burden, all other ideas for a moment give place to one so dear, so heartfelt, I feel my resolution revive; and urged on by such incentives, think nothing too arduous for me to attempt, or impossible for me to succeed in." [72] Rachel interpreted her efforts as proof of her affection for her father, as if something in their relationship remained to be proved. Yet Rachel embarked on a partnership with her father; she assumed an active role as manager and teacher. Rachel believed that her contribution was part of a family venture, but her participation revised her self-perception and inspired self-confidence.

The Warrenton Female Academy offered grammar, reading, writing, arithmetic, composition, history, geography, literature, and languages. Advanced students read the *Iliad* in the original Greek, an innovation at Warrenton, since only male academies taught the classics as an entrance requirement to the professions. [73] Formal science courses such as chemistry, astronomy, and biology were not offered as American educational reformer Benjamin Rush proposed. [74] Nonetheless, Jacob Mordecai recruited his son Solomon, who attended nearby St. George's Academy, to teach, and he informally taught first principles in science to his sisters and students. The school relegated needlework, drawing, and painting to second place. Perhaps to elevate standards in the ornamental arts, the dance instructor taught his pupils to dance "scientifically." [75]

Dialogue as represented in *Practical Education* remained the primary pedagogical tool. Rachel's diary bears evidence of that, and Solomon delighted in the exchange of ideas with his students. Questions about twilight may have prompted the meticulous graphs drawn to explain the mathematical relationship between the sun and the horizon. [76] Moreover, the school stressed the use of maps and globes. [77] Maps and globes reinforced scientific precision with a specific spatial sense. When Samuel, Jacob and Judith's second son, sailed to Portugal on a business mission, he sent the family a detailed map of the coast; he then used the map to pinpoint the locations of his business ventures, especially in the port of Algeciras in Spain. [78] The use of practical tools such as maps and globes and scientific and mathematical experiments to hone observation and enhance inductive skills demonstrated the Mordecais' understanding of progressive educational reform.

In spite of such progressive educational ideas, the school's pedagogical method varied. The school retained rote learning; recitation of place-names associated with historic importance played an important part in the curriculum. In addition, Jacob's sense of propriety or traditional wisdom suggested the necessity of strict discipline; the school paid careful attention to bathing and personal hygiene.

Initially, the Mordecais taught thirty-two scholars, a number that increased daily. Success became apparent almost immediately as more young women enrolled in the school. Ellen noted that family solidarity resulted: "We expected it [the school] would be a great deal of trouble, but really, I think the family is more regular than it was before; and upon the whole I like it very well." [79] Certainly, the success of the school rested on the collective family endeavors. The rising number of scholars meant an increased demand for teachers. Moses, Jacob's eldest son, who, along with Solomon, attended St. George's Academy, studied law in 1807 and began practice in 1808 at the same time that his father opened the school. Moses assisted his father in negotiations for buying the school building. Later he participated in a play the family put on to entertain students after their public examinations. Solomon remained at the academy as long as his health lasted. He quickly became one of the children's favorites, teasing them into an understanding of mathematics. Jacob planned to keep Solomon at the school for a year and then send him to Princeton or some other northern college. [80]

Solomon also kept the accounts, a job that entitled him to an office. The office afforded him peace and quiet so that he could continue his medical studies. It also offered a haven to his sisters, whom he tutored. [81] Rachel became an apt and determined student. In her memoirs she wrote: "Amiable in youth and in manhood, [Solomon] took delight in bestowing the time alloted for recreation to impart to his sisters the lessons he had been receiving, . . . and I, with the strongest motives to sustain me to exertion, found nothing too difficult to be attempted for the acquisition of knowledge." [82] Solomon taught his sisters science and mathematics, areas of advanced learning traditionally closed to women. Rachel found it "inspiring" to learn the forbidden subjects, and she hardly knew herself for entertaining such ambition. Grateful to Samuel for leaving his library at home while he traveled, Rachel proudly noted,

If you have ever thought of their station at all, you have probably supposed Hume, Shakespeare, Fielding etc. ranged in neat shelves round the office, but you must cast your eyes a little farther, & a little higher, and you will find a small press in my room converted into a book case, into which if a stranger was to peep, the sight of Encyclopaedias innumerable, Classicks, and History, would at once establish my fame as a learned lady. The books you borrowed of Mr. M[arx] papa has perused with great satisfaction, and as he read them to me, I too may boast being somewhat skilled in ancient lore.[83]

Rachel, a conscientious student, regularly devoted her free hours to study; she usually had a book or some educational material in hand. She retained an interest in optics throughout her life. Her preoccupation with science and enlightened rational discourse marked her as an uncommon republican woman.

Rachel's intellectual discipline as well as her teaching method allayed her insecurities as a teacher. Her approach to teaching differed from her father's. Although Jacob Mordecai admired progressive theory, he observed a stringent disciplinary regime likened by one historian to an English public school overlaid with the strictures of a Jewish patriarchy.[84] In contrast, Rachel's insecurities as a teacher forced her to temper fear with kindness. She recalled how she overcame the difficulty of not being old enough to command respect. She said, "I would seek to substitute for it a desire of pleasing which could only be obtained by implanting love instead of fear. By being kind as well as just, by entering into the little pleasures and sympathizing with the little troubles of children, we soon obtain their confidence and affection."[85] Kindness, the mark of her mother's teaching, perhaps remained instilled in Rachel's memory. Rabbinical literature distinguished between fear out of love and fear out of punishment. The latter proved inferior, according to the wisdom of the sages.[86] Republican idealism, influenced by Protestant morality, assumed that in a postpatriarchal world love would replace fear among virtuous individuals.[87] Benevolence—the desire to do good out of a sense of fairness, not out of exaggerated sympathy or sentimentality—characterized Rachel's kindness.

Increasingly, objectivity took hold of her perception and judgment of the children, causing her to gain self-confidence. Not without irony, she noted in a letter to Samuel, "'Tis strange how people will sometimes forget themselves; here am I seated in my chair of authority, where tomorrow my frown (very awful I assure you) will be the ordainer of sadness, and my smiles the harbinger of happiness and good humour to a score and a half of little animals who look up to me with all due deference and respect."[88] Although writing in jest, she wished her brother not to hold her remarks as a stain upon her character, known for "sedateness and wisdom."[89] Rachel remained protective of her character because her usual mature demeanor elicited confidence in her counsel. Although Jacob Mordecai managed the school, advertising for pupils, hiring faculty, and ordering supplies, Rachel tended to the details and gave advice. In effect, she acted as assistant manager, although she regarded her role as a necessary measure of family agency, to act for "the best of fathers."

For instance, when Jacob asked Samuel to hire an aide or assistant teacher, Rachel provided the job description. Rachel instructed Samuel:

> I believe he [father] mentioned to you his wish that you would endeavour to procure a proper assistant should increasing numbers render one necessary; I should not suppose that this would be very difficult, as the qualifications requisite, are merely correctness of deportment; a knowledge of Arithmetick, and writing.—$300 would I suppose be considered a sufficient salary, and such an assistant, ten or fifteen more [pupils] could be done strict justice to.—This I give as my real opinion, and you know I am very conscientious, at least Moses says so.[90]

Obviously, Jacob involved Rachel in the business of the school, and Rachel felt entitled to discuss such important matters as salary. Yet, careful not to overstep the bounds of gender, she added an ironic line to dispel the purely executive nature of her letter. On another occasion, Rachel took the initiative and commissioned Sam to advertise for and hire an embroidery teacher. Since Rachel regarded such a teacher as auxiliary to the faculty, she believed her agency would only relieve her father of one more care.[91] Jacob never countermanded Rachel's directives.

The source of Rachel's confidence in herself and in her own opinions lay in her experience and in her faith in Providence. The cares of the school weighed upon the young teacher, but she trusted that her actions would not go unrewarded. "May we not . . . rely on that merciful providence, which with a benignant eye watches over its creatures, and believe that virtuous endeavours will not be suffered to pass unheeded or without their just recompence," she wrote.[92] When her brother Samuel embarked upon a long business trip to Spain, Rachel expressed her concern for his safety and added: "They who submit to circumstances, and place a constant and undeviating confidence in the protection of Heaven, are surely most worthy of its favour, the latter I feel in its full extent, the former has long been, & still is my study, and I think I find it proved, that to seek is to gain; for I am more patient now than formerly, and to what other cause can it be attributed?"[93] Certainly, hers was not a passive faith; she expected reward for virtue and only gradually accepted her circumstances. And as often as she struggled to reconcile "reason and affection,"[94] rational control over her mind substituted for spiritual serenity in her soul.

In her early maturity Rachel displayed an uncommon self-possession. When Samuel, crushed by the rejection of a young woman, appealed to his sister for sympathy and encouragement, Rachel wept over Samuel's plight but counseled him, "The more you acquire the mastery over your own mind, the less powerful will be the conflict, and the sooner will you find it returned to its accustomed equanimity."[95] In short, Rachel discovered the power of self-control. She wrote:

"I cannot conceive a sensation more grateful, more animating, than that of having gained a victory over one's self—not in action alone, but in feeling, to be able to look down in contempt on the littleness of selfishness, of envy, which by the weakness and imperfection of our nature, had arisen and threatened to hold us captive." [96] Having gained self-control, Rachel internalized her father's values and thus achieved a righteous character. Overtaken by the power of rational restraint, Rachel absorbed an ideology of virtue that allowed her to conceal her emotional conflict about grief and loss.

Self-mastery allowed Rachel to dream of autonomy, an exceptional desire in the new republic dedicated to women's domestic virtue. In the summer of 1816, soon after she began to write her diary, she dreamed that she challenged a proud male. The dream excited her and prompted her to recount her dream experience in detail to her sister Ellen. She claimed that "not one word of embellishment" tainted her recounting of it. She also explained the dream to Sam:

> I had gone with a large party to hear an oration on the fourth of July. Major Gibbons came up to our party and after paying his compliments generally, passed individually along the row saying something appropriate to each lady. I happened to be the very last, and the two just before me, were very silly, insignificant girls; to the first of them he said, "don't you think you are the finest girl in the room?" She replied in the negative, and he repeated the same enquiry to the next. I now seemed to be reflecting that if he addressed it to me, he should have an answer, and when he said immediately after, "and don't you?" I laid my hand on his arm and looking up at him said, "Oh, Major! have not you something new to say to me?" He looked a little confounded, and said, "No." "O, then," said I, "you have not so much address as Mr. Jefferson . . ." It was pretty smart for a dream. The Major I thought went off, and I heard him say, I had behaved most shamefully. A little after this, the ladies rose to go. "What," said I, "are we to have no oration?" "I think," said the major, who stood opposite, looking at me, "I have heard an oration, at any rate." I then went up to him and said, "I think Major Gibbon I was severe, perhaps a little rude but I acknowledge it was intentional, for I thought you had not sufficient respect for my feelings, and wished to make me appear ridiculous. However, I do not wish to think any more of it and hope you will not." I held out my hand to him, which he took with one of his sweet smiles and we parted good friends. [97]

In the dream Major Gibbon affected a patronizing manner; Rachel openly challenged him out of her own resentment and won. She dreamed of a patriarchy that accepted and understood her feelings. The dream ends in reconciliation. Rachel may have imagined a society where women commanded a status equal to men, for instance, a society where her father recognized her contribution to the Warrenton Female Academy as being as invaluable as his.

Ellen commented on Rachel's dream that Rachel was "not half so smart awake." [98] In reality, the self-possessed Rachel remained discreet. Common wisdom demanded propriety, the right moment, the right action. The antebellum southern patriarchy rarely allowed public circumstance to present a subversive sexual challenge; thus Rachel relegated the struggle for autonomy to the dream world. But the enthusiasm lay in the recounting of her victory, a victory she obviously relished. If wisdom presented itself in Rachel's dream as contradiction, [99] then Rachel would have to learn through experience the way of wisdom.

The family's scholarly enthusiasm generated an excitement and pleasure in learning. Students never forgot their encounters with Rachel, Solomon, Moses, and the kindly Rebecca Mordecai. [100] The school flourished, and by May 1809 Jacob Mordecai, who was steward of the Warrenton Male Academy, decided to devote himself full time to his own school. He declined management of the boys' school because management of the Female Academy proved more profitable. The problems of management convinced Jacob that no advantage existed in supervising the two schools. Instead, he made plans to buy the house from Judge Oliver Fitts and expand the academy to include about one hundred preadolescent and adolescent girls who attended elementary and secondary divisions within the school. The school included Jewish girls among its pupils. [101]

The Warrenton Female Academy prepared for its first examinations in the spring of 1809. Rachel experienced "much anxiety . . . not unmixed with confidence." Her confidence lay in the numbers of students whom Rachel believed were a credit to the academy, students Rachel trained. At first the faculty decided on a private semi-annual examination, but since many parents indicated they would be present at the end of term, the instructors changed their plans to a riskier public examination. Samuel Nicolson, the retired principal of the Warrenton Male Academy, presided over the exercises. [102]

Public examinations received reviews much like plays or novels. The *Petersburg Intelligencer* gave the Warrenton Female Academy's academic performance high marks. Rachel exulted at the "most ample success" that crowned "our unremitted exertions." Only the praise and commendations calmed the "violent" inner turmoil and the fears of Rachel, an inexperienced teacher. Her relief at the pupils' performance gave her confidence. The success of the school prompted Samuel to remind Rachel, "Do you recollect the dissatisfaction you used to express at occupying uselessly a space on this planet?" [103] Few women in the early republic received such public affirmation as Rachel did.

The judges and all the parents present signed a letter expressing their "highest satisfaction" with the examination. The pupils acquitted themselves so well that the judges could not decide among them. Most gratifying to the Mordecai family, however, was the case of the Fayetteville mother who had earlier informed the school that she planned to transfer her daughter to the well-regarded Raleigh Academy. But the mother, impressed with the examination and her daughter's progress, assured the Mordecais that she would not remove her daughter. Rachel noted that the Fayetteville mother "was convinced that she would not derive equal advantages at any other seminary." [104]

Laudatory reviews continued during the school's existence. The *Raleigh Star* called the Mordecai school an "excellent Seminary" and commented upon the faculty's exemplary literary taste. Students read Addison and Pope, not "silly novels." The critic's comments on literature communicated the academy's serious purpose. Young women did not waste their time on reading romances or, worse, cultivating their emotions. [105] Academy women, then, were trained to be sensible and reasonable. Moreover, the academy advanced enlightened art. The *Raleigh Star* effused that student artists "are copyists, but they only copy from nature," [106] which suggests innovation and the ability to rely on one's own powers of observation for creativity. William Crawford, principal of the Warrenton Male Academy, credited "very accurate Knowledge" and "unmistakable progress" to the students. The parents appreciated the blooming health of their children and recommended the school as a "nursery of virtue." [107]

What convinced Rachel of the school's productivity and its power to compete against other local academies was its method. "I know that our method is excellent and that if children are capable of receiving instruction we must improve them, I also know that our perseverance is not of a nature to be subdued by obstacles, or to wear away with time." [108] The Mordecais followed Orthodox wisdom and enlightened assumptions that scholastic accomplishments rested upon virtue and wisdom. Jewish wisdom assumed that all knowledge began with fear of the Lord. The Lockean first principle advised the inculcation of the true notion of the nature of God cultivated by prayerful devotions. All other relations, to self and others, followed upon the first principle, according to Locke. Locke admonished scholars, "if anyone should wish to make this virtue his own, there are two chief places that must be frequented early and often: the hall where men may learn to debate and the temple where they may learn to pray." [109] The first principle fostered diligence, innocence, and obedience, and the effects of such virtue overflowed to others. Thus virtue, "hard and valuable," directed education, and the school became a "nursery of virtue." [110]

Jacob Mordecai encouraged attendance at religious services; most of his students were Protestant Christians. In addition, he instilled regular habits by insisting that students wash their own eating utensils, bathe regularly, and attend to their personal grooming. Mordecai laid the hard lesson of discipline upon the recalcitrant and indifferent. He kept a record of student habits in a system of "checks and blocks" and made each pupil accountable for her behavior. [111]

Strict discipline and sensible, not sentimental, behavior characterized virtue at the Warrenton Female Academy.

Warrenton supported the academy's advanced educational and disciplinary methods; the proof lay in the town's response to a fire at the school. On 29 April 1811, one of the pupils left a candle burning in her room. The fire that resulted reduced the Mordecais' "extensive range of buildings" to ashes. The prompt action of a number of Warrenton residents saved much of the furniture. In addition, the students of the Male Academy acted with exemplary "alacrity and zeal." Judge Fitts offered a spacious building he owned as a refuge for the dispossessed Mordecai family. Neighbors kindly took in the female students. The school reopened in a rented building a few days after the fire.[112] A Wilmington paper hoped "that the confidence which has hitherto been deservedly bestowed on Mr. Mordecai, in entrusting a part of the rising generation to his care, will be so far increased as to make him forget his present loss, in future and increased emoluments."[113]

Despite the crises and problems, Ellen Mordecai recollected the period before 1816 in the academy's existence as the "Golden Age when every pupil was a sister and friend."[114] Yet even with the school's renowned reputation, family cooperation, and community support, internal tensions and external pressures exerted a powerful inclination in Jacob Mordecai to close the school. By 1816 the school's growth reached its natural limit. The increase in size increased the responsibilities and trials of the Mordecais. That year an especially vindictive thirteen-year-old girl who had been reprimanded set the school on fire and wished "all the Mordecais burned up in it!"[115] When confronted, she coolly replied, "I do not care if I have set the house on fire."[116] The school was forced to expel the unrepentant arsonist.

One hundred children attended the academy, and approximately 30 percent boarded. "Not a moment of our lives is free from anxiety and the apprehensions of evil," Ellen complained.[117] Rachel wrote an ironic commentary on the variety of responsibilities the family endured for their pupils. She complained to Sam that parents expected the Mordecais to follow all their different charges, such as: "I will thank you to see that my child does not eat snow, I know she is mighty apt to do it at home . . . My little girl, Miss Mordecai has a habit of biting her nails, which I will thank you to attend to."[118] In addition to caring for the numerous children, trouble of a different sort occurred when a Mr. Price started rumors that the children were overcrowded and received insufficient food. Alarmed parents attempted to remove their children, but the pupils insisted upon staying; thus the young women themselves scotched the rumors.[119]

Despite the family's cohesion under adversity, members felt the strain. "Our poor Rachel is almost worn out. What a life hers has been!" Ellen noted. Caroline, too, appeared overworked, as she had taken over Ellen's household duties in addition to teaching. Caroline and George replaced Solomon, whose delicate health forced him to give up teaching in 1817.[120] The family's arduous task ended in 1818 when Jacob sold the school. One resident commented that the sale of the school "seems like a death in the town."[121]

The Mordecai Family's Social Isolation

The Warrenton community held the Mordecais in high regard, but the town's support did not obscure the Mordecais' intellectual and religious isolation. Warrenton remained an insular town, despite the presence of male and female academies. Ellen commented on a relative's visit to Fayette, North Carolina, and compared that city to Warrenton. She wrote, "The inhabitants there [are] not like Warrentonians but polite, hospitable, friendly and amiable; that is they can speak of something else besides the defects of their neighbors."[122] Ironically, later in life Ellen wrote a thinly disguised novel about Warrenton in which her neighbors are portrayed with less compassion than humor. She wrote, "Hastings [Warrenton] was composed of a most choicely original collection of people, such as are seldom to be found in a much larger community."[123] Neighborly visits amused and appalled the Mordecais; the family wished for more refined company. Rachel worried that perhaps the family was "too refined." She said,

> [N]othing can be more certain than that we perceive a great difference between ourselves, and the generality of those with whom we associate, either here or elsewhere. . . . [I]f we are not exactly like the fluttering, unthinking herd who pity us, & whom we pity, it must be attributed to circumstances alone. Misfortune opened our eyes to the deceitfulness of the world, reflection taught us, that most of its boasted pleasures were vain, and unworthy the pursuit of a thinking mind; and the want of other society, made us look for it within our domestick circle.[124]

The Warrenton Mordecais bristled when Richmond family and friends did not appreciate their cultured status. When Richmond visitors praised the society of the Mordecais, Rachel chafed, "They know not that we were known. Thought of us as a family of mushrooms who started now and then in their gay city just to glimmer a faint light and sink into our grave . . . Warrenton again."[125] Intellectually and culturally, the Mordecai presence proved a contradiction in the provincial town. Certainly, the Mordecais minded intellectual deprivation, but anti-Semitism increased their isolation.

Rachel Mordecai insisted in a letter to Maria Edgeworth that the success of the school proved "the estimation in which persons of our persuasion are held in this country." As an example she mentioned that her father served as county and town justice of the peace for twenty years.[126] Jacob Mordecai was one of the first generation of Jews allowed to hold office. Furthermore, Samuel, Jacob's son, occupied a prominent place as a merchant in Richmond. When a fire in a Richmond theater claimed the lives of sixty persons, including several Jews,[127] Samuel delivered a memorial in the synagogue on behalf of the victims. His "Discourse" reflected the patriotism of Jews who had gained citizenship in the Revolution. Samuel expressed his "admiration of the liberality which exists in this our happy country, among members of conflicting religions, and of different sects: a liberality superior to vulgar prejudices, and which marks a man's actions, not his particular religious professions, nor his wealth the criterion of his respectability."[128] Thus Samuel spoke in terms of Revolutionary idealism that included a rational concept of virtue and toleration. He ignored the more blatant forms of bourgeois liberalism that upheld class distinctions based on property. But Samuel, a successful merchant, represented status and respectability. Jacob Mordecai would later note, ironically, "As citizens of the United States [Jews are] entitled to equal privileges with others but in many of the states . . . their political rights depend more upon courtesy than upon constitutional equality or privileges."[129]

The American Revolution provided a receptive context for the adoption of enlightened practices, within limits. Before the Revolution American Jews had enjoyed civil rights—naturalization, mobility, and economic rights. The colonies, however, denied Jews political rights. Although religious toleration was practiced throughout the colonies, in many the established church taxed all colonists, regardless of religious affiliation. After the Revolution the Jews achieved political equality on the federal level since the First Amendment guaranteed freedom of worship. In the next struggle American Jews witnessed the realization of political rights—the franchise and the right to hold office at the state level.[130] Virginia's Bill of Rights, which included freedom of religion, necessitated the passage of an enabling act in 1785 and granted Jews the right to vote. Virginia and New York were the only states that allowed full political participation.[131]

As Jewish citizens pressured state and local governments for equal rights under the law, families and individuals increasingly dealt with the forces of assimilation. Ethnic diversity absorbed Jewish distinctiveness, and commercial identity submerged Jewish identity as gentiles increasingly patronized Jewish businesses. Prosperity encouraged Jewish social mobility and assimilated rising middle-class Jews into the prevailing bourgeois culture. The merchant, not the Talmudic scholar, gained prominence among Jews. Business partnerships with gentiles and social acceptance promoted greater American rather than ethnic or religious identity.[132]

The Evangelical Challenge

Despite evidence of Anglo-American liberality and Jewish assimilation, the Mordecais experienced anti-Jewish sentiments in Christian proselytization efforts and Evangelical belief in divine judgment against those not "born again." At the turn of the century, the Second Great Awakening aroused Christian missionary efforts that extended to Jews. Scandalized, Rachel reported to her brother in 1810, "Methodism is at present the rage . . . what do you think of its being reported all over the county that papa has become one of the elect, many will swear to the minister whose eloquence converted him, and some one positively contradicted Dr. Gloster the other day and offered him any bet of its being the case! What would our grandmama say should her ear be profaned by the report?" [133] Jacob Mordecai blamed reports of his conversion not on his deportment, which he characterized as unimpeachable, but upon the zealous rivalry between Evangelical religious sects in Warrenton, where there were few converts. Evangelical proselytization efforts only reinforced his beliefs and strengthened his faith and hope "in the only true God—the lord of hosts the God of Israel." Now his consciousness as a Jew went beyond dogma, and he expressed a deep desire "to follow the divine commands and conform to the precepts of our holy religion." [134]

Jacob Mordecai read Jewish apologia intensively, especially the work of David Levi, whose polemical work galvanized American Jews isolated in cities and towns familiar with only the most fluid notions of Judaism. Jacob I. Cohen, Jacob Mordecai's stepfather, owned copies of Levi's work. Since that work rested on biblical scholarship, Jacob Mordecai intensified his study of the Scriptures.[135] The Mordecai family also used Rabbi Solomon Jacob Cohen's catechism, *Elements of Jewish Faith*,[136] to train the younger children. Jacob presided over a household that followed the dietary laws and observed the High Holidays. The family also possessed a copy of "On the Festivals, Games, & Amusements of the Ancient Jews," an essay, apologist in tone, that described ritual joy and reverence in the observance of ancient practices. The essay may have been written by one of the Mordecai daughters.[137] American culture attenuated the Mordecai family's strictness of observance, however; members of the family read novels and wrote business letters on the Sabbath.[138] The child Eliza nonetheless evinced guilt about carrying heavy planks on the Sabbath.[139]

Despite his family's less than strict observance, Jacob continued his scholarly efforts. Perhaps his religious renewal redoubled Evangelical proselytization efforts. In 1814 Richard Blount, a former student who was an Evangelical, exhorted Jacob to study the prophets. Jacob replied emphatically that "he had studied them." The Reverend Adam Empie, an Evangelical Episcopalian preacher and organizer of the Diocese of North Carolina, made overtures to proselytize him. Rachel, by this time accustomed to Evangelical overtures, reflected, "It is curious enough and somewhat flattering too, that so many should feel themselves so much interested in papa's conversion and eternal welfare. There is no doubt that it was Mr. Empie's sole object in visiting Warrenton about a week ago."[140] Discussions between the two men led to a published dialogue on the subject of Jewish religion.[141] In addition to Reverend Empie, a converted Jew also directed his religious arguments to Jacob Mordecai.[142]

The case of a Mordecai cousin, Henrietta Marx, gave evidence of persistent Christian proselytization efforts. Henrietta Marx was a cultured, very learned woman who suffered from childhood neuroses. Her instability grew in her adult life, and she often relapsed into bouts of insanity. The family suspected that a Baptist servant baptized Henrietta during a bout with delirium. The servant told a member of her congregation that Henrietta had converted, and the story then circulated that Henrietta was baptized.[143] In another instance a family friend volunteered to stay with Henrietta, but family members discovered that the friend's intent was to convert Henrietta. The family felt keenly betrayed.[144] Ellen Mordecai believed that the cause of Henrietta's malady was "the want of fixed religious principles."[145]

Henrietta's plight marked a family crisis. Christian proselytization threatened to destroy the Jewish family. The family members drew together to protect one another against both the strains caused by Henrietta's illness and the intrusive Christian environment. Evangelical insistence that those not born again would suffer damnation presented the most dogmatic stance to the beleaguered Jewish family. On Washington's birthday in 1818 Samuel Mordecai mused that for all of his virtues, "Washington himself is probably consigned to eternal damnation" because he was not born again.[146]

Cultural isolation raised the question of salvation or projection into the world. Only in the collective would prophetic morality find its unique voice, yet to embrace American culture meant the eclipse of Jewish tradition, language, ritual. Additionally, individual solitude posed a threat to the salvific collectivity.[147] Such contradictions bred insecurities within the Mordecai family as they faced the difficulty of remaining a religious minority within American society.

The Effects of Cultural Isolation

According to rabbinical literature, an individual lives among the people, and the "Children of Israel" bear a singular personality. God made the covenant with a chosen people, not a chosen individual. In addition, dyadic rather than individual relationships characterized traditional Mediterranean peoples. The individual within the early modern Jewish family might apply reason to the precepts of faith yet never deny traditional authority. An individual might differ intellectually with Jewish tradition, but Jewish authority would not tolerate behavioral deviation.[148] The process by which an individual moved toward differentiation occurred with subtle power in the Jewish family at the turn of the century.[149] Assimilation affected men and women differently; men had greater opportunities to differentiate themselves from family authority, since they inhabited the public world of business and the professions. Women, with less chance to lead independent lives, faced a more difficult task of differentiation.

The patterns of dependence and independence may be traced in the Mordecai family. Solomon and Ellen Mordecai demonstrated a psychological and emotional dependence that disrupted family harmony and the family enterprise. Ellen never surrendered her devotion to her brother until he died. Solomon entered a profession, married, and moved away; thus he effectively severed an overly intense familial tie. In contrast to Ellen and Solomon's intense relationship, Rachel accomplished a more balanced intimacy with her brothers and sisters. She often intervened in matters of the heart and urged greater independence among intimates. Her preference for less dependent relationships may have resulted from her responsibility as eldest daughter in the family and teacher in the school.

Within the Mordecai family, Solomon, Ellen, and Rachel, Judith's children, were especially close and offered each other the nurturance they craved. Thus all three interpreted their emotional security in terms of each other. Solomon's study brought them a measure of privacy in an overcrowded household; it was there they studied and huddled together before the fire. Ellen made a brown straw carpet for Solomon's "Office Chamber" from the broomsedge found in the vicinity of Warrenton.[150] In Solomon's office the trio developed a new level of intimacy expressed in a deep concern for each other's welfare. When Ellen complained of constant pain in her side, Rachel, "in her kindest, gentlest manner," urged Ellen to "give up [her] business." Rachel advised Ellen to hand over her household tasks to Julia, a younger sister: "She is young, and has never known trouble in her life. You have been laboring and struggling ever since you were born—now you are unable to bear it longer. Therefore think of it no more as your business."[151] Both Solomon and Ellen were in frail health, but at one point, when Rachel fussed over them too much, they laughed at her. Although Rachel addressed Solomon as "dearly beloved," she advised him to leave home for medical school lest he should be interrupted in his studies by domestic affairs. When Solomon did depart for Philadelphia Medical College, Rachel and Ellen met alone in the dining room, threw their arms around each other, and wept.[152] Solomon's departure demonstrated the intensity of family unity. As Rachel noted, each family member was acutely identified with the others, so that the experience of one was the experience of all. Rachel explained to Solomon the reason why the family eagerly awaited his letters:

> Your hopes, your fears, your intentions is the occupation which most tenderly awakens ours and so well is each, acquainted with the strain accordant to the mind of each, that let one note be struck and the whole chord forms itself insensibly, and fills the ear and the heart . . . all that you say of yourself is reciprocated, or rather anticipated in our ideas . . . We have from our peculiar situation so completely imbibed the habits and sentiments of each other that it has . . . unfitted us for the enjoyment of common every day intercourse with a heartless world: we sigh in vain for that delicacy, that correctness of principle and warmth of feeling, which implanted by nature, has been cherished by books, with which we have conversed more than with man.[153]

Intellectual and social isolation reinforced identification and intimacy within the family.

Intermarriage

Rachel's intervention in Ellen and Solomon's relationship demonstrates her role as family broker. She counseled separation of Ellen and Solomon, encouraging Solomon to persevere in his studies and supporting Ellen in her teaching and writing. But earlier Ellen had negotiated the family's acceptance of Moses' marriage to a Christian. Rachel and Ellen acted similarly to enlightened German Jewish women who used their secular education to facilitate family members' adaptation to the host country's intellectual and cultural values. Rachel and Ellen both played key roles in influencing parental acceptance of their siblings' mixed marriages.

The question of mixed marriages presented the most problematic issue for Jews. At stake lay Orthodox tradition—the sacred collective and the preservation of prophetic morality. Rachel and Ellen weighed tradition against American demands of personal happiness and negotiated freedom of choice for their siblings. With these individual choices the contradiction of Jewish morality and culture to American society remained less clear. The early republic provided few Jewish marital partners. Family resistance to non-Jewish partners ultimately collapsed under pressure from children who insisted upon marriage to the person of their choice. Marriages to Christians resulted in crises of Jewish family identity.

Evangelical southern culture, tolerant of Jewish practice, nonetheless set up barriers to mixed-faith marriages. In the context of such assimilationist pressure, Rachel and Ellen steered a delicate course. They perceived no impediment to mixed marriages, provided the partners held equal social and intellectual rank.

Thus among third-generation Jewish American women status as well as religion complicated the prospects of a mixed marriage. Rachel's and Ellen's views affected Samuel's and Moses' decisions regarding marital partners.

When a Christian woman rejected his marriage proposal, Samuel struggled out of depression and despair. Rachel helped him put the affair in perspective. She wrote to him, "When I thought she pitied, and would love you, if she could, it was my first desire, that you should seek to improve the regard of kindred into the affectionate requisite for a closer and more dear connection but when I hear that a name could create an objection, I begin to be impatient and dissatisfied." [154] Rachel approved of the match until she had to reckon with the family's snobbery. She betrayed her own social insecurities when she suggested to Samuel, "This name is not, I allow, the one I would select from all others." Nonetheless, she continued, "but when it has been and is borne by our revered father with so much respectability, a respectability which his sons have rather added to, than diminished—it ought not to be thought of." [155] She tentatively agreed with Samuel that once he was permanently established in his profession, his difficulties with social acceptance might disappear. [156] And when her brother Moses won an honor, Rachel enjoyed a wicked irony. As she explained to Samuel, "We were elated to see Moses' honorable mention in the Compiler—I wonder how *Mrs. Greendy* thought the shocking un-tonish name of Mordecai looked then." [157]

The name Mordecai itself betrayed the anomaly of Jewish identity. Rachel responded from her perception of the family's privileged position within the southern social hierarchy, a hierarchy defined by skin color. Moreover, Jacob Mordecai could claim a southern honor, respectability, won through upward mobility from merchant to honored scholar. Nonetheless, Jews existed as both white and Other. Some southern matrons may have regarded Jews as unassimilable, a mongrel breed. And in the early-nineteenth-century South religious difference weighed heavily in the definition of Other. Regarded as "un-Christian" and "infidels" in overheated public discourse, Jews experienced political and social restrictions. [158] Southerners may have perceived whiteness as Protestant and Jews as "not-yet-white." [159] Thus whiteness was seen through a religious lens.

Beneath the pride of American citizenship that defined Jews as white, Jews struggled with social acceptance and religious anomaly. The practice of Judaism united the Mordecai household, and Richmond, where Sam lived, presented the greatest opportunities for involvement with the larger Jewish community. Samuel, who had access to a luah, a Jewish liturgical calendar, supplied the family with information on the holy days. The family celebrated the High Holidays and kept the Sabbath. Furthermore, Jacob and Samuel were occasionally called upon to perform Jewish nuptials. [160] Thus the Mordecais evolved as a traditional Orthodox Jewish family; Jacob Mordecai stood as patriarch. None-theless, early republican tendencies toward contractual family obligations gave women, especially German Jewish Mordecai women, opportunities to broker new freedoms.

Jacob Mordecai's portrait depicts a man of substance and solidity animated by quick, intelligent eyes. His children revered him for his kindness and be-nevolence, but like all patriarchs, he sometimes took his children for granted, as mere extensions of himself. He wounded Ellen when she returned from a trip and found her father completely indifferent to her. On another occasion, when Eliza attempted to put out a small fire in the living room, Jacob intervened and directed her to get a turkey wing, used to extinguish sparks. Eliza couldn't find it immediately, and her father called her stupid. He never apologized to Eliza for his momentary lapse, and Rachel counseled submission.[161]

Rachel, however, insisted that her father remained a man "happy in his chil-dren."[162] Regardless of the choices his children made in life, Jacob never aban-doned them. His love of family and dedication to Jewish Orthodoxy forced him to choose between the two. The mixed marriages of Moses and Caroline threat-ened to break down family unity. But ultimately, given the choice between the marriage or the loss of a son or daughter, Jacob chose his children's happiness. Rachel and Ellen played important roles in the painful process of reconciliation. Although Orthodox in their views, the sisters ultimately held the personal bond to be equal to religious ideology.

Moses, the eldest of the family, born 4 April 1785 in New York and educated in Warrenton, studied law in 1807 and was licensed to practice in 1808. He taught only briefly at the Mordecai school. After residences in Petersburg and Tarboro, he finally settled in Raleigh in 1815.[163] His practice grew rapidly, and he purchased a house.[164] He rode circuit, and this may have impaired his health. Within a year of his arrival in Raleigh, he met Margaret Lane, daughter of Henry Lane and Mary Hinton. The Hintons and the Lanes represented two of Raleigh's wealthiest and most socially prominent families.[165] The match pre-cipitated a family crisis. Jacob objected on religious and social grounds; other family members believed that Margaret was intellectually inferior to Moses. Rachel wrote to Moses on 4 October 1817 and expressed her fears: "Heaven grant that I am unjust and that my fears mislead me. But my beloved Moses, is she, let me ask, is she a Sally Kennon, is she a Mary Long, is she in short a woman capable of comprehending your sentiments, of appreciating your worth? Can she converse with you?"[166] A very young Ellen Mordecai concurred in Rachel's estimate of the match. She recorded in her diary that Margaret Lane was "a sweet lady" but that the world "acknowledges she is not sensible—she is the eldest of five sisters who all reside near Raleigh with their grandfather and Aunt—What a connection! Could we be intimate with people whose minds, whose manners are so uncongenial to our own?"[167] Obviously, Moses' sisters cared more about intellectual compatibility than religious scruples.

Moses determined to pursue his own course; he wrote his father that he would be the best judge of his own affairs, "not accountable to any."[168] Jacob Mordecai exclaimed in anguish, "The pride of my life is throwing himself away."[169] Moses admitted that his father's and Rachel's letters distressed him. He believed that although he put aside religious scruples, he had not acted precipitously but prudently, his decision supported by friends. But he told Solomon, "Rather than occasion our father one pang; I would relinquish every thought of my own happiness." Moses clearly recognized the lines of patriarchal authority and understood his duty. Solomon rejoiced at Moses' conciliation and believed that the matter would soon be resolved. The family supported Jacob in the matter of Moses' marriage, but Jacob did not act in an authoritarian manner. Rather, he joined a family conference assembled on the evening of 4 October 1817 with the hope of resolving the affair.[170] At that meeting family members spoke "freely and honestly," but Moses determined not to break his engagement, a connection he said he would not have formed had he known how the family felt. The issue threatened family unity until Ellen promised Moses she would attempt to reconcile their father to Moses' decision. Although Ellen knew her father would not change his principles, she believed that "now he is better prepared to bear it than before."[171]

Jacob at last reconciled with his son, a reconciliation that prompted Rachel and Solomon to attend the wedding.[172] "We should be cheerful," Ellen solemnly recorded in her diary. In fact, Ellen never reconciled herself to the marriage and criticized Margaret after the wedding: "Margaret is not pretty, dresses plainly—says she is at home with us—Can't say the same for her—she never opened a book in her life. How can a man marry a woman so far his inferior?"[173] In this marriage the family had two concerns: religion and intellectual compatibility. For the parents, religion remained the primary concern, but for the third generation, intellectual compatibility carried great weight. Moses' siblings influenced Jacob's path to reconciliation. Family politics tempered patriarchal control; contractual rather than patriarchal values led the process of family negotiation.

As to Moses, his marriage ended tragically: Margaret died from complications in childbirth on 11 December 1821. In 1823, echoing Orthodox practice, Moses married Margaret's sister, Anne Willis Lane. Moses' health, never good, began to deteriorate that year. Feverish and weak, he sought relief at Saratoga, a health spa. He continued to travel, however, to Massachusetts, Connecticut, Philadelphia, and Mobile, but by the summer of 1824 his poor health forced him to give up most of his legal practice. Alfred accompanied him back to Saratoga, and Samuel stayed with him at White Sulfer and Sweet Springs. Despite everything done to encourage his convalescence, he died on 1 September 1824.[174]

Moses' marital crisis demonstrated Ellen's and Rachel's inclination toward peaceful, rational reconciliation of family problems. Ellen acted as broker, while Rachel, along with Solomon, attended Moses' wedding. The sisters, especially Rachel, displayed restraint, cool judgment, and delicate diplomacy. As family matters became more complex, Rachel emerged as family counselor. The third generation exerted a powerful influence on the patriarchal family structure. Moses chose his own marriage partner against his father's wishes, but he had powerful family allies to support him.

The case of Caroline, the daughter who lived at home, followed Moses' precedent. Initially, Caroline Mordecai obeyed her father's wishes concerning her marriage, but not without anguish. Rachel's intercession and advice aided Jacob's decision to allow Caroline's marriage to a Christian. As the youngest of Judith Mordecai's children, Caroline remained, until Solomon's departure, on the outside of the school operation. Caroline was a difficult young woman, and her training was, at times, problematic. Sam referred to her as his "dear, charming, lively, obdurate, cross, be-blue-deviled sister."[175] Caroline did well in school, except for an occasion when her composition was not chosen for exhibition during the public examination period. The family felt the composition did not do her credit, and furthermore, Jacob Mordecai wished to avoid a charge of favoritism. But Caroline excelled in French, especially under the tutelage of Achilles Plunkett, a teacher at the Warrenton Female Academy.[176]

The Mordecai family experienced alarm, however, when Plunkett, a middle-aged, former Santo Domingan planter, began to court Caroline. Achilles Plunkett's behavior at the academy had proved a trial. Jacob Mordecai believed him to be a lazy teacher who didn't hear his students' lessons. When reprimanded by Jacob, Plunkett replied that he was responsible only to parents. Jacob assured him he had authority in the school.[177] Rachel, who had been tutored by Plunkett, found him "an agreeable teacher" who sacrificed his leisure time for her. Ellen learned that the man had a *"heart"* since he demonstrated a fondness for children.[178] Plunkett, an eccentric, talented man, simply lacked the discipline of an experienced teacher.

In January 1820 Caroline fretted because she did not receive "weekly assurances of love" from Plunkett. Ellen thought the affair somewhat ludicrous. She debated the issue in her journal: "When we think of it reasonably would it not be a most ridiculous thing for an old man of at least fifty, to cherish a romantic passion which whatever C[aroline] may think of it, is nothing more nor less than love, *hopeless love.*"[179]

Jacob Mordecai disapproved of the match on religious grounds: Achilles Plunkett was a French Catholic. He forbade correspondence between the couple. Although Caroline's sheer misery and storminess eventually moved him to allow them to correspond, he still disapproved of the marriage.[180] Finally, during a long walk with Rachel, he broached the subject of Caroline's marriage. Despite his religious scruples, Rachel persuaded her father to consent. When Rachel returned from the walk, she told Ellen to meet her at the dairy; there Rachel told Ellen that their father had given in. The sisters then went to tell Caroline. Ellen set the stage: "We went up in the room where Caroline all gloomy and desponding was bearing in silence her mental sufferings. Rachel said to her, 'Caroline do you wish to be happy?' Imagine the melancholy voice which replied, 'Yes, to be sure I want to be happy.'—'Then be so for Papa has given his consent,' [said Rachel.] 'To what?' [Caroline asked.] 'To your marrying Mr. Plunkett,' [Rachel responded.] 'Impossible!' [cried Caroline.]" Ellen explained that it took some minutes to convince her, then Caroline threw her arms around her sisters' necks, and they all held each other in sympathy and relief. Caroline thanked her father in tears. She said he had extended her life. He reminded her of her religious responsibilities, and indeed her religious principles remained fixed while Achilles Plunkett lived.[181]

The match scandalized the Jewish community; therefore, Jacob requested that Plunkett hold the ceremony in Raleigh, where Moses Mordecai lived.[182] However, Moses and Margaret objected to the match. Margaret admitted to a "decided aversion to the man" and refused to have the ceremony at her house. She objected to Plunkett on the grounds that he was "a foreigner—a french man and a music master, a disgrace to the family." Moses then wrote a five-page letter ridiculing Plunkett's profession and his family and Caroline's choice. He urged his father to stop the marriage. Under such duress Jacob withdrew his consent.[183] But Richmond family members Joseph Marx and Samuel Myers persuaded Jacob to relent. They argued that "unless some new objection presented itself, . . . he would not now be justifiable in withdrawing his consent . . . he had done all that a parent could to oppose it and now it was best to yield."[184] In this case Jewish elders added to female family members' influence. After discussion with his relatives, Jacob returned home, embraced Caroline, and told her "her feelings should never be tortured" on his account; he would not stand in the way of her marriage. He accompanied her to the home of an old friend in Warrenton, where she was married.[185]

Jacob sacrificed his deepest religious sensibilities for the happiness of his child. His wife understood his anguish. She wrote from the Mordecai home in Spring Farm, near Richmond, "Your letter from Warrenton informs us that your task is accomplished and I hope my Dearest Husband [that] your heart [is] relieved of a heavy burden of which it has so long been opposed. Surely no parent could have made a stronger effort to secure the happiness of a child and may heaven reward you for the sacrifice but I will not say more tho my heart is full." [186]

Jacob Mordecai interpreted the law strictly. He wanted to prohibit his children from marrying non-Jews. But Jewish ethics are not independent of human circumstances. Since obedience to the Commandments implies free consent, honest intent rather than strict conformity is the spirit of the law. Compliance is "beyond the strict letter of the law" and left to the human heart. Mercy and compassion are divine attributes also applicable to the relationship between fathers and children, according to rabbinical wisdom. One school of thought argues that a man may deviate from truth for the sake of peace. [187] Peace came slowly to Jacob Mordecai.

The Mordecais in Retirement

Jacob sold the school in 1818 to investors Joseph Andrews and Thomas P. Jones, who overextended their enterprise. Subsequently, the property was sold under mortgage to Caroline and Achilles Plunkett in 1822. Moses Mordecai congratulated his family on their "prospect of departure from the land of Egypt, and out of the house of bondage." [188] Samuel congratulated his parents and his brothers and sisters on their release from a toil "too great for your strength but borne with patience and strength unparalleled." He wished his family "years of repose." [189]

After a brief sojourn in a rented home, the Mordecai family moved to Spring Farm, a neglected property near Richmond. Some whitewash made it look less shabby. But after setting the home in order, the Mordecais settled into an uneasy domesticity. Farming was an occupation in which Jacob had little experience, and he never succeeded at it. Slave labor, both domestic and agricultural, supported the new enterprise. Thus the Mordecais assimilated their southern neighbors' economic and social values, which maintained a household hierarchy and guaranteed some leisure time. Although their lives at Spring Farm were never comfortable, the Mordecais believed farming afforded them the time to read, practice, study, and write. [190]

Rachel felt grief rather than disappointment at the end of her tenure. [191] The children had done well in their last examinations, and she knew she would never again experience public affirmation of her teaching ability. But she did have the satisfaction of rising above the condescension of some parental factions. Not without a certain pride she noted, "We were surrounded by enemies, we have changed them not into friends, for of friendship many of them are incapable but they have found themselves compelled to acknowledge our merit, and to patronize the institution." [192] Rachel's observation implies the extent to which tensions related to cultural isolation afflicted the Mordecai family. The difficulties of living within a majority culture fostered crises of conscience and identity, and instead of family unity and stability of character, paradox, ambivalence, and contradiction harassed and muted family cohesion. Nonetheless, the experience of ordinary existence, fraught with tension, influenced Mordecai teaching and encouraged wisdom and the ability to question, reason, and imagine beyond accepted precepts.

The Mordecais' struggle with assimilation during the school period challenged family unity. Certainly, cultural isolation, family reconstitution, Christian proselytization, and, according to historian Myron Berman, the lack of training in Hebrew distanced the Mordecai siblings from their Orthodox faith. Throughout this period Rachel Mordecai acted as counselor and transition facilitator. She enjoyed her position within the family because of her piety and deference.

The Enlightenment gained a ready acceptance among the Mordecais, a German Jewish family who inherited secular learning and experienced Revolutionary upheaval. Nonetheless, the Jewish precepts held firm in a household that maintained kashrut and observed the High Holidays. Judith Mordecai instilled the practice of virtue with a loving kindness that brimmed with holy intent. Jacob Mordecai tended toward the practice of strict discipline in obedience to Orthodox precepts. While the family struggled with academic concerns, anti-Semitism, and mixed marriages, the source of tension offered a dilemma: how to adapt, modify, or reject the enlightened model of education and social relations. Mordecai discipline overlay a tradition of holiness that permeated the teaching and lived experience of the family. Greater exposure to enlightened Edgeworthian method only exacerbated the subtle dialectic that offered a choice between disciplined virtue and faith-filled holiness.

The Mordecai practice of enlightened pedagogical method that privileged criticism, scientific observation, and practical experience received reinforcement from Rachel's correspondence with educational reformer and novelist Maria Edgeworth. The Edgeworths' pedagogical and literary texts, in addition to their correspondence, linked the American and Anglo-Irish families in the cause of educational reform. Nonetheless, the Edgeworths' complicated family history and Maria Edgeworth's ambivalent female fictional characters created an uncertainty about female gender roles that influenced Rachel Mordecai's educational experiment and her moral formation.

CHAPTER 2

ENLIGHTENED WISDOM

Rational Pedagogy and
Irrational Impulse in the
Edgeworth Family

ɿɔɑɿɔɑɿɔɑɿɔɑɿɔɑɿɔɑɿɔɑɿɔɑɿɔɑɿɔɑɿɔɑɿɔɑɿɔɑɿɔɑɿɔɑɿɔɑɿɔɑ

Rachel Mordecai's Challenge

"How can it be that she [Maria Edgeworth], who on all other subjects shows such justice and liberality, should on one alone appear biased by prejudice: should even instill that prejudice into the minds of youth!"[1] Twenty-seven-year-old Rachel Mordecai, outraged by Maria Edgeworth's stereotypical portrayal of an unscrupulous Jewish villain, "Mordecai," in her 1812 work *The Absentee,* thus expressed her dismay at the celebrated novelist and educator. By the summer of 1815, when Rachel wrote her indignant letter to Maria Edgeworth, she had taught in her father's academy for six years and had adhered to the principles of the Edgeworths' book, *Practical Education,* in her teaching. Rachel's admonition exposed the shadow in the fair sunlight of Edgeworthian enlightenment.

Chastened, Maria Edgeworth replied that she was then engaged in a work entitled *Harrington* that would make amends.[2] Maria Edgeworth, a lively contributor to Rachel's intellectual life, then became a faithful correspondent and mentor, writing to Rachel until Rachel's death in 1838. Their relationship drew Rachel into a transcontinental enlightened discourse that enlivened her pedagogy and her scientific study and challenged her social values. Edgeworthian method revealed the ethnic and religious content of enlightened education in America.

In truth, the two women shared many parallel experiences even though separated by a generation and transatlantic culture. Both women formed a part-

nership with their fathers and learned excellent managerial skills. The unusual
closeness of father and daughter that developed in their mutual enterprises left
the daughters emotionally dependent upon their fathers and therefore ambivalent about their own independence. Competition within their respective extended families taught them strategies of dealing with rivals for their father's
affection, especially their stepmothers. Each woman learned that rational restraint at the cost of emotional expression earned them greater paternal esteem. This greater fatherly esteem resulted in increased responsibilities such as
the teaching of younger siblings and, eventually, partnership in an educational
venture.

Despite comparable experiences, Evangelical controversies in the United
States fractured the Mordecai family in a way that the Edgeworth family, insu-
lated by their secular culture, avoided. In the introduction to *Practical Education*
the Edgeworths demurred, "On religion and politics we have been silent, because we have no ambition to gain partisans, or to make proselytes, and because
we do not address ourselves exclusively to any sect or to any party."[3] Assuredly,
the enlightened neutrality of *Practical Education* drew the Orthodox Mordecai
family to its tenets, yet assimilation of enlightened education only complicated
Orthodox family cohesion.

Rachel Mordecai wished she could visit the Edgeworths and engage in their
intellectual and literary discussions. Most of all, she admired the closeness of
their family ties.[4] The Edgeworths, especially Edgeworth women, appeared to
have achieved greater domestic unity because of their class status and the success of their literary enterprise. Rachel's consistent and warm regard for the
celebrated family drew her more closely into their orbit of Edgeworthian enlightened moral principles. Those principles, constructed in Edgeworth family
experience, however, contained ambivalent notions about gender roles that
contributed to Rachel's conflicted ideas about family and marital relationships.
Nonetheless, the Edgeworths existed as an increasingly lionized model of the
enlightened and progressive family; their joyous domestic life was a pattern for
Maria Edgeworth's fiction.

The Edgeworth Family Model

A cheerful family gathered around the breakfast table in the Edgeworth household during the early decades of the nineteenth century. The breakfast table
acted as something of an icon. When Maria Edgeworth wrote home, as she
often did during her travels, she inquired where the family members sat. She
said to her young stepmother, Frances Anne Edgeworth, "I want to know at
what table you & Harriet dine? oval? small oval? & do you sit at each end? or
how?"[5] The memory of the breakfast scene created a family continuity, inti-

macy, and security as the absent Maria imagined her domestic "friends" around the table.[6] Also, she needed to know the shifting manner of domestic relations and family diplomacy.

Always new, always refreshing family conversation turned to literature, science, politics, agriculture, and family news. Hilarity often punctuated intellectual discourse. At one point Maria's half sister Honora penned an ambitious family satire and hand printed the "Edgeworthstown Weekly Register." Honora conceived of the circle as a royal family: "We are happy to state that his Majesty appears in perfectly good health . . . Her Majesty & the rest of the royal family are in good health . . . Her royal Highness Maria is recovering from her late indisposition."[7]

Family members (known as the "Parliament"), however, challenged royal prerogative. When, according to the "Register," "His Majesty," Richard Lovell Edgeworth, proposed that a poem be read, Mrs. Frances Edgeworth and all the family members objected. Maria made an especially clear argument. Nonetheless, the book of poems appeared, and Maria read one, only to be interrupted by her father, who asked his young daughter Fanny if she understood the poem. Fanny then read the poem and interpreted it herself. The lesson might have continued had it not been for the arrival of Mr. Robert Wiggins, who demonstrated a scientific model. A long consultation ensued between the father and Wiggins. Mrs. Edgeworth occasionally interjected remarks.[8] Breakfast ended as family members slipped away to their own morning diversions.

The "Edgeworthstown Weekly Register," like a witty constitution, describes the family's parliamentary challenge to the controlling monarch, Richard Lovell Edgeworth. However, the pleas of his female constituents are unheard as the father carries out his wishes; Maria, then Fanny, reads the poems. Fanny is instructed in interpretation, and the lesson continues until the father is distracted by the more important scientific exchange with Wiggins. Young Honora's ironic sketch imputes the opposite of playful reporting and establishes her real intent, to challenge her father's benign yet sovereign power. Her irony suggests a way of "reading" the distinguished Edgeworth family: beneath the rational manner, pedagogy, and scientific method lay frustration, passion, and rebellion expressed in gendered terms.

Historian Roger Chartier describes enlightened monarchic relations that may also be applied to family relationships. He argues that individuals are "linked by a specific mode of reciprocal dependence . . . the reproduction of which supposes a mobile balance of tensions."[9] Such a definition eludes the imbalance of tensions within families to which a benign yet patriarchal power responded. For instance, Edgeworth men rebelled against family and social convention. The patriarch, Richard Lovell Edgeworth, abandoned his first wife, Anna Maria Elers, the mother of five of his children, including Maria, and engaged in a scandalous affair with Honora Sneyd, whom he subsequently married after the death of his first wife. Richard Lovell Edgeworth's disastrous tutoring of his son Richard according to Rousseauian theory led to the young man's unmanageable behavior and flight to America. Lovell Edgeworth attempted to practice his father's pedagogical theory, but competition with his father only drove him to alcoholism and failure. Francis Edgeworth, after a promising start at Charter House, a private school, wasted his Cambridge education and entered into a liaison with the daughter of a Spanish general. Married young, he never took up a profession but toiled as a tutor of university students and later managed the Edgeworth estate. Richard Lovell Edgeworth's own scandalous past plagued his sons; the father attempted to exercise power over them, but he lost the battle.

Edgeworth women, in contrast, maintained a domestic harmony and female network that not only sustained Maria Edgeworth's literary work but preserved a stable environment for the unruly men, who disturbed family relations.[10] The disparity between rational family ideology and impassioned behavior provided the context in which Maria Edgeworth dedicated her pedagogical and fictional work to the art of self-control. The family chasm did not leave the author unscathed; her writing bears the unmistakable mark of schism, of a writer at odds with herself. At issue in this enlightened family remained the question of authority. Few children in the family achieved independence, and Maria Edgeworth, one of the most celebrated British authors of her day, wrestled with her own self-definition. She took pride in her writing as an independent source of wealth, yet she maintained an intellectual and emotional dependence upon her father.

The Edgeworths reproduced an enlightened cultural pattern that enabled scholars to attribute an "oddly double" reputation to Maria Edgeworth's literary works. Maria Edgeworth has been identified as a moderate feminist and a patriarchal apologist, a thoroughgoing individualist and a dedicated traditionalist. Scholars have attempted to ameliorate these contradictions, which counterpose enlightened scientific ideology and corporate family values.[11] Historians Lenore Davidoff and Catherine Hall suggest that although early-nineteenth-century society recognized property as commercial and utilized credit and liquid capital, "personality," founded upon real property, land, remained the basis of virtue and status.[12] Davidoff and Hall's suggestion prompted scholar Teresa Michals to interpret the relationship between personality and property somewhat differently in relation to the Edgeworths. She argues that "[Maria] Edgeworth embraces economic individualism without seeing individuals themselves as autonomous. For her the family has a corporate personality, one underwritten by the market value of its members' good characters rather than by its inheritance of land, the traditional basis of such a corporate personality."[13] Edgeworth's language of family, coded in market terms, however, suggests a family history that encouraged a preoccupation with character, virtue, and the preservation of a fractured family's integrity.

The Anglo-Irish gentry family of Edgeworths occupied a unique place in the history of education and literature at the turn of the nineteenth century. Maria Edgeworth's didactic novels excited the loyalty of an expanding and influential middle class. Edgeworth family history coincides with the rationalization and repression implicit in a growing commercial culture. Free market production spurred a prosperity tied to middle-class consumption of goods and services. Production entailed the separation of home and business, public and private space that increasingly forced class and gender distinctions. Appeals to religion and rationality justified such distinctions.[14] Maria Edgeworth, by opposing impulse and self-discipline in her work, addressed the social tension between laissez-faire individualism and moral constraint. Consequently, Edgeworth's conflation of moral questions and rational method acknowledged female intellectual ability but confirmed women's domestic role.

Edgeworth's ideological contradictions may also have been rooted in the changes that occurred in the British educational system at that time. Institutional and professional schools had not yet replaced informal and domestic arrangements. Parental education retained its standing because patronage often undermined the standards of the dominant church school system. Some schools existed as family enterprises in which women assisted by teaching or supervising boarding students. Such schools were literally extensions of the household. In contrast, dissenters established academies that competed with the dominant Anglican school system and offered a more practical, scientific curriculum that prepared men for business.

Richard Lovell Edgeworth joined the enlightened educational debate through the Lunar Society, a dedicated group of businessmen and scientists influenced by Rousseau's ideas on education.[15] Richard Lovell Edgeworth appealed for changes in the divisive British educational system; he proposed a parish system of inspection that educated both Protestant and Catholic pupils in basic reading and computational and trade skills.[16] Edgeworth family members Lovell and Harriet established schools,[17] and brothers William and Francis attended the Charter House school; however, Richard Lovell and Maria Edgeworth's enlightened guide, *Practical Education,* concentrated on parental education. Thus Maria, exposed to enlightened pedagogy, remained vitally interested in domestic education, increasingly the duty of the mother. Parental education offered the earliest opportunity to shape moral character, a concern of both enlightened and religious, especially Evangelical, audiences.

Richard Lovell Edgeworth's Irish estate, Edgeworthstown, a household of talented and intelligent family members, provided a model environment for educational experimentation. Edgeworth encouraged his children to test their assumptions about natural phenomena, collect fossils, and build accurate scales. The parents rewarded the children with the pleasure of participating in experiments. The family's work and play inspired *Practical Education,* an enlightened guide to children's education that won critical acclaim on the European Continent and in progressive enclaves in America. The work, co-authored by Richard Lovell Edgeworth and his daughter Maria, further encouraged Maria's children's fiction based upon *Practical Education*'s precepts. Erasmus Darwin's adage "A fool is a man who never tried an experiment in his life" served as the family motto, yet rebellious family members escaped the application of a rigorous rationality. The family both supported and limited individual attempts at autonomy. Each attempt had to be carefully weighed against the desires of the father. Children chose marriage, education, and career only with the consent of the patriarch. Conflicts within Richard Lovell Edgeworth's personal history account for both his keen endorsement of liberal ideology and his practice of benevolent paternalism.

Richard Lovell Edgeworth and Enlightened Education

Richard Lovell Edgeworth's mother, Jane, raised him in the Lockean tradition according to the dictates of self-control and self-discipline. Paralyzed after her son's birth and unable to use physical force, she exercised control over Richard Lovell's violent temper with her reasoned discourse alone. While still in the nursery he nearly killed his older brother by flinging a hot iron at him. His mother's chastisement and warning remained with him all his life.[18] She admonished him:

> You have naturally a violent temper: if you grow up to be a man without learning to govern it, it will be impossible for you then to command yourself: and there is no knowing what crime you may in a fit of passion commit, and how miserable you may in consequence of it become. You are but a very young child, yet I think you can understand me. Instead of speaking to you as I do at this moment, I might punish you severely: but I think it better to treat you like a reasonable creature. My wish is to teach you to command your temper; nobody can do that for you, so well as you can do it for yourself.[19]

Although Richard Lovell later claimed he never forgot his mother's words,[20] he unfortunately remained capable of rash behavior. He demonstrated a taste for self-indulgence that ended with a hasty marriage in 1783 to Anna Maria Elers, daughter of an impoverished judge. His first marriage proved unhappy but produced five children: Richard, Lovell, Maria, Emmeline, and Anna Maria. Maria, born 1 January 1768 at Black Bourton, Oxon, was the eldest of the daughters.[21] Restless and impatient, Richard Lovell Edgeworth then fell in love with Honora

Sneyd. In his memoirs he remembered "the violence of love" he felt for Honora. Consequently, he spent time away from his wife and family. The children, with the exception of Richard, remained with their mother's family in England; Richard lived with his father, who, preoccupied with building bridges in Lyons, France, neglected young Richard's education.[22]

The change in Richard Lovell Edgeworth's life uprooted his assumptions about family life. The educational theory outlined in Rousseau's *Emile* seemed to offer a new way to stabilize his own restless nature and at the same time develop a relationship with his son Richard. Rousseau, after all, had warned, "To be a child's master you must be your own master."[23] The French philosopher attempted to reconcile self and civic interest with an education according to nature rather than principles or conventions. Instead of harsh discipline in the training of habits, Rousseau recommended necessity as the source of learning. "The truly free man wants only what he can do and does what he pleases," Rousseau argued.[24] Necessity is freedom's only obstacle. According to Rousseau, punishment does not deter the child, experience does, since the child must live with the consequences of bad behavior. Passions, then, balanced by the experience of natural limits, lead to virtue, Rousseau maintained.[25] Tragically, Edgeworth's son could not comprehend "natural limits" and instead remained obstinately defiant.

For five years young Richard Edgeworth lived out *Emile*. As a child of nature he worked with his hands, adopted a trade, sharpened his senses, believed himself his own master. But he grew into a rebellious, unruly adolescent. His father finally packed him off to boarding schools. Ungovernable, the raging son fled to America. Thereafter, his father sought a system that balanced self-reliance with discipline. Although the experiment ended in failure, Richard Lovell gained a richer understanding of the practice of education. He learned the enlightened method—that action, not principles, is the means of education; that in doing good one becomes good, as Rousseau counseled.[26] The senior Richard Lovell, a mechanic and engineer, discovered the education of common sense—that the senses, the raw experience of making things or making one's way, determined perceptions. Ideas, Edgeworth believed, were merely simple associations of perceptions.

Like the bridges he built in Lyons, Edgeworth developed an educational structure, a method of learning that attempted an expansive and solid understanding of experience. Edgeworth adapted the scientific method as the best model for teaching the understanding and analysis of the material world. Edgeworth's educational scheme included a dynamic association between mentor and pupil that breathed life into mundane subjects. But most important of all, Rousseau's lesson was to speak to the heart; at stake was self-mastery, the command of one's emotions, an elusive goal for Edgeworth men. The aim, a peaceful, well-ordered citizen, responsible to self and others, necessitated a moral dimension in the method.[27] Thus "the education of the heart" took on new meaning in the training of impulse and self-will. Richard Lovell applied his chastened understanding to the education of his children, especially his eldest daughter, Maria.

Maria Edgeworth, the Apprentice

The educational practice and even literary ideas developed by Richard Lovell Edgeworth and Maria Edgeworth were based upon an enlightened partnership. What Maria Edgeworth contributed to pedagogical theory filtered through the experience of her relationship to her father. Perhaps the same impulsive nature, disciplined but energetic, bonded father and daughter. Richard Lovell, by turns improvident and rational, attempted to rein in Maria's impetuous spirit. Frances Edgeworth noted: "The most remarkable trait in her [Maria Edgeworth's] character was the prudence with which she acted; the command which she had acquired over her naturally impetuous nature and boundless generosity of spirit."[28] The making of Maria Edgeworth's character lay in her father's response to Maria's conflict with her stepmother Honora. Four months after Maria's mother's death, Richard Lovell Edgeworth married Honora Sneyd. Maria then accompanied her father and stepmother to Edgeworthstown. Family politics had shifted, and her father had found a new marital ally. Richard and Honora had two children, Honora, born in 1774, and Lovell, born a year later. The five-year-old Maria, isolated and abandoned, had no way to express her grief. Maladjusted in her new surroundings, Maria exhibited tantrums—she cut up a checkered sofa cover and trampled down hotbed frames.[29] Maria's behavior prompted her parents to send her to several fashionable schools. From a distance Honora sent advice to the banished Maria. Her tone is unmistakably cool. Honora wrote, "Your being taught to dance may enable you to alter your common method of holding yourself. If you pay attention to it, & I must say you wanted improvement in this respect very much when you were here."[30] Her banishment and alienation from her family taught Maria to hide her emotions. Maria's repression enabled her to resist further interference from Honora. Honora simply could not fathom Maria and found it frustrating to deal with her. "It is in vain to attempt to please a person, who will not tell us, what they do and what they do not, desire," Honora said.[31] The unbearable tension between Maria and her stepmother led to Maria's emotional withdrawal.

Richard Lovell Edgeworth countered his wife's coolness toward Maria. He implored Maria to write more "*familiarly,*" to express her likes and dislikes.[32] "Continue to cultivate your heart," he told her. "It is from the heart the fruit of happiness must spring."[33] The father's request that she write stories to enliven her dispirited correspondence awakened the young writer. While apart from her father, Maria developed an eye inflammation that a doctor diagnosed as serious and leading to blindness. Alarmed, Richard Lovell sent for his daughter, and she arrived at the family home at Edgeworthstown, Ireland, in 1782, an awkward and shy fourteen year old. Richard Lovell's concern, affection for, and increased appreciation of his daughter guided Maria toward greater responsibility.

When Richard Lovell Edgeworth undertook the restoration of the family estate, supervision and estate management demanded his attention. He therefore entrusted the accounts to his daughter Maria. Richard Lovell Edgeworth proved an expert manager of his tenants and thus an excellent teacher for Maria. Maria, who had gained self-discipline, learned to manage others well.[34] During this period an unusual trust developed between father and daughter, and Richard Lovell Edgeworth delegated the important work of education to his daughter.

Maria served her pedagogical apprenticeship under her father's tutelage within the domestic circle. She was given young Henry as a ward. Henry was the oldest son of Richard Lovell Edgeworth and his third wife, Elizabeth Sneyd, the sister of Honora Sneyd whom Richard Lovell had married after Honora's death. Her parents, Maria said, "trusted him to my care to teach me the art of Education & instructed me every day all day long, in the Theory & practice."[35]

Richard Lovell supervised not only Maria's teaching and writing but her management of the estate as well. He thought in terms of "joint endeavors."[36] In their work relationship they expressed a "balance of obligation," so necessary to the domestic monarchical figuration that restrained willfulness. Naturally, Richard Lovell Edgeworth found great satisfaction in so invaluable a daughter. He then turned "his whole mind" toward forming her character—"for her happiness," he explained. If she did not find a "rational creature" worthy of her, his care would secure her serenity and, he said, "whilst I live will rivet the affections of a fond parent and a steady friend."[37] That riveting attention both inspired and bound Maria Edgeworth. In a rare critical moment Maria said that her father's excessive attentions made all others pallid by comparison. She scribbled on a piece of torn paper, "I acknowledge that he gave too much praise and that his expressions of affection were too warm & too strong an excitement. All others seemed insipid compared with this, and his pupils have felt the want of this stimulus when it was no longer to be had. There was danger that they should sink & flag for want of it as from my own experience."[38] The fatherly gaze doubled Maria's image; in his eyes she was both herself and his mirror-image. The split in her self-image carried over to her literary and pedagogical output. Her educational works such as *Practical Education* and the didactic children's stories based upon Edgeworthian pedagogy, *Early Lessons, Moral Tales, Parent's Assistant,* and *Popular Tales,* clearly suggest the binary voice of father

and daughter. Richard Lovell provided the pedagogy, criticism, and plot suggestions for Maria's writing. Her statement, "I am my father's pen," gives evidence
not only of her filial devotion and her indebtedness to his educational ideas and
narrative imagination but also of her self-deprecation. However, the moral animus of her adult fiction suggests much less paternal collaboration and greater
focus upon her inner conflict between self-control and impulse, dependence and
self-determination.[39] Practical method provided the framework of discipline,
adapted to the individual nature, that trained and nurtured the Edgeworthian
spirited temperament.

A Practical Education

Practical Education grew out of Richard Lovell's vigorous scientific curiosity.
Richard Lovell Edgeworth abandoned the Rousseauian system after the failed
experiment with his son, but he found the ideas of his colleagues in the Lunar
Society more conducive to his scientific inclination. Within this intellectual cli-
mate, Anglo-Scottish pragmatism adapted all forms of knowledge to scientific
experiment. Joseph Priestley, a teacher of note whose *Essay on a Course of Liberal
Education* suggests the modernization of academy curriculum by the inclusion
of the sciences, most influenced Edgeworth. A more liberal rather than classical
education prepared pupils for the newly developing commercial and professional world. Priestley's edition of David Hartley's *Observations on Man* alerted
Edgeworth to the psychological importance of Hartley's "association of ideas"
in placing education upon a more scientific basis. By paying attention to a
child's responses to stories and parents' clear, accessible language, Edgeworth
hoped to develop simple associations derived from a child's own experience. A
pupil's mental associations formed his or her nature and character.[40] Edgeworth
said that Hartley "put us upon our guard to prevent false associations in early
education and has encouraged us to employ this faculty of the mind in forming . . . character."[41]

Edgeworth abandoned educational theory for practical experiments that
would yield positive results. Honora and Richard Lovell Edgeworth recorded
their observations of children's responses to learning in an endeavor to decipher
the most practical methods of learning. Honora wrote tales about "Harry and
Lucy" that offer depictions of well-behaved but curious and intelligent children.
After Honora's death Maria kept up the family notebooks; they became the basis
of Maria's writings on education, especially "Harry and Lucy." The "Notebook
for *Harry and Lucy*" became a family enterprise.[42] Maria kept a writer's notebook in order to collect odd pieces of information or useful dialogue. The notebook contains English and Latin inscriptions, recipes, and dialogue written in

hands other than Maria's. Maria transcribed her sister Harriet Butler's description of a day at the races and wrote down a scene of children playing at the seashore. Out of this rich mixture Maria perfected her stories. The notebook represents literary archaeological evidence: remnants of family conversations, jests, arguments, inspired thoughts recorded with intent and care because they mattered and made an impression. Most of the jottings did not make it into the stories, but the existence of the notebooks attests to a family contribution to and interest in the family's literary enterprise. Thus Richard Lovell Edgeworth, with the aid of Honora, Maria, and his numerous progeny, inspired and devised the first practical guide to education.[43]

Empiricism dominated Richard Lovell and Maria Edgeworth's educational manual. The authors conceived of their work as experimental. Each chapter on toys, tasks, attention, obedience, temper, truth, rewards and punishments, sympathy and sensibility, vanity, pride, and ambition sets forth the experiments they had tried within their own family. But some general principles emerged. The utilitarian principle of pleasure and pain guided the educational experiments; that is, the application of either pleasure or pain was decided by the circumstance and the nature of the child. Every child, of course, experienced the pain of going to bed. Edgeworth believed that going to bed taught the child to avoid the pain of resistance. Ultimately, the child would learn to "forego present pleasure for future advantage."[44]

The Edgeworths cautioned patience and education by degrees. Once a child reached the age of reason the Edgeworths suggested teaching the child to spell by sounds and marks. The idea was not original with Richard Lovell Edgeworth; however, he published a simple and workable system that became popular on the Continent.[45] The system operated in order to create in children "a love for mental employment."[46]

Edgeworthstown existed as an experimental schoolhouse. There the practical relationship between scientific method and moral values worked through intimate family ties. In addition to his seven children Richard Lovell Edgeworth had nine more children with his third wife, Elizabeth Sneyd. Edgeworth's generous nature and his genius held his extended family together. The atmosphere, brimming with affection and excitement, provided a challenge to young curiosity. The children engaged in all the adult activity of the household—readings, plays, tasks.[47] The household's planned activity fostered initiative as a way of teaching self. Thus by necessity the Edgeworths cared as much about method as content.

Edgeworthstown, or wherever the clan gathered, buzzed and hummed with the joyful noise of children at play, a very special kind of play. Richard Lovell introduced his children to the excitement and wonder of science through play.

The scientific experiments may have occupied the boys more than the girls, but the girls enjoyed planting a garden, too. Maria divided up a garden into "territories" where each child had a share. Gratified, Maria observed, again to her cousin: "I assure you it is very cheerful to see the merry, scarlet-coated, busy little workwomen in their territories, sowing, and weeding, and transplanting hour after hour."[48] The children naturally led each other to a further interest in science, and Maria observed the process. On a journey Henry entertained Fanny, his half sister, with a description of the process of tanning. Maria recorded the scene: "As we passed by the crooked wood he [Henry] took her on his knees and shewed her the oaks stripped of their bark & the heaps of bark piled up on the ground & he explained the whole art & use of tanning to her so well that I wish I could have written it down word for word for Harry & Lucy. She repeated what she understood of it to Sophy today. There is a tanpit here which she is to see."[49] The Edgeworths expanded an enlightened notion that children learn through play. They recommended the use of "rational" toys such as carpenter's tools rather than store-bought toys. In a letter to a Mrs. Tabart around 1809 Richard Lovell enclosed a list of rational toys. It included a paste brush and pot, a horseshoe for making stay laces, a loom, windmills, wheelbarrows, microscopes, locks, pumps, jacksbell ropes, hooks, and joints.[50]

The Edgeworths took pride in the fact that their playroom looked more like a carpenter's shop than a nursery. Maria Edgeworth described a typical family scene to her cousin Sophy Ruxton:

> There are . . . a great many good things here. There is a balloon hanging up, and another going to be put on the stocks: there is soap made, and making from a receipt in Nicholson's Chemistry: there is excellent ink made, and to be made by the same book: there is a cake of roses just squeezed in a vice, by my father . . . There are a set of accurate weights, just completed by the ingenious Messers Lovell and Henry Edgeworth, partners: for Henry is now a junior partner, and grown an inch and a half upon the strength of it in two months.[51]

Toys in the Edgeworth estimation were a means of occupation, that is, employment.

Edgeworthian children were busy children, occupied with constructive play, designed to help them think and enter the burgeoning commercial world. When the child's attention fixed upon a subject, then teaching began. The Edgeworths advised short, repetitive lessons for the young with extended sessions for the more advanced that included the introduction of theory and experiment. Laboratory time might take as long as the child needed. The experimental method cautioned against too much abstraction or theorizing. Whatever was taught, such as values, for instance, was conveyed in the particular, never in the general. Individual acts learned by habit and repetition were the preferred method rather than officious rule making. A gentle, decisive hand with the use of reason rather than force would succeed in making children happy—happy to be obedient, rational children. Richard Lovell Edgeworth boasted to his friend Erasmus Darwin, "I do not think one tear per month is shed in this house, nor the voice of reproof heard, nor the hand of restraint felt." [52]

The Edgeworthian emphasis upon rationality adapted to the circumstance of the individual child replaced shame as a general principle applied to the training of children. [53] Recent scholarship contends that shame as an inhibiting technique produces diminishment of the individual and can lead to alienation from self and emotions. [54] The Edgeworths advised that shame be applied only in exceptional circumstances and not as punishment for "slight faults." [55] But Maria Edgeworth did not hesitate to counter violent behavior with forceful discipline and shaming. For example, she once wrote to her aunt: "Whenever the passion of children breaks out into personal violence it should be returned with tenfold resentment. Impatience should be treated with patience and gentleness, a soft method of refusal and their own experience will by degrees teach them that time is necessary in all things. We stroke a fiery horse on the neck & slacken his reins—it is only the slow and stubborn Garron that requires the heavy bit and goaring spur." [56] Usually, however, a parent's indignation free of passion and petty concerns represents punishment enough, the Edgeworths counseled; thus "the pupil should feel that it is indignation against his fault, and not against himself." [57] *Practical Education* avoided condemnation of the person and instead primed the child's conscience by building good habits and inducing guilt over destructive actions. The Edgeworths did not forbid recourse to shame but only cautioned parents that shame presented a powerful tool to be used sparingly. [58] Nonetheless, the power of rationality, systematically applied, produced as repressive an effect on the emotions of children as shame.

The Edgeworths spoke of the economy of sympathy, which limits parental indulgence. They wrote, "Instead of lavishing our smiles and our attention upon young children for a short period, just at that age when they are amusing playthings, should we not do more wisely if we reserved some portion of our kindness a few years longer?" [59] The advice to withhold such ordinary pleasure indicates a certain suspicion of the emotions. Indeed, the Edgeworths distrusted "instinctive" feelings such as children's love of animals; they argued that such love never prevents children's cruelty toward animals. In addition, the Edgeworths criticized children's spontaneous charity because children must learn the difference between deserving and undeserving requests. In short, only trained emotions and habits ensured trust, according to the Edgeworths. These enlightened preceptors labeled heartfelt emotion sentimental and dismissed any demonstration of feeling. "The amiable feelings of the heart need not be displayed," the Edgeworths claimed. [60]

"The Mental Thermometer"

The seriousness of the Edgeworths' assertion concerning emotions may not be overstated. For example, the Edgeworths devised a family metaphor for restrained emotions that found its way into one of Maria Edgeworth's stories. Prior to the publication of *Practical Education* the Edgeworth family speculated about the invention of a "mental thermometer" that measured emotions and allowed its user to regulate any excessive feeling. Edgeworth enthusiasm viewed the mental thermometer as a fit device for self-control and a moral governor. *Practical Education,* "the education of the heart," attempted to make the connection between mind and body, reason and emotion, experience and virtue by reducing experience to a science. But the passionate, unstable, marginal, ambivalent, and idealistic qualities of human nature eluded scientific measurement. The Edgeworths still imagined such a perfect qualitative instrument and confidently believed that the possibility of qualitative measurement opened the way for a wonderfully ordered system of virtue and morality. In short, the Edgeworths considered how to move from experience to conscious moral construct and found their answer in the mental thermometer, a fictional measurement of human emotions.

The accurate measurement of heat had been a conspicuous triumph of enlightened science as early as 1612. Eighteenth-century inventors refined the instrument by substituting mercury for alcohol and adding a uniform scale of measurement, the Fahrenheit scale. Most upwardly mobile English households in the first few decades of the eighteenth century displayed handsomely decorated thermometers. Popular imagination immediately associated the volatile substance mercury with the vagaries of human emotion.[61] The Edgeworths habitually used thermometers as a measure of good health. Charles Sneyd Edgeworth, the son of Richard Lovell and Elizabeth Sneyd, took his own pulse and compared the rate with the doctor's examination. Charles also took his sick father's pulse and reported the results to the family.[62] When one of Maria Edgeworth's stepbrothers went to India, he took along a thermometer, and after it was destroyed, Maria replaced it since she considered a thermometer indispensable to good health.[63] Abstract concepts such as health yielded practical meaning only in measurement. The purpose of experiment and observation was to organize and interpret cognitive experience, not to theorize. The measurement of the emotions, and an instrument to manage and control them, presented the Edgeworths with their greatest challenge.

In 1787 thirteen-year-old Honora Edgeworth, daughter of Richard Lovell's second wife, composed a story in which an old gentleman offered a prize for the best picture to his two artistic daughters. One painted well, the other ingeniously. The father awarded the prize to Cordelia, who painted clever portraits of her sister and her sister's heart. But when the narrator applied a "crystal" to Cordelia, it measured her embarrassment; she then yielded to her better intentions and pleaded that the prize be given to Clarissa, who had produced the best, if not the most technically correct, painting. The father praised Cordelia for her virtue.[64] Cordelia precisely understood her emotions; therefore, she responded with admirable virtue. Female experience with the crystal demonstrates the most rational use of it.

Maria Edgeworth retold Honora's story and transformed the ambivalent crystal into a mental thermometer, a more precise measure of human emotion. In addition, Maria substituted male characters. The young male who narrates the story raises the question of "the problem in the history of the human mind—whether different people feel the same positive degrees of pain or pleasure with equal intensity: whether all men have the same capacity for happiness or misery?" The narrator continued to speculate that "it seems further to suggest a moral idea that many are led to pursue what others falsely call pleasure merely from their want of the power of comparing & reflecting on their own feelings, & thus of deciding for themselves in what their real happiness consists."[65] Maria Edgeworth might have been describing her father's and her brothers' capacity for selfish disregard of their own best interests and the interest of their family. In Maria's story it is uninhibited male emotion that ultimately breaks the mental thermometer.

The narrator of Maria's story told of his father's friend, a philosopher of "remarkable serenity" who "seemed to penetrate with a single glance into the inmost recesses of the human heart." The philosopher revealed the secret of his happiness and serenity—an instrument, resembling a thermometer, that registered the range of pleasure and pain from "perfect felicity" to "indifference." The extremes, warned the philosopher, were most dangerous. The young man questioned the significance of the instrument; he cited ordinary reflection as sufficient to understand one's emotions. The old man suggested that without precision, the young misjudge pleasure and follow false pursuits, since they are guided by others' expectations and opinions. According to the philosopher, the mental thermometer unraveled the most complicated emotion and avoided needless repetition in finding one's true happiness. When the youth understood the marvel, the philosopher presented the mental thermometer to him as a means of attaining greater virtue and wisdom. Unfortunately, the youth revealed the secret to a "metaphysician," who claimed that he could "perfect his theory of mankind" if he possessed the thermometer. The metaphysician's excitement at such a prospect burst the instrument, and "the world and the metaphysician were deprived forever of . . . intended experiments on the Mental Thermometer."[66] In a rational male world only a philosopher would find serenity with the mental thermometer. In the hands of a sentimentalist or metaphysician who deals in supernatural speculation, the attainment of serenity and happiness is impossible. The irrational male bursts the instrument with his excitement. The story comments upon the danger of male passion and the necessity of a mental check upon such destructive emotion.

Maria Edgeworth's transposition of gender coincided with the changing nature of eighteenth-century literary conceptualizations. With the feminization of male subjects, maleness increasingly included emotional sensibilities previously attributed only to women. Moreover, "the feminization of discourse," the language of feeling and sensibility, increasingly pervaded British novels of the eighteenth century. For instance, Samuel Richardson's novel *Clarissa, or, The History of a Young Lady* evoked new subjectivity in the victimization of a female character.[67] However, Maria Edgeworth, educated in the neoclassical aesthetic tradition and a reader of Edmund Burke's *Philosophical Inquiry into the Origin of Our Ideas of the Sublime and Beautiful* (1756), Lord Kames's *Elements of Criticism* (1762), and Joshua Reynolds's *Discourses,* rejected such subjectivism. She held to traditional, dispassionate form,[68] and, therefore, in "The Mental Thermometer" she implicitly condemns the sentimental sensibility usually attributed to women.

In their desire to balance "sympathy and sensibility" the authors of *Practical Education* recommend particular care with regard to the management of "female sensibility," a tendency toward sentimentality and affectation.[69] Thus the Edgeworths viewed gender definitions in hierarchical terms that privileged the public life of rational men and relegated women to the domestic sphere. In effect, the authors acknowledged female exceptionalism, certain moral habits and emotional tendencies that necessitated gendered training. Although the Edgeworths accepted few natural distinctions in children, they adopted conventional ones. Their enlightened principles emboldened them to prescribe more than a superficial education for women; they exhorted parents to encourage girls to rise higher than mere copying or memorization. Both sexes should be taught science and mechanics, according to the authors. Such trained reasoning ability gave a woman a moral power, command over herself. Thus practical training discouraged women from the idleness and mischief of reading romances. The use of reason also obviated the necessity of cunning, usually attributed to women.[70] Nonetheless, the Edgeworths assumed that young women were "naturally full of chastity" and therefore needed no intensive moral training on that score. However, women were to be taught caution, albeit through the use of reason. Again, the moral nature of the training decided in favor of distinct training for women, since women have "particular morals," which were acquired, not innate.[71] In another instance, the Edgeworths assumed that a reasonable training educated women's temperament to employ argument. The

Edgeworths warned that an attempt to "thunder like Demosthenes, would not find her eloquence [or] increase her domestic happiness."[72] And since domestic happiness remained women's goal, the Edgeworths advised that women learn the domestic arts, including the art of cooking.[73] Thus the Edgeworths implied that women's role specified a sex-determined destiny.

The split between rational training and women's cultural destiny in Maria Edgeworth's fiction eventually fractured the author's vision. It polarized her characters and her own self-understanding as a woman. Ultimately, her refusal to write after the critical failure of her novel *Belinda* suggests an alienation of self, an inability to integrate the rational and emotional parts of herself.

Edgeworthian Children's Literature

Caution may be attached to the training of self-control and the repression of spontaneity and legitimate emotion, especially if the sexes are assigned varying degrees of self-discipline. Maria Edgeworth's children's fiction elucidated Edgeworthian pedagogy, applying discrete categories to gendered roles. Her stories such as "Harry and Lucy," "Forester," "Rosamund," and "Angelina" may be regarded as fictional case studies of the impulsive personality, of how boys and girls learn self-control through experience and experiment.[74] Harry and Lucy, brother and sister, shared the same household tasks such as bed making. When Harry objected that "he did not know that boys or men ever made beds," his father explained to him that sailors made their own beds.[75] Although the parents expected their children to dress themselves and make their own beds, the children learned different gender roles throughout the course of the day. Lucy accompanied her mother to the dairy, while Harry went with his father on his business rounds and to the brickyard. Once the children reunited, Harry shared his new-found expertise with his sister. The children set about at once to make bricks. With the help of both parents the children tried several experiments in the art of brick making. Thereafter both children learned about science and technology from their parents, mostly their father. The Edgeworthian method educated young children of both sexes in science, yet the gendered message implicit in the story demonstrates that girls use their knowledge in the domestic sphere, while boys explore the public sphere.

Edgeworthian male characters rather than female heroines enjoyed a wider venue for training the mind and learning character. Forester, for example, impulsively leaves his guardian's house and tries several vocations in his search for character and his place in life. Young women may travel, as Anne Warwick and Angelina did in search of an ideal friend, but in Edgeworthian fiction, females did not find self-realization through a vocation but, rather, in rational relationships. Anne Warwick, a girl whom "it was scarcely possible to manage by common sense," entered into a highly charged correspondence with a girl who signed herself "Araminta."[76] With dreams of living with her unknown friend, Anne flees from her guardian and hastens to meet Araminta, who turns out to be Rachel Hodges, a self-absorbed writer with a masculine voice and a preference for brandy and servile men. This "moral tale" suggests danger outside the domestic sphere for women alone. Moreover, to seek heartfelt emotion is to seek disaster. Anxious to find a kindred romantic spirit, Anne Warwick ran away from home and met with calamities, the loss of her purse and disillusionment with her friend. Rachel Hodges represents the independent woman, a masculine and vulgar sort, the perfect foil for the addled Anne. Here Maria Edgeworth projects two negative images of sentimental women, the fool and the tyrant. The tyrant manipulates emotion to exert power over the weak-minded sentimentalist.

According to Maria Edgeworth, the proper course for young women, as for Rosamund, remains the preservation of good character in the midst of domestic power struggles. Rosamund and her brother enter into the family lists for nine days as Godfrey batters Rosamund's judgments about character. In the end, Rosamund triumphs over Godfrey's incessant criticism and maintains her good judgment about the true character of friends.

Edgeworthian pedagogy offers a classic guide to the management of impulsive children. Foremost in Edgeworthian ideology is the principle that mentors themselves require mental discipline and self-criticism in order to judge individuals accurately and respond accordingly. Teachers must take care that the underlying character of the child changes; this constitutes the heart of the stories. Such change of character is the responsibility of both the tutor and the pupil. The relationship draws on the teacher's ability to measure the child's inner strength or resources. The hardship of the struggle increases self-esteem in the child. For example, Madame de Rosier in "The Good French Governess" confronts three difficult children, Herbert, Isabella, and Matilda. She opens their capacity for critical thinking by tailoring her instruction to their interests. She prevails upon Herbert to investigate the "Rational Toy Shop," teaches Isabella literary analysis, and develops Matilda's mathematical prowess.[77] In contrast, Mademoiselle Panache taught her pupil, Lady Augusta, only the externals, the art of appearances. Character training had no place in the tutor's scheme; consequently, the tutor thoroughly corrupts Lady Augusta.[78]

Edgeworth's children's fiction sets the domestic parameters for the female role, while she converts childhood spontaneity into training for moral struggle. In the process, female characters split into the wise and prudent heroine who remains within her sphere and the selfish, imprudent antiheroine who ventures far from her happy domestic life. The author implies that at all costs women

had to maintain domestic stability and rationality; successful male-female relationships depended upon women's moral strength. Edgeworth carries these
themes into her adult fiction, but here the gap widens between the rational and
irrational female characters, until what the antiheroine represents, emotionalism
and autonomy, is utterly abandoned or ignored. In this way her novels preserve
the relationships between men and women; men depend upon the stability and
domestic virtue of women.

The Novels of Maria Edgeworth

Maria Edgeworth's novel *Ormond* is the story of a young man who desperately
needs a stable environment. *Ormond* traces the moral development of a young
man deprived of parents, home, and a suitable upbringing. Harry Ormond decides to become the Irish Tom Jones. Harry is described as "a warm-hearted,
imprudent young man with little education, no literature, governed more by
feeling than principle, never upon any occasion reasoning, but keeping right by
happy moral instincts."[79] He develops a moral sense, the ability to see people as
they are, when he compares the "real and factitious, both in matter and manner."[80] He learns, in effect, the difference in women; Dora Ulick, manipulative
and changeable, contrasts obviously with the generous and principled Florence
Annaly. Ormond chooses Florence because she represents "simple pleasures and
domestic virtues," the sight of which recalls Ormond to "his better self."[81]

Much of Edgeworth's fiction turns on the nature of principled women of
such depth of character and sure judgment that her tales quietly pivot on their
unperturbed axes. Of Florence Annaly the author wrote, "The face never expressed any thing but what the mind really felt."[82] Grace Nugent of *The Absentee* is described as a person who "with plain unsophisticated morality, in good
faith and simple truth, acted as she professed, thought what she said, and was
that what she seemed to be."[83] Her irreducible simplicity of character held to
principle and with graceful wisdom protected the marginalized society dame as
well as the exploited tenants. And no one had more courage than Grace Nugent,
said a male acquaintance.[84] Caroline, a heroine in *Patronage* who is compelling
because of her beauty and character, is immediately recognizable as the foil to
the impetuous Rosamund. It is Caroline who detests the "duplicity and piti-
ful meanness of a character, which was always endeavoring to seem, instead
of to be."[85] Edgeworth's heroines demonstrate the courage of independent
judgment and sympathy that emanates from a deep solidity of principle and
character.

In contrast to the principled heroines, the pride of their families, are the
troubled female protagonists who subvert marriage and family for their own
selfish interests. Dora Ulick in *Ormond*, along with her husband, is a partner in

a faro bank that cheats gamblers. Hers is a marriage of convenience to gain the social recognition she craves. *The Modern Griselda* is a disturbing tale of a neurotic woman "of too much sensibility" who uses emotional blackmail and intimidation in an attempt to dominate her husband.[86] The story recounts the slow deterioration of a marriage. In contrast, in the same story Emma and her husband demonstrate an enlightened marriage. Emma protests she would never vow to obey a husband's tyrannical rule, because she would "never respect a husband who demanded it."[87] The reasonable husband contends, "I wish to live with my wife as my equal, my friend. I do not desire that my will should govern; where our inclinations differ, let reason decide between us; or where it is a matter not worth reasoning about, let us alternately yield to one another."[88] The story suggests the strength and endurance of a reasonable relationship based upon the principled woman and the inherent democracy of such relationships.

Maria Edgeworth contrasts the equity of the reasonable relationship with the feminist notion of freedom and the rights of women. Harriot Freke, a traitorous and boisterous character in *Belinda,* illustrates the devastating effect of women's liberation and autonomy. The impetuous Harriot often dresses as a man because, as the narrator explains, "Harriot had no conscience, so she was always at ease; and never more so than in male attire, which she had been told became her particularly. She supported the character of a young rake with such spirit and truth, that I am sure no common conjurer could have discovered any thing feminine about her."[89] The treacherous Harriot, dressed as a man, compromises her friend Lady Delacour and then betrays her, causing a duel between Lady Delacour's husband and Colonel Lawless, the would-be seducer. The duel ends tragically with the Colonel's death. Harriot then prompts a duel between rivals Lady Delacour and Mrs. Luttridge. Luckily, a friend provides a diversion, and nothing comes of the women's affair of honor. By instigating role reversals, Harriot Freke causes despair and destruction. At bottom, according to Edgeworth, is Harriot Freke's refusal to feel shame for her actions or her existence as an independent woman. To hide her guilt she states that "all virtue is hypocrisy." She recognizes no positive value in shame. Yet hidden in the odious character of Harriot Freke is her refusal to accept shame for her gender. Her resistance to positive shame and responsibility for her actions negates Harriot's righteous stand against the negative aspect of shame—blame cast upon the woman.

In a revealing dialogue with two gentlemen, Mr. Percival and Mr. Vincent, Mrs. Freke contends that "shame is always the cause of the vices of women."

> "It is sometimes the effect," said Mr. Percival: "and as cause and effect are reciprocal, perhaps you may, in some instances, be right." But Mrs. Freke insists, "shame is the cause of all women's vices."
> "False shame, I suppose you mean?" said Mr. Percival.

"Mere play upon words! All shame is false shame—we should be a great deal better without it. What say you, Miss Portman?—Silent, hey? Silence that speaks." Belinda Portman, an admirer of Mr. Percival's domestic virtues, and present during the exchange, blushes.

"Miss Portman's blushes," said Mr. Vincent, "speak for her."

"Against her," said Mrs. Freke: "Women blush because they understand."

"And you would have them understand without blushing?" said Mr. Percival. "I grant you that nothing can be more different than innocence and ignorance. Female delicacy—"

"This is just the way you men spoil women," cried Mrs. Freke, "by talking to them of the delicacy of their sex, and such stuff. This delicacy enslaves the pretty delicate dears."

"No, it enslaves us," said Mr. Vincent.

"I hate slavery! Vive la liberté!" cried Mrs. Freke. "I'm a champion for the Rights of Woman."

"And I am an advocate for their happiness," said Mr. Percival, "and for their delicacy, as I think it conduces to their happiness."

Mrs. Freke then raises a pointed issue. "Why," she asks, "when a woman likes a man, does not she go and tell him so honestly?"

Belinda, surprised by this question from a woman, was too much abashed instantly to answer.

"Because she's a hypocrite. That is and must be the answer."

"No," said Mr. Percival; "because, if she be a woman of sense, she knows that by such a step she would disgust the object of her affection." [90]

Belinda Portman blushes as a woman who understands her subordinate place; she remains a silent and shamed witness, deferential to the gentlemen's definition of gender conventions. Harriot's "freakish" suggestion, the abolition of shame, is set in the context of "delicacy," the constriction of female mores. Evidence that those mores inculcate female self-hatred is found in Percival's assumption that if a woman initiated sexual contact she would arouse only contempt and disgust. Harriot, who abandoned her domestic role as a woman, took on the more violent liberty of men. Her uncontrolled "manly" character made her dangerous indeed. Harriot arouses disgust because she acts like a man. Men cannot be trusted because of their unstable emotions, unless they are aligned with reasonable women. In a sense, Maria Edgeworth reverses the traditional assumption of manly reason and female emotionalism. The Edgeworths introduced experimental rational training for women, yet underlying Maria Edgeworth's empiricism is an anxiety that women will not prove stable and thus undermine the social order, as in the case of Harriot Freke. Her anxieties relate to gender tensions within the Edgeworth family history. The connections between Maria Edgeworth's fascination with role reversal and her family structure require further investigation.

Edgeworth Family Tensions

Male and female members of the Edgeworth family experienced a rational environment differently. Passion, death, the rebellion of young Edgeworth men broke the calm exterior with the unwelcome insistence of inner imperatives. Maria Edgeworth's family literary establishment, however, provided the domestic stability and management necessary for a rational solution to family problems.

The life of Francis Edgeworth is a case in point. The son of Frances Anne and Richard Lovell Edgeworth, his prototype, the well-behaved "Frank," became one of the best-known and loved of Maria Edgeworth's stories, yet Francis Edgeworth contradicted his image of the well-trained, rational male. His passion overruled his reason, and he accepted a forced marriage. The domestic circle welcomed him back as the only way to restore his lost virtue. However, his choice forced upon him a marginal life.

Maria believed Francis Edgeworth most clearly inherited her father's character; if that was the case, Francis inherited both instability and a capacity for logic and reason. The young boy received a Lockean education from his guardian, his brother William. Richard Lovell counseled William to attend to the development of Francis's reasoning ability—"the first object to be attended to." "Habits of application & attention are the tools with which we must work," advised the father. Articulate, engaging, learned, Francis appeared to be the embodiment of his fictional alter ego. Lord Carrington, upon meeting Francis, exclaimed, "Frank—this is Frank—dear little Frank!"[91]

Francis seemed to be the picture of self-confidence and control, yet, like his father, his romantic passions interrupted a rational, secure course of life. Certainly, Francis demonstrated a well-trained mind. His father wished Francis to know classical and English literature. Edgeworth had no preference for Francis's profession but wished him to go to a public school in England and then on to Cambridge.[92] Francis followed his father's wishes. He attended the Charter House school, which he hated. Only the presence of his brothers and scientist uncle and namesake, Francis, made life bearable. When he moved up to preceptorship, he found a true interest in teaching. At Cambridge, Leigh Hunt, the well-known artist and rake, counted himself among Francis's friends. Hunt introduced him to the poet and addict Coleridge. At the end of his career at Cambridge Francis wrote to William and reflected upon his advantages: "a peaceful, free, & happy childhood, a good & kind family home, an open & unshakled education, that has fixed my roots deeply & strongly like a tree that is left open to the wind . . . they & my natural disposition & powers have formed me, made me—and I now am to govern this form that has been given me."[93] He decided to become a philosopher and to pursue wisdom. "And this wisdom," he said, "is my love." He planned to forsake all other earthly loves or ambitions.[94]

Unfortunately, Francis discovered instead the reality of a philosopher's existence. Unable to bear being shut up and lonely in a room in Italy, he became involved in romantic intrigues that led to a family scandal. Francis inherited his father's passionate nature. In one incident, the family invited two young women to the family estate after Francis had returned home. Francis courted them both; he settled on one and then decided on neither, much to the embarrassment of the girls' and Francis's families. After that Francis left again for Italy and met Rosa, a young Spanish woman with whom he had an affair. Scandal forced him to marry Rosa, much to the family's distress, though they ultimately accepted her.[95] Maria judged that Francis would never make much of literature as a profession because he lacked discipline and flexibility. She saw a future for him as a tutor.[96] He wrote a well-received article on architecture, and Maria hoped that success would encourage him. He then planned to finish a Cambridge degree.[97] Francis lived a philosopher's life, a life of poverty, and received family support; ultimately, he managed the Edgeworth estate.[98]

Lovell Edgeworth, the son of Richard Lovell Edgeworth and Honora Sneyd and the heir-apparent, dedicated himself to the advancement of the lower classes by teaching the Edgeworthian moral system presented in *Practical Education*. Lovell's opportunity came when Richard Lovell proposed a state education scheme to reconcile religious, ethnic, and economic differences. Richard Lovell Edgeworth applied to the archbishop of Armagh and proposed a school that would teach the basic mathematical and literary skills and "moral and prudent conduct." The elder Edgeworth was willing to contribute land and money (five hundred pounds) and suggested that the Erasmus Smith Charities contribute the remainder.[99] The Smith Charities fund proved exhausted; undaunted, Richard Lovell revised his proposal and offered a house, a thousand pounds, and his son Lovell as master of a school.[100]

The legatee of his father's educational schemes, Lovell proved competent and hardworking. Lovell taught poor children at Bristol, England—"wretched children," liars, and thieves, as he categorized them. He inculcated "moral feeling" as a preliminary step in the advancement of Irish education. His enlightened experiment consisted in making the children feel that "if they [were] good they [were] happy, & that if they behave[d] ill they [were] unhappy."[101] His was a rational system of education based upon the pleasure/pain principle. He encouraged his pupils to reinvent the system of rewards and punishments and established a trial by jury for those guilty of bad conduct. The system forced the children to reflect upon their own behavior.[102]

With the success of his early experiments in England, Lovell imagined himself the equal of his father. When Richard Lovell proposed a school at Edgeworthstown, Lovell replied to his father, "I am eager to enjoy you as an agreeable, clever companion."[103] Lovell usually expressed himself with an inflated rhetoric, a mark of insecurity, while he struggled to live up to his father's expectations.[104] His egalitarianism rested more on personal insecurity than ideology. When Lovell's aunts Mary and Charlotte visited, he lined up the poor from the village and the boys from the school to give his relatives a rousing welcome.[105] Despite his class bias Lovell insisted upon the enlightened principle that every child must be treated differently and gently led to learn.[106]

School debts and increasing drunkenness ended Lovell's experiment. According to Maria Edgeworth, merchants wondered, "How could so much wine be drunk in one house?"[107] Maria felt the pain, because the school represented the Edgeworthian model outlined in *Practical Education*. Moreover, she knew the great care Lovell had taken with his pupils. Nonetheless, Lovell's mismanagement of the estate also contributed to strain the household finances.

Throughout the 1820s Maria Edgeworth mastered the outstanding debt by a combination of family loans and tenants' extension of credit.[108] Lovell's irresponsibility and alcoholism disgusted the family and eventually resulted in his exile to England. Later Maria pleaded his cause to the rest of the family in the most reasonable terms. She argued that his letters had acquired a more sincere, less exaggerated tone and that he had abandoned his bad companions and acquired better health; the family could tolerate an "experiment in his favor." He had paid his debts and had done nothing to justify perpetual banishment, she insisted.[109] Lovell chose a dissolute life; a rational environment did not save him. But he found redemption in a system of values that erased his moral debts. Lovell, like Francis, went home. With the settling of accounts, Maria justly inherited her father's preeminent position in the family. And in league with Maria's beloved Frances, the fourth wife of Richard Lovell and the only wife to survive him, the family continued to operate as one corporate soul.[110]

Erring Edgeworth men went home to a well-integrated domestic household. In addition to ordinary family affairs, the Edgeworths supported Maria Edgeworth's literary enterprise. Frances Anne Beaufort Edgeworth, Richard Lovell's fourth wife, acted as chief housekeeper and peacemaker; she integrated the children of the previous marriages and managed a household of over twenty people—"a whole family of people of different ages & humors, and tastes all together."[111] Maria Edgeworth depended upon her extended family and stepmother for intellectual and emotional support. The women in the family maintained a literary subculture; Frances occasionally copied work for Maria. Honora, Harriet, and Fanny edited and criticized Maria's work. Aunts Ruxton and Margaret, cousins Sophy and Lucy, and sisters Harriet, Fanny, Lucy, and Honora read novels and literary criticism and kept up a literary dialogue across several estates—Edgeworthstown, Trim, and Black Castle. Maria delighted in moving from one stimulating atmosphere to the next during her family visits.

To understand the family content of Edgeworthian pedagogy, then, is to understand the balance of power within the household. Maria Edgeworth's voice is the most accomplished among those who contributed to the final product. Edgeworth family life was a continuous dialogue; pedagogic, scientific, and literary themes were shared and became part of lived experience. The family lived the texts of *Practical Education,* "Harry and Lucy," and "Frank." Maria acted as maestro, orchestrating family voices into her fictional product.

The family that revolved around Maria's axis provided her with the literary discussions so vital to her creative imagination. After a day spent at Trim in the company of her half sister Harriet Butler, Maria wondered in her letter to Fanny Edgeworth "how people get along without literature and what is much more extraordinary without the least taste for literature! . . . The conversation here and the taste for literature are so refreshing and inspiring to me." [112] The Butler household at Trim offered literary diversions to family members. Harriet read biography to her half sister Honora and a fairy tale, "Le Oiseau blue [*sic*]," to her mother, Frances. [113]

Harriet served as one of Maria's most important editors, especially in Maria's later life. The young woman began as something of an apprentice to Maria, copying letters for her. She graduated to editorship because Maria trusted her judgment and her friendship. [114] Maria once encouraged Harriet by passing on to her the comment of Aunt Ruxton, who said Harriet had "a great mind." [115] Harriet aided the publication of *Harrington* and *Ormond.* In addition, Harriet inspired Maria with a story theme and continued to edit her work. The pattern of family criticism was important to Maria. She rewarded Harriet's work for her by copying the story that Harriet suggested into a notebook just like the ones in which she wrote for her father. Harriet's link to Richard Lovell probably increased Maria's trust of her judgment and reinforced her love of her half sister and her respect for her intellect. [116]

Honora, daughter of Richard Lovell's third wife, followed the same apprenticeship as Harriet, starting as a copier and graduating to editor. Honora also acted as confidante to her half sister Maria. Maria Edgeworth stated that she would entrust her own diary to no one but her "mother" (Frances Anne) or Honora. [117] Honora received "sovereign power" over one of the lesser *Early Lesson* stories, "Blind Kate." Maria, prompted by her aunts at Black Castle, advised Honora to shorten it. Honora acted more like a lieutenant than a general, however. She received direct orders from Maria and carried them out. [118]

After the death of her father in 1817, Maria's "chosen companion" remained Fanny, the eldest child of Richard Lovell and Frances Anne Beaufort Edgeworth. [119] The age difference made the relationship between them more like aunt and niece than sisters. Nonetheless, Maria relied on Fanny's fresh point of view and listened to her literary commentaries. Fanny offered sharp criticism and put Maria back on "the right path." Maria had to assure Fanny, however, that Fanny's criticism did not discourage her and, on the contrary, inspired and excited her. Often Fanny got into a passion about the inclusion of a chapter, or she insisted upon excising examples that she believed would not work. The second series about Harry and Lucy, especially, benefited from her editing.[120] Maria wished the sequel to "Harry and Lucy" to be especially well written since the original was her father's "own and first book." [121] Perhaps Fanny's special role in this series had as much to do with her intimacy with Maria as well as Fanny's interest in science. Maria wrote with a more self-conscious scientific approach than in her earlier works. Fanny remained an editor for Maria; [122] moreover, their fondness and shared enthusiasm for literary criticism continued over the years as they exchanged commentaries on their reading. Although Maria and Fanny disagreed about style, it was important to them to acknowledge what had touched them.[123]

Trim, Harriet's estate and part of the literary enterprise mentioned above, functioned as an editorial board with Harriet as chief editor. Black Castle, the home of Maria's beloved Aunt Ruxton and cousins Mag and Sophy, offered a safe haven. Aunt Ruxton provided maternal care to the young Maria during her father's abandonment and after her mother's death. Once the Edgeworth family stabilized, Aunt Ruxton offered both family warmth and a pleasant literary hospitality. The household read Maria's work and responded with criticism and pleasure. Maria referred to the Black Castle family as her "dear correctors." [124] Maria Edgeworth wrote from Black Castle to Frances Anne Edgeworth, "My aunt & Sophy & Mag are all reading Harry and Lucy and all reading in a way that delights me—bit by bit—the only way it can be fairly judged." [125] The Black Castle circle had a good deal of trouble with the tedious scientific account of sugar refining and said so.[126] Aunt Ruxton demanded accessibility, color, and simplicity, characteristics that humanized the scientific tales.[127] Sophy made corrections on "Rosamund," and she and Aunt Ruxton made stylistic suggestions, which Maria followed.[128]

The theme of family unity animated the Edgeworth literary enterprise and pedagogical experiment. Richard Lovell Edgeworth described family harmony in terms of his relationship with Maria and her relationship with his wife, Frances: "[Maria] is my pupil, my literary partner & my friend . . . Her constant attention to all of [the family members] is undoubtedly of the utmost service, & her strong attachment to my wife gives a unanimity to all our pursuits that has a most salutary effect." [129] Even after the death of Richard Lovell, Maria Edgeworth observed that the family continued to operate as "one whole—one great Polypus [an octopus] Soul." [130] Like the tentacles of an octopus, family criticism supported the one great moral enterprise of being good by doing good.

Nonetheless, family training, example, and experience shaped moral character but not necessarily psychological or emotional independence. Maria Edgeworth may have achieved fame on the Continent and illuminated many a soirée, but she eschewed a public life of literary criticism or political comment. Rather, she relished her domestic life and in her work attributed creativity and moral strength to family stability and regularity.

Family cohesion meant that Maria Edgeworth remained ambivalent about her personal independence. Maria claimed ownership of her work. She acknowledged that independence was her father's legacy. She insisted on her reason for writing:

> It certainly is my principle never to write for money—but it certainly is my principle that it is just and proper that I should earn money by writing. The distinction here I think is not a futile tricky distinction but—fair and solid—writing for money I take it means making money the sole or principle object—not considering fame or the service to be done to our fellow creatures or any other motive. This I hold to be base—I never did it & I never shall. But my father constantly exhorted and excited me to exert myself to earn money by writing.[131]

Moreover, she treasured the annuity her father set aside for her. It enabled her to live well and take care of family members.[132] However, she did not judge her independence by personal wealth but rather by her independent moral judgment and personal integrity.

In the Edgeworth family, emotions were denied, measured, and restrained in order to allow moral space, both internal and external. Maria Edgeworth never forgot her mother's death and "being taken into the room to receive her last kiss."[133] No other memories of Maria's early childhood survive except perhaps indirectly in a poem Maria sent to her niece Emmeline King. In her old age Maria copied Mrs. Norton's poem "The Daughter's Recollection of Her Widowed Mother Teaching Her Children" from a collection entitled *Dream*. The verses describe the long-repressed grief of abandonment and privation:

> Oft through that hour in sadness I retrace
> My childhood's vision of thy calm sweet face;
> Oft see thy form, its mournful beauty shrouded
> In thy black weeds, and coif of widow's woe;
> Thy clear expressive eyes all dim and clouded
> By that deep wretchedness the lonely know,
> Stifling thy grief, to hear some weary task
> con'd by unwilling lips with listless air . . .
> Hidden forgotten by the great and gay
> Enduring sorrow and by fits and starts
> But the long self denial day by day
> Alone, amid thy brood of careless hearts.[134]

The poem may have been evocative for Maria. Surely, Maria Edgeworth shared the sadness of her abandoned mother, a life hidden and full of grief. Too young to understand, Maria may have blamed herself for her mother's unhappiness and identified with the "careless hearts." Nonetheless, a lifetime of forgetting produced an aged heart full of compassion for her mother. The memories of her mother may have induced a certain shame for her mother's predicament.

Yet Maria often encouraged members of her family not to enter into self-recrimination. She once made a critical comment to Frances Anne concerning her daughter, "I am glad she [Harriet] never repents—or beats her head—that is the only thing in which I dont wish her to resemble her mother." [135] Occasionally, she acknowledged that denial or emotional restraint could not contain the irrational. She had only to observe her own circle. Maria Edgeworth was shocked to learn of the suicide of Lady William, a sensitive, reckless, high-spirited, aggressive woman. Maria reflected, "How little we know of others— or ourselves—or of the wonderful & fearful manner in which we are made! It is awful to see how little power the Reason has over the Will or the Will over the Reason." [136] Emotions did lead Maria, but she allowed them to do so only if they were minor or nondestructive. After receiving particularly disturbing news Maria returned to the ordinary concerns of the day; she cherished the ordinary. "Is it not wonderful," she wrote to Frances Anne, "that after great emotions, little things can interest us so! and is not it a blessing such tiny emotions spring up before us to rouse us again however foolishly and lead us on—on through life." [137] Respect for another's interior life or the allowance of moral space did not mean isolation since that would make a mockery of social ethics. Rather, Maria allowed for an intuition, a sympathy "by which the higher order of minds know each other." [138] Class, education, and talent counted for sociability; however, she respected virtue wherever she found it, among Irish tenants or Jewish correspondents.

The individual balanced the inner and outer attitude and manner. "Take care of yourself," Maria cautioned her brother Charles Sneyd, "& dont let your feelings wear out your body." [139] She admired her half sister Honora, who she believed survived an illness because of her "equanimity & great self-government." What impressed Maria was Honora's "power of keeping objects & feelings in just proportions . . . judging always with a calmness . . . [and supporting] herself with a touching fortitude." [140] The Edgeworth family assumed the difficulty, repression, control, and supervision necessary to develop an enlightened moral character. The family experience, transcribed and transformed by genius, contributed social guides to moral development. In effect, the family produced a secularized wisdom literature.

As the scale tipped increasingly toward the rationality and stability of Edgeworth women, that is, as Maria and Frances Anne gained greater control over the management of the household, Maria Edgeworth distanced herself from the "oddly double" nature of her character. After *Belinda* Maria Edgeworth never wrote another novel and instead gave in to her comfortable domestic existence. Only shadows and memories reminded her of her painful past, impetuous youth, and impulsive actions. Nonetheless, Edgeworthian fiction and pedagogy left a paradoxical legacy for the "textual community" of women educators who admired her principled heroines but struggled with the emotional repression and limited domestic context her moral ideology reinforced. The Edgeworthian moral model applied, after all, in circumstances where men or male surrogates acted badly and irrationally and women provided the rational balance. However, a new generation that demanded greater personal and political expression for women, that defined moral standards in subjective religious terms, and that insisted upon changes in the domestic partnership confronted the inherent gender conflict within Edgeworthian pedagogy. Edgeworthian principles contributed to the contention between generations; the controversy introduced different perceptions of goodness, justice, and morality associated with Victorian social constructs.

Maria Edgeworth's first contact with Rachel Mordecai occurred in August 1816 just as Rachel had launched her Edgeworthian experiment with her half sister Eliza. "Education of the heart" took on new meaning for Rachel the teacher; she had touched the sensibility of the author of her method and engaged in a transcontinental dialogue with an enlightened family source. Now Rachel's test took on new meaning; her work joined Continental educational reform, which promised moral direction and character formation. However, she discovered the conflict inherent in enlightened practice between egalitarian discourse and traditional gender roles. Rachel also encountered what enlightened scholars ignored: the limitations in the training for "goodness" and the challenge of teaching the practice of holiness.

CHAPTER 3

WISDOM
TESTED

Rachel Mordecai's Practice

ɪɔɔʊɔɔʊɔɔʊɔɔʊɔɔʊɔɔʊɔɔʊɔɔʊɔɔʊɔɔʊɔɔʊɔɔʊɔɔʊɔɔɪ

Say to Wisdom, "You are my sister,"
And Call Understanding a kinswoman.
—Proverbs 7:4

Republican Female Definitions of Self

"I THOUGHT YOU WERE conceited yourself." A sullen remark by ten-year-old Eliza Mordecai to her sister-mentor, Rachel, on 19 August 1819 indicates more than petulance after being rebuked for a proud, wrong-headed intellectual challenge.[1] Definition of self in the early republic carried with it ethnic and religious tensions that complicated a preadolescent's path to maturity. Generational challenge occurred during a period of transatlantic reform of women's role. Such challenges, however, remained safely within certain moral limits, the practice of virtue to preserve the republic. The "republican mother" as an educator of civic virtue suggests only one category of multivariant social reform; the "republican wife" as a virtuous companion suggests another.[2] The evolution of a female self, played out on a battleground of pedagogical relationships, makes any categorization of diverse republican women difficult. Ethnic and religious adaptations of enlightened notions of republican womanhood demonstrate the intense negotiation and compromise that shaped republican women. The pedagogical experiment of Rachel Mordecai, an Orthodox Jew of German descent who taught her half sister Eliza according to enlightened pedagogy, transformed Protestant female ideology into enlightened Jewish practice. Her experiment reveals the struggle to accomplish the creation of a moral and religious self in the early national period.[3]

Edgeworthian principles and methods emerged in the pragmatics of learning, the practice, operation, and structure actors experienced and developed in the educational process. The wisdom gained in the instructional process joined enlightened and religious practices, since the Edgeworthian method concentrated upon "education of the heart," or the training of character, important to evangelical and Jewish as well as secular educators. Post-Revolutionary American educational theory, practiced in the home, tied method to familial relationships bound up in a particular religious culture. Wisdom, the discerning ways that profited the student and enlightened the teacher, endured at a very deep level in the relationship between sisters and between parents and children. Scholars note the egalitarian changes in American and British family structure that wore away patriarchal hierarchy and introduced parental friendship with children.[4] However, these changes took place gradually in educational contexts fraught with conflict as mentors struggled to reconcile religious and rational values. The interpretation of virtue as "goodness" or "holiness" generated friction between generations.

Rachel Mordecai's experiment, carried out in an Orthodox Jewish household, imbricated Jewish pietism in enlightened method. Traditional Jewish literature, the Bible and the Talmud, does not recognize ethics outside the notion of holiness. Holiness, according to classic Jewish scholars, indicates a more inclusive term than the enlightened value of "goodness." Full and free assent to the will of God enjoins the individual in social action for God's sake. The call to holiness, in the context of a choice between good and evil, then, is a call to intimacy with the divine. Human response is measured in the depth of compassion an individual might have for the marginal, the poor. In the struggle to respond willingly is a hidden desire to become what Divinity intended. Bahya ibn Pakuda's eleventh-century treatise, *Duties of the Heart,* counsels an inner godly response that corresponds to the outer obligations of Jewish law. In addition, Pakuda advised pietists to teach the terrors of evil and God's punishment in order to edify the soul that struggles toward purity.[5]

The Enlightenment may have moderated the disciplinary force of Jewish pietism and redirected social ethics from community to democratic nation, but the call to holiness remained a part of Jewish Orthodoxy. In contrast to Orthodox holiness, the enlightened precept of "goodness" ascribes no inner godly response to external behavior; outward behavior manifests inner virtue, conformity to natural law or God's laws. Leniency, not severity or fear, governs the manner of enlightened discipline. And rather than covenantal responsibility for others' welfare, enlightened ethics prescribes natural concern for social harmony and welfare. The aim of enlightened education is the development of a "free and intelligent agent." [6] In the enlightened tradition, free agency did not apply to women, who were identified as inseparable from families or marriages and therefore dependent. [7]

In May 1816, in the midst of her teaching and domestic duties, Rachel entered upon her experiment, teaching her half sister Eliza according to Edgeworthian method and pious Orthodox tradition. At stake in her character training lay the very nature of freedom and the meaning of independence for herself and her charge. Mentor and pupil absorbed the implications of rational method incrementally, moving from authoritarian discipline to shared, consensual learning. They did not always move in unison but in ways that responded to deeper intimations about who they were and what they were about. Initially, protectiveness for a dependent child motivated Rachel, since she had always been charged with Eliza's care and felt a certain responsibility for her. As she confided to her sister Ellen: "Eliza says her lessons almost every day but does not go into school regularly, I do not think she is quite so engaging as she used to be—I am afraid that as she grows larger such a variety of companions will be an injury to her. We must try and let her be among them as little as possible—her disposition is naturally so good that I cannot bear the idea of its being injured." [8] Rachel's reservations about schooling reveal her concerns for the child's virtue. White southern families feared that schools might corrupt their daughters. Even one errant child in a class might taint the group, according to common opinion. [9] Ironically, Rachel held to the common bias against schooling despite the good reputation of Warrenton Female Academy. Perhaps Rachel feared that the challenges to the child's virtue might mature her too quickly, an indication of Rachel's overprotectiveness.

The Edgeworthian pedagogical scheme, devised as home tutoring, offered closely supervised training of character and an engaging dialogic method. Rachel deeply appreciated Edgeworthian practice and told her brother Sam: "Everything from the pen of Miss Edgeworth contains so much good sense, so much instruction, & so many useful hints on the subject of Education, that to those earnestly engaged in that pursuit they are invaluable." [10] In addition to Rachel's enthusiasm, the child Eliza presented unusual opportunities because of her attitude and interest. Six-year-old Eliza had read and understood many of the stories of *Early Lessons*. [11] And since the family marveled at Eliza's good nature, she seemed predisposed to accept intense tutoring. Ellen remarked, "I have seldom seen such a disposition as hers. It is the greatest blessing heaven bestows." [12] Such a rare "bud" of unblemished quality needed special care, and because of it Rachel exhibited a certain anxiety about tutoring Eliza. She felt she could not do the child justice, as she confided to Maria Edgeworth, with whom she had recently begun a correspondence: "Eliza, a child of seven years has always been particularly my charge. She possesses an excellent disposition and a degree of intelligence which, while it delights, often causes me to sigh, at my incapacity to cultivate it as it deserves. I seek by fixing your principles and precepts in my mind and making them as far as I can my guides, to supply in part my own deficiency." [13] Rachel's insecurities perhaps made her cling to enlightened precept, but tradition kept her faithful to the practice of true virtue, the attainment of holiness.

Evident in the very first entry of Rachel's journal is a combination of enlightened method and religious consciousness, her reason for writing the diary. On a Sunday, 19 May 1816, Rachel described her intention "to commence writing juvenile, I should rather term them, 'nursery anecdotes,'" about Eliza. Rachel borrowed from the Edgeworths the didactic technique of recording her teaching dialogue. Her expectations also mark the progressive, Lockean teacher; she wished to observe Eliza's growth through childhood's successive stages. Metaphorically, she wrote, "I wish too to see if the tender bud which promises so fair, will bloom into a fragrant, lovely, and unfading flower." Her expectation took the form of a prayer:

> Should it seem good to the Most High to suffer *it,* and *me,* to continue on this great theatre of existence, I will watch over, and mark its daily progress, I will endeavor to destroy each canker that would enter its bosom to render it less sweet and lovely, And O! may I be rendered capable of forming the materials which nature has bountifully placed in my hands; may reason, combined with virtue, and nourished by education, form a character eminently fitted to discharge every duty of this life, and when called from this transitory state of being, worthy to repose eternally in the presence of its Creator.[14]

Proper reverence for the divine name indicates the depth and seriousness of Rachel's prayer, and Rachel invokes divine Providence as a sacred presence in her efforts to train Eliza's character. The elder sister directed the voice of authority, of God's law, to the child's bosom, or heart. Development of character involved a conscious moral choice on the part of the individual. Thus Rachel endeavored to remove each "canker," or obstacle to virtue. Jewish tradition stressed that in the proper fulfillment of the precepts, the obedient individual became a partner with the Almighty in the work of creation.[15] Rachel's own obedience to God's will allowed her to participate in the creation of Eliza's character. The education of reason and virtue aimed at a responsible life that would be rewarded with the eternal divine presence.

Throughout the diary Rachel listens for the child's deeper response to duty and obligation that reveals the divine presence. When Rachel teaches her the commandment "Thou shalt not take the name of the Lord thy God in vain," Eliza notes how frequently and carelessly the name is used. Rachel counsels her sister that "no address should ever be made to God, but what is serious, & with all our hearts." Eliza concurred, "Yes sister Rachel & when I meet with *that word* in books, I would rather leave it out, or say some other instead of it." [16] When Eliza replied, she did so not only as an obedient child but as one perhaps trained to know Hashem, the name, in Hebrew. The sacred word expresses divine power and might. [17] Avoidance of the use of the name attributes power to God and not to the frail self. Eliza learns the infinitude of mercy that covers human vulnerability when she questions a hymn that praises past mercies but begs for ten thousand more. [18] The hymn, according to Rachel, does not imply human greed but blesses God for commanding his people to petition for mercy.

Perhaps the most transparent example of response to divine presence occurred when Eliza complained of distraction in prayer and examined the cause. She said, "Sister Rachel it is so hard to keep *my thoughts from wandering*. I read in the 'Misses Magazine' . . . where Lady Witty said that she would always try to think of God when she was praying to him. But thinking of that very thing makes my thoughts wander, for then I begin to think of the 'Misses Magazine.'" [19] Eliza's self-analysis impressed Rachel; here was a self-conscious process to get at the root of distraction and eliminate it in order to pray. The method is rational, but the concern is Orthodox. Edgeworthian ethics demanded an intentionality that prescribed moral behavior but not necessarily divine intercession.

Eliza easily identified an enlightened distinction between "true charity" and "its image," of doing good for its own sake or for the sake of praise. She recounted the incident in Maria Edgeworth's "Mademoiselle Panache" where Lady Augusta flaunted her generosity, whereas Helen Temple and her sister nursed an old woman privately to "do all the good they could." [20] Enlightened charity aimed at the greatest good possible for social well-being. That Eliza understood ethical integrity pleased Rachel, but she listened more closely for a divine intimation. In a subsequent anecdote, Eliza admires clouds at sunset and notes, "when I looked at the cloud[s] I felt *afraid*, they looked so beautiful." Rachel believes this is the "first impression of Sublimity." [21] Out of the reconciliation of divine intimation and rational method emerged the early republican female self.

Maria Edgeworth's Literary Prototypes Applied

In her diary Rachel describes Eliza as a "good girl," a "Rosamund" figure. Rosamund, a character in Maria Edgeworth's children's fiction, makes impulsive choices but learns through painful experience the necessity of obligation and the pleasures of benevolence. But within the historical reality represented in the diary, Eliza challenges authority, thereby defying the literary norm. In the "strawberries anecdote," Eliza is offered some strawberries through the kindness of her sister Caroline. But a servant mistakenly removes them, and Rachel decides not to pursue the matter. Eliza, momentarily disappointed, recovers her composure and is just as satisfied with her sister's alternative, playing with but not eating filberts. When Caroline returns the strawberries, Eliza is given her share, and Rachel remarks that Eliza receives the strawberries because "goodness is always rewarded." But Eliza evades literary expectations when she qualifies her sister's assertion and replies, "No sister Rachel not *always* you know." In the cool tones of a mentor Rachel replies that virtue is its own reward.[22]

Literary convention breaks down under the spontaneous challenge of the child. Eliza fights literary representation. Here is a seven-year-old child who typically enjoys arguing or challenging the rules of a game. Eliza's confidence is based upon trust in her own observation; she speaks from a new self-contained stage as a thinking child. But like the parent in Edgeworthian children's fiction, Rachel maintains authority. When she argues that virtue is its own reward, Rachel establishes a clear hierarchy: first, that she is the authority, and second, that a principle exists that can be grasped only by children older than Eliza. Eliza accepts the rule because it is from her older sister and reveals her good nature as well as her submission by offering some strawberries to Rachel.

Eliza's resistance and submission suggest something beyond literary convention and didactic assumptions, namely, the development of a self out of inner conflict. Literary convention illustrates "the good girl"; historical observation records the fact of resistance. The question is how to interpret resistance in the midst of didactic language that generally devalues, circumvents, and transforms resistance. What is significant is the pattern of resistance. Eliza rejected enlightened values—reason, good sense, orderliness, intellectual achievement, shaming techniques. Nonetheless, she used critical method and differentiation to construct her own religious, social, emotional, talented self. Eliza confronted the human struggle—the will to do good or evil—and chose family harmony. Additionally, since she caused Rachel some anxiety by her challenge, she offered a kind of restitution: she shared her strawberries. The offer appeased her sister but did not quite cancel out Eliza's criticism of the idea of a beneficent world where goodness is always rewarded. Her recognition of a more ambivalent world originated in her awareness that goodness was not a simple choice. Eliza admitted that at times she felt she couldn't help being good.[23] Her dilemma may have been provoked by the depth of her internalization of "good" and aversion to antisocial behavior. Yet Eliza's socialization came at a cost. Rachel equated goodness with docility; she compared "good girl" to "good servant."[24] Mentors reminded critical children of their place in the family hierarchy.

Nine-year-old Eliza confronted the code of paternal hierarchy one cold morning in February 1818 when she attempted to put out a small fire started by sparks from the fireplace. Her father directed her to get a "wing,"[25] and when

Eliza had difficulty finding it, he called her stupid. Eliza complained to Rachel that the remark made her angry because she did not think she was stupid. Rachel's reply contains the hierarchical family code, a code that demanded strict obedience:

> It is the duty of the child to submit, without complaining, to the blame or punishment which a parent thinks proper to inflict. We should feel sorry for having displeased our parents, but never allow ourselves to feel *angry*, at any thing they say or do to us. They are very seldom unjust, & when they are so, they are sorry for it, & shew by their kindness that they wish to make us amends. But even if they do not, we *must be wrong* in blaming them, & we ought to submit with as much gentleness as possible.[26]

The father, under the duress of the emergency, gave no explanation of his behavior, nor did he apologize. Instead, when reminded of his behavior, he simply said "Oh" and left the room.[27] The patriarchal family code demanded more than simple obedience: it required suppression of any subversive feeling or thought. Repression of feeling was a cost of family unity.

The family hierarchy, once established, nonetheless competed with a rational intellectual standard. The Mordecais accorded no deference to age or gender in studious pursuits. In this respect, the Mordecais pursued standards of enlightened female equality, a social equality that acknowledged the importance of advanced education for women.[28] When Eliza corrected her older brother Augustus during a geography lesson, he became angry and resentful. Augustus claimed that Eliza was "proud," but Eliza defended herself by answering, "I did not say [the correct answer] because I was proud, for I know it was not any thing to be proud of, just to know my lesson." [29] Solomon, the teacher in this case, reprimanded Augustus. Rachel agreed with Eliza and Solomon that Augustus was wrong, but she reconciled the children by stressing Eliza's hurt feelings. Rachel apologized for Augustus. Augustus admitted only that he was no longer angry with Eliza; later he gave way and rejoined Eliza. The family considered Augustus ill-behaved, but he remained impervious to Rachel's insistence that he admit his error and that he graciously repair the damage.[30] Individual male personalities may have been reluctant to relinquish the privileges of their sex even in this enlightened age. The family, however, insisted upon intellectual standards at the expense of deference. This single incident suggests that the ideal of benevolent patriarchy contained within it fractures of authority. In educating Eliza, Rachel used an ethical model, Edgeworthian pedagogy, that encouraged children's individuation but within the context of a benevolent patriarchy. The model itself was not internally consistent. Moreover, Rachel's own conflict between autonomy and authority undermined the coherence of the enlightened model with which she was educating Eliza.

Philosopher Michel Foucault situates modern (enlightened) discipline and punishment not merely in its repressive regimen but in a whole series of positive and negative effects where punishment may be regarded as part of a "complex social function."[31] Repression demonstrated power relations within the family, but so did affection during the early republic. Rachel kissed Eliza when the younger sister demonstrated good behavior and withheld affection when she exhibited bad or childish behavior such as temper tantrums or lying.[32] "Goodness" entangled with emotional well-being confuses parental and teacher roles and prompts the child to wonder if she deserves love.

The conversation between Rachel and Eliza on 26 July 1818 illustrates the "gentle way in punishment," the reminder or symbol of surveillance reinforced by tentativeness of affection and dominance.[33] Dressing for bed, an embarrassed Eliza admitted she had not been "as good a girl yesterday & today as I was in the week." She continued her litany of faults: "Oh, I have been out of humour with Emma a good many times, & I did not feel right when you kissed me last night, because I had not told you." Rachel cautiously replied, "Well my dear you may have your kiss now, but you must try & be as good on Saturday & Sunday when you are not employed, & when I do not generally set down your conduct, as you are on the other days in the week, when you are busy with your studies & when I do [set down your conduct]."[34] Eliza perceives emotional blackmail as natural, a positive, consistent force that somehow will propel her toward safety and well-being.[35]

The Orthodox use of God as the ultimate judge and punisher is a variation on the hierarchical theme. When Eliza lied about her lesson preparation, Rachel wrote in her list book, "God does not love people who tell *lies,* nor will any one have confidence in them."[36] The Supreme Being implicated in human retribution then reinforces patriarchal notions of authority. Rachel conflates love and justice in such absolute notions of authority that fear replaces love in teaching ethics. Such intimidating weapons reinforced the family hierarchy and challenged the egalitarian method.

Rachel represented punishment, especially self-recrimination, as an exercise in virtue—to "destroy each canker" that threatened character. Sometimes, however, such discipline elicited only confusion in Eliza and fear of Rachel's anger. Eliza's response depended upon the weight of the offense. Her recital of week-old slights against Emma suggests an easier admission than her confession to carelessness. When confronted with neglect of her dew plant, Eliza hesitated telling Rachel because, as she said to her sister, "I thought you would be angry with me."[37] Eliza's routine responses to discipline appear mechanical because of her overly scrupulous training in self-recrimination. Locke suggested shame as an antidote to force in the foundation of discipline.[38] The Edgeworths cautioned that shame not be used for slight faults; rather, they leaned toward positive reinforcement. "Children who are zealous in defense of their perfections are most stationary in progress," argued *Practical Education*.[39] According to the Edgeworths, self-recrimination represents progress because it bolsters pride. For the sake of a repentant child the Edgeworths addressed this observation, "To confess that you have been in the wrong, is only saying, in other words, that you are wiser today, than you were yesterday."[40]

The Mordecai family insisted that Eliza admit her faults. Self-recrimination may have been cultivated by the family as an example of affection. Locke recommends leniency—better to forgive twenty times a self-confessed fault than forgive an excused or self-justifying one.[41] Renowned child psychologist Jean Piaget contends that seven-year-olds consider rules sacred because adults command them. Appeasement is the only way to reconcile breaking the rule and regain the trust and affection of the parent. Children then love recrimination, according to Piaget.[42] Nonetheless, family environment interprets practice. Eliza's confessions took place within a carefully supervised environment. Rachel notes, "[Eliza] has been also constantly sent by her other sisters to her sister Rachel with messages indicating the manner in which her different employments had been executed."[43] Her mortification in having to admit "'I have been very inattentive' or 'Sister E[llen] says I am too impatient'" led her to develop a silly voice for her confessions.[44] Silly means lacking in good sense. Silliness subverts rational order. The family operated as a system that defined power in an organized hierarchy. By her silly voice Eliza resisted being defined as subordinate in the family hierarchy. However, the Mordecai sisters' "constant" intervention in Eliza's care suggests that adults are intimately involved in Eliza's welfare. In this atmosphere Eliza is overcome by the circle of elders who expect her compliance, and she begins to break herself of the habit of speaking in a silly voice. Internalization in this case assimilates command but does not demonstrate a fully developed sense of responsibility. Eliza accepts adult authority in rule making; rules are then externalized. In contrast, liberty is an advanced stage that reflects upon an internalized rule.

Eliza's Challenge

Eliza's internal struggle for self-control and a sense of self created a crisis within the Mordecai household, a crisis that propelled Eliza toward greater self-affirmation yet firmly implanted her within the familial hierarchy. The unstated but compelling issue remained the power struggle between child and mentor. At stake, according to Rachel, was not simply her own but divine authority. Rachel invoked a potent dual parental authority: a maternal teaching authority and a paternal religiously sanctioned authority.

Rachel relates the incident of a temper tantrum that occurred while she was teaching Eliza a lesson in "recollective memory." According to Rachel, Eliza tended toward heedlessness, the unconsciousness of a seven year old. Determined to instill motivation, Rachel promised to finish a story of Peter the Great's marriage only if Eliza reminded Rachel of it before bedtime. When Eliza requested the story after being put to bed, Rachel refused: Eliza hadn't remembered to request the story at the proper time. Humiliation and disappointment fueled Eliza's tantrum—she railed at having to remember everything in order to have any pleasure and insisted that she had remembered to request the story but not at the precise moment Rachel required. Rachel denied more than Eliza's impulse to have a story told; she denied Eliza's very self. Seven year olds are governed by the need for immediate gratification and expect punishment in a world of rules and reciprocity, but they are still creatures of impulse with an inability to mediate between self and object. The denial of an object is also a denial of self. Tantrum, according to Robert Kegan, is the result of a conflict of impulses when "the impulses are the self." [45] "[Eliza] would not *listen to reason*," Rachel despaired. [46] In Kegan's terms, Eliza rejected Rachel's insistence upon reason because reason contravened Eliza's impulsive self. Shut off from the family and miserable, Eliza eventually apologized to Rachel and "prayed to God to make her a better girl." Rachel reassured her that God "would assist her." [47] Reasonable instruction and discipline had limits that only divine intervention could remedy. Divinity had the power to reshape and redirect character and animate a true self.

The crisis left Eliza pale and thin, enervated, depressed. She may have been reevaluating her earlier truce with Rachel, her earlier pattern of behavior as the pliant, apologetic child. A more defined sense of self may have suggested to Eliza the possibility of a different relationship with Rachel. Such a relationship, however, is not clearly perceived by the reader of the diary. A crisis theoretically could evoke a radical change in a child's outlook, but Rachel does not record Eliza's private thoughts in her diary. Rachel observes listless, depressed behavior, but it is unlikely that Eliza redefined her relationship with Rachel because she was still, at age seven, so embedded in family life and was caught between separation and integration, independence and compliance.

Eliza experienced such a crisis and probable ensuing imbalance in the middle of her seventh year. In subsequent entries in the diary Rachel records that Eliza misrepresented the amount of work she had done in her mathematics exercise and on her poetry and French lessons and evaded responsibility in the care of her dew plant. Rachel severely reprimanded Eliza for her lies and shamed her in front of family and playmates. Rachel instilled further measures of shame by depriving Eliza of a good-night kiss and threatening her with the loss of God's love. [48]

Eliza's behavior may have been connected to her anger over the Peter the

Great incident and the feeling that Rachel acted precipitately and harshly. The Edgeworths observe that lying results from servility, often practiced in the presence of masters. In contrast, they observe honor and truth telling among children and their peers. Here the Edgeworths' class-bound notion that only servants lie fit in well with the slaveholding Mordecai household and its gender hierarchy. As a female, Eliza learned that she was included but not fully accepted into the world of white male values.[49] The Edgeworths stated that if a preceptor is unjust, the child will conceal his or her thoughts and deceive.[50] Certainly, children respond more honestly to adult discipline if it is developed in an atmosphere of reason and affection.[51] According to the Edgeworths, family context determined children's integrity: "[I]n families where sincerity has been encouraged by the voice of praise and affection, a generous freedom of conversation and countenance appears, and the young people talk to each other, and to their parents, without distinction or reserve; without any distinction but such as superior esteem and respect dictate. These are feelings totally distinct from servile fear: these feelings inspire the love of truth, the ambition to acquire and to preserve character."[52] Trust and affection among siblings pervaded relationships within the Mordecai household; however, the distinctions of "superior esteem and respect" may have been overplayed in the tutoring process, especially in the Peter the Great incident. Thus the limitations of hierarchy proved subversive of the relationship between Rachel and Eliza.

Rachel noted that Eliza responded to discipline with indifference, a defensive attitude that wounded her sister. Eliza's behavior thereafter followed a double course of scrupulous obedience along with independent reflection. Thus while she was painfully correct in self-recrimination, she adhered to her sister Ellen's caution to think for herself. Although shame encouraged submission, reflection reinforced independence.

Eliza obeyed but criticized the rules, giving Rachel evidence for inferring independent reflection. Rachel had a name for Eliza's habit of criticizing, namely, Eliza's "criticizing cap." Eliza questioned the use of singular and plural and the nature of poetic license. Her confidence stemmed from her ability to apply rules and to question those rules.[53] Rachel observed that Eliza, on the eve of her eighth birthday, was both conscientious in admitting her faults and heedless in listening to commands, as if Eliza were reserving her energy to formulate and invent a self.

Eliza's New Possibilities

If identity, as Henry Louis Gates says, is influenced not only by the past but by the objects with which one identifies, one's liveliest attachments,[54] then Eliza's ties to new family relationships shaped her identity. A trip to Richmond presented Eliza with new possibilities of engagement and relationship. In Richmond she met the cousins and her friend Louisa, whom she dearly loved, and she experienced the excitement of a big city. Richmond captured Eliza's imagination, especially the allurements of society. Her uncle Samuel Mordecai, her father's brother, owned a thriving mercantile business and provided for his family in style. Most importantly, the Mordecai cousins gave Eliza the sense of belonging to a group beyond Jacob Mordecai's household. The identification with the group and group values would eventually set Eliza apart from Rachel and determine Eliza's independent course. As she left Richmond, she expressed the wish that if her parents and all her brothers and sisters could live there, "I should want to stay in Richmond always." [55]

Eliza had found another world on which to fix her attention. Richmond became the unspoken desire around which the child fitted all else in her young life. Richmond, after all, was everything Warrenton was not—cultured, stimulating, leisured, congenial. Their crowded, busy life left the family little time to pay attention to Eliza. Later, when told that her father planned to sell the Warrenton Female Academy and that the Mordecais would move to Richmond, Eliza expressed great glee. She rejoiced to her sister Rachel: "Then we could live in a house by ourselves, and we should not have such a large family, and there would not be so much noise sometimes, & every body would not have so much to do, I mean papa, & brother Solly & you & sister Caroline & all the family." [56]

The Mordecai school existed on an island of culture and learning, isolated from the larger intellectual ferment a city might provide. Most importantly, however, Eliza found an extensive Jewish community in Richmond. The Mordecais were related to the prominent Richmond Marx family. Moreover, the Richmond Mordecais had connected their families through marriage to the wealthy mercantile Myers family of New York and Norfolk and to the Cohens of Philadelphia, Baltimore, and Richmond. The eastern Jewish community remained in close contact. For example, noted author and educator Rebecca Gratz knew of Rachel Mordecai's correspondence with Maria Edgeworth. [57]

The Richmond experience helped Eliza focus on self-definition, what was essentially herself, her values, her delight in Richmond, yet she struggled with a family too intent upon unity and discipline. Since she distinguished more effectively between herself and others, her self-preoccupation may have made her thoughtless of others. After the Richmond experience her family found Eliza more heedless than ever. Rachel, determined to break the bad habit, used an extraordinary weapon, family ostracism. "No one would send Eliza on an errand, declaring that they feared she would forget by the way, even her good and kind father, who seldom blamed her, said, he could not trust her to do any thing for him," Rachel wrote. [58] Edgeworthian theory advised that parents must alter habits of thinking, change the view of the object, before patterns of feeling could be changed. The Edgeworths also cautioned not to "overawe the child by authority but to take the child's feelings into consideration."[59]

Whatever feelings Eliza may have experienced are not recorded in the diary; what is noted is the change in Eliza's habits, so much so that Eliza is rewarded for her efforts. With a family so intimately involved in her growth, Eliza's sense of her changing self barely had a chance to emerge. Yet Eliza controlled her impulses; she did not become her impulses.[60] The unfriendly environment changed to a rewarding one when Eliza gained this new self-assurance. Her self-assurance, however, was predicated upon submission to the family hierarchy. There remained in her submission an ambivalence exhibited in the February 1818 confrontation with her father over the turkey wing episode. Eliza reacted with anger and insisted to Rachel that she was not stupid, as her father called her, yet she repressed her anger. Rachel noted that "several times within a few days," Eliza admitted, "I was going to say something cross to Emma or, I was beginning to get a little out of humour, but I thought how bad I should feel to tell you of it this evening, & then I got over it directly."[61]

Eliza repressed her anger but expressed the one emotion sanctioned in an enlightened household—benevolence. Benevolence restrained the disorder but did not bind family members to Eliza with a deeply held emotion. In that context Rachel feared that Eliza lacked deeper feeling, a "kind and affectionate heart." Eliza believed she knew what charity meant. She regretted that there were not "*any* poor people about here . . . that any body can do any good to."[62] And she distinguished between "true charity" and "only its image."[63] Yet she did not equate slaves with "poor people." So entangled in her family was Eliza that slaves appeared as merely lesser members of the household. Certainly, Eliza demonstrated an enlightened sensibility and a regulated sympathy, but her anger flared when challenged by an authoritative intellect. After all, the family supported her in her battle with Augustus and the right of intellectual contest. Emotions suppressed gave way to a sharper rationality, but Eliza's reason led her back to her emotional sense of fairness and passionate defense of right.

An argument on the definition of "betimes" concentrated upon not just the definition of a word but the claims of authority. During her reading lesson Eliza came upon the word and insisted it meant "*all times.*" Rachel, irritated at the interruption and Eliza's lack of understanding, sent Eliza to fetch a dictionary. When Eliza did not cheerfully comply, she was ordered to run up the stairs again with a proper attitude. Rachel demanded internalized obedience, so that even feelings must comply to command. Orthodoxy compelled an inner godly response to duty. In addition, Rachel admonished Eliza not to challenge her sister's authority, saying: "You see you were wrong to interrupt me, for as I supposed, the line without explanation would either have been misunderstood, or have made a wrong impression: besides it has an appearance of conceit to interrupt one who is making observations to you, to suggest your own opinions, if when I had finished you had something to say, you know I should listen to you with pleasure." [64] But Eliza's anger simmered at the arbitrariness of Rachel's intellectual authority. Told she was conceited to interrupt her sister's speaking, a sullen Eliza mumbled something under her breath. Fearing Rachel's anger, Eliza only reluctantly admitted what she had said by writing on a slate, "I thought you were conceited yourself." [65] Rachel demurred and replied, "No, Eliza I believe I am not conceited, for I am very sensible that I have many faults & I am very glad when any one is so good as to point them out to me. You know, when I am doubtful about any thing, or do not know it, I tell you so. Therefore when I tell you that something is wrong you ought to believe that I know it to be so. Think that I am older & must have more knowledge & experience than you, & you will be willing to submit. Now go on with your lesson." [66] Eliza, fearful of Rachel's anger but assured that Rachel felt only sorry, admitted her "one great fault" that day.

Two versions of conceit undermined the relationship between Rachel and Eliza. Rachel planned to explain "betimes," but the child initiated her own, albeit wrongful explanation. Rachel counseled patience instead of conceit or pride. But Eliza interpreted the incident as an overweening display of power on Rachel's part—to stifle challenge and to demand humiliation and cheerful submission to humiliation. Eliza considered Rachel conceited. Two hierarchies conflict: the rational hierarchy accepts questioning even if it is inconvenient; the patriarchal family hierarchy eschews questioning. In effect, Rachel presented Eliza with two different cues, enlightened and patriarchal, a condition ripe for subversion. If her older sister refused questioning except at appointed times, then enlightened rational values concealed another form of authoritarianism. Eliza's challenge to "betimes" and her temper tantrum reveal an inchoate but very real anger at an authority that administered moral training by an unequal family order.

The Critical Mode Applied

Growing awareness of a context larger than the family encouraged an understanding of democratic order. During a grammar lesson that considered the pronoun "I," Eliza said, "I don't think it ought to be the *first* person to speak of *ourselves,* because we ought not to think of ourselves, before we do of any body else; ought we?" [67] Social responsibility formed a precept, an "ought." By the age of ten Eliza had begun to grasp the social cohesion that the rules supported. Her understanding first emerged in the context of the Jewish faith. When Eliza first understood and questioned anti-Semitism, Rachel repeated the commonplace narrative of the time: Europeans persecuted Jews, depriving them of rights or employment or education and thus making them a marginal, despised lot, but in America, where each individual was judged by merit, Jews were treated equally, and toleration characterized society. In fact, the family, especially the father, Jacob, endured proselytization attempts by earnest Christian devotees. And the family lamented their intellectual and religious isolation within American culture. Despite these obstacles, Eliza formed an enduring loyalty to Judaism and to her family's perception of American democracy. She said, "There are two things sister Rachel that I love better than any thing else in the world . . . my *religion* & my *country*." Eliza proclaimed her belief with all the vision of a ten year old who suddenly understands that she belongs to and has a special standing in a larger world of faith and civic responsibility. The relationship between faith and community lay in the teaching of the commandment "Thou shalt not bear false witness against thy neighbor." Eliza recognized reverence toward others; the spread of scandal was a sin.[68]

Eliza's moral development culminated in civic identification, a direction clearly delineated in Edgeworthian children's fiction. In Maria Edgeworth's story "Frank," the parents of a seven-year-old boy move him from egoism to reciprocity. When Frank takes on role-playing he learns the social implications of the Golden Rule. Frank disturbed his mother while she was writing at a table, and she sent him away. He complained that he could not read his book as well where he sat under the table. His mother replied: "If you had not disturbed me . . . I should not have sent you away from the table. You should consider what is agreeable to others, or they will not consider what is agreeable to you."[69] When Frank later helped his brothers and cousins with a shuttlecock, the lesson he had learned from his mother had social consequences: his siblings then helped him clean out a garden house to make a playhouse.

The basic enlightened ethic of exchange, the Golden Rule, taught by constant repetition, is then a reflection of a developmental stage, a moral process, that seven-year-old Frank had to learn. Who the child is is not the subject of Maria Edgeworth's fiction; rather, Edgeworth has captured the bundle of impulses children are at this stage. "Frank" conveys the necessity of choice with which the child is repeatedly confronted. But the child's dilemmas are never suffered alone; rather, the adult always accompanies, consults, guides, and distinguishes moral dichotomies for the child. The aim is to teach virtue, generosity, and integrity as extensions of the Golden Rule. Very young children perceive the Golden Rule as a simple exchange, but once role-playing is understood, the opportunity for family and social harmony is greater.

The ethical foundation of the Golden Rule, or simple exchange, matured into generous application and a consensual pattern in Rachel Mordecai's lessons. Rachel noted with pleasure the change in Eliza, who as a young child displayed a kindly consideration. When Eliza noticed that her sister was tired or busy, she readily sacrificed her story time to accommodate Rachel. Rachel recorded the dialogue:

> At such times she has repeatedly said to me, "If you please sister Rachel, not to tell me my story tonight, I would rather not hear it when you are tired." I have sometimes yielded to her with a kiss of approbation, but oftener said, "No, my dear, we should always endeavour to perform our promises, and I will now exert myself to give you pleasure, as you have been good, and deserved it. At some other time when *you* do not feel altogether inclined to do something which I wish, *you* will think of this, and exert yourself to give pleasure to *me*." [70]

With the help of fiction, a story in Thomas Day's *The History of Sandford and Merton,* Eliza easily identified the consequences of a lack of reciprocity. Squire Chace unmercifully beat Harry Sandford, but the boy subsequently saved the squire's life. Eliza proposed that the squire must have been ashamed "when he found that it was Harry, who had helped him, and that such a little boy, was so much better than he was." [71]

Children's literature established the didactic principles of the Golden Rule, but fiction also served to fix a conventional form that alternately conveyed biblical and enlightened themes. The stories of both "Frank" and "Harry" suggest type-scenes, conventional situations upon which character or destiny depended, made interesting by their variation and interpretation. The enlightened fiction of Maria Edgeworth and Thomas Day drafted the venerable biblical (and Homeric) type-scene that heightened revelations of meaning while conforming to conventional moral narrative. [72] For Eliza, Squire Chace's comeuppance appears so devastating because his vanquisher is a little boy. The prosaic event resonates with biblical portentousness as moral constancy uproots caste or established order.

"Jacob at the Well" offers an example of enlightened perception endowed with biblical meaning. Rachel recounted the anecdote as an ironic type-scene: "Eliza saw one day at the well, two old Negro women, a black boy (Robin), who was drawing water for them, and several dogs. 'Look sister Julia,' said she, 'there is *Jacob* drawing water for the *maidens;* and the dogs, you see, are *for* the sheep.'" [73] No matter that Genesis 29 : 1–13 recounts only the unmarried Rachel at the well in the betrothal scene or that the Warrenton scene presented nonvirgins; Eliza transposed convention into a more inclusive application. The slaves at the well do indeed represent bondage just as Laban tricked Jacob into voluntary servitude in order to win the hand of Rachel. But that was hardly Eliza's point. Eliza saw only a representation of a biblical tableau, but the fact that she elevated her subjects to biblical archetypes dignifies an otherwise ordinary scene of servility. Rachel's emphasis in the narrative suggests castelike condescension; blacks' servile pastoral practices marked them as racially inferior. [74] Rachel's subsequent observations on slavery taught Eliza to distinguish between slave and mistress.

Rachel complimented a considerate slave and said, "You are a good soul, Lucy." Eliza mistakenly believed that Rachel praised Lucy as a "good servant" and proceeded to give Rachel this observation: "Sister Rachel when any of the servants do any thing for me I never say, you are a good *servant* or any thing like that, because it seems as if it would make them feel bad, to put them in mind that they were our servants, would not it[?]" Rachel replied, "No, my dear, I believe not, they have always been servants, and do not feel their situation a disgrace as they might do if they had ever been in different circumstances."[75] Eliza, who had experienced submission as a female child, identified with the slave and felt as Lucy must have felt. If the practice of reciprocity extended to all in a democracy, why did it not extend to slaves?

Rachel's class and racial insecurities may have prompted her patronizing reply, since Jews, regarded as "not-yet-white" in the antebellum South, carefully distinguished themselves from African Americans.[76] Rachel, with disciplined sensibility and conformity to household authority, placed slaves in a discrete category beyond the reach of egalitarian sympathy. In a southern family, justice accommodated the pursuit of harmony and order. Reciprocity applied to external behavior, which preserved peace in families as well as their social and economic independence and well-being.[77] According to southern patriarchal ideology, slaves' dependent status limited their rational understanding; slaves, like children, needed supervision and a secure placement in the household hierarchy. When Eliza complained to Rachel that the slave Rosina insisted upon dressing Emma, Eliza's younger sister, first, Eliza admitted, "I was very angry & I told her [Rosina], I would slap her if I could."[78] Rachel restrained such angry, disruptive impulses with the caution that power included limitations over the dependent. Rachel said,

> Well, Eliza I need not tell you that you were wrong, because you know it; but you should be careful to check yourself whenever you feel any thing like ill temper, or when you are older it will get the better of you. You may easily see that the same feelings which made you *wish* to slap Rosina, might have tempted you to do it, if you had been older & her mistress. She was wrong, but you know she is a poor, ignorant servant, & does not know right from wrong as well as we do. I shall tell her to dress you first, whenever you are ready first, and then there need be no more said about it.[79]

Careful training placed slavery in mental and linguistic brackets; benevolent patriarchy cordoned off egalitarian considerations of dependents within the household. Such a predisposition, however, did not eradicate progressive education. Historian Christie Farnham suggests that female education in the early republic, including the Mordecai academy, heightened white racial superiority without fear of white female superiority since women had few career opportunities to advance themselves in the public sphere.[80] Thus Rachel fostered enlightened method and patriarchal authority, an anomaly destined for criticism and revision. Democratic alterations in family governance, namely, the family conference, that emerged during the crisis over Moses' engagement surely created a model for consensual governance and prepared the way for Rachel to introduce participatory instruction in her ticket system.

The Enlightened Goal Accomplished

In the hopes of providing stimulation and competition in her private tutoring, Rachel devised a ticket system, rewarding good behavior ("early rising . . . bad habits overcome") and punishing bad habits ("carelessness, heedlessness").[81] Faults incurred the penalty of forfeiting two good tickets. Seven good tickets obtained a reward—something the child viewed as pleasure, such as reading a book. Eliza's initial enthusiasm with the system pleased the family, but the sense of fairness began to break down as the system grew more complicated. Eliza earned a reward and chose to have a story read to her the next night. In the meantime, she misbehaved and had to postpone her reward. But Rachel assigned an exercise designed to make up for Eliza's deficit so that she might receive her reward more immediately. Nonetheless, Eliza considered the burden too heavy, and to punish her impatience Rachel postponed the story even longer. Fortunately, Rachel regretted her decision and discussed it with Eliza. She admitted her misgivings and asked Eliza exactly what she thought. Eliza replied with the candor to which she had been trained, "Why, sister Rachel, I will tell you, I thought it was not quite *just* for you to deny me my reward, for what I did today, because you know I had *earned* it three days ago, & if I had chosen something else, I should have had it then, so it does not seem right that I should lose it for not being attentive today."[82] Rachel readily agreed and promised to read the story that night. Thus the fixed system of rewards and punishments existed only with Eliza's free consent and her ability to challenge and change the rules. The rules are no longer arbitrary, at the will of authority, but they conform to Eliza's notion of autonomy.

What Rachel noticed in Eliza at ages ten and eleven was a rapid growth in intellectual and emotional maturity. She wondered at her deepening sensibility, her affectionate and delicate regard for a friend, and the fact that she wept to hear of an accident in Warrenton, and she delighted in Eliza's appreciation of poetry and plays.[83] For the most part, Eliza behaved as a "good girl," scrupulous in admitting her faults and considerate of family members and friends. The "good girl" role meant a greater integration into family values, an appreciation of family solidarity but with an understanding of self-sacrifice, taking the other person's part. Eliza cared enough about her brother Samuel's feelings that she did not tell him she had already read the book he gave her as a present.[84] Eliza carefully kept the secret of her own injury in an accident caused by a companion, Miss H. Her discretion was meant to console the other child. Eliza did not reveal the secret for three years until the girl's reputation was safely secured. According to Rachel's estimate, self-esteem held the greatest value for Eliza; she often demurred in accepting "undeserved" praise but found pleasure in simply doing good.[85]

Rachel's final assessment of Eliza is one of deep satisfaction with her intellectual progress. "The tender bud," so lovingly introduced at the beginning of the diary, has now burst forth "in new born loveliness." Rachel pinned her hopes of "future excellence" upon ten-year-old Eliza's "docility, candour, & good sense." And of her moral progress, Rachel considers Eliza a child of good sense, self-reflective and docile. Rachel desired that Eliza "be sensible, well informed, mild, sincere, . . . & I would have her beloved for being amiable, rather than admired for being brilliant."[86] At the age of twelve Eliza exhibited alacrity and reflection, Rachel noted. In short, confident, intelligent, deferential, Eliza represented the middle-class version of the ideal female of the early republic. Yet Rachel, who commented upon Eliza's heedlessness, failed to see Eliza's pattern of resistance, which defied self-recrimination, refused to "listen to reason," questioned the paternal hierarchy, and rejected religious assimilation.

From her religious and enlightened perspective, Rachel viewed positively only the reasonable pattern of accommodation and deference and not the contraries that shaped Eliza's highly individual context of meaning and selfhood. Later in life Eliza chose an alternate model of self-definition, one grounded in consensual family governance and domestic intellectual pursuits, translating French and German fiction into English and writing stories for her children. Eliza accommodated enlightened method to the domestic order. However, the same critical energy that determined Eliza's steadfast Judaism in a predominately Christian culture propelled Rachel toward rejection of family Orthodoxy. In Rachel and Eliza's experiment historians might see the conflict of generations that introduced Victorian American cultural values.

Eliza represents the dissident voice, the struggle to overturn ambiguous enlightened notions of "goodness" that promoted critical thinking yet accepted conservative notions of household hierarchy. Orthodox precepts emphasized duties, but enlightened education implanted individuation and the desire for rights. Eliza used enlightened method, the insistence upon rights, to secure what she desired by nature, the wider pursuit of Jewish family ties and connection. In her defense of rights she learned heartfelt expression that went beyond the pallid benevolence of Edgeworthian ideology. Unexpressed longing for a secure home, for self-definition, for Jewish community settled into the heart of the child and emerged in adulthood with deep intensity. Eliza transformed her education into a medium for domestic religious and intellectual expression; that is, Eliza adapted enlightened and Orthodox principles on her own terms.

Rachel's diary coincides with the end of the "golden age" of the Warrenton Female Academy in 1816, the period that demanded considerable energy from family members, especially Rachel, who taught at the school and indirectly administered it. Family observers noted her exhaustion and rejoiced with her when Jacob Mordecai sold the school. The sale of the school made Eliza happy because it meant the family might pay more attention to her and to each other. Rachel's experiment, wedged in between her more pressing business, may not have been as systematic as classroom exercises, but the experiment changed the lives of pupil and teacher. It marked them with critical perception and the desire for holiness.

CHAPTER 4

WAYS OF WISDOM

Separate Paths of Holiness

ЮСИЮСИЮСИЮСИЮСИЮСИЮСИЮСИЮСИЮСИЮСИЮСИЮСИЮСИЮСИЮСИ

A House is built by wisdom,
And is established by understanding.
—Proverbs 24:3

Jacob Mordecai's Orthodoxy

RACHEL AND ELIZA matured in Jacob Mordecai's household, a house built by the wisdom of the Law. The measure of Jacob Mordecai's dedication to the Law may be demonstrated in his most emphatic statement: "All is uniform. All inculcates one doctrine, the unity of God, obedience to his laws, charity to the poor and needy, whether he be of thy people or a stranger among you—for this saith the prophet Micah, 'He hath shewed thee O Man! what is good, & what doth the Lord require of thee, but to do justly & to love misery, & to walk humbly with thy God?'" [1] Rachel's understanding of patriarchal wisdom shaped her enlightened experiment. She counseled Eliza in the ways of Jewish Orthodoxy and family hierarchy; however, as a teacher, she adapted to the consensual education of Eliza. Unconscious of the internal contradictions in her method, Rachel placed her practice under the direction of Providence. Practice, according to the ancient sages, even that conforming to religion and ethics, must accord with Providence in order to assure the desired results, since only God knew the future. [2]

The future revealed sisters at odds religiously; Rachel converted to Christianity, and Eliza maintained her Jewish Orthodoxy. Circumstance and character contributed to their divergent paths: Rachel moved into a tightly knit community of Evangelical Protestant women; Eliza remained close to home, marrying her Richmond cousin. Rachel devoted her most acute intellectual powers to criticism and debate with a larger enlightened community of Edgeworth interests and connections. Eliza, as child and adolescent, experienced ambivalence between the pull of unity and embeddedness in family and religion, on the one hand, and individuation, inherent in enlightened notions of family and education, on the other. Thus Eliza found her own individuality in an enlightened domestic and religious life; she translated neoclassical and Romantic texts that both elevated and bound women within an Orthodox home. Rachel's childhood, tragically marked by the death of her mother and separation from her father, healed in the partnership with her father that successfully launched the family's enterprise, the Warrenton Female Academy. Rachel's experience in public life contributed to her maturation and individuation. She married an Orthodox Jew, Aaron Lazarus, who had a large number of children from his first marriage. Rachel then continued her task of educating a household of children in an enlightened Orthodox Jewish environment.

Most importantly, each sister interpreted her spiritual destiny in disparate terms. Eliza maintained her ethical understanding of Providence, such that by her conscious acts to do good she followed the will of the Most High God.[3] She carved out her own standard of ethics, a more romantic sense of passionate liberation combined with an idealized family unity that recognized female ability and potential. Thus Eliza remained within her redefined Orthodoxy. Rachel, largely self-taught but deeply influenced by the enlightened pedagogy of the Edgeworths and her father, entertained doubts about Orthodoxy and contravened both her husband's and her father's authority. For Rachel, the call to repentance for self-will, doubt, and inaction bruised her soul and forced her to seek salvation in the finding of a new self.

In Judaism, sages are teachers who stand between humanity and God. Theirs is a Talmudic science. They speak the language of ethics, a dialectic precise in the conscious attempt to define and do good in order to draw believers closer to God.[4] In his later years Jacob Mordecai, an educated man, expanded his role as sage by writing a two-volume guide for young people "perplexed" by Christian proselytization. In the guide he refutes Harriet Martineau, the famous traveler and proponent of Unitarianism who argued that assimilation would end the "Jewish problem." The second volume includes a commentary on the New Testament.[5] Jacob Mordecai rejected any path but the traditional one in order to preserve "a united Jewish family."[6] In this way, he distanced himself from Christian and enlightened precepts that criticized Jewish religious tradition. In the early republic, Edgeworthian practitioners offered a moral dialectic for the natural development of children and the inculcation of good habits. Rachel Mordecai, daughter of the sage, discovered that enlightened pedagogical dialogue enhanced freedom; Rachel and her pupil Eliza eventually adhered to a consensual method of learning that respected their different needs and natures. At the same time, Rachel and Eliza recognized that their pedagogical dialogue unfolded an ethical order that led them to separate paths of holiness.

A sage recognizes contradictions. Jacob Mordecai, whose family flourished in the religious liberty of the early republic, suffered the pressures of proselytization and the grief of his children's mixed marriages. In the early nineteenth century, enlightened ideology competed with Protestant revivalism; the Second Great Awakening unleashed powerful religious emotions that slowly undermined religious restraint. Traditional Judaism identified the heart with yezer, or the natural inclinations in humanity, and believed that the Law as set forth in the Torah countermanded evil inclinations. According to Orthodoxy, the wicked were ruled by their emotions, whereas the righteous restrained their desires. But the intense heat of Protestant revivalism weakened the careful constraints of accommodation, formality, and rational piety. In the wake of the great religious divide of the early nineteenth century Jacob Mordecai, stung by the challenge of Evangelicalism, awoke to the necessity of the Law. If idolatry meant the enthronement of the evil inclination, then a man of righteousness must speak out against it.[7] Jacob Mordecai reconstructed his ethnic-religious identity and attempted to redefine familial and religious boundaries between himself and Anglo-American culture.[8] The teacher and sage became an apologist for Judaism.

For twenty-five years Jacob Mordecai evinced indifference to Orthodox Jewish observance until the mixed marriages of his children and Evangelical Christian proselytization threatened family unity. His apologia, written later in his life to defend Judaism against Evangelical challenges and strengthen the faith of the younger generation, underscored the necessity for corporate family structure. Jacob Mordecai maintained a visionary belief in Jewish family unity. He claimed that Jesus, who came to send fire and sword upon the earth, divided father and son but that in the Messianic Age family enmity would be healed when Elijah the prophet converted "the heart of the *Fathers* unto the *children*, and the heart of the *children* unto the Fathers."[9]

At stake in patriarchal unity lay the survival of the Jewish nation. In his work Jacob Mordecai documents scriptural support for the proposition that Providence manifests itself through Israel as a nation: "I have poured my spirit upon the house of Israel, saith the Lord God."[10] According to Jacob Mordecai, the writings of the prophets, especially Isaiah, "speak of a *nation,* its sufferings and degradation, and not of an individual."[11] Jacob Mordecai refuted Christian writers who attributed prophetic revelations to the person of Christ and not to the Jewish nation. For example, he points to the Gospel of Matthew, which claims that Joseph and Mary's flight into Egypt with the infant Jesus fulfilled Hosea's prophecy, "Out of Egypt have I called my son."[12] According to Mordecai, Hosea 11:1 refers to the nation: "When Israel was a child then I loved him and called my son out of Egypt." [13]

The fragmenting effects of Christian teaching and practice upon Jewish family life in the early republic returned Jacob Mordecai to an acceptance of the traditional dyadic model of family structure and definition of self. Traditional Jewish family patterns eschewed individualism and assumed that a person defined self in relation to others. Family members remained undifferentiated, subsumed in a patriarchal family. For Orthodox Jews cohesive family identity demonstrated the moral gap between Jews and non-Jews, assimilated and unassimilated Jews. [14] To ignore the prophets and to walk outside traditional ethics is to encourage idolatry, according to Jacob Mordecai. Often "the customs of the people" included idolatry, he wrote, warning the younger generation of Jews tempted by assimilation. [15]

Abhorrence of idolatry and fear of fragmentation led Jacob Mordecai to denounce Reform Judaism. In 1824, when Isaac Harby and his band of reformers in the Charleston Beth Elohim congregation proposed changes in ritual, language, and liturgy, Jacob Mordecai wrote a commentary upon the proposed reforms entitled "Remarks on Harby's Discourse." He attacked reform as an attempt to shatter Jewish unity by destruction of faith and worship. Jacob Mordecai referred to reformers as "subverters of every established system." [16] Furthermore, he contended, in an integrated system truth is seamless, convention originates from the Law, and the Law emanates from the source of "Goodness and Wisdom"; therefore, ritual is changeless. [17] Reform disturbed sacred unity and pointed toward assimilation. If Jews adopt the "customs of the people, they will cease to be Jews," and Judaism will cease to exist, warns Mordecai. Yet Mordecai trusted that Jewish ceremonies and ancient customs would never perish because they "have dipped deep into the heart." [18] In effect, Jacob Mordecai repudiated enlightened secular and anti-authoritarian impulses. He attacked Harby's sources as "deist calumniators, canonized authors and heathen philosophers." [19] But Mordecai carefully excluded the enlightened Jewish philosopher Moses Mendelssohn from his list of recreants. As a "strict conformist and Talmudist," Mordecai argued, Mendelssohn retained the ways of wisdom and holiness—reason and observance.

Jacob Mordecai spoke with the voice of unicity and tradition: the wisdom of the past shaped behavior in the present. As Mordecai adapted Scripture to contemporary problems, his living texts invested him with greater authority, much like a rabbi who stands between the people and God and teaches a kind of divine revelation. [20] Although Jacob Mordecai respected the rationality, tolerance, and benevolent paternalism of the post-Revolutionary period, he nonetheless denounced the divisive social and spiritual consequences of enlightened ideology. His efforts to reclaim Orthodox integrality and strengthen traditional authority made his daughters' attempts to differentiate themselves as persons a complicated task.

Separation: The Edgeworthian Imprint

Rachel Mordecai's early intellectual attachment to her father and her subsequent partnership with him at the Warrenton Female Academy assured her identification with him and with traditional values. Trained in the moral discourse of her father, she retained his strict discipline and Orthodox observance. She learned that in doing the will of God, in teaching, in study, in performing moral acts, she drew closer to God. Moral training, especially, according to Jewish tradition, led straight to the vision of God, not in a mystical sense but through mundane experience.[21]

For Rachel moral life had broad consequences. She found the workings of God in Edgeworthian moral discourse and fiction and in the commonplace female friendships she formed with Edgeworth and later with her Evangelical Wilmington neighbors. Through her friendships, enlightened and Christian values created a dialogic interaction in her that resulted in a new formulation of self in relation to the social forces of her Evangelical community.[22]

Rachel's friendship with Maria Edgeworth flourished with their lifelong correspondence. Their dialogue, which lasted twenty-three years, began with Rachel's first letter on 7 August 1815, which was critical of Edgeworth's Jewish stereotypical characters in *The Absentee,* and extended to Maria Edgeworth's affectionate, literary letter of 16 June 1838, written a week before Rachel's death. Their correspondence represents a moral dialogue expressed in terms of domestic virtue, idealizing Rachel's perception of domestic virtue and family harmony. Rachel rejoiced in her recognition by the Edgeworths because she felt "deemed worthy of affinity to the Good."[23] From the Edgeworths Rachel derived comfort that rested in the security of Richard Lovell Edgeworth's moral vision. In a sense, the Edgeworths completed the moral context Rachel needed in order to define her own moral self. Such lovers of domestic virtue required family narratives to keep alive the deeper moral purpose of ordinary life.

Maria Edgeworth imparted her own family stories because of Rachel's intense interest in them. Maria remarked to Rachel, "You have such taste for domestic happiness and [are] so kindly sympathetic in ours that I must tell you . . ." and here Maria relates news of her sisters' health and her brothers' schooling.[24] For Rachel, Maria Edgeworth's letters created an immediacy and intimacy that led her to form a less formal attachment. Commenting upon Sophy Edgeworth's marriage, Rachel wrote, "the terms in which you mention her are so sweet and engaging that I seem to have seen, to know, and to have learned to love her too."[25] Rachel identified with Edgeworth family members and idealized them as a "domestick unity, combined with all the charms of intelligence and culti-vation." [26] She longed to join the Edgeworth family circle around "a cheerful fire in the Library." [27] Her easy adoption of the Edgeworth family ignored the distinct differences of class, religion, and culture that existed between the Edge-worths and the Mordecais. However, at the same time that Rachel considered the relationship to validate her own moral life, she also differentiated herself from the Edgeworths as a Jewish American.

On the other side of the Atlantic, the relationship with Rachel Mordecai enhanced Maria Edgeworth's role as moral guide and social arbiter. Maria Edge-worth desired Rachel's attention partly as intellectual and emotional gratifica-tion. Not without vanity, Maria Edgeworth professed pleasure in the young woman's concern: "I am quite pleased and touched by your being so constantly awake to whatever interests me. You seem to be always up to whatever I am doing and to know where I am and all my domestic concerns as well as if you were near me and one of ourselves." [28]

Enlightened discourse with Maria Edgeworth sharpened Rachel's critical and intellectual powers but left little room for emotional expression. There is no mention within the Edgeworth-Lazarus correspondence of Rachel's marital problems or of her religious doubts. Rachel often surrendered her own interest and sense of self to the genius and concerns of the novelist. Rachel's brush with death and her subsequent dialogue with her Christian neighbors on the subject of mortality, however, opened a vast reservoir of feeling and longing. Rachel's emotional life, repressed in her youth, struggled for expression amid the con-straints of enlightened discourse and Orthodox ideology. But whatever key her voice intoned, certain themes remained the same: common sense, moral integ-rity, and domestic virtue. Like the character Ormond in Maria Edgeworth's novel by the same name, Rachel's own persistent cultivation of rational virtues enabled her, later in life, to claim moral authority even as she experienced a spiritual and psychological crisis.

What did tie the elder author to the young North Carolina teacher, however, remained their identification with their fathers. [29] Their allegiance to their fa-thers and paternal values shaped the women's character and personal life. Both Maria Edgeworth and Rachel Mordecai entered into partnerships with their fathers that had public consequences. Their correspondence served to widen Rachel's ethical understanding and sharpen her critical powers beyond the do-mestic, provincial world of the early republican southern frontier. Thus the correspondence exists as a formal discourse that examines the domestic appli-cation of practical morality, a morality based upon criticism. It was this con-sistent questioning along with a desire for emotional expression that opened Rachel to a redefinition of religious values.

Maria Edgeworth, chastened by Rachel Mordecai's criticism, which reinforced her own determination to write a novel about anti-Semitism, nonetheless failed to challenge social convention by portraying a mixed marriage. She lacked an understanding of Jewish religious character. Rachel presented a model of Jewish piety; she sympathized with Maria's grief after her father's death and counseled resignation to the "Orderer of the Universe."[30] In addition, Rachel offered the assurance of shared values and delicate sensibility. Rachel praised *Harrington* and claimed she was inspired by the "warm admiration of goodness" evident in the novel. To her surprise, the novel reveals that, after all, Berenice, its heroine, is not Jewish, a surprise too convenient in a plot that called for a Christian, Harrington, to marry her. Rachel delicately broached the topic of the turnabout in the religious affiliation of Berenice, a subject of disappointment to the Mordecai family. She added diplomatically that her father, Jacob, believed that making Berenice a Christian was a testimony to her father's benevolent intentions, since it allowed Berenice to choose between her mother's and her father's faiths. Such diplomacy pointed out Maria Edgeworth's error but preserved the honesty of her intentions.[31] Rachel Mordecai appeared to be a trustworthy informant whose father displayed an uncommon wisdom. Unmistakably, too, Rachel identified herself as a Jew and defended Jewish rights and reputation out of a sense of corporate identity.

Rachel's tact did not prevent her from providing a realistic accounting of the plight of American Jews. She discussed a Maryland law, in effect a test act, that barred Jewish candidates from public office. At the same time, Rachel mentioned Christian support for a change in the law.[32] Most important, Rachel resisted conventions and myths concerning Jews. Lucy Edgeworth wanted to know more about the popular eighteenth-century myth that Native Americans were descended from the "Lost Tribe of Israel." Rachel quite plainly labeled the theory "visionary" and suggested reading material on the subject. When Maria Edgeworth solicited Rachel's views concerning Sir Walter Scott's character Rebecca in *Ivanhoe,* Rachel answered that she admired Rebecca's delicacy, firmness, and rectitude, but she evaded the question of a romantic relationship between the hero and Rebecca. Nonetheless, Maria Edgeworth pressed the issue and sent Rachel a ring inscribed to "Rebecca." Rachel replied, "As to the name in the motto it would be much easier to imagine my own in its place, than to transform myself as you advise into the Rebecca of Sir W[alter] S[cott]."[33]

Although she refused characterization as a conventional, self-sacrificing Jewish heroine, Rachel nonetheless admired and chose to emulate Edgeworth's fictional characters. On her part, Maria Edgeworth tacitly identified Rachel with the moral integrity characteristic of the author's heroines, the "good daughters." When Rachel announced her engagement to Aaron Lazarus, Maria Edgeworth invented her late father's wishes and claimed he would have said, "Happy the man to whom she is to be united. She will make an excellent wife as she has been an excellent daughter."[34] On her part, Rachel claimed to "imbibe" Edgeworth family principles of unity, benevolence, kindness, and wisdom from reading "Rosamund" and "Frank." In those principles, espoused by the fictional character of the "wise and benignant father," Rachel identified "the excellent and ever-lamented Mr. Edgeworth."[35]

Maria Edgeworth imprinted her relationship with her father upon Rachel and Jacob Mordecai and thus engaged Rachel in complicity with and resistance to patriarchal values. In exchange for a father's benevolent tutelage, an enlightened daughter developed dependencies upon paternal love and esteem for self-definition. Paternal empowerment meant that the daughter spoke through the rational discourse of the father and devalued feminine or maternal attributes of speech or thought. However, on some level, self-doubt and anger undermined the "good daughter's" self-esteem, as she found worth only in the identification with her father's values.[36] Thus daughters who wished a separate identity resisted paternal domination often in implicit, indirect ways. Edgeworth's fiction conveys these contradictions within the female character. Edgeworth heroines exhibit a tenderness of heart that expresses "female" vulnerability and tentativeness, yet they possess a "manly" courage. Count Altenberg, the suitor of Caroline Percy in *Patronage,* describes Caroline and the perfect mate as "unobtrusive, mild, yet firm."[37] Caroline derives her character from the patriarchal notions of both her parents, who, in the face of fashionable pressure, insist upon preserving their daughter from the marriage market. Mr. Percy suggests his daughter remain in the "bosom" of the family, where "without seeking to entice or entrap, they can at all events never be disappointed or degraded; and, whether married or single, will be respected and respectable, in youth and age—secure of friends, and of a happy home." Mr. Percy extends paternal protection and, hence, continued dependency upon himself. Mrs. Percy invests her husband's argument with her own plea for rational choice. She declares to an intrusive cousin, determined to introduce Caroline into society,

> The warmest wish of my heart . . . is to see my daughters as happy as I am myself, married to men of their own choice, whom they can entirely esteem and fondly love. But I would rather see my daughters in their graves than see them throw themselves away upon men unworthy of them, or sell themselves to husbands unsuited to them, merely for the sake of being *established,* for the vulgar notion of *getting married,* or to avoid the imaginary and unjust ridicule of being old maids.[38]

Freedom of choice in this case does not mean independence; the father protects his daughter against potentially destructive social norms but secures her within his household and sphere of influence.

Maria Edgeworth draws the balance between vulnerability and strength differently in the character of Grace Nugent in *The Absentee*. Of her strength an admirer says, "No one has more courage," but she also appears "unprepossessing."[39] As Maria Edgeworth writes, "This young lady was quite above all double dealing; she had no mental reservation—no metaphysical subtleties—but, with plain, unsophisticated morality, in good faith and simple truth, acted as she professed, thought what she said, and was that which she seemed to be."[40] Grace Nugent, an orphan cousin attached to the Columbe family, appears independent of paternal influence. Edgeworth assigns strength of mind and character to Grace Nugent, as if to suggest that paternal virtues could exist without the father. Here is either a declaration of the universality of patriarchal values or a wish for appropriation of those values without dependence upon the father. Edgeworth's heroines display firmness of character whether or not they are closely allied to their fathers.

Maria Edgeworth saw in Rachel Mordecai Lazarus the same balance of character she attributed to her female protagonists. In their correspondence Edgeworth reassured Rachel that her "letters have given me an increasing opinion the more I have seen of them of your understanding, plain uprightness of character and real tenderness of heart."[41] On her part, Rachel expressed delight in Edgeworthian complex heroines, especially Emma Granby in *The Modern Griselda* and Lady Davenant in *Helen*. Of Lady Davenant Rachel writes, "Lady Davenant's character pleases me particularly—such dignity, such genuine greatness of mind combined with feminine tenderness of feeling and with just enough of human frailty to keep it on a level with its kind."[42] The character Lady Davenant, the wife of a British ambassador, establishes a warm intimacy with her young friend Helen. Lady Davenant thanks Helen for her sympathy and states, "You can understand me, you can feel with me."[43] Lady Davenant's passionate plea is coupled with rational restraint, however. As a kind mentor, Lady Davenant teaches Helen the importance of principled behavior. When Helen surrenders her moral judgment to Lady Davenant, the latter admonishes Helen: "It must not be what I please, my dear child, nor what I think best, but what you judge for yourself to be best; else what will become of you . . . ? It must be some higher and more stable principle of action that must govern you. It must not be the mere wish to please this or that friend;—the defect of your character, Helen, remember I tell you, is this—inordinate desire to be loved, this impatience of not being loved."[44] Perhaps Rachel, motherless at a tender age, understood Helen's temptation—to be loved at all costs, even forsaking her principles. Rachel may even have hoped that the elder Edgeworth author would act as Lady Davenant and check this tendency in her. Certainly, Rachel looks to the Edgeworth family as moral paragons.

In her relationship with Eliza, Rachel tried to carefully control the child's desire to be loved at all costs. Warm and sympathetic by nature, Rachel nonetheless acted toward Eliza with rectitude, fearful that too much love, like that of Eliza's mother, Rebecca Mordecai, for Eliza, would ruin the child. Rachel's dilemma, affectionate regard versus strict discipline, suggests a longing suppressed, a desire unfulfilled. Edgeworthian heroines, especially Helen, illustrate character in the making, unfinished subjects who choose good out of a rational exertion of their wills, often against their own desires. Through her teaching, Rachel discovered the power of her intellect and the mastery of her will. Yet she recoiled from the coldness of self-containment; she looked for simple human kindness in Eliza and directed the child toward consideration of others. The task of balancing disciplined self-control with the expression of love and affection challenged Rachel's teaching and parental skills.

Lady Davenant conveys the strength of character that is accomplished only by checking a deep-seated weakness, the longing for power. She explained to Helen that she decided to attain fame by ruling her husband, Lord Davenant, in his role as ambassador. She claimed she fancied herself "a female politician." [45] Lady Davenant warns Helen, "So long as ladies keep in their own proper character . . . all is well; but, if once they cease to act as women, that instant they lose their privilege—their charm: they forfeit their exorcising power; they can no longer command the demon of party nor themselves." [46] The temptation to power existed in female self-possession and confidence; thus Maria Edgeworth counseled women to have only a reactive response. Such conventional advice must have reinforced female deference; nonetheless, the novel is about moral courage, about telling the truth at any cost. Helen's admirer, Beauclerc, holds less conventional notions of the kind of woman Helen is. Beauclerc compares his notions of Helen's character to those of his guardian, General Clarendon: "The general, with his strict, narrow, conventional notions, has not an idea of the kind of woman I like, or of what Helen really is. He sees in Helen only the discreet proper-behaved young lady adapted, so nicely adapted, to her place in society, to nitch and notch in, and to be of no sort of value out of it. Give me a being able to stand alone, to think and feel, decide and act, for herself." [47] Through the general's words, Edgeworth intimates that female independence may be valued by men. In this she may express her hope rather than social reality. This same ambivalence characterizes the heroine of *The Modern Griselda*.

Rachel considered *The Modern Griselda* one of her "prime favorites"; she particularly identified with the domestic morality of the heroine. Rachel admits to her esteemed friend: "Many years ago, before I dreamed of being allowed the happiness of thus conversing with you, after reading 'Griselda' again and again, I copied into a commonplace book the delineation of her character, as if by transcribing I could have claimed some property in that which attracted so strongly my love and admiration." [48]

In the novel *The Modern Griselda* the sophisticated circle of a deeply neurotic and destructive woman ridicules Emma Granby as *"the pattern wife, the original Griselda revived."* Emma Granby is the ideal wife whose timidity attracts the attention of "every gentleman present." [49] But upon hearing the story of the original Griselda, a woman who agreed to a marriage of enslavement, Emma said that she "could never have wed or esteemed the man who required such a promise." [50]

Rachel dearly wished to claim the property of self-possession, to defend herself well against a hostile or indifferent society. It was this wish that prompted her dream of witty rapprochement with the condescending Colonel Johnson. [51] In traditional relationships one defense against domination is moral prepossession. Although the pursuit of goodness drew its power from the patriarchal definition of the moral horizon, women of the early republic claimed virtue as their very own path toward that distant end. Edgeworth's heroines offered Rachel her own way within a patriarchal culture. At this juncture, Rachel claimed Judaism and marriage as her identity; she struggled to claim self.

Rachel's Marriage

On 21 March 1821 Rachel married Aaron Lazarus, an Orthodox Jew and a prosperous businessman. Aaron Lazarus, the eldest child of Marks Lazarus and Rachel Benjamin, was born in Charleston, South Carolina. Later he entered the lumber business with a partner, William Calder. Anxious to strike out on his own, Aaron immigrated to Wilmington, North Carolina, a growing shipping center, where he married Esther Cohen in 1803. They had eight children, seven of whom survived into adulthood. Aaron's planing mill prospered, and he established himself as a social and civic leader. The home he built near the center of town covered a city block. Since no synagogue existed in Wilmington, the Lazarus family attended the fashionable St. James's Episcopal Church. Tragedy struck when Esther Cohen Lazarus died in 1816. [52]

Several years after Esther's death Aaron began to court Rachel Mordecai. Aaron's daughters attended the Wilmington Female Academy, and he often visited there. Rachel hesitated to marry an older widower with seven children; she harbored no romantic illusions and expected only a "reasonable share of happiness." [53] When she finally consented to his proposal of marriage, Rachel found, unexpectedly, much happiness. The nature of her partnership with Aaron gratified her very much; the honeymoon made Rachel and Aaron's relationship almost too perfect. She joked to her brother Samuel: "With a partner kinder, more affectionate, more amiable than mine, no woman was ever blest— one failing he has I must own, that of a sort of partial blindness, for I do believe he thinks there are few such wives to be had as his own, & tho' this day completes 3 months since our marriage, all my efforts have been ineffectual to draw forth one word of reproach or displeasure—you had better write him a letter on this subject."[54]

Rachel and Aaron shared the same principles of child rearing. Although Aaron's application of those disciplinary measures may have been less systematic than Rachel's, nonetheless, the parents did not contradict one another.[55] Aaron also discussed his business interests with Rachel; she accompanied him on an inspection tour of his salt works.[56] Besides the salt works, Aaron operated a successful international trade in shingles and naval stores. His extensive business holdings occupied a greater part of the Wilmington waterfront.[57]

However, their marriage suffered a crisis when Lazarus's business collapsed due to a subordinate's misconduct. Throughout the difficult affair Rachel took comfort in the fact that the business community regarded Aaron Lazarus as a man of strength and integrity, no small recognition in the nineteenth-century commercial world that regarded character as essential for a business reputation. Their relationship deepened as Aaron reposed greater and greater confidence in his wife. Rachel explained: "I find a constant source of comfort and happiness [in Aaron], and far from repining at our lot, I daily rejoice that our union by taking place when it did, has given him a faithful friend, to whom he can confide his every thought, and who by the gentle offices of affection may alleviate his troubles."[58]

The happy partnership between Rachel and Aaron eased Rachel's acceptance in the Lazarus household. The Lazarus family responded warmly to Rachel, beyond her expectations. Contentedly, Rachel assured her sister Ellen: "The children do not tell me in words of their affection, but they evince it in a thousand ways, more grateful to my heart; they love to be near me to assist, to oblige me; are as obedient and orderly as I could desire."[59] Setting about to "derange and arrange" her new home, Rachel reported with confidence to her sister Caroline: "Our little girls have proved excellent assistants and I already find myself comparatively settled. Momma and her children are perfectly well acquainted, and every request meets with ready and cheerful obedience: how happy am I in not having allowed unreasonable scruples to weigh too heavily, and overbalance the whispers of affectionate partiality."[60] Phila Lazarus, Aaron's daughter, never felt that Rachel showed any partiality among the children. When Rachel and Aaron added four children of their own to the seven from Aaron's first marriage to Esther Cohen, Rachel made family harmony a priority. The task of knitting together the family was "serenely and lovingly accomplished, . . . guided by the wise Rachel," recalled a family member.[61] Rachel believed that "domestic unity," a highly prized virtue in the Mordecai and Edgeworth families, existed in the Lazarus household.

The extended household also included Eliza Mordecai. As Rachel prepared to leave her father and family to begin the daunting task of setting up a new household, she requested continued guardianship of Eliza, age twelve. Ellen Mordecai observed that Eliza "would derive many advantages by remaining with [Rachel] which at home and in our retirement she could not possibly have. She is a fine child and with her sweetness of disposition cannot fail making friends, and being loved." [62] In exchange for Rachel's tutelage, Eliza would help with the housekeeping and provide companionship for Rachel. Rachel expected only the resumption of "old habits and former pursuits" in her mentorship. [63] Separation from her family only confused the adolescent Eliza and divided her feelings. When Rachel asked her if she wished to move to Wilmington with her, Eliza, blushing and weeping, replied: "I don't know how I feel sister Rachel. I am glad & sorry. I do want to go with you, but I cannot help crying to think of leaving all at home." [64] Before she was twelve Eliza had experienced the move to Spring Farm and mourned the loss of familiar places and friends in Warrenton. Now she faced a second upheaval. In her expectation of adventure she encountered loss. If she had no home, where was the sense of connectedness that made her feel worthwhile? [65] Eliza could not imagine the changes that would take place in her that would replace her childlike dependencies with more mature independence.

Nevertheless, Eliza adjusted well in her new surroundings. Rachel reported, "Eliza is happy with her companions, they live in perfect unity, and I rejoice to see them so pleased with each other." [66] Eliza's presence during Rachel's transition period must have been of great comfort to Rachel. Rachel felt that a maternal bond tied her to Eliza; she referred to Eliza as "my child." [67] The elder sister once confessed a fondness for Eliza bordering upon indulgence; she admitted to her brother Solomon, "I cannot bear to withhold from her even for a few hours her best and dearest gratification." [68] Neither could Rachel part with Eliza. She explained to Solomon that Eliza was "superior in mind and disposition to any child I have known." Rachel deeply regretted the fact that her marriage would leave "so fair a flower . . . to waste its sweetness on the desert air." [69] When Eliza accompanied Rachel to Wilmington, they clung to each other; Eliza slept in Rachel and Aaron's apartment. [70] And as a mother-teacher Rachel greatly wished to observe the growth of the child. She confided to Maria Edgeworth: "I have pleasing anticipations of what her maturity may prove. Still watchful solicitude perceives various errors, which to the best of my ability I seek to correct, and trust my cares may prove successful." [71] Despite Rachel's concern for Eliza's mature character, the pattern of love and discipline she imposed upon Eliza's childhood and adolescence proved crucial in Eliza's resistance to and accommodation of Rachel. Eliza, who shifted between childish heedlessness and adult responsibility, nonetheless quietly constructed her own conscience and set of values. She did so at psychic cost; at times, she accepted guilt. [72]

Rachel nurtured Eliza's talents, but she maintained strict discipline. The elder sister sought out the best sheet music that would show off Eliza's musical talent and exposed Eliza to musical culture, such as the Lewis boys' piano concert in Charleston. However, Rachel insisted upon discipline; for example, she sought Ellen's reinforcement in reminding Eliza to practice her piano lessons. Rachel feared overconfidence and unwillingness to improve on Eliza's part, since she exhibited talent superior to other children.[73] The old problem of discipline occurred also with regard to Eliza's reading. Rachel believed that Eliza's habits and manners had deteriorated and that Eliza neglected her reading in favor of her companions. The adolescent Eliza had entered the period of socialization that would lead to a transformation of self. Socializing meant more to the adolescent Eliza than to the matronly Rachel. Rachel believed Eliza should practice more self-control. Eliza complained to Ellen that Rachel forbade Eliza to interrupt her reading in order to open a letter from Ellen. "I almost cried," Eliza said. Nonetheless, she felt guilty and conceded that "a little self-command is necessary at all times."[74] The old guilt feelings associated with self-accusation permeated Eliza's sense of self.[75] Eventually, Eliza did settle into a more structured routine of reading, one in which she and all the Lazarus girls participated. In the afternoon the girls read to each other while they worked. Reading and sewing occupied their day. By the fall of 1821 Eliza reported she had finished Cowper's letters and was currently involved in Blair's lectures. She looked forward to learning mythology and reading the *Iliad.*[76]

Work followed a rational routine within the Lazarus household. Rachel disapproved of any activity that disrupted her domestic system. She remarked to her sister Caroline that "idle business consisting in dressing, visiting and receiving company, is the greatest foe to rational employment of any kind."[77] With her large brood Rachel placed a premium on household efficiency. She devised money competitions for the completion of work despite Edgeworthian prohibitions and her own mother's bias against such prizes. Anna, Maria, and Eliza competed for the first prize of half a dollar, second prize, twenty-five cents, and third prize, twelve and a half cents. Typically, Eliza procrastinated and gave up hope of winning the prize, but, working industriously the last two days of the competition, she completed her work and won the prize. Since the other two finished only an hour later, they were rewarded with the same prize. The competition replaced slave or paid household labor, a valuable reward for Rachel. As Eliza matured, she contributed more to household productivity. As an adolescent, she was capable of substituting for Rachel as housekeeper in Rachel's absence, joining communal work such as quilting and sewing clothing and household linens.[78]

Household chores held fewer charms for Eliza than the excitement of an introduction into society. Eliza and the Lazarus girls attended their first assembly in the winter of 1823. Attendance at an assembly meant recognition of status both personal and economic. At the age of fourteen, Eliza entered the marriage market. Eliza and the Lazarus girls practiced cotillions to the music of the piano. And like Rosamund in Edgeworth's *Moral Tales,* she confronted the dilemma of adolescence, to enter society but not be drawn into its passions and idleness. Eliza enlivened Wilmington society throughout the 1823–24 season.[79]

Eliza the Adolescent

As Eliza prepared for the business of marriage and family, she struggled to define her own domestic character. Rachel, thoroughly imbued with her father's progressive ideas and disciplinary practices, offered Eliza the model of intellectual accomplishment and domestic stability achieved through paternal and marital partnership. But Eliza experienced mixed emotions, both shame and validation, within the enlightened framework of female instruction. Her task of self-definition, then, involved the positive experience of female support and the necessary steps toward separation. Her own personality longed for a passionate solution of her dilemma. Eliza's English translations of popular Continental French and German texts reveal the dimensions of her struggle between reason and emotion, differentiation and attachment.

Translations provoke a transliteration of words and ideas; the translator attempts to understand creatively the substance and meaning of the author's intent but also to remain true to exact language and to keep a distance from the text. The intent to balance subjective meaning within objective limits allows creative dissonance and the translator's own meaning to emerge.[80] The translator's task closely resembles the adolescent's, in that both must deal with newly discovered, almost alien emotions and place them within a learned objective framework of meaning. Eliza translated Stéphanie Félicité de Genlis's play *Queen of the Rose of Salency: A Comedy in Two Acts;* Johann von Goethe's *The Sorrows of Young Werther;* and Friedrich von Schiller's "The Criminal from Lost Honor" and "The Revolt of the United Netherlands."[81] These largely romantic works challenge traditional ideas of family and society while upholding the necessity of a family and a free state. Genlis wrote a neoclassical allegory that demonstrated the centrality of women in family networks, the liberating possibilities of virtue, and the importance of merit rather than inherited status.[82] Goethe's *Sorrows of Young Werther* expresses Romantic detachment and alienation while extolling the joys of married and family life. Schiller's "The Criminal" examines the psychological make-up of the criminal and his revolt against society, while "The Revolt" analyzes the economic and political foundation for the uprising of the Netherlands against Spain.

Queen of the Rose presents a comedy, a happy ending to a fable about the town of Salency, which awards a hat of roses to a young woman of irreproachable conduct. Each candidate's family must prove a lineage of virtue. Helen, a candidate for the prize whose female ancestors have won the hat of roses since the fifteenth century, lies about her good conduct in order to protect her friend Theresa's cowardly conduct. Theresa saves Helen's integrity by revealing Helen's heroic exertions in saving an old woman's life; at the same time, she publicly admits her own irresponsible actions in refusing to help the elderly woman. Theresa redeems herself by her selfless action on Helen's behalf.

Eliza translated a story in which a young woman's self-accusation restores trust in herself and reconstitutes women as a moral force. Although the author reinforces a traditional hierarchical practice, self-accusation, the primary focus of the story is upon the importance of women within the family system.[83] When the young woman is crowned, "a whole family is crowned upon the head of one; the triumph of one is the glory of the whole."[84] Here Genlis preempts a French Revolutionary ritual that illuminates the band of brothers as the unifying force of the society and government.[85] Men emulate women in Salency. According to the play, everyone dreads, "by an indelicate action, to dethrone either his sister or his daughter."[86] In the end the festival exists to celebrate the merit of women. Genlis writes, "The distinguishing characteristic of this festival is, that every part of it is referable to the queen . . . her splendor is direct not reflected; her glory borrows nothing from the distinction of rank; she has no need of any one to make her great and respectable; in one word, it is the image of virtue which shines, and everything disappears before her."[87] Merit, not marriage, is women's prize in Genlis's post-Revolutionary allegory.

If Genlis undermined the patriarchal hierarchy, Goethe in *The Sorrows of Young Werther* idealized the traditional family, even as he attacked and criticized it. Werther longs for an ancient patriarchy as he watches the activity of young girls by the side of a fountain. His fascination with Lotte, one of the young women, is as a mother figure, a substitute mother for her siblings. The domestic analogy pervades a literary discussion in which Werther engages with Lotte. Lotte expresses her preference for the author, "who takes me into my own world, where everything happens as it does around me, and whose story, nevertheless, becomes to me as interesting and as touching as my life at home."[88] Enamored by her intelligence and talent as a musician and dancer, Werther desires greater intimacy, but Lotte marries Albert. Rejected, Werther later returns to intrude upon the marriage; thereupon Lotte requests distance between herself and Werther. Werther, "determined to follow his own ambition, his own need,"[89] accepts a post as a diplomat but tires of the attention paid to his intellect rather than his sensibility. He scoffs, "Anyone can know what I know. My heart alone is my own."[90] Alienated and aggrieved, he wastes his talent and sinks into depression. He then decides upon suicide but first forces his attentions upon Lotte one last time. She responds ambivalently. Unable to tell her husband of the nature of her parting with Werther, she remains silent when Werther requests Albert's set of pistols. Werther then commits suicide and leaves Lotte in a perilous state.

The formal construction and rational restraint of a neoclassical allegory such as Genlis's story pose a contrast to the indulgence and subjectivity of Goethe's Romantic text. For Eliza, Goethe's Romanticism may have opened the possibility of risk, to dare the extreme, openly to express need and passion as a way of affirming her own individual nature. While the Romantic text allowed her to risk, the neoclassical text provided her with a solution for dealing with risk. The combination of texts allowed her to imagine a reconstituted family, egalitarian and woman-centered.[91] Thus Eliza selected from neoclassical formalism its family text and from the Romantic code its creative energy.

Schiller's "The Criminal" attacks form itself. Desire, for example, takes on protean shapes even though Schiller posits an innate moral sense. In a psychological appreciation of the origin of criminality, he examines the human heart and explains: "The heart of man is something so simple and yet so complicated! One and the same faculty or desire can operate in a thousand different forms and directions, can produce a thousand contradictory phenomena, and may appear in the same character in a thousand different combinations, and thousands of unlike characters and operations be elaborated from the same disposition, even though the individual who is the subject of all may be utterly unconscious of the existing relationships."[92] Schiller created ambiguity in the character of Christian Wolf, a murderer-robber whose vice does not wholly extinguish his remorse. A mischievous, ugly child, Christian learns to extort his needs and later steals to satisfy his wants. Jailed and impoverished for his crimes, he becomes a hardened criminal, bent upon revenge against a townspeople who scorned him. Alienated, he kills his rival and pursuer and joins a band of robbers. Fear of betrayal by the outlaws forces him to feel remorse. Wolf writes to the king and asks for rehabilitation, but the local prince ignores his plea. Finally, with self-surrender, he binds himself to a last moral act. His surrender to the authorities constitutes a moral act since it is a measure of his feeling for the necessity of justice.[93]

Schiller wrote "The Revolt of the United Netherlands" as "a history with historic truth"; he borrowed his Romantic theme of freedom from literature but stopped short of writing a romance. His purpose, he claimed, was to incite in his reader a "spirit-stirring consciousness of his own powers," that is, a psychological sense of individual and national empowerment.[94] The author's subversive intent framed the First Book, "The Earlier History of the Netherlands up to the Sixteenth Century," as he traced the dynastic foundations and commercial developments of the Netherlands. The Netherlands' prosperity and stability fostered a critical attitude toward Spain's despotism and led to eventual revolt.

Adolescents seek "moral authenticity" in a context of physiological change and sexual desire. In the chaos of feelings and contradictory longings the adolescent attempts various strategies to deal with the new and extraordinary urgings. "The Criminal" offers one such strategy, surrender to authority, as a way of dealing with guilt and remorse. "The Revolt of the United Netherlands" proposes yet another method of dealing with authority, namely, revolt. Such a course, however, requires a deep sense of righteousness, "a spirit-stirring consciousness of [the individual's] own powers."[95] Schiller appealed particularly to adolescents struggling to separate from family on their own moral terms.[96]

The literary texts presented expectations or horizons of possibilities of freedom and individual moral definition for Eliza, whereas circumstance introduced the means of realizing these complexities already existent in her adolescent self.[97] Rachel respected Eliza's growing maturity and believed she had "taught the right" and thus desired "to let the character in a manner form itself." She claimed that necessity taught her to practice the lessons of the Edgeworths with regard to a child's independence. Rachel explained Eliza's growth pattern to her sister Ellen: "Since she has been less habituated to depend on me, she has become more capable of judging and acting for herself, of walking alone, as I term it; and it seems to have given her a degree of ease which she did not before possess. She looks up to me but without constraint and I see the more of her as she will be, than would otherwise have been possible."[98]

At the time Eliza began to emerge into womanhood, her mother hinted to Rachel that she and Jacob desired their daughter's return. With delicate tact, Rebecca Mordecai hoped Eliza lightened Rachel Lazarus's household burden but mentioned, "Father is lonely." Rebecca Mordecai left the decision to her stepdaughter's judgment. She wrote feelingly: "I know the struggle it will cost you to part with her, yet this must one day be, and both your Dear father and myself are willing to leave it to your decision and believe me when I say that my own individual feeling shall never be suffered to proponderate to her disadvantage; a life of grateful affection will scarce repay the tender care which you have lavished on her."[99] The mother preempted Rachel's claim to Eliza, yet this request involved a four-way interest in the child's development: the parents, the eldest daughter, and the child herself. Rachel attempted to keep the child from identifying with Rebecca, whom Rachel regarded as incompetent to raise and educate children because she was too indulgent. Nevertheless, Rachel did not undermine Eliza's strong tie to her fond mother.[100] Rebecca Mordecai, whose love for Eliza made separation unbearable for her, pleaded with Rachel, "I scarce dare trust myself; my anxiety to have her with me is indeed great and the fear that she will become in a manner estranged from home, often intrudes itself upon my mind, and make[s] me almost impatient for her return."[101]

Rebecca's fears of Eliza's alienation may not have been groundless; the moves in quick succession from Warrenton to Spring Farm to Wilmington disrupted Eliza's childhood and threatened dislocation. Rebecca and Jacob consented to Eliza's loss for the sake of their daughter's education and opportunity. Despite Rebecca Mordecai's pleas, Eliza remained in Wilmington for another year. Amid piano and French lessons, housekeeping and parties, Eliza kept up an "accomplished" appearance. Nonetheless, for Rachel Lazarus, whose family had grown too large to sacrifice any more time for Eliza, the parting was a necessity.[102] The guardianship came to an end in 1824.

When Rachel prepared for the journey to take Eliza back to Spring Farm, she considered the character of the child she had raised. Not surprisingly, Rachel had a sense of failure; enlightened pedagogy assumed character as much as ideas derived from external or sensate experience. Locke himself believed that of all the individuals "we meet with, Nine Parts of Ten are what they are, Good or Evil, useful or not, by their Education."[103] Eliza had been "taught the right," yet her habits belied "the education of the heart," a trained, virtuous, benevolent sensibility. Rachel compared Eliza to her younger sister Emma and admired Emma's amiability and affection. Rachel said that Emma "always possessed more of that than Eliza shews. I do not believe she wants the right feeling but it does not evince itself in those little nameless unteachable ways that gain so powerfully on our affections, a few more years may render her more as I could wish her to be—mean time, I do not endeavor to make her seem more than her feelings prompt."[104] That poignant moment when Rachel gave Eliza her last lessons dissolved without sentiment on Eliza's part. Rachel said nothing; Eliza had not noted the change in their relationship.[105]

Eliza's silence may be attributed to embarrassment and guilt upon leaving her sister. Her emotions may have been too complex or mixed to express; she both loved and resented her elder sister. Surely, too, Eliza would have missed her new companions within the Lazarus family; they constituted her peer group, her refuge from Rachel's demanding authority. The business of separation, while a necessity with adolescents, still prompts a mourning period, a realization of loss. However, Eliza's removal meant a return to her parents, whom she dearly loved; thus Eliza faced an ambivalent event, loss and gain.[106]

Rachel may have wished a fonder heart for Eliza as she herself struggled to enlarge her own capacity for warmth and companionship. Eliza's adolescent imagination shifted from the domestic to the social, from confinement to expansion, from order to impulse. Rachel disapproved of Eliza's fascination with the provincial, nonintellectual, and fashionable world of North Carolina, but Eliza's curiosity drew her to new connections and new freedoms that generated her originality and creativity.[107] In a sense, Eliza used the removal as a flight, a way of distancing herself from the past, and yet she chose a paternal figure, Samuel Myers, an older man, on whom to lavish a new passionate attachment.

Thus the young Eliza married but still remained within the orbit of her extended family.[108] In 1824 Eliza and Rachel parted, each to their separate lives.

Once at Spring Farm Eliza exercised her talents and found new confidence in her abilities. She resumed her music lessons with her sister Ellen. Ellen had a gift for teaching, and Eliza distinctly improved her singing and instrumental talent. Also Eliza's self-confidence grew as she assumed the task of teaching Emma, the youngest child. Most importantly, she began to take stock of her life and attempt to make some meaning of it. She used the writing of fables to work out her personal identity.

She wrote children's narratives, set mostly in thinly disguised versions of her family homes, Spring Farm and Warrenton. "Foolish Stories by the Foolish Old Woman for Good Little Foolish, Old Fashioned Children" is an allegorized family tale. Gaffer and Goody Mason and their children, Johnny, Dickey, and Margery, resemble the large and good-natured Mordecai family in their attempts to establish Spring Farm as a stable enterprise. Eliza writes: "They settled on this small portion of land which was the best their scanty means enabled them to purchase and with sincere affection for each other, strong hands and stout hearts and a cheerful reliance on God, they resolved to build themselves a home."[109] Their hard work, cheerful cooperation, and acts of kindness earn the family recognition by neighbors and townspeople. The appearance of a giant, Lilyda, who carries Margery away, interrupts this prosaic tale. Eliza's subversion of form marks a departure from Edgeworthian children's fiction, which condemned the use of fantasy.[110] Yet in Eliza's tale the fantasy enhances the idealization of family life. Even the threat of a giant cannot shatter this family's harmony. Nonetheless, the fairy tale contrasts with the enlightened realism Eliza had been taught to admire. Moreover, her tale "Pierot and His Dog: A True Story" warns of the dangers of self-absorption in scientific study and wholly goal-oriented behavior.[111] "Pierot" counters the scientific method so essential in Eliza's training.

As if to gain an inner freedom, Eliza wrote about fairies and giants.[112] Clearly, Eliza sought freedom in imagination and adventure, a Romantic imagination that nurtured self-development and adventure and threw off her childhood constraints.[113] Eliza employed fantastic and antiscientific themes to subvert the rational, pragmatic, enlightened method she had been taught. Instead, she relished a stable domestic life without the rigor of enlightened intellectual discipline.

Eliza's Marriage

While at home Eliza reestablished the happy connection with her uncle Samuel Myers in Richmond.[114] Shortly after her return she became romantically involved with young Samuel Myers, her cousin; Eliza was then fifteen years old. Samuel Myers had spent a reckless, dissolute early youth and met Eliza when he was a twenty-five-year-old bachelor. Eliza's mother wrote to Rachel and attempted to make the best of their engagement. Rebecca Mordecai suggested that Samuel Myers was an "amiable, sensible man who having passed through the fiery ordeal of youthful dissipation, there is less to apprehend from the want of stability in his future course . . . S[amuel] only want[s] something to stimulate him to exertion, to prove him a superior character; he has . . . for the first time an object that will inspire him with the interest necessary to secure an attainment which he knows will depend entirely on his own exertions."[115] Samuel Myers appealed to Eliza's free-spirited temperament. Her mother described Eliza as "gay as a lark and not less innocent . . . but free and artless."[116] Eliza wrote Sam a verse in which she declared, "I will go on loving thee."[117] But during their courtship Eliza formulated just what character she needed if she contemplated a union with Sam. In 1825 she penned "My Idea of a Woman with Character." She argued:

> Her disposition must be warm and enthusiastic, her heart, affectionate and sincere. The temper must be mild and forbearing, for her trials will be many; yet mindful of her dignity, she must not be too passive to maintain her own rights and privileges which are so apt to be ungenerously trampled upon. Gentle, yielding, open to conviction, she yet must form her own opinions, and when confident of their correctness, act with firmness according to them. In her ideas of religion and of duty she must be governed entirely by her own reason.[118]

Although Eliza was determined to act the principled individual, she yielded to Romantic ardor and traditional notions of clinging dependency. She noted finally in her essay: "She must possess deep feeling and exquisite sensibility, without parade or affectation . . . Her first love must be her last . . . her only wish will be to live for him and him alone, to bless him, and to die with him."[119] Eliza's declaration represents a departure from Edgeworthian feminine models. Edgeworthian heroines remained "unobtrusive yet firm," that is, rather passive in their principled behavior. Moreover, the liveliest of heroines such as Lady Davenant and Helen suffer drastic consequences when they display reckless abandonment. Eliza's ideas of womanhood, however, demonstrate a certain Romantic tilt or imbalance that preserves enlightened dignity and reason, the fight for rights, but tends to favor "deep feeling and sensibility" as the last, best moral expression. The adolescent contradictions between past moral stricture and present sexual compromise are evident in Eliza's passionate essay.[120]

The couple postponed their marriage until Samuel established himself in business. He engaged as a tobacco broker with Mr. Massey in Richmond. Two years after their engagement Samuel told Eliza that "he hoped the day would come when he could ask her to make something else beside sacrifices for him."[121]

Rachel Mordecai Lazarus harbored fears of the match. She admitted that the approach of Eliza's wedding threw her "into a complete tremor and . . . cast a chill through [her] heart." Rachel insisted to Ellen Mordecai that "this is not and cannot be right . . . I have never felt entirely as if her happiness would be secured by this union." She fretted about Samuel's lack of business sense and want of stability. "I do not entirely like this change of business, it seems too variable to be prosperous," Rachel said.[122] Nonetheless, after the wedding Rachel glossed over her misgivings and wrote Maria Edgeworth:

> Do you recollect my sister Eliza, my child of whom I have sometimes spoken to you? Ten days since she became a wife; she has married Mr. Samuel Myers, an amiable, well educated, intelligent young man, sufficiently her senior to be her friend and guide as well as her chosen companion for life. Her path thus far has been a flowery one; her sweetness of temper and innocent gaiety of heart have rendered her a favorite with the many, while other qualities of sterling value have bound her still more closely to the hearts of her friends and of her family.[123]

The young couple married on 21 November 1827. However, as she prepared to meet guests after the wedding, Eliza felt dizzy, as if she hung over a precipice. Her reaction, less foreboding than shyness, nonetheless exposed the precarious nature of adolescent choice, the constant state of "betweenness."[124] As if to demonstrate their ambivalent independent status, the newlyweds first set up housekeeping with Eliza's half brother, Samuel Mordecai, in Petersburg, where Eliza expected to establish a school.[125] Family members hoped the couple eventually would settle in an independent household, but business success eluded Samuel as he spent an increasing amount of time away from home. In addition, Eliza's school never materialized. Instead, Eliza depended for emotional support upon her parents, who resided only twenty-five miles from the young couple. With Samuel's frequent business trips from home, Eliza visited her family, made preserves, played her guitar, and managed a useful existence. The couple's re-unions, however, produced the happiest of circumstances. Jack, a Mordecai bondsman who visited the Myerses, observed to Ellen Mordecai, "The most they [the Myerses] do ma'am, is to laugh, ma'am."[126]

Eliza blossomed in the marriage. When the couple visited Rachel and Aaron in Wilmington, Eliza radiated so much vitality that Aaron referred to her as "a dangerous article." Three years after their marriage Eliza and Samuel expected their first child. Eliza spent her confinement at Spring Farm.[127] Rachel confided to Maria Edgeworth that the birth of Eliza's son, Edmund, caused Rachel to feel "almost as if I were a grandmother in reality."[128] And Eliza fondly reported to

Rachel the child's exploits: crawling, imitating cows and crows, and blowing out candles. The latter skills left the family totally in the dark.[129]

Described as a "sweet little fellow," Edmund followed his father everywhere, and Samuel Myers cultivated a companionship with his son. Eliza noted Sam's philosophy: "Sam says he has no idea of being an awful spirit-queller, or anything to his son but a friend to whom he may at any time naturally and confidently appeal."[130] Eliza still held to enlightenment ideals of beneficent paternalism, a hierarchical order in the early mentor-child relationship; she thus shared her misgivings about Sam's approach with her former teacher, Rachel: "I hope he [Sam] may find that he has the art of inspiring this confidence and at the same time of preventing a degree of improper familiarity which I should be apt to fear from incautiously adopting such a course with a child, and more especially a boy."[131] Whatever caution Eliza may have addressed with regard to familiarity, she neglected it when it came to her own relationship with Edmund. She delighted in his prattle and recorded it for the family, but she mocked her own maternal demeanor. She wrote to Ellen: "Well, now, let me tell you how sweet Edmund is—he can kiss his hand & make a bow, & say 'bye' for goodbye—& when he drops any of his playthings he looks about for it & says 'Whay is it'—& when he finds it he says 'dare tis' and ever so many more things he can say & do that kill Jane [a slave] with delight, but only fill me with calm & *dignified maternal pride*—a-hem!"[132] However sweet the care of Edmund, nonetheless, the drudgery of household chores continued to plague Eliza. On one gray day in 1833, Eliza penned a satire of Lord Byron's *Childe Harold's Pilgrimage,* in which she substituted the poet's paean to solitude for a woman's unceasing work. In the second canto of the poem, Byron wrote, "To sit on rocks, to muse over flood and fell," which Eliza parodied, "To sit on frocks, to muse o'er stitch and fell."[133] Not even domestic drudgery could dampen Eliza's sense of fun.

Rachel and the Evangelical Circle

In contrast to Eliza's warm and familial but sheltered life, Rachel expanded her domestic concerns beyond the household. Several of Rachel's and Ellen's acquaintances from the Warrenton Female Academy resided in Wilmington, North Carolina. Ellen Mordecai had visited Wilmington in 1818 to regain her health. At that time, Aaron Lazarus had accompanied Ellen and courted her, but Ellen disclaimed any interest in Aaron's suit.[134] Ellen provided the link between Rachel and the Wilmington women's circle. When Ellen went to Wilmington she visited her friend Jane Vance, but the Vance household, crowded with boarders, proved unacceptable, and Mary Orme, Jane's sister, invited Ellen to stay with her. Ellen described Wilmington as once all "gaiety and levity" but now a place presided over by the formidable Reverend Adam Empie, the rector of St. James's Episcopal Church. Ellen noted, "He has checked them by degrees in all those amusements which excess only can render sinful, but to which opinion Mr. E[mpie] does not subscribe." [135]

Ellen Mordecai observed the effects of an Evangelical revivalism that had revolutionized everyday life in Wilmington. In 1808 revivals infused a new fervor into Protestant denominations, including the High Church Episcopalian. Evangelical enthusiasm succeeded in making Wilmington a center of Low Church activity; Reverend Empie, an Evangelical Episcopalian, organized a diocese in 1817. Evangelicals experienced a deep consciousness of personal sin and acknowledged their helplessness before God, but they believed that Jesus atoned for their sins, and thus they turned to God with new understanding and a new life of service. Convinced that they were transformed by God's love and power, "born again" Christians reformed their social order. A more stringent morality attested to the new order of holiness, one that, incidentally, attacked upper-class pleasures. [136]

Reverend Empie's Low Church movement attracted Wilmington's female communicants in record numbers but largely alienated the traditional male communicants. Wilmington's High Church male gentry refused to sacrifice the patriarchal order for what they regarded as emotionalism and asceticism; for instance, the gentry supported local drama productions, whereas Evangelical Episcopalians shunned the theater. [137] Only once did Ellen's circle of Evangelical friends "stray" for her sake and attend an amateur theater production. Aaron Lazarus escorted her. Ellen believed there was "more austerity than religion" present in such attitudes. She abhorred the religious exclusiveness that led to intolerance. Ellen found Mr. Empie "very much prejudiced against our poor race." [138] His born again credo preached no salvation outside belief in Jesus Christ. Ellen bristled and kept to her own belief that "he [Jesus Christ] was only a man and a mortal." She dismissed her unpleasant encounters with Reverend Empie's sermons. [139] She noted in her diary on 5 January 1818, "So much for Mr. E[mpie]—and so much for the religion of Wilmington . . . I do not subscribe!" [140] Evangelical Christianity challenged traditional religious and gender relationships in Wilmington and sought a moral order that excluded non-Evangelicals.

The repressive social order did not entirely preclude entertainment, as Ellen discovered. She delighted in the dinner parties and sailing excursions. [141] Mrs. Orme's home remained the center of social activity in a cheerful, hospitable neighborhood. A fence separated her from Anna Cochran, formerly Anna Green, who had been a student at the Warrenton Female Academy. Phlegmatic and particular about company, she tolerated most in her offhand, absent way. Mr. Cochran, who struck Ellen as "unsavory," departed from his home for long periods of time. Anna endured her husband's absences and lived with her mother, an energetic, kind woman and an excellent household manager. Mrs. Cochran's lively, literate conversation sparked even the dullest circles, and, as Ellen observed, Wilmington had the dullest cast of characters.[142]

When Rachel moved to Wilmington, the neighborhood women immediately provided her with a familiar intellectual and affectionate companionship. Her neighbors read contemporary British women writers such as Fanny Burney and Maria Edgeworth and delighted in literary discussion and exchange.[143] Rachel never mentioned their dullness. Of Jane Vance, Rachel wrote, "Jane has a pretty little man for her husband, is comfortably settled, & appears quite happy." She found Anna Cochran "just as she always was, an amiable, pleasing, little silent woman." Anna, Rachel's former student, could never bring herself to address Rachel with anything more familiar than "Miss Rachel." Anna's mother chatted happily with Rachel, even though she was somewhat deaf and blind. Rachel's mere presence made all the difference to the old woman.[144] Catherine DeRosset, who lived practically next door to the Lazaruses' large and pleasantly imposing home, provided Rachel with a kind and hospitable companionship.[145]

The Education of Marx Lazarus

Rachel's happy domesticity intensified with the birth of her first child, a son, Marx Edgeworth Lazarus, in 1822. Self-conscious about Marx's training and education, Rachel approached her responsibility not as a dedicated practitioner about to perform an "experiment" but as a mother faced with a child's fixed habits and potential abilities. Her lack of confidence with her first-born affected her method; she reverted to rigid discipline. Her belief that at the age of six months Marx's "dispositions and little habits" were already formed and therefore it remained her responsibility to train them rightly caused Rachel anxiety. She described herself as "watchful and diffident in undertaking a task so interesting." [146] Fully absorbed but fearful, Rachel tried to abide by Maria Edgeworth's observation that "children are sometimes injured by our too great anxiety to render them exactly what we wish." Rachel acknowledged her own behavior in this regard: "This danger will now increase, and I must be more than ever vigilant in training myself, that I may become the more competent to guide usefully and judiciously the early years of my son." [147]

Her father's discipline and affectional pattern, often repeated in Eliza's training, erupted in Rachel's education of Marx. Rachel's anxiety prevented her from successfully countering Marx's extreme anti-authoritarian stance. When Marx established a naughty pattern, Rachel slapped him. She also used shaming. Sometimes she had only to say, "my son," and Marx quietly took notice. But later, when he was set in his unmanageable ways, Ellen encouraged shaming and even instilling fear in Marx by letting him know his cousins were fully informed of his progress or negligence.[148] This ploy had little effect. When told how well his cousins were progressing, Marx replied, "I love my cousins too well to feel anything like Emulation, I want them to do better than I do." Rachel hastily explained the difference between envy and emulation. Sadly, Rachel regarded her son as a "strange heedless boy." [149] In effect, she regarded Marx as a distinct, although eccentric, personality.

Rachel's strict disciplinary method contrasted with her more spontaneous and progressive teaching, a pattern established earlier with Eliza. The teaching of reading particularly interested Rachel. Educators Bolmar and Murray recommended teaching phonetics before reading, and Rachel attended phonetics lectures in Wilmington. But Rachel believed that teaching the sounds of words or letters was much too tedious for a child, and she taught words and phrases after Marx had absorbed a general knowledge of word sounds.[150] Whatever her technique, Rachel succeeded probably because of the amount of attention she paid to Marx's lessons. Rachel's attentiveness arose out of her need to "know the child as he really is." [151] At the age of eight he read mythology and the stories of Washington Irving, recited his French lessons, and worked diligently on a map of Asia.[152] For sheer pleasure his mother allowed him to read allotted portions of Sir Walter Scott's poetry, *The Lay of the Last Minstrel* and *The Lady of the Lake*. She believed children should read whatever they could assimilate. The delight, she maintained, lay in the unexpected; anticipation, in this case, proved the best teacher. To make the study of arithmetic more interesting, Rachel sent a special request to the New York publisher of *Colburn's Arithmetic* for plates of their illustrations.[153] An enlightened teacher, Rachel adapted her instruction to her child.

Within the Lazarus household Rachel labored to dispense discipline and learning, but the number of children and her duties overwhelmed her. She complained to Ellen Mordecai: "What a charge it is to educate a child! and how impossible to educate properly any but your own, or one who like Eliza and Emma, is given completely to your direction. This I often silently acknowledge, for tractable as the girls are, to whom my cares are now given, I find it indispensable to overlook a thousand little errors, & deficiencies which in a child of my own I would labor to correct." [154] She worried that she could not extend a more exacting method over all her charges.

Marx, the most burdensome of her charges, might have foundered without constant supervision. His willfulness grew uncontrollable as he matured. His attendance at Chapel Hill and later the University of Pennsylvania Medical School did not stabilize him; rather, he inclined toward alcoholism, vagabondage, and the advancement of quack cures. Marx's enlightened education led to social criticism, socialism, and a brief encounter with Brook Farm, the socialist experiment in West Roxbury, Massachusetts, that lasted from 1841 to 1847. He married, attempted farming, and died in poverty in 1895, a burden to his family, who thought him mad.[155]

Marx's sisters proved equally difficult to train. Rachel reported that Mary Catherine did not improve at an infant school she attended, forcing Rachel to teach her at home. Julia and Ellen Lazarus occupied a great deal of Rachel's time. The weary mother admitted that Ellen was "a difficult child to manage," although she considered her less "wayward" than previously. Rachel confided that Ellen cost her "many a sigh." [156] Ellen and Julia shared Marx's enthusiasm for alternative medicine and reform movements. Ellen married John Allen in 1848, a man interested in Brook Farm and other communal movements. Against family counsel, Mary Catherine entered into a tragic marriage to an abusive Mobile planter.[157] Thus the second generation of Rachel's pupils adopted the more critical method of enlightened education that allowed greater freedom of choice, yet, like Eliza, Rachel's children rebelled against enlightened discipline.

Rachel's Faith

Only an abiding sense of faith sustained Rachel as her cares and household responsibilities intensified. She retained her unmistakable regard for holiness, careful to choose the good for herself and others by observing religious precepts. Thus she labored to instill in Marx strong ethical boundaries, and she succeeded in building a harmonious and cooperative family. Her religious inclination followed an earlier pattern of humility and religious resignation. For example, during the War of 1812 as she worried over the safety of family members, she wrote to her beloved brother Samuel, "let me endeavor to be resigned to His will, be grateful for general good, and bear every evil with patient resignation." [158] Then again, she explained to Samuel Mordecai her success in teaching as a resignation to divine will. She wrote: "They who submit to circumstances, and place a constant and undeviating confidence in the protection of Heaven, are surely most worthy of its favour, the latter I feel in its full extent, the former has long been, and still is my study, and I think I find it proved, that 'to seek is to gain' for I am more patient now than formerly, and to what other cause can it be attributed?" [159] Moreover, she prefaced her diary, which contained her pedagogical "experiment," with a prayer that consecrated her work of shaping Eliza's character to the will of the "Most High." Rachel heard Eliza's prayers, taught her the principles of Judaism from Rabbi Solomon Jacob Cohen's *Elements of Jewish Faith,* conveyed Jewish history, helped her to observe the Sabbath, and fostered an awe of the divine.[160] Rachel's diary may be read as wisdom literature, training the child in the precepts of the Torah. Eliza was trained in the precepts of truth telling, honesty, obedience, and respect for the name of God.[161]

The Mordecai and Lazarus families practiced their faith in southern villages and towns where no community of Jews existed. Once settled in Richmond, however, the Mordecai family attended the Beth Salome Synagogue. In Warrenton and Wilmington, Christian, especially Evangelical, influence impinged upon Jewish daily life. Jacob Mordecai accompanied his Christian students to services on Sundays, thus opening him to proselytization on the part of Christians. Aaron Lazarus attended St. James's Episcopal Church with his family as part of his position as social leader in Wilmington. Rachel's easy camaraderie with Christian women followed naturally upon her status as Aaron's wife. Thus the Mordecai and Lazarus families accommodated themselves in various ways to Christian culture.

The tensions and threats of Christian proselytization disturbed Rachel, but she tended to maintain an enlightened perspective. She insisted to Maria Edgeworth that in Warrenton she maintained friendships with "those of persuasions different from her own; yet each has looked upon the variations of the other as things of course—differences which take place in every society." [162] She believed that open discussion with Christians did not necessarily lead to conversion. Her method in dealing with unbelief may be clearly seen in her advice on how best to deal with cousin Henrietta Marx's madness and fixation upon conversion. In 1817 she considered Henrietta's state:

> She muses, when she does not speak her doubts, if she has any, or her anxieties, are increased, until becoming insupportable, they for a time overpower her reason. I am much inclined to believe that if she were permitted to speak freely on religious subjects, to read the letters of [David] Levi to Voltaire & others, his evidences of the truth and correctness of our faith, and other works of the same kind that it would have the effect of calming her mind, & restoring it to even more than its wonted tranquillity. [163]

Nevertheless, dialogue with Christians led to the exchange of religious language and phrases that found their way into Jewish discourse. On the death of her brother Moses in 1824, Rachel sent her family the prayer "Form O lord, the inward thoughts of thy servants, & prepare their hearts to serve thee, Thou who hast planted eternal life within us, & who daily loadeth us with benefits, enable us to observe thy statutes, firmly fix thy love & thy fear in our hearts, & teach us to obey thy precepts in this world, so that we may be worthy to live, & inherit with the good, the blessing reserved for the life of the world to come." [164] "The life of the world to come" is a common Christian phrase, perhaps derived from Jewish origins, associated with the doxology and final blessing. Eliza, as a child familiar with the poetry of the Christian hymnist Isaac Watts, remarked on the theological implications of the lyrics. [165] Christian custom, language, and literature found a place in the common discourse of Jews in the early republic.

Rachel's intimacy with Evangelical women and her dependence upon them during her three confinements presented no exceptional association for a Jewish American woman. Rachel gave birth to three daughters within the space of five years; Ellen was born in 1825, Mary Catherine in 1828, and Julia Judith in 1830. With each birth Rachel lost strength, but the presence of her family and especially her loyal friends buoyed her confidence. She faced death during Mary Catherine's birth. Mrs. Orme wrote to Ellen and explained that Rachel's life seemed "to hang on a single thread," and she questioned if Rachel should have more children. Mary Orme's solicitude and tender care drew Rachel to her; in gratitude, Rachel named the child Mary Catherine after her and another friend and neighbor, Catherine DeRosset. The neighborhood women, including Mrs. Orme, Mrs. Hooper, and especially Catherine DeRosset, nursed Rachel through the illnesses that followed her pregnancies.[166]

The attendance of Rachel's friends during Mary Catherine's difficult birth sustained Rachel in her struggle for life. The experience changed her, and she determined to be "daily more devoted to my God." She related her close encounter with death to a friend, Lucy Ann Lippett. She wrote:

> Yes, my friend, truly may I say, that I have walked "through the valley of the shadow of death," and as truly may I add, in the sweet words of the psalmist, "I feared no evil, for Thou wert with me—Thy rod & Thy staff, they comforted me"—I was conscious of my critical situation, that my life was suspended but by a thread—and I deem it a blessing that I was perfectly collected—that tho' almost unable to articulate, I was capable of reflection & endeavoured to prepare my mind & my heart for the awful change—trusting all that was dear to me on earth to the care of my Heavenly Father—confiding in his mercy for pardon of my sins & transgressions, & wholly submitting myself in resignation to his most Holy Will.[167]

The Twenty-third Psalm comforted her, and she resigned herself to death confident in the God of mercy. Her feelings and spiritual preparations expressed Jewish sentiments and principles. That experience in childbirth invested her with a longing for the deep serenity she had known in the face of death. Instead she found only bitter struggle. Her emotional and spiritual intimacy with Christian women impelled her in new spiritual directions that surfaced as doubts of faith. Between 1828 and her death in 1838 Rachel investigated the tenets of Christianity.[168]

Nat Turner's Revolt

During several years of spiritual crisis in which she questioned her Orthodox faith, Rachel experienced a moral testing in the Nat Turner uprising. This event opened her cherished assumptions to debate through profound psychological shock. The Southampton slave revolt revealed a wider conspiracy in Wilmington. The shock waves turned Rachel's rational opinions concerning slavery upside down and replaced her moral complacency with fears of a future uprising.

Thereafter she questioned slavery's existence in the South and the economic motivations that fastened the peculiar institution to the region.

The Wilmington white community, bound by its friendships, kinships, and church, was built upon the labor of black bondsmen and bondswomen. The Nat Turner slave revolt in Southampton County, Virginia, on 22 August 1831, which resulted in the brutal slaying of sixty white men, women, and children, exposed racial oppression, challenged the premises of patriarchal social hierarchy, and contested the existence of slavery.[169] Rural southern communities like Wilmington experienced the Nat Turner revolt intimately as authorities implicated household slaves in the conspiracy and white families protected their members against potential violence. The Lazarus household, however, held firm against the hysteria and dared question the necessity of slavery. Rachel's criticism of the South's peculiar institution suggests her enlightened perspective, but she rejected immediate abolitionism as impractical and dangerous. Her dialogue with Maria Edgeworth on the question of slavery reinforced her own doubts about slavery, advanced her critical abilities, and contributed to her moral, intellectual, and spiritual crisis.

Maria Edgeworth offered abolition as an enlightened response within the limits of an Anglo-Irish patriarchal formulation. The moral reform of families within the British empire rested upon their right relation to marriage and property. Inspired by the Burkean proposition that masculine authority and privilege secure proper order and women's fidelity insures legitimate heredity, Edgeworth argued her case.[170] Maria Edgeworth used Lord Byron's work for the Greek cause as her case in point. She wrote to Rachel:

> The Greeks like the Spaniards have been so long degraded by slavery that they cannot exert themselves sufficiently to regain or deserve liberty. This is the greatest evil and injury done by tyranny. It induces the vices of falsehood and cunning. . . . In the Greeks, the West Indian slaves, the Irish "poor slave" as he often calls himself, the same defects of character from the same causes appear. But we must not do the cruel injustice of supposing that these faults of character are natural and inherent and incurable, and make this imputation a plea for continuing the wrongs and oppression by which the faults were produced.[171]

Tyranny defies proper order because men cannot claim their property either in themselves or their estate, Edgeworth intimated. Without legitimate inheritance morals cannot reform or affection increase within families. Instead, among oppressed families dependence, not innate character, encourages corruption, lies, and cunning. Obliterated in Edgeworth's argument is any consciousness that whiteness alone allowed an accumulation of property and wealth. Even among the propertyless, whiteness, the claim to white superiority, acted as a "wage," a consolation in lieu of economic consideration.[172]

Although Rachel Mordecai Lazarus believed that "the Negro" was not inherently weak, she defended the slave system's benevolence. She wrote:

> The condition of our slaves both in this and the sister states is far less miserable than that of the poorer classes of white people. They are comfortably maintained and with very few exceptions kindly treated. So long as the benefits of education are denied them, their state must be abject, and the necessity of retaining them is by all admitted to be an evil tho' at present an unavoidable one; but their usually cheerful demeanor argues well for the humanity of their masters.[173]

Even though a necessary evil, slavery mitigated its profane consequences by benevolence, according to Rachel. This assumed slaveholder identity, created for the distribution of wealth, took on not just the trappings of class but an ideology of benevolence.[174] Thus the moral animus rested with the slaveowner, not the seemingly acquiescent individual, who in reality struggled against the implications of dependence and servility. Rachel consistently defended the slaveowner and did not discuss the nature of the system. "Much has been humanely urged in the British Parliament on the subject of Negro slavery; yet is the condition of the Irish poor incomparably worse than that of the slave, either here, or as far as I am informed, in the Islands[?]" she asked.

Maria Edgeworth reduced the abolition argument to the moral necessity of property rights and legitimate authority. Tyranny disguised as paternalism did not allow the slave the right to ownership of self or property and therefore did not insure morality. Once free to express the moral cause, however, "The Negro does more for the Negro race than any English act of Parliament can do. The one affects opinion, far above law in its range of power," Edgeworth argued.[175]

True to Edgeworth's observation, Nat Turner's revolt expressed the African American slave's oppression in brutal but unmistakable terms. Yet Rachel Mordecai and her family responded in rational ways; experience and serious thought on the matter prepared them for the crisis. One month after the Southampton revolt, alarms arose in the North Carolina counties of Samson and Duplin. Rachel refused to escalate the fear as some of her neighbors did. "I am fortunate in being a stranger to terrors on this score & I fervently pray both that I may remain so, & that there may be no real grounds of apprehension. Many of our females make themselves wretched by anticipation," she wrote.[176] As families fled for safety to the bank on the night that disclosures of a Wilmington slave conspiracy were revealed, the Lazarus family remained at home. However, as county authorities submitted overwhelming evidence of a Wilmington conspiracy, Rachel grasped the reality of the threat. She wrote, "The horrible disclosures which have subsequently been made have made a total change in my feelings, and I view the condition of the southern state as one of the most unenviable that can be concieved." [177] Rachel believed that she or her descendants faced certain murder or outrage at the hands of slaves, for whom rampage seemed just retribution. Rachel concluded that some form of abolition provided the only solution. She argued: "The United States government might possibly find a remedy by rendering some equivalent to slave owners and exporting the slaves in as large numbers as practicable to Africa. But I do not know whether if such a plan were proposed it would be acceded to by any considerable majority; people are too short-sighted, too unwilling to relinquish present convenience from fear of future ill or for the prospect of future good." [178] Ironically, Aaron Lazarus wished to immigrate North but found his business and property too extensive and complicated for such a move. [179]

Circumstances drew the Lazarus family ever more deeply into the volatile environment. Further investigations uncovered conspirators within the Lazarus household. Billy, Aaron Lazarus's slave, and another man belonging to the family joined with Jacob Cowoen, the leader, in plotting revolt. An informant betrayed Jacob Cowoen before the group carried out their plan; nonetheless, the Lazarus slaves suffered execution for their role in the conspiracy. Despite the danger and community outrage, Washington Lazarus, the twenty-three-year-old eldest son of Aaron Lazarus and a member of the bar, defended several of the accused conspirators. He had ridden with the slave patrols and observed the trials. His participation in events convinced him to defend the slaves. But the physical toll of the defense proved too much for the frail young man, and he died after a short illness.

Rachel, torn by the untenable position of southern slaveholders, prayed that Providence would enlighten the minds of leaders with a solution. [180] Personally, Rachel hoped for the "gradual and judicious emancipation of slaves." Rachel concurred with Maria Edgeworth in deploring the inconsistency of "American liberty and slavery." Although Rachel laid the blame for the existence of slavery upon the English trade and upon northern business interests' inability to reimburse slaveowners, she explained that she would willingly sacrifice all domestic help to rid the South of slavery. [181] Rachel upheld an enlightened environmental argument associated with colonization (the idea that freed slaves could be resettled in Africa) already considered naive by southerners at the turn of the century. Consistent with colonizationists' lack of vision for an end to white racism, Rachel abhorred revolutionary change, as her white family had been its victim. Thus she would sacrifice her domestic help to retain the trappings of social hierarchy. [182]

The Wilmington conspiracy and Rachel's subsequent dialogue on the subject insinuated doubt in her mind about slavery and the order it represented. Nonetheless, Aaron's business precluded the family from divesting themselves of the necessary evil. Moral ambiguity then rooted itself deeply in Rachel's soul, already troubled by religious uncertainty. Consequently, when she experienced a spiritual conversion, the ordeal acted like a conspiracy that shattered the stability of her mind and her family's peace. She suffered a nervous breakdown during the ordeal.

Rachel's radical response also resulted from the political and social disorganization and reformulation of the early nineteenth century. The Nat Turner rebellion occurred within the context of subversive pressures that exposed the disequilibrium of the southern system. The Nullification Controversy, debated in 1830 over the tariff issue, challenged the nature of the Union and explored the causes of national disunity. Only President Andrew Jackson's threats to invade South Carolina and his recommendations to reduce the tariff staved off civil war in 1832. Thereafter, partisan conflict enacted the social drama within the states and became the surrogate means of resolving racial, economic, and sectional tensions.[183]

Rachel's Conversion

Historian Mary Ryan's groundbreaking study *Cradle of the Middle Class* linked economic and social changes in a commercial northern county, Oneida County, New York, to the Second Great Awakening, an Evangelical revival that penetrated the countryside in the East and spread west during the period from 1800 to 1840. Questions of religion and class during this period, she argued, remained intimately tied to issues of family and gender. Men and a greater majority of women debated the "nature, relationship, and legitimacy of their awakening to grace."[184] The younger generation rebelled against an older Protestant patriarchal order, converted to Evangelicalism, and were baptized as adults without the benefit of parental religious authority. Attacks on established churches followed in the South as well as in the North.[185]

Evangelical conversion transformed women initiates from anguished sinners to self-confident communicants. The conversion experience shared among converts formed the basis of social relationships within an Evangelical community.[186] As a result, women charted their own religious course. Catherine DeRosset, Rachel's neighbor, for instance, left the Episcopal Church and converted to Methodism, despite the fact that her husband remained Episcopalian. By the second decade of the nineteenth century the Second Great Awakening, which had unleashed an attack upon established churches at the turn of the century, fought counterrevolutionary measures of High Churchmanship and patriarchal order. Reverend Adam Empie represented the forces of Evangelism subverting High Church Episcopalianism. His message, which expressed religious emotionalism and practiced social asceticism, attracted women followers.[187]

Reverend Empie had connections to the Mordecai family. He had debated the tenets of Christianity in correspondence with Jacob Mordecai; later they published their debates. He visited Ellen Mordecai during her stay in Wilmington and left some religious books with her. She, as noted earlier, remained highly critical of Reverend Empie's anti-Semitism.[188] Reverend Empie converted Gershon Lazarus, Rachel's stepson, but Aaron Lazarus protested his son's conversion to the Right Reverend Bishop Richard Moore in Richmond. During time spent with Jacob Mordecai reviewing Reverend Empie's arguments, Gershon changed his mind, and he did not continue as a Christian.[189]

Reverend Empie's Low Church influence endured in the association of Evangelical women in Wilmington; Rachel remained close to them. As Jane Orme Vance lay dying in May 1828, she requested mourning rings to be made for her friends Rachel Mordecai Lazarus and Anna Green. And when Mrs. Hooper's husband faced financial embarrassment, Mary Orme, her husband, and Catherine DeRosset rallied to undertake an "infant school" to help matters.[190] Rachel relied on the women during her confinements, but her health never quite recovered from the births of her daughters in 1828 and 1830.

When Emma Mordecai, Rachel's youngest half sister, visited the Lazarus family in 1832, she found Aaron playing with the children in the dining room, but Rachel appeared thinner than Emma had ever seen her. A bout of illness returned in May 1835. Aaron reported to Ellen Mordecai that Rachel's debilitation occurred "in one short week." Jane Robertson of Philadelphia, a friend of Ellen Mordecai, inquired about Rachel's health that spring. Julia Mordecai, Rachel's younger half sister, regretted that Rachel's illness separated her from her husband and children. Emma expressed relief on 5 June 1835 that Rachel had recovered. Although Rachel reported improvement in her health on 26 June 1835, she wrote with a shaky hand. On 22 July 1835 Rachel joked to Ellen Mordecai in a letter that she presided as mistress over her household sitting in dress and cape, directing the servants. Nevertheless, she added that she had no illusions about her health; she wrote, "My constitution is far from invulnerable."[191]

During this time period it is difficult to determine whether Rachel suffered from physical or psychological illness or both. Jane Robertson asked Ellen if Aaron Lazarus lost a great deal of property in a warehouse fire. No other allusion to such a fire exists, but Rachel rarely reported about Aaron's business dealings in her later correspondence. If a fire had occurred, it might have devastated his enterprises and caused strain in the marriage. In addition, Rachel's confinements did weaken her constitution. However, the separation between Rachel and Aaron commented upon by Julia Mordecai suggests something more troubling between the couple.

Rachel confided to Ellen on 29 July 1835 that her crisis was a religious one. "I have as you know long been in an uneasy and anxious state of mind, caused by the change in my religious sentiments, & the impossibility under existing circumstances of acting up to them," she wrote.[192] For a decade Rachel had studied Scripture to confront her religious anxieties. Continuity between her Jewish and Christian beliefs guided her, yet Ellen sensed Rachel's new conviction. Ellen recalled that Rachel asked her if she read the Bible, and Ellen replied, "If my reason could be convinced and satisfied I should like to study it." Rachel then asked Ellen if she "could give a satisfactory reason for the motion and the origin of the power that influenced [the mind]." When Ellen admitted she could not give a satisfactory explanation, Rachel then asserted, "If you cannot give what mathematicians would call a demonstration of this simple action, which you see me perform can you not accept in some things, the mere assertion of our Maker, who does not think it necessary to give us a reason for all he does?"[193] Rachel relied upon revelation rather than reason in her inspired reading of the Bible. "A belief in Scripture appears to me the only solid basis of religion—and if there is a weakness in the belief in miracles, it is a weakness I would not exchange for all boasted worldly wisdom," Rachel said.[194]

Rachel's trust in the Creator and her belief in revelation and miracles attested to her grounding in Jewish faith. Her piety remained the same, obedience to divine will, but her reckoning of salvation changed from a distant but revered God of mercy and justice to a personal savior who promised the immediate experience of forgiveness and reconciliation of self with God. Good works followed upon metanoia and the assurance of salvation.[195] In effect, a transformed soul entered a new community of faith that prefigured the entrance into eternal salvation. Such a step defied Jewish concepts of divine unity and Orthodox corporate existence.

Although the Jewish and Christian communities shared the same enlightened values prior to the nineteenth century, revivalism, which insisted upon a Christocentric, emotional religion and largely anti-establishment, nonhierarchical authority, discouraged rapprochement between the two groups. Rachel entered the psychic borderland between Orthodox Judaism and Evangelical Christianity.[196] Salvation meant release for Rachel. Ever controlled and controlling of herself, her children, and her charges, Rachel found in her new apprehension of holiness a power other than her own to chart the course of her life, a power as close to her as her own nature, which yearned for tranquillity and generous love. The question of salvation, although doctrinal in form, remained particular in nature as she searched for identity in the changing context of the early republic.

Rachel's conversion, if interpreted in traditional assimilationist terms, assumes her passive incorporation into the dominant culture. Her decade-long inner debate about conversion, however, implies intentionality on her part. A third-generation German Jew, Rachel's ethnicity resulted less from a sense of "belonging" to an ancestral clan than claiming a culturally constructed understanding of herself as a pious, albeit enlightened Jew.[197] Rachel adapted enlightened ideology to the strictures of Orthodox Judaism and moved from an authoritarian discipline to mutual consent in the process of educating Eliza. The introduction of free agency into her educational scheme coincided with her support for freedom to choose marital partners. Freedom of choice and obedience to the Most High proved no contradiction in Jewish tradition; divine Providence, or foreknowledge, did not negate responsibility for one's actions. St. Paul, however, suggests the priority of election as opposed to deeds "in order that God's purpose of election might continue, not because of works but because of his call" (Romans 9:11).[198] Rachel wrestled with her pending conversion; the journey from rational argument to spiritual conviction involved retreats and misgivings.

Years of prayer and study then led her to the crisis point in the spring and summer of 1835. Technically, according to Evangelical precepts, Rachel remained unsaved. She had not yet had the opportunity to respond to God's grace and accept baptism and admission to the body of believers.[199] Thus, Rachel determined to resolve her spiritual and emotional crisis by revealing her change of heart to her father. She explained to a dear friend: "I wept & prayed and resolved to take the step which I have so long dreaded even to abandonment, of writing to my father, disclosing to him fully my sentiments, & entreating his forgiveness, his indulgence, & his sanction to pursue the course which my feelings & convictions dictate. I felt as if under the influence of the Holy Spirit, I was strengthened, prepared for the effort, & I would not delay to act in obedience to its dictates."[200] Naively, Rachel planned to obtain her father's permission for her conversion and then to win her husband's approval. She chose what she considered a reasonable course with her father. She informed Ellen, "I have written such a letter as I think cannot irritate the mind of our father, my arguments appear to me mild, just & reasonable, in pleading for freedom of conscience & stating the long probation I have undergone. I shall anxiously await the result."[201] A sense of atonement impelled Rachel to take such a risk. As she told Catherine DeRosset, she yearned to fall at the foot of the cross and "be washed in the purifying blood of atonement."[202] Convicted of her sins, she keenly wished to act openly according to her new understanding. In addition, filial duty, both to her father and her divine Father, compelled her drastic action.[203] At this point, however, Rachel hesitated to break from patriarchal authority.

Jacob Mordecai received Rachel's letter with anger and bitter pain. The news of Rachel's intention also sent shock waves among her sisters Eliza, Laura, and Emma. The father immediately made plans to travel to Wilmington, plans that alarmed Rachel. She knew how disturbing such a visit would be to her own family, so she suggested that she travel to Spring Farm instead. In the meantime, she promised not to make any open declaration of intent and to investigate again the reasons for her desire to convert to Christianity. She hoped that by her actions her father might relent. She pleaded with him: "I will do anything in my power that may in any degree tend to comfort or reconcile you my beloved father." Rachel struggled, torn between her conviction and filial duty. Concealment, she felt, amounted to duplicity.[204]

The visit to Spring Farm proved volatile, a nightmare to Rachel. In a rage, Jacob met her at the door, cursed the letter, and then tore it "in a thousand pieces."[205] The severity and madness of those days left Rachel unstable and deeply disturbed, but she blamed herself for rashly bringing on her own trouble. She promised later in a letter to Emma never to avow openly her opinions and to reinvestigate her father's and other Jewish writers' opinions and arguments. Such promises, however, were made "under the most awful & harrowing circumstances."[206] Nonetheless, Rachel did not promise to give up her opinions. She argued with her father that her decision was not the result of youthful enthusiasm but the product "of study & mature reflection."[207]

Rachel remained in Raleigh, separated from her husband and family, and she stayed with her brother George and her deceased brother Moses' Christian wife, Nancy. While there, Rachel reviewed the collision with her father. She stubbornly refused to be convinced on purely rational terms. She admitted to Ellen: "To persons who have accustomed themselves to believe the whole of Xtianity to be a system of priestcraft, it may seem an easy matter for a rational mind to become disabused, & if this were indeed all, I believe I may say, it would never have attracted me."[208] During their separation Aaron Lazarus threatened Rachel with the loss of her children if she converted to Christianity. Deeply disturbed, Rachel struggled to regain her "equilibrium and composure."[209] Despite considerable strain, she believed the scene with her father had had some positive advantage—it had relieved the minds of her father and husband. Both men believed the subject closed.[210]

Nonetheless, tensions continued to affect Rachel's marriage. Although Rachel defended Aaron against her sister Ellen's criticism, Rachel admitted to unhappiness. Rachel kindly submitted to Ellen: "You do not do him [Aaron] justice in believing that he has ever been unkind, he has not, but his views were so different from mine that his strong [opinions] could not fail to distress me. It is in fact a subject on which unless one is at liberty to pursue his own course, distress of mind must ensue."[211] Prophetically, angry scenes between Aaron and Rachel ensued. "If I speak freely," she said, "it occasions him to use sinful expressions in his opposition to & disavowal of my sentiments . . . this discordance forms a sad barrier to our happiness."[212]

Thus Rachel lived with a divided heart, silent with her husband and family on the subject of religion. Only to her sister Ellen did she unburden her true feelings. By 1836, Ellen herself had experienced a conversion. Rachel rejoiced at

her sister's conversion yet worried about the obstacles she faced.[213] Rachel cautioned her not to reveal her choice:

> My sister be circumspect . . . be on your guard against exciting suspicion in those who would endeavor to oppose the course of reasoning you have pursued, & to convince you by counter arguments of its fallacy. They would not convince, but they would unhinge your mind, harry it with doubts where none should exist, rob you of the comfort of believing & reposing your hopes of salvation not on any merits of your own, but on those of the Savior who was bruised for our transgressions, & by whose strokes we are healed.[214]

Robbed of her peace of mind, Rachel felt her orderly life destroyed, replaced by chaos. With her mind only "partially restored," she trusted in the mercy of God to guide her actions. Yet she could not abandon her family for the sake of Christianity. "I cannot impose misery on all and risk my children," she confided to Ellen. "My sin is ever before me," Rachel lamented over her piercing dilemma.[215]

Rachel worried about salvation for herself and her children: Marx, age thirteen; Ellen, age ten; Mary Catherine, age seven; and Julia Judith, age five. She reproved herself for failure to "lead [her] children to righteousness."[216] Aaron, quite naturally, forbade proselytization. Hence, her children presented Rachel with a moral dilemma. Rachel worried that if she taught the children Christian doctrine, the children would be taken from her, and if she taught them nothing, they would be raised without religion. Since her teaching consistently included the practice of holiness, the prospect of secular teaching distressed her. She claimed that "the moral duties are insufficient for the mind to rest on."[217] Hence Rachel disclaimed a purely enlightened or Edgeworthian approach to character training. To solve her dilemma, Rachel decided not to defy overtly her husband's authority. Thus she led her children in traditional Sabbath prayer and kept the festivals.[218] Nonetheless, Aaron did place their daughter Ellen with another family but relented when he believed the girl received no discipline there.[219]

Paternal and spousal pressure afflicted Rachel with doubt, yet she prayed in the words of Scripture, "Lord I believe, pardon thou mine unbelief." Bitterly, she explained her anomalous behavior to Ellen:

> Yet I could go foreward, were there not so many obstacles, so many contending duties, such necessity for concealment, almost for the practice of duplicity towards those to whom we owe our first earthly duties. We boast of living in a land which permits freedom of conscience, habitually we express our rejoicing—but individually how are we benefitted, when those who would shudder at Spanish persecution, unwittingly practice the same in kind if not in degree. Surely our Heavenly Father will hearken to our supplications, and will point us out a way & make our crooked paths straight.[220]

Rachel, who took pride in self-possession, experienced abject humiliation, guilt, and crises of faith. Her sense of unworthiness and helplessness, which precipitated her trust in the will of God, followed the Evangelical conversion pattern. As an individual "under conviction" she suffered extreme distress because she could not act: make a public declaration of sinfulness and faith. By this act she would have declared her intent to join an Evangelical church. This she could not do or she would risk losing her children.

However, in her inner intent Rachel possessed a desire for holiness. Evangelicals believed that, infused with God's holiness or the indwelling of "his own moral nature," converts lived with the hope that their trials sanctified them.[221] Rachel's life-long self-disciplined pursuit of a moral life culminated, for her, in conversion. Holiness shattered any presumptions of "goodness," of acting as a good daughter or dutiful wife, and instead left her submissive to divine mercy.[222] Rachel, resigned to her state, reminded Ellen that "we could not be like Asa perfect in the Lord, because we are denied the power of acting up to or obeying his most Holy Word." She believed that "a way will be open for us." Despite her faith, she admitted that her strength faded at times, and "darkness" overcame her spirit.[223]

During her period of trial from 1828 to 1838, Rachel remained in the company of her Evangelical women friends, who counseled and consoled her. Rachel admired the pious fortitude of Mrs. Cochran in bereavement, "resigned to her Redeemer's will, finding consolation in his word, aided by her minister and books of devotion."[224] Mary Orme advised Rachel concerning Ellen's conversion. And as Rachel tended to the dying Catherine DeRosset and prayed with her, Catherine, too, discussed Ellen's change of heart and possibilities for the conversion of the rest of the family. Evangelical responsibility entailed changing all relationships, directing them toward salvation.[225] That subject also absorbed Rachel and Ellen; Rachel complained to Ellen about what she considered Eliza's "inexplicable [religious] state."[226] She wished Eliza would read the Twenty-fifth Psalm: "Show me thy ways, teach me thy path" and then be led to the Fifty-first Psalm, a prayer of repentance.[227] Rachel believed that conversion would be an antidote to Eliza's moodiness, but she cautioned Ellen to wait in God's time and not disturb their family's convictions. Rachel disclaimed the family's fears that conversion would estrange Ellen and herself from the family. Rachel contended, "Are not the baptised children of our dear deceased brother [Moses] objects of deep interest to us all?" Estrangement, Rachel knew, would come from her husband's family if she openly professed Christianity.[228]

The death of Catherine DeRosset especially impressed Rachel. Catherine experienced death as devotional—another means of discipline and prayer. Mrs. DeRosset consciously strove for an exemplary death, enduring great pain but praying for others. Rachel recounted the experience. It was, she said, "a privilege to witness such a scene which I would not exchange for any pleasure that the world has in its gift to bestow. Indeed the whole of her illness has afforded lessons of patience, fortitude, forgetfulness of self & consideration of others, with faith & hope and a pious confidence in the mercy of her heavenly father such as I trust never to forget—'precious in the sight of the Lord is the death of his saints.'"[229] Ironically, Rachel's own death opened the way for her religious conversion.

Her spiritual journey began with the news of her father's serious decline in health. She made arrangements to be at his bedside with her children.[230] But the boat to Richmond filled, and Rachel had to wait for another. Her final message to the family expressed concern for her father and submission to Providence: "Oh that I could hope my beloved father were ever as he has been for months past, but submission is our duty, & the Almighty will order as He knows best— May his merciful kindness & grace be with you all."[231] The Mordecai family's attention was focused upon the grave condition of Jacob Mordecai when Mr. Maury, a friend who accompanied Rachel from Wilmington, arrived and calmly informed the family of Rachel's illness. Only Eliza and Rachel's daughter, Ellen, reacted with alarm. Ellen Lazarus could not be comforted.[232] Stricken on the train, Rachel was removed and taken nearby to her brother Samuel's house in Petersburg, where she lay helpless.

In her last moments Rachel struggled with her religious dilemma. She desired to be baptized as a Christian but felt honor bound to her husband. When asked if she desired baptism she replied, "Oh what a sting it would be to my husband." Ellen Mordecai counseled her that soon all earthly ties would be broken; she should do as she wished. Rachel then consented to be baptized and asked the minister to bury her in his churchyard. With calm faith in her redemption she felt "released from all fears."[233] Rachel died in Ellen's arms on 23 June 1838.[234]

Death proved only a final transformation in the life of Rachel Mordecai Lazarus. Rejected by father and husband, a scandal to family members, she died a paradox to her family. She lived an anomalous life, deliberately choosing the borderland between enlightenment and Judaism, between Judaism and Christianity. The borderland offered freedom to choose. She freely followed the precepts of Judaism and taught them, one upon the other, with disciplined intent. Such resolve augmented the desire for sanctity, the avoidance of the evil inclination. Her desire far outstripped the Edgeworthian notion of self-restraint, since goodness did not imply mere conformity to "autonomous ethics" but adherence to God's Law.[235]

Precepts test.[236] In the crucible of Rachel's pedagogical experiment she weighed the necessity of discipline against the demands of freedom. Rachel chose freedom; she allowed Eliza full participation in the making of rules and thus gave her her own independence, the ability to choose her own way. Both Rachel and Eliza invented themselves in the process of rational dialogue, but the venture only increased observance (observance of the Sabbath, for example) that fortified holiness.

Rachel's life suggests a persistent desire for holiness. Evangelical ideology assumes that sanctification or holiness follows upon repentance. Rachel remained in a repentant state because she could not accept baptism or join a church, but she exhibited a sanctified life, caring for dying friends and trusting in the Providence of God. Evangelicals refer to holiness as "experimental" or "experimental piety," by which they mean a practical, concrete, everyday piety.[237] Similarly, Jewish observance, the daily practice of precepts of the Law, is the practice of holiness. However, Judaism does not distinguish one act of conversion that leads to salvation and holiness but, rather, addresses all acts as holy that fulfill the Law. Rachel's change of heart, her desire to surrender self in one sacrificial act of conversion, adjusted her notion of holiness. Her pedagogical experiment and her conversion are of a piece. In both she experimented with holiness. Her enlightened teaching method imbricated Jewish pietism, the practice of the presence of God. Her conversion embraced experimental piety, the second leap of Evangelical faith, to trust in one selfless act of repentance that insured a sanctified life.

Conversion, a process that introduces the liminal state of "no place and no time," defies categorization; the potential convert discovers the painful anomaly of existing betwixt and between religions and cultures. During her conversion period Rachel Mordecai Lazarus lived as both Jew and Christian. Her ethical identity, her ancestral origin, distinguished her as Jewish. She lived in a community of mutual recognition, where one Jew acknowledged another as sharing a common descent. In addition, the Jewish community bound her to the ties of family and the demands of benevolent patriarchy. Of her faith, Rachel Mordecai Lazarus retained, in addition to holiness, the Jewish notion of Providence or the presence of God, which she clung to with reverence. She remained obedient to the will of God despite her anguish.[238] Only Providence could contain the contradictions of Jew and Christian, nonduty and duty.

Rachel's removal to Wilmington's Evangelical circle placed her within a communitas where her ordinary and everyday relationships achieved a level of depth and seriousness that bound her to other women in an egalitarian, religious company. Here she experienced heartfelt friendship, free from family strictures and hierarchies. That freedom suggested a different kind of love, an affection unburdened by the merely useful, domestic, or agreeable, a condition of feeling apart from the Edgeworthian ideal of well-regulated sympathy and benevolent affections. If Rachel sought forgiveness and experienced it in the context of Evangelical *communitas*, she sought a certain love in communion with others that heightened her notion of Providence. Christian religion, and Evangelicalism in particular, emphasizes conversion as life-in-process and rejects past connections. Rachel, however, continued to act according to Jewish ritual for years until she worked out forgiveness—forgiveness for loving yet forsaking past connections. Rachel's pilgrimage culminated at the end of her life; only then was she freely able to choose apart from the religious structure of her previous life. Providence and penitence converged in the rites of passage when, as her pastor noted, "twice born" Rachel accepted baptism and death.[239]

Grief

Eliza grieved over the loss of "the best sister, the best friend, the best mother—all those bright endowments, all those rare qualities, all that sterling sense, all that surpassing goodness."[240] When Eliza looked after Rachel's children's wardrobe, she discovered the infinite care Rachel took of her children's clothing.[241] Deeply moved yet intimidated by Rachel's standard of perfection, Eliza said she felt she had never lived up to Rachel's expectations of her. She confessed to Caroline: "Oh if you knew what a sense of unworthiness I feel whenever I think about her, when I think how far different I am, from what she wished to make me and in fact how far inferior to a much more ordinary standard—in many many points . . . you really would feel for me."[242] Evidence suggests that Rachel, the eldest daughter, set a supreme example for her sisters. Of Rachel's virtue Emma recorded in her diary: "How is it possible that I can know of such excellence without making one feeble effort to imitate it—I am wickedly weak."[243] Years after Rachel's death, Caroline remembered her father returning from a visit to Rachel and telling his daughters: "What a fine well-informed girl sister was, how beautifully she expressed herself, how correct she was in her whole deportment & that when she came home he wished us to have her for our pattern."[244]

Rachel's enlightened mold, her exacting standards of virtue and intellect, her critical ability and managerial talents made imitation almost impossible. Eliza, a musician, created her own life in a different key; her art and social consciousness found expression in domestic and religious life. She imbued mundane and ordinary practices with awareness of the presence of God. Her wisdom followed a precept that bound her to family and nation and rested in covenantal promise of deliverance. The southern Victorian family system, which valued kinship connections above all, reinforced traditional Jewish family patterns.[245] In addition, Jewish religious isolation in the Evangelical South strengthened internal family associations and kinship connections. Eliza remained close to her natal family, especially to her father during his illness. She deeply grieved over Jacob's death. He died three months after Rachel on 4 September 1838. Eliza wrote to her sister Caroline:

> I saw somewhere the other day, a remark which my heart could not acknowl-edge the truth of—"grief for the loss of the aged is never lasting"—it may not be called grief perhaps—but the same feeling of regret, of deep, deep sorrow pervades my breast when I think of papa, as at the first—and I am sure it is so with all of us—and I believe we could not have lamented him more if he had left us at an earlier period—indeed I do not know but that our sorrow for his loss was deepened by his very infirmities—his sufferings seemed to endear him to us so peculiarly.[246]

Eliza's closeness to her family did not preclude an independent spirit. On the last day of Succoth, while the rest of the family went to the synagogue, Eliza remained home and wrote to her sister Caroline, who taught school in Mobile, Alabama. Eliza hoped Caroline, a widow, would return to Spring Farm, and the two might join forces. As Eliza admitted, "You can imagine better than I can tell you, how I long for an independent situation." The young mother accepted her father's offer to remain at Spring Farm only as a temporary expedient until Sam Myers stabilized his business career. Nonetheless, in 1839 Eliza confessed the dwindling of her last fifty dollars. Although she imagined the possibilities of teaching,[247] she kept up her nomadic existence as she visited among her family until Sam's death in 1849, when she moved permanently back to Richmond.

Eliza's Domestic Piety

The routine of Eliza's domestic life included care of Sam's gout, attendance at women's confinements, management of the Mordecai household during emer-gencies, and the preserving of jams and jellies. And whatever household Eliza attended she graced with music. Emma Mordecai remembered that the sound of Eliza's music accompanied all the stages of Emma's life.[248] That Eliza regarded her duties as sacred and a means of holiness may be seen in her response to her sister-in-law Rosina's delivery. She felt moved to record a prayerlike gratitude for the life of mother and child: "I thought how we had been blessed in her safety and that of her child, and with all that we had suffered, how gently & with how many alleviating circumstances our misfortunes, great as they are, had been sent to us how could I but feel the deepest gratitude to the Almighty for his great mercy? And there is not a day that I do not feel this."[249]

Eliza's heart remained especially generous since for her duty or service to her family constituted a holy practice. She regarded the simple creature comforts as blessings: fire, bed, friends—they filled her with gratitude.[250] When Ellen Mordecai attempted to convert Eliza to Christianity, Ellen argued that Eliza's first duty was to God as savior, but Eliza professed a more immanent theology: that service to others served divine purpose. Eliza refused to visit Ellen in Petersburg because of Ellen's pressure and Eliza's responsibilities. Eliza said her first duty was to her husband, "and he has too few comforts, to allow me consistently with that duty, to leave him for any considerable time." Hers, she felt, was a humble course. She explained to Ellen, "I have not forgotten my Creator—but I cannot but believe that I serve him best, by performing my earthly duties as well as I can—oh how imperfectly they are performed who knows and feels as deeply as I do."[251]

Eliza's ethic of service issued from a well-disposed heart. She best defended her religious predilection by addressing her attitude of devotion. To Ellen she stated her habits and direction. She said, "I have not been by any means inattentive to the subject in question [religion]. I have read & I have reflected & I shall continue to read & to reflect—but on the subject of religion, 'let me commune with my own heart, & be still.'" Although she developed opinions about religion, she declined to debate them because, she said, "they are sacred and lie in the depths of my soul." She continued, "There is a sense of something like immodesty, or at least indelicacy, in bringing my sentiments foreward & I never speak of them or write of them—but communicate them only to Him to whom alone they belong." She cautioned Ellen to refrain from engaging in a "controversy" between them, a controversy that originated in "the deep and terrifying importance" Ellen attached to religion. "Would it were otherwise," Eliza wrote, "deep but not terrifying."[252] Ellen's proselytizing of Eliza amounted to trespass upon a sensitive and committed soul. Eliza followed her own mundane yet graced path to holiness.

Yet depression, a lifelong difficulty, presented one of the more serious obstacles to Eliza's peace of mind. Depression intermittently interrupted Eliza's round of duties and her pious reflection. Sometimes she believed her trials might end. She once cautiously rejoiced: "My mind I hope is permanently cured of a habit of despondency which was once but too characteristic of it."[253] Unfortunately, the depression returned, and Eliza admitted to Caroline, "I haven't written because there are times when I think everything I see & hear is vapid & hackneyed." She felt, she said, like a "human machine, full of negativity."[254] The birth of her daughter brought joy but did not break the chain of depression. When her baby slept, Eliza had a sense of awe for her child. But soon, "a hard crust" formed over Eliza's sensibilities. She complained that her love of books, music, poetry, and people had evaporated, and she remained apathetic, alienated, dissipated.[255] Her despondency may have been provoked by lack of occupation or an outlet for her talents. Her circumstances further depressed her. Sam never made a success in business; consequently, he and Eliza endured financial instability. George Mordecai, Eliza's brother, contributed anonymously toward Eliza's household expenses.[256] Eliza gave music lessons briefly, but later the settlement of a family estate left her with an annuity.

Despite the difficulties of her life, Eliza taught her children, especially her son, Edmund (known as Ned), the importance of service and domesticity. When Edmund accompanied his mother on her rounds to find a seamstress, the pair discovered the desperate living conditions of poor women, one dwelling more wretched than the next. Mrs. Brown, who agreed to do the work, explained that she could not come to the Myers home since she had no shoes. Her palsied hands indicated her painful difficulty with her work. Like the mother in the "Rosamund" stories, Eliza gave Ned a choice—to use his money to buy a parrot in a cage or do something useful. Eliza reminded Edmund of the women who went barefoot; three-year-old Ned deliberated and said, "Yes, I believe I'll give 'em the next pair of shoes I have." Then remembering the money in his purse, he exclaimed, "Mother, I *great* mind to buy 'em some." Later, he shyly presented Mrs. Brown with a pair of shoes. Mrs. Brown responded, "Thank you my love."[257]

Eliza hoped that Ned's benevolence would develop a wholesome domestic and family life. As Edmund matured, he gained much success as an army engineer. He constructed the Washington Water Works and rose to a supervisory position despite the politics of the job.[258] During the Civil War he assumed the command of a Confederate Army Corps of Engineers. But Eliza insisted that domestic values counted more than material success. She wrote Ned: "You will have another [home], one of these days I hope my son; just as dear to you as that was—with a good sweet wife to bless it for you, and maybe another little Carrie [his sister]—but you must love to stay at home and comfort your wife and take care of your children, and then home will continue a blessed place to her and to them and to you."[259] Eliza's admonition suggests an idealization, a desire for the secure domestic life she never really enjoyed.

The Civil War altered Eliza's idealized view of domesticity. Initially, the war appeared a distant concern, a subject for Eliza's satiric eye. She described a meeting with Jefferson Davis to her sister Emma:

> The Sunday School went off well yesterday and the *Meetn* in the afternoon. Our Liege was *so* gracious as to dispense with kneeling & even backing out of the presence—No business of any importance transacted—Rebecca & I did not have quite as much to make fun of when we came out as we usually have, and should have returned to our respective homes quite spiritless, if the President had not fortunately spoken of Dr. *Cullens* in the course of the sitting.[260]

Evidently, conversation about "Dr. Cullens" provoked a comical response, and the women gave in to laughter and giggles.

The war added only a mock heroism to pleasant family gatherings. At one event her grandchildren begged Eliza to write an epitaph for Fawn, a dog the children had buried. Eliza declined, but Edmund proposed, "Here lies Fawn— aged 8 years—who passed through life honorably, and died fighting." [261] The drudgery and rigors of domesticity, however, intensified during the Civil War, when households converted to hospitals for the care of the sick and wounded. Eliza, who lived at Spring Farm after Sam's death in 1849, tended to the wounded soldiers brought there. Eliza especially cared for one patient, her nephew, whose hand had shattered in a shell explosion. Refusing to rest, she died exhausted, nursing the sick in 1863. Her generosity tested in the war, Eliza knew no rest until she had given herself completely.

The wisdom of the Law tests the human good inclination. If the father built his house upon the Torah, his children inherited the shelter that preserved the worship, family unity, and national cohesion so essential for moral life to exist. Jacob Mordecai's daughters lived in his house, then married and moved away to establish their own households. Eliza remained practically and psychologically within her father's house. She visited Spring Farm frequently when her husband, Sam, went away on business trips; she then returned to Spring Farm when Sam died in 1849. She lived in the orbit of her father's household. When her own household collapsed like a temple destroyed, she reverted to a piety of generosity reminiscent of the prophet Hosea, who said of God, "I desire loving kindness, and not sacrifice" (Hosea 5:6).[262] Eliza's conduct went beyond Rachel's expectations of thoughtfulness—"little attentions"—toward her elders. Eliza followed precept upon precept and fulfilled the practice of holiness.

Rachel departed from her father's house and entered an Evangelical community. The danger of assimilating the values and beliefs of strangers may be summarized in the words of an ancient sage who warned against idolatry, the enthronement of the evil inclination. He said: "There shall no strange god be in thee; neither shalt thou worship any foreign god," that is, "make not the stranger within you your sovereign." [263] When Rachel found in Wilmington a ready circle of friends, pious women whose example she cherished, she did not feel she had strayed into an alien community. And when she struggled with conversion and intensely desired salvation, she found what was truly and uniquely herself. Her trials unleashed the holy affections, profound emotions that Rachel had so assiduously regulated. She ultimately chose the nonrational "peace that surpasseth all understanding," [264] which freed her from enlightened restraint and Orthodox discipline. She died with a peace that hallowed the education of her heart.

The trials of Rachel and the lessons of Eliza provided the material for didactic narrative. L.N., clearly moved by Rachel's life and death and influenced by Edgeworthian pedagogy, wrote a curious account of the Mordecai family. The narrative transposed a family tragedy into an Evangelical tract and obscured the Mordecais' Jewish identity. The history of the tale is important in understanding the change in meaning of mid-nineteenth-century educational method.

CHAPTER 5

WISDOM
TRANSFORMED

The Evangelization of
Edgeworthian Pedagogy

ΩΟΠΟΟΠΟΟΠΟΟΠΟΟΠΟΟΠΟΟΠΟΟΠΟΟΠΟΟΠΟΟΠΟΟΠΟΟΠΟΟΩ

Evangelical Didacticism

"'Business first, pleasure afterwards,' says the good and wise Miss Edge-worth."[1] This Edgeworthian aphorism found its way into an Evangelical tract, "Past Days," published in 1840 under the pseudonym L.N. The text neatly bridges enlightened and Romantic Evangelical discourse. The enlightened moral system juxtaposes pleasure and pain; work may be its own reward, or one may anticipate a pleasant occupation after the completion of the work. The Evangelical moral interposed not a natural but a supernatural source of pleasure. The text reveals that "it is God who gives us our duties to perform, and that the more difficult they are, the more pleasure He will let us feel for having done them faithfully!"[2] The enlightened moral system is framed within a Romantic Evangelical context; rational models of discourse fortify a sentimental story. The story "Past Days" contains the family and religious history of Rachel Mordecai Lazarus. Yet the author's deliberate attempt to present Rachel and the Mordecai family as Evangelicals forces readers to consider the gap, the hermeneutic, the enigma at the center of the story.[3] "Past Days" tells an Evangelical story without conversion as its dramatic climax.

Didactic family histories along with Evangelical conversion stories shaped the post-Revolutionary and Victorian generations' notions of moral identity. Victorian Evangelicals transformed early republican didactic literature into exhortatory and religious tracts that redefined the purpose and nature of virtuous conduct. *Practical Education* and Maria Edgeworth's tales of "Rosamund,"

"Frank," and "Harry and Lucy" cultivated the enlightened guide to character formation at the same time that Evangelical Protestants published conversion narratives. The religious books and pamphlets admonished readers to repent and experience the "operations of the spirit."[4] Through experiment the enlightened method taught that experience reinforced parental example and directed rational dialogue toward a child's development. The Edgeworths' pedagogical discipline purposefully initiated critical thinking and creative self-identity in order to undermine parental authoritarianism and promote more contractual relations between parents and children. Evangelical didacticism initiated an affectional and experiential mode that enhanced a child's introspective inclination and prepared a youth to recognize spiritual movements leading to salvation. The individual's experience of salvation would lead to a decision to join an Evangelical community where covenanted souls submitted to church discipline.[5]

Scholars consider Romantic Evangelicalism the religion of the heart, because it fostered cultivation of feeling or sensibility as a necessity in establishing the truth of religion. Since Victorians assumed women possessed greater sensibility than men and therefore greater potential for religious conversion, Evangelicals advocated a particular female pedagogy. Hannah More's "Strictures on the Modern System of Female Education" suggested the cultivation of female sensibility. She believed that "genuine feeling" fostered "a warm, tender, disinterested, and enthusiastic spirit." However, the English author warned of the necessity of governing sensibilities, since uncontrolled feeling produced mayhem and self-destruction. According to Hannah More, under direction by the Holy Spirit such sensibilities led to religious devotion and holiness.[6]

"Past Days"

This narrative, which both inscribed and transformed Enlightened pedagogical method, itself became a didactic narrative that transferred an Orthodox knowledge of holiness along with enlightened educational practice to an Evangelical context. In 1841 L.N. completed a children's story called "Past Days" about Rachel Mordecai Lazarus's teaching and her moral dilemma. The narrative related the account of a mature Aunt who instructed her inquisitive and "warmhearted" niece, Fanny, in the mercies of God and the lessons "upon the heart" prescribed by Maria Edgeworth.[7] The "story within a story," called "Past Days," read by the Aunt to Fanny, began with Lucy Neville grieving at the graveside of her sister, Mary Neville Layman. It then lapsed into an account of Mary Layman's early life: the death of her mother, her subsequent banishment from home and the difficulties of living apart from her father, her return home to raise the younger children, her partnership with her father in the family school, her marriage, her "trials," and her early death twenty miles from her dying father's bedside. L.N.'s narrative retells essentially the same story Mordecai family members explained in their correspondence and Rachel recounted in her diary, in her recollections, and in her 25 September 1816 letter to Maria Edgeworth.

The story told in its various forms, however, assumes different meanings. Rachel's family narrative established her credibility with Maria Edgeworth. Her initial letter to Maria Edgeworth that challenged the stereotypical Jewish character "Mordecai" confused Richard Lovell Edgeworth when Rachel signed her name "Rachel Mordecai." Richard Lovell, in his only letter to Rachel, complained, "Whether I am addressing a real or an assumed character is more than I am able to determine." He then asked, "Pray make us better acquainted with your real self." [8] Flattered but hesitant, Rachel narrated the family history. She wrote:

> Will you be interested to hear of one who, deprived of maternal care ere its value or its loss could be known or lamented, was for years dependent on nature and chance for the cultivation of her understanding and the forming of her heart and principles? To whom a second mother proved a blessing, and who in riper years learned patience, perseverance and cheerfulness in the school of adversity? My father, formerly a merchant, was in 1799 involved in the general ruin which attended the shippers of American produce, and after struggling under difficulties for several years, was prevailed on by many who had known him in better days to open an academy for young ladies. But just turned nineteen, I was sensible rather of requiring a governess myself than of possessing the capacity to become one, but the case was urgent, the best of fathers sought to encourage me, the confidence reposed by others inspired me with zeal, and with the commencement of the year 1808 we engaged in the all important business of education. . . . In the improvement of our pupils, acknowledged by their parents, we often receive a reward the most grateful, and the number of applicants constantly exceeding that to which we have limited ourselves gives a satisfactory proof of publick approbation. [9]

Maria Edgeworth sent Rachel a copy of *Harrington* and later a letter announcing Richard Lovell Edgeworth's death. Thus, through family events and narratives Rachel connected in a more personal way with Maria Edgeworth's work and intimate family relations. The correspondence itself initiated a moral dialogue in which the writers debated the legitimacy of slavery, the moral efficacy of certain literature, and the ethical dimensions of personal behavior.

Rachel Mordecai's diary and recollections defined her identity as a dutiful daughter and a wise and judicious teacher. Written between 1817 and 1821, the "Recollections of Rachel (Mordecai) Lazarus" recounts her reactions to her father's plight. She remembered, "How often did I wish that I had been a son, that like my brothers I might at least relieve him by doing something for my own support." [10] She notes, too, her solution for gaining the students' respect when she herself was so young. Not old enough to command respect, she decided, "I would seek to substitute for it a desire of pleasing which could only be obtained by implanting love instead of fear. By being kind as well as just, by entering into the little pleasures, and sympathizing with the little troubles of children, we soon obtain their confidence and affection." [11]

The family narrative that she set forth in her diary, recollections, and letters to Maria Edgeworth confirmed her worth, her value to her father, her importance in the maintenance of the school, her sense of belonging in a worthy Jewish family, and her faith in the Almighty. In addition, her diary especially established the enlightened dimensions of her educational practice; it may be read as a didactic text. Moreover, the diary narrative suggests a teacher's struggle to accept both the individuality of each pupil and the necessity of a child's independence. Ultimately, however, the diary addresses the hidden but deeply experienced Providence of God.

Edgeworthian pedagogy and fiction and Rachel Mordecai's moral educational principles expressed the tenets of white middle-class female virtue. Virtue defined as masculine in the new republic only gradually associated white female values with republican motherhood. Although religious and enlightened ideologies contributed to the assemblage of female moral attributes designated "republican motherhood," literary sentimentalism encouraged the same "qualities of the heart"—prudence, temperance, faith, and charity, to name a few. [12]

L.N.'s narrative expanded the "qualities of the heart" and thus relocated republican virtues within an Evangelical female context. In this narrative enlightened precepts remained the same: the Aunt admonished Fanny, "Happiness is the reward for doing right" and "Our Duties are our pleasures." [13] Moreover, Edgeworthian principles guide the young reader in "Past Days." The heading of chapter 2 reads: "'Business first, pleasure afterwards,' says the good and wise Miss Edgeworth." Fanny refers to "my lessons for the heart" and adds, "as that lady [Maria Edgeworth] calls it." Edgeworthian principles, however, are transposed to an Evangelical order. The Edgeworths suggest that education of the heart is a practical matter, a matter of experience, practice, and habit, in short, a natural, rational process. L.N. contends that duties give "lessons *for* the heart," as if an outside, not a natural force, guides the individual in the attainment of moral consistency or good habit. "Past Days" reveals the source of habit in a dialogue between the Aunt and Fanny: "'Now Aunt look here,' said Fan, pointing to the place in her prayer book that teaches a moral lesson—'and do my duty in that state of life, into which it shall please God to call me.'" [14] Duty occurs within the context of a divine call, thus behavior takes on a heightened sense of responsibility, and good behavior fulfills divine intention. In Evangelical texts holiness, a divine presence and direction, takes precedence over virtue, a human quality.

L.N. constructs two narrative levels in "Past Days." The "story within a story" contains the Mordecai family history, which demonstrates the Evangelical principles explained in the primary narrative of Fanny and her Aunt. The fictional personages identify with the characters in the story within a story, thus providing further reinforcement for the Evangelical themes promoted in the text. The narratives, however, are orchestrated by an unknown voice.

As the story within a story begins, Lucy Neville weeps beside her sister's grave. Lucy Neville's initials, L.N., would suggest her authorship of the story. However, Fanny asks her Aunt, "Who is it that is talking so sorrowfully about it all? Is it the lady who was sitting at her sister's grave?" The Aunt replies, "It is the history of that lady and the sister by whose grave she sat and of some of the other members of the family, but—whether it is Lucy Neville who wrote this story I do not know." [15] The masking of authorship serves an important purpose: to disguise the voice that tells the details of a personal family tragedy. Ellen Mordecai wrote *Fading Scenes Recalled,* reminiscences of Warrenton, North Carolina, using her grandmother's name, Esther Whitlock, as a pseudonym. [16] Later, she also wrote "History of a Heart," her own conversion narrative. [17] "Past Days" combines memory and religious concerns to commemorate Rachel's spiritual crisis and also to contribute to Christian Evangelization and education.

Ellen Mordecai

Ellen, daughter of Judith and Jacob Mordecai and closest to Rachel in age, admired and loved her sister for her steady and affectionate influence. Rachel attempted to lead Ellen toward greater emotional detachment. Ellen, one of the most vulnerable of the family members, had difficulty in achieving independence. Ellen plainly indicated her predicament: "I am sure if or when I am ever married I shall love my husband too much." [18] Ellen also had problems in parting with friends. [19] She did not identify with independent women. Ellen viewed an independent woman as an anomaly. She recorded in her diary a social call at a Mrs. Ruffin's, where she met "one of the completest characters I ever saw—a female Botanist." [20] Later Ellen copied or wrote in her diary a satire of Margaret Fuller's opinions on the independence of women. [21] Ellen's dependence on family and friends led to certain confusion about her own identity. She pondered Addison's line "nature does nothing in vain" and asked of "what use or purpose was I intended?" [22]

Ellen may have been particularly vulnerable to dependency needs, since she felt most strongly the loss of her mother. She remembered only two instances of maternal care, but they were enough to attach her to her mother's memory. Her deep maternal devotion caused her to violate Jewish practice. When the family left Warrenton for Richmond, Ellen insisted on exhuming her mother's remains and having them reinterred in Richmond. The sight of their mother's coffin evoked intense pain in the family, but the sight filled Ellen with joy. As she knelt by the coffin she felt as if her mother were restored to the family. She idealized memories of her mother. She recalled her mother teaching Rachel to forgive an injury, and, most telling, she remembered an instance of her mother's anxiety for her health.[23] Perhaps Ellen then interpreted solicitude for health as love. Unexplained illnesses plagued her throughout her life.

Her brother Solomon affected maternal care in his solicitude for Ellen, especially in his concern for her health. He also concerned himself with her emotional needs and her intellectual growth. She measured their intimacy by the progression of their bonds as playmates, schoolfellows, and constant companions.[24] Ellen's dependence upon Solomon led to fantasies about living with him, acting as his housekeeper and companion. Each felt "a craving void" without the other.[25] Solomon declared his steadfast devotion to Ellen when he was separated from her in Richmond. He assured her that "our affections burn as bright as ever. I believe that mine is supplied with fuel for life, and I must lose either my senses or my feelings or both if the flame ever flickers."[26]

Separated from Solomon for a time, Ellen became ill and depressed. A pain in her side reduced her usual "allegro[/]adagio" spirits to inactivity.[27] Kind Aunt Richa Marx promised to care for her, and Rachel gently persuaded her to give up her duties at the school to Julia. Silent but unresigned, Ellen anxiously awaited Solomon's return. She believed that if only Solomon could be with her, "sickness and cares would be strangers" to her.[28] Aunt Richa cared for Ellen for several months. Solomon rewarded Ellen's convalescence by his return. He embraced Ellen in her sickbed and said, "I cannot live without you."[29]

Ultimately, of course, Solomon left home to pursue his career; Ellen had no such option. Rachel offered a salvific message and counseled Ellen to accept separation and recognize that her brother must "seize his prospects in life." She urged Ellen to trust the Almighty to protect Solomon from "danger and death." Finally, Rachel gave some straight sisterly advice: "Now let me tell you one thing, and remember I lay my positive commands and they must be obeyed— do you keep up your spirits—One good cry I will allow you, and even one whole day to sigh, and look as you feel, dejected—but this is the extent of your Privilege—when you retire for the night offer up your prayers for his safety— rise in the morning cheerful."[30] Rachel's rational counsel followed Orthodox thinking. Primary dependence rested on the Almighty. Without the primary order all other relationships are disordered, even foolish. The purpose of rational counsel was to lead Ellen to the collective social order. The chief argument against idolatry was its irrationality and self-centeredness.[31] Ellen achieved marginal independence; she taught and wrote while living with family members and others. With conversion she used her literate skills for Evangelization and the support of the Christian community.

During the family's residence at Spring Farm, Ellen occupied her time teaching her nieces and nephews. Later, in 1822 she moved to Warrenton to assist her sister Caroline in managing Caroline's school and household. For a period of years beginning in 1834 she lived as a housekeeper with her brother Samuel in Petersburg.[32] In Petersburg Ellen received baptism on 2 December 1838, only six months after Rachel died. Ellen explained to her brother George how relieved she felt "to throw off the mask of dissimulation & appear what I had long been—Christian in heart and hope." During the long conversion process Rachel ever remained her sister's confidante. Ellen's brother Samuel "calmly and patiently" accepted her conversion and informed the family. Her stepmother, Rebecca Mordecai, found Ellen's actions indefensible but spoke of her kindly.[33] Perhaps Ellen assumed the pseudonym L.N. in deference to her family's feelings. "Past Days" received a limited circulation; one thousand copies were printed and distributed among church societies and groups. Only three copies of "Past Days" sold between November 1845 and 30 April 1846. Ellen received four dollars in royalties for both of her works that quarter.[34]

The Story within a Story

Ellen framed her story in the context of struggle, trial, and chastisement, reminiscent of the Jewish Exodus. However, in Evangelical terms, the trials indicate a state of justification that instills the sense of humility, unworthiness, and guilt experienced prior to conversion, regeneration.[35] According to Evangelical theology, conversion is a grace bestowed upon a sinner who cooperates with God in the individual's personal salvation. The Aunt declared that faith necessitated a life-long struggle; she said: "If you live to be a woman . . . and God sees that you wish to become better and better, He will be your friend, and cause such things to take place, as will be of use to you . . . such as are called trials." [36] The story within a story of Mary Layman exists as a model of forbearance during trials. As Lucy Neville wept upon her sister's grave and remembered her sister's troubles, the biblical verse comforted her, "God loveth whom he chasteneth." [37]

The trials of Mary Layman fill the pages of "Past Days." When her kind and beloved mother died, her father, overwhelmed with the parenting of six children, sent Mary and Lucy to those who could care for them. "They were therefore sent away from their home, and went to school; but they were not well taught," according to the story. The father took the girls home again only to assist in the work of the family. Burdened by household responsibilities, young Mary had no teacher and "had therefore to depend much upon herself." [38] Although she was inexperienced and largely uneducated, her father asked Mary to teach with him in the school he decided to open after his business failed. Happy to oblige her father yet fearful, she stammered to him, "Oh!, my dear Father, how can I teach others, when I know nothing myself?" The father explained that he, equally unprepared, would have much work to do. He asked his daughter to do the same as he, and she willingly consented. In a tender scene described by L.N., "He [the father] pressed her to his bosom; called her a blessing to her father; and said, as his eyes filled with tears, 'Your dear mother told me, my child, that you would be, a blessing to me, and so you are.'"[39] Deeply moved, she persevered in love and duty; she readied the house as the school term approached, yet she had little time to study.[40]

Faced with students her own age, Mary doubted her ability but gained confidence in the teaching experience. In addition to teaching academic subjects, Mary taught sewing and tended to the younger members of the family. At night she studied for the next day. According to the story within a story, as the school prospered, the health of Mr. Neville "and that of the Children suffered from the unceasing labour and close confinement. Often after the fatigue of the morning, Mary would feel so feeble she could scarcely creep up stairs to dress for dinner."[41] Despite her fatigue she tutored her bright young sister Sally. Mary gained some respite, however, when her brothers joined her in the school and lightened her teaching load. The narrator commented that "it was very, very touching to see such good children wearing their young lives out, and never feeling discontented nor uttering a complaint of their own sufferings."[42]

Some of Mary Layman's greatest trials occurred after her marriage and remain largely unexplained in the text. The mention of the trials suggests that as death approached, Mary taught an Evangelical message to her receptive children. The narrative reveals that Mary married a widower with many small children whose care was especially burdensome. In addition, Mary and her husband had four children of their own. Mary's relationship to her children is told in a series of their reminiscences. Mary admonishes her family: "Listen to that emotion, that speaking to the heart which in the Bible is called the still small voice!"[43] To encourage them in their own difficulties, Mary guided the children spiritually along the Evangelical religious path. She says: "You may have many troubles my dear children, as I have had, and when it pleases God to afflict you, and send to you, your trials, you will find, as your mother has that true Religion, pure and holy as God has been pleased to give for our benefit in the Bible. His own Divine direction will be a comfort to you when all others fail!"[44]

The narrator attributes Mary's decline in health to "the injury sustained by her school labours" and her residence, after marriage, in "an unhealthy environment."[45] But there is nothing in the text to indicate the psychological or spiritual reason for the crisis that develops. The text only hints at Mary's dilemma and says: "Mary often thought of her duty to God. To perform it, was the first wish of her heart. She would seldom say, but often, often feel—'I am faithful in the discharge of my duties to my family, and to my fellow creatures, but alas! How imperfectly do I fulfill my duty to the Maker of us all! I set my earthly house in order but I am not ready to appear before Him who solemnly warns and exhorts us to make preparation. O Lord because of my difficulties, make my way straight before me.'"[46]

The primary narrative of Fanny and her Aunt does not uncover the reason for Mary's distress. Fanny asks her Aunt, "But Aunt why did not Mary do what she thought right? Why didn't she do her duty to God?" The Aunt replies, "I cannot tell . . . but . . . Mary never acted willfully wrong, and I cannot think she did so now." The Aunt cautioned her niece not to judge since it is impossible to know anyone's motives.[47]

"Past Days" then relates the events of Mary's premature death. As she was hastening to the bedside of her dying father, a fatal illness overcame her twenty miles from her father's home. The text notes that on her deathbed Mary "spoke of her husband and left a farewell message for him." She also spoke of her children, of whom she said, "God would provide for their eternal welfare."[48] Most telling of her character, according to the narrator, was her reply to her sister concerning her children's education. When her sister Lucy suggested, "Let your sisters be their teachers," the text describes her response: "Mary! Mary! even in death's dying hour still the same, looked with grateful tenderness on her sister, and with the last spirit-like expression of that 'beaming smile' now, though faint, so sweet, she slowly feebly, gently, moved her small, soft hand and passing it over her cold forehead whispered 'It is too great a charge.'"[49] At this poignant moment the narrator intervenes and exclaims, "Dear reader, this is true—true!" The meaning of "too great a charge" is not interpreted for the reader but is supposed to be self-evident.

At once the fictional world erupts as the author makes a truth-claim in order to establish contact between the author and the reader. Until the late nineteenth century and the introduction of fictional realism, fiction had little credibility in the estimation of the reading public, who preferred the truth-claims of history. Ellen, undoubtedly, abandoned her story to make a factual claim and thus a stronger case for religious meaning and Evangelical proselytism. In a sense, the Mary Layman story works as an allegory, the narrative serving larger symbolic purposes.[50]

Truth no longer lies in the facts of the narrative but in the motives, purpose, and argument of the author and in the spiritual assumptions of the Evangelical audience the story addressed.[51] The author's motive establishes the virtue of sacrifice. At the point of death Mary Layman thinks of her sisters, not herself. Mary places her values above life itself and achieves what few achieve: transcendence in the face of annihilation. The text argues that the ultimate trial, death, may be transcended by virtue and sacrifice. Virtue, the performance of unrelenting, ordinary duties, proves a steady foundation for the spiritual equilibrium needed to let go of life itself.[52]

The Jewish Dilemma

Although the text slips into reality at the death of Mary Layman, the full truth of the story is never told. The characters of the story within a story are never perceived as Jewish, whereas the story upon which the text is based is the story of a Jewish family. The anguish that Mary Layman suffers is never identified as a conversion dilemma, although the Evangelical community must have been keenly aware of Rachel Mordecai Lazarus's acutely painful conversion decision. Why did the dilemma remain obscure in the text? How is it that Fanny asks, "Why did not Mary do what she thought right? Why didn't she do her duty to God?"

Discretion no doubt played a major part in Ellen's reluctance to embarrass Jewish family members further by publicizing their anguish. Rumors of Rachel's conversion reached her brother Alfred Mordecai, commander of Watervliet Arsenal near Albany, New York; he expressed his disappointment if the rumor proved true. "It is almost the only act of her life that I look back on with dissatisfaction," he wrote.[53] Whether or not the family confirmed his suspicions is unknown. Aaron Lazarus, who arrived in Richmond after his wife's death, expressed shock to learn of her burial in an Episcopalian cemetery. The Mordecai and Lazarus families would have been mortified by any public discussion of the circumstances of Rachel Mordecai Lazarus's death.[54]

Perhaps another reason Ellen did not reveal Rachel's religious dilemma had theological implications. The power of indeterminate anguish indirectly raises the Job-like dilemma of the suffering of the just in the face of a wrathful God. How much greater the triumph or transcendence over death and the dissolution of self if an individual can face even an angry God with affirmation. Self-recognition occurs at the point of death because there are no illusions, only a hope born out of conflict and acquired through a long and difficult apprenticeship that the individual will encounter a living God.[55] Mary Layman's suffering, her sacrifice, her final duty affirmed her virtue and her self. Her life of striving toward virtue, her faithfulness to duty, enabled Mary Layman, even in the face of death, to go beyond the suffering self and create herself anew.

Self-creation, historically the burden and responsibility more often undertaken by Jews caught in hostile cultures, appears as a leitmotif in "Past Days." The story contains episodes of self-creation: the abandoned child raises herself, the unlettered girl becomes the skilled teacher, the dying woman transcends self. Such invention of self suggests why the author, Ellen, never recognizes the Jewishness or the ethnicity of her characters and thus the deeper poignancy of the story. More significantly, for Ellen the characters represented an Evangelical identification with justification or salvation. Yet recurrent self-invention set against final ambivalence obscures the deeper question of identity: if the main character constantly changes, who is she? Ellen narrated the account of the Mordecais using analepses, or flashbacks, as a story device. Thus Ellen imagined the story as a point of departure from the event of the death when the character Mary Layman/Rachel Mordecai Lazarus struggled between two worlds. Ellen witnessed Rachel Mordecai Lazarus approaching a borderland not only between heaven and earth but between Christianity and Judaism.

The borderland between cultures presents an anomalous category for Jews, since the question of Jewish identity in the early national period is especially elusive. Traditional scholars, taking a cue from Heinrich Heine, contend that assimilation all but dissipated Jewish identity since "as the Christians do, so do the Jews."[56] Sociologist Benjamin Kaplan's 1957 study of assimilation notes, "It has been wisely said that the Jew himself does not exist—he is 'becoming.'"[57] Philosopher Emmanuel Levinas admitted that in the nineteenth century Jewish morality "more and more resembled the generous but general formulae of the European moral conscience."[58] Historians William Petersen, Michael Novak, and Philip Gleason explain the invisibility of religio-ethnicity in the new republic as a result not so much of assimilation as of the nature of citizenship and nation building. They argue, "The fact that the American people were of diverse ethnic strains was not overlooked in discussions of nationality, but because of the nature of the events that brought the nation to birth, the American identity was conceived primarily in abstract ideological terms. Ethnic considerations were subsidiary."[59] Nationality derived not from place of origin or religious affiliation but from consent to certain principles: liberty, equality, the pursuit of happiness.

More recent interpretations of historic Jewish identity, however, do not discount assimilation but offer more complicated notions of enlightened Jewish identity. Historian Michael A. Meyer notes: "Enlightenment thus manifested itself as a force that could draw Jews further and further away from Jewish identity, across the territory where one was a Jew and at the same time something else as well (European, German, Kantian, socialist) to the border where Jewish identity became vestigial or disappeared entirely. Yet in the border regions countervailing forces arose that sometimes reversed the trajectory." Professor Meyer refers to anti-Semitism or Jewish nationalism that historically drew Jews back from the brink of religious or ethnic abnegation.[60] Assimilation never occurred in a linear fashion nor as completely as scholars suggested. In addition, Meyer raises the more relevant issues about Jewish identity, addressed pointedly by scholar Charles S. Leibman. Although Leibman does not deny the historic adaptation of Jews to the surrounding culture, he shifts direction to more important questions, such as, "Which elements of that culture have [Jews] simply assimilated without change; which elements have [Jews] transformed in the process of absorbing them; which elements have [Jews] resisted; and which have they ignored?"[61]

The Mordecai family trajectory initiated during the Revolutionary period readily accepted liberal tenets of citizenship. Liberty, equality, and consent to government assured them of citizenship and religious toleration. The Mordecais evidenced a subdued ethnicity in the early republic: there is no evidence in their correspondence that they used German as their lingua franca; rather, Eliza and Rachel read German to expand their literary range. Perhaps Rachel Mordecai, a third-generation German Jew, identified with her German heritage on a purely symbolic or intellectual plane, hence her easy adaptation of enlightened method and thought. However, the Mordecais, Rachel in particular, transformed enlightened pedagogy into an instrument of religious instruction even as they accepted the enlightened method of rational change. In these actions the Mordecais remained invisible, their agency as German Jews dedicated to education only a subtle motion on the landscape of American monoculturalism. However, Jewish identification with American and enlightened precepts obscured their religious and cultural affiliations, placing them at odds with early-nineteenth-century culture.

The Mordecais resisted the dominant culture by Orthodox observance of ritual, kashrut, and the High Holidays. And the Mordecais supported the Jewish community: Samuel Mordecai acted as a Jewish spokesperson and officiated at Jewish marriages. Moreover, Jacob Mordecai's refusal to convert in the face of Evangelical pressure to do so and his apologia signified his antithesis to Christian proselytization arguments. Although the father ultimately accepted the interfaith marriages of his children Moses and Caroline, he rejected completely Rachel's desire to convert. Rachel's husband also demonstrated an unyielding stance with regard to Rachel's religious decision. And despite her enlightened education and training in criticism, Eliza remained an Orthodox Jew.

Anglo-Americans did not see or understand Jewish conflict and resistance perhaps because Jews established their identity in dialogue with Anglo-Americans. The Edgeworth-Mordecai correspondence strengthened ideological and family ties between the two families. Furthermore, the Mordecais taught the daughters of Evangelical planters and encouraged their faith by seeing to it that they observed Sunday services. Jacob Mordecai sometimes attended Evangelical services with his students. Accommodation, however, did not always forestall resistance. Anglo-Americans identified Jews with accommodation, whereas Jews developed their identity not only in conformity with but in opposition to Anglo-American culture. The liberal tradition accounted for Jewish counterculture.

The Didactic Purpose

L.N. perceived Mary Layman's entire life as faithful to Evangelical precepts. The night before Mary Layman teaches, filled with anxiety, she resigns her cares to Christ the Savior. She prays:

> O Lord! thy suppliant turns to Thee,
> With gracious words still comfort me;
> Be Thou my hope, my first desire;
> Free me from every weight: nor fear,
> Nor sin can come, if Thou art here.
>
> In suffering be thy love my peace,
> In weakness be thy love my power:
> And When the storms of life shall cease,
> Oh, in that important hour,
> In death, as life, be Thou my guide,
> And save me, who for me hast died? [62]

L.N. imparts to all of Mary Layman's trials a quiet center, a Christian equanimity. L.N. frames the chapter concerning school hardships with this verse:

> Religion's rays no clouds obscure,
> But o'er the christian's soul;
> It sheds a radiance calm and pure,
> Though tempests round her roll. [63]

Nonetheless, after her marriage Mary Layman confronts how "imperfectly" she carries out her (unnamed) duty toward God. L.N. notes the discontinuity, the different nature of Mary's anguish toward the end of her life, and suggests the guilt and suffering Mary endured prior to her conversion. However, since conversion of Christians, a change of heart, remains central to Evangelicalism, the text masks the drama concerning conversion to another faith. At the same time, holiness and equanimity preserve a sameness about the character of Mary Layman.

At the end of her life, Mary Layman desires to make her children "religious, useful, & happy." [64] The narrative demonstrates her primary concern with religion; she exhorts her children to obey the will of God and their conscience. The "still, small voice" of divine inspiration and the Bible, the inspired Word of God, remains their guide. The mother projects her own struggle with her conscience upon the children and bequeaths them her internal conflict. Perhaps the author reconciles the discontinuity and continuity of Christian and Jewish tension implicit in the story when she "quotes" a passage from Mary Layman's correspondence to her sister Lucy. It reads: "Beautiful and consoling is the language of the Psalmist: 'He who goeth forth and weepeth bearing precious seed, shall surely return in joy bearing home his sheaves.'"[65] Rachel cited the passage in one of her last letters to Ellen; Rachel derived much comfort from the psalm as the hymn promised a happy end of her sufferings.[66]

Evangelical triumphalism belies the suffering Rachel Mordecai Lazarus endured during her ten-year struggle with the seeds of her conversion. Rejected by father and husband, a scandal to family members, she died a paradox to her family. Who was she after all? If she died a new creation, true to herself, was that self undivided? Conversion, a process that introduces the liminal state of "no place and no time," defies categorization; the potential convert discovers the painful anomaly of existing betwixt and between religions and cultures. During her conversion period Rachel Mordecai Lazarus experienced the conflict of living as both Jewish and Christian. Her ethical identity and ancestral origin distinguished her as Jewish. She lived in a community of mutual recognition, one recognized by others as people of a common descent. In addition, the Jewish community bound her to the ties of family and the demands of a benevolent patriarchy.

Rachel Mordecai Lazarus retained the Jewish notion of Providence, or the presence of God, which she clung to with reverence, and she remained obedient to the will of God, which she held to despite her anguish. Thus there is in Rachel's religious transformation a certain familiarity, a sense of continuity, that Providence guided her life.[67] Rachel's removal to Wilmington's Evangelical circle placed her within a communitas that bound her to other women in an egalitarian religious company. Here she experienced heartfelt friendship free from family strictures and hierarchies. The security of the community encouraged self-creation, and that self-renewal bonded her to others. If Rachel sought forgiveness and experienced it in the context of Evangelical communitas, she sought a certain love in communion with others that engaged her notion of Providence, the mundane experience of the presence of God.[68]

Only Providence could contain the contradictions of Judaism and Christianity, nonduty and duty. Contradiction implies that nothing is known for certain; rationality remains circumscribed in a liminal state. L.N. asserts, "God knows what is good for us."[69] Cooperation with divine Providence exists for L.N. not on a rational but on an expressive plane. The Aunt explains to Fanny how to know the will of God: "Your ears would not have heard him; but the inward feeling, that you say makes you 'feel like singing when you are good,' is that happiness which God gives us, to let us know we are doing, or have done right. It is what people call conscience. But the Bible tells us it is the Holy Spirit. And it is proper to call it so, as it comes from God, and He has given It the name!"[70] Whereas pleasure or pain determines the rational conscience, harmonious feeling engages the Evangelical conscience. For both, however, the knowledge of right or wrong can be known by the subject only in the doing, by experience. Interpretation of that experience, however, depends upon formation of character.

Mary Layman's character and the Aunt's character do not develop as much as they demonstrate the Evangelical message, the importance of salvation. Character and action are drawn together in order to derive the moral lesson. Character, then, is essential in determining direction, and direction reveals the design of the didactic text.[71] The author introduces Mary Layman as a "very sensible and very sweet tempered" girl for whom "study was never a trouble. Her trouble was not having a teacher! She had therefore to depend much upon herself . . . However she had good sense and the desire to improve it, she caught and kept what came in her way." The text continues, "This child grew up to be a young lady. She was very pretty; she had light brown hair, a clear complexion, a very sensible countenance, and a most delightful smile, so sweet and so bright, that Lucy always called it a 'beaming smile.'" Mary's smile made "all feel more cheerful."[72] Mary demonstrates a sensible nature, open and responsible, whose character improved society and therefore proved useful. Mary's optimism contrasts with her father's diffident nature, "uncertain of his own powers to effect what he wished or attempted." The result, according to the narrative, was that "he had often been unsuccessful in his endeavours, he was more inclined to fear, than to hope."[73] Her natural disposition inclined Mary to hope, to place her confidence beyond unhappy experience.

Teaching further refined Mary's personality. The narrator explains, "Mary was so sweetly tempered, so kind, so reasonable, and so patient, that all the girls loved her; and so did their parents, who were very glad to have so good a school for their children." The usefulness of Mary's disposition accounted for the success of the school; thus, her very nature has social consequences. At the end of Mary's life the narrator sums up her contributions: "Mary discharged her duty as stepmother most faithfully. She was a treasure to her amicable husband, she was beloved by the community in which she lived—an example to the young— a companion to the middle aged—a benefit to society—a comfort to the afflicted—a friend to all—sympathising tender, active and efficient. Such was the matured character of Mary Neville."[74] Evangelical character moves increasingly from the individual to the community. Ultimately, relationships define the individual and prove salvific.

Ellen Mordecai's character is hidden or only indirectly alluded to in references to "the Aunt." It may be that Ellen, changed by her relationship with Rachel, sees herself only in relation to her sister. Ellen derives her moral authority from relating her sister's story; Ellen's story is not yet told. Ellen's purpose is to reach an Evangelical audience, to catechize. Her focus is not upon the Rachel-Eliza relationship or the enlightened pedagogical method (she only briefly mentions Mary Layman's teaching of her sister Sally); rather, the author reveals an inner dialogue. The voices of the story are Ellen's inner conflict—the true dimensions of the tragedy that she longs to share but cannot. She stands in the present as the Evangelical teacher, the Aunt, but relates the past, an inner history, or story within a story, of herself as a sister, a Jew, who witnesses the conversion and death, the cutting of all earthly family ties, of Mary Neville Layman/Rachel Mordecai Lazarus. The shock of the death and the sacrifice disrupts the narrative, and the author begs the reader with intense emotion to understand the truth; the truth, however, is not plain. Ellen interweaves fictional and true experience to approximate the actual temporal experience. Despite the gap between the knowing and the telling, Ellen experiences a transformation, an empowerment that leads her to tell her own story, "History of a Heart." [75]

The Narrator

The character of the Aunt facilitates mimesis: she tells the story, and she allows Fanny's discursive disruptions in order to teach and demonstrate the story's moral. In so doing the Aunt reinterprets the family story and gives it new spiritual direction. "Past Days" can be compared to Rachel's diary as a didactic text. Both Rachel and the Aunt engage in the home education of a child, and although recitation occurs, the dialogic method predominates in establishing educational and religious precepts. The manner, formal, authoritative, yet affectionate, offers support and guidance to the pupil. However, method, manner, and discourse in "Past Days" support Evangelical religious assumptions, including free will, immortality, and salvation.

L.N. employs Edgeworthian dialogue and example to show the proper manner for the education of virtue. Fanny, anxious to ask her Uncle a question when he returns home for dinner, is told by her Aunt, "Shorten the time by employment, little girl, that will at least make the dinner hour, seem to come sooner." The nature of employment is then demonstrated by the Aunt, who carries a breakfast tray to her Father. The Aunt says, "Prepare your lesson ready for me to hear when I return. Learn from your prayerbook, 'My duty to my neighbor.'" [76] The narrator then continues: "And the lady with her Father's breakfast, left the room; mentally hoping, her little niece might learn, both by heart and by practice, that beautiful lesson, which no one was better calculated to teach both by precept and example; than the lady who had assigned it to the little girl." [77] The narrator describes the Aunt as "good and wise," [78] the perfect complement to Rachel's exemplary behavior.

In the primary narrative of "Past Days" Fanny acts spontaneously, she jokes about her creaking shoes, and the Aunt tells an amusing anecdote about women who gently chide a shoemaker for his manufacture of squeaking shoes.[79] Fanny's spontaneity insures that her responses to her Aunt's suggestions for alternatives are free choices. Fanny learns from Mary Layman that helping her father teach fulfills the Golden Rule, "doing unto others as you would they should do unto you!" When the Aunt invites the child to accompany her to visit a friend in trouble, she says, "Will you run out to play, or walk with me Fan? Take your choice," and the child readily agrees.[80] The scene is reminiscent of Rachel's invitation to Eliza to oblige her by accompanying her downtown. Romantic Evangelicalism fully accepted the notion of individual responsibility for salvation and therefore readily assimilated enlightened notions of free choice. Example permits a moral lesson, but experience also teaches the deeper lessons of virtue. Experience as interpreted by Evangelical texts is never random or neutral, since "God loveth whom he chasteneth." However, an Evangelical may choose how to respond to God's will. According to the Aunt, "to chasten, means to correct; to make a person better, by curing them of their faults." Fanny inquires if "faults make us sick?"[81] The Aunt carries her didactic lesson through a discussion of the existence of the soul that assumes a more profound apprehension of experience. The Aunt asserts, "Faults do not always make our bodies sick, but they always injure our minds, in the same way that different diseases hurt our bodies." Fanny inquires what a mind is, and the Aunt responds, "You have a mind. It has another name, but it is the same part of us; the other name of this part is soul; and it is that something inside of us which thinks it will never die. Our souls will live forever."[82]

Mary Layman's death prompts discussion of the soul, and the Aunt explains that the soul exists in the body as a kernel lives in a shell. Comforted yet still inquisitive, Fanny wanted to know if Mary Layman had any faults. "It seems to me she was good, quite good, for her sister loved her so much," observes Fanny. "My dear little girl, no one in this world is quite good; though some persons are better than others," replies the Aunt. Fanny wonders how she compares to other little girls, then she answers her own question in her Aunt's voice: "Sometimes, Fanny you are better and sometimes not." "I believe I should not say exactly that," rejoins the Aunt, "but that some times you are better than other little girls who do not try to correct their faults."[83] In typical enlightened fashion Fanny answers, "I am happiest when I am the good little child." This rejoinder included an Evangelical premise that attributed happiness to the soul and not to the natural experience of the body. Fanny continues, "'I feel like laughing and singing then, there is something merry in my bosom—away inside of me Aunt,' said the child, pressing the ends of her small fingers against her heart, as if she wished to show the spot." The narrator interposes, "Her Aunt smiled at the little girl's effort to communicate, what language cannot express."[84]

Although the Aunt presents a metaphysical issue in dichotomous terms, the separation of mind (soul) and body, Fanny illustrates her understanding of the soul by pointing not to her head but to her heart. She grasps at the idea as if that part of the mind called soul exists not as a kernel but as something more diffuse and elusive, namely, feelings in the body. Goodness registers not simply in the effort of will to be good but in the soul that inclines toward holiness. The Aunt indicates that goodness can be discerned in the soul by the Holy Spirit. The Aunt explains:

> When God went to Heaven, after he had been in this world, and told people how to do right, and showed them, too, by his example, he sent to all who wish to be good, this Holy Spirit, that they may feel when they are even trying to wish to do right, and know by its effect on them, that they are not mistaken. As if God said to their ears—you are right!—People feel, though they do not hear, him. Blind persons, you know, feel what persons who have eyes, can see: So we, while we live, are blind to God, yet we feel his direction.[85]

The character of the Aunt fulfills two didactic purposes: first, to demonstrate the method of character education, and second, to reveal the salvation process in the formation of character. The formation of Evangelical character follows a specific direction; the Aunt acts as an agent in fostering divinely directed holiness. She accedes that "the Holy Spirit is God's direction to us to show us which way we are to go, to get to Heaven." [86]

According to "Past Days," then, transformation is achieved through spiritual direction, which alone transforms the suffering soul. The dialectic of struggle, of choice, suggests a soul unturned, a perception relenting, bound in a liminal state. The enlightened model of instruction, a critical mode that utilizes creative doubt to invent endless possibilities, assumes a restless pursuit of virtue, a noble ambition subdued only by constant acts of will. Self-creation acts as a marker, a test of possibilities, in the natural development of enlightened individuals. Enlightened individuals are as busy as Edgeworthian characters as they seek secular goals. Evangelical moral purpose discounts the improvident use of energy. "Trials" deplete the extraneous matters that encumber the soul and reduce choice to a single alternative, anguish or salvation (conversion). Christian holiness, never fully achieved, however, offers tranquillity, a godliness, that originates in the choice for salvation and in the surrender of all other choices to the Divinity. Self-identity ceases to compel anxious concern; complications and contradictions within the human person are left to divine Providence.

Thus Rachel Mordecai Lazarus's pedagogical and religious history is not recounted as enlightened and Jewish but represented as Evangelical and Christian. For the author of "Past Days," Ellen Mordecai, the truth lies only in transformation; thus method, character, history, and experience serve a specific didactic purpose—Evangelization. Through the message the author is transformed; no longer embedded in the past or in the person of her sister, Ellen assumes an independent life of teaching and Evangelization. The family narrative offers Ellen the hermeneutic, the interpretation that bridges the gap between the experience lived and the expectation of the heart.

AFTERWORD

THE WAYS OF WISDOM, of seeing, are diverse: tangible and intangible, scientific and religious. Perception can be an immediate recognition of a material object or an intuitive sense of a moral quality. Whether by experiment, an empirical test, or spirit, "the breath of God," the ways of seeing, imbricated in mind and body, contain the power of transformation. Wisdom reveals its effusive ability much like the refractive capacity of light, which can change direction when passing obliquely from one medium to another. The diary of Rachel Mordecai Lazarus, composed in the early nineteenth century and deeply informed by the enlightened Edgeworthian method, nonetheless shifted understanding of pedagogical technique according to Orthodox Jewish precepts. Ellen Mordecai, Rachel's sister, adapted Rachel's practice to yet another didactic model: Evangelical instruction.

The European Enlightenment carried its experimental method and educational theory to a diverse ethnic and religious American environment, where secular and rational values competed with traditional folkways and Orthodox piety. The result, as observed in the Lazarus text, is neither synthesis nor fragmentation but syncretism, an attempt at reconciliation that is resisted, challenged, ignored, and adapted at various times. The link between Orthodox Jewish and Edgeworthian pedagogies lay in rational dialogue, recognition of stages of development, and acceptance of natural order, but the connection broke with Jewish covenantal ethics, faith in Providence, and the pursuit of holiness. The internal contradiction of republican pedagogy, which adapted secular method and values to religious ends, revealed itself in the conflicted lives of students of the method.

The education of the heart absorbed Rachel Mordecai as much more than a practical guide to home education. Edgeworthian practices offered a moral context for the commonsense approach to childhood training. These "common truths" made room for sympathy and benevolence, albeit "well regulated." [1] Jacob Mordecai's German Jewish background and his revolutionary fervor inclined the family toward an enlightened path. However, Rachel's most tender memories conveyed the recollection of her mother, Judith Mordecai, as a woman of righteousness who trained her children in the path of virtue and the presence of God. Judith bequeathed the model of holiness, of faithfulness to God and divine precepts. Thus Edgeworthian pedagogy presented a familiar parental pattern of attention to mind and heart. With the death of her mother, Rachel's attentiveness to concerns of the heart declined in the face of the demands of mind and body, namely, teaching at and managing the Warrenton Female Academy. Although Rachel taught lovingly, she took pride in self-possession, self-control. With rational intent she accepted the secular and personal advantages in the mixed marriages of her siblings, and she remonstrated with her sister Ellen for her overinvolved emotional attachment to their brother Solomon. Edgeworthian lessons of well-regulated sympathy and habits of benevolence fell upon a receptive, grieving heart.

The Edgeworthian moral model evolved out of a family divided, delicately balanced to insure reciprocal dependence. Frances Anne and Richard Lovell Edgeworth, who moved home to Edgeworthstown, belied the enlightened goal of a responsible, independent self. Edgeworthstown housed a remarkable family culture known for pedagogical experiment but structured in a way that inverted enlightened gender order. Women maintained the stable, rational domestic shelter for the unruly and dissolute men. The Edgeworthian model, later refined and developed into a body of fiction by Maria Edgeworth, carried an ambivalent theme for women, that in rational independent thinking lay a moral course; such thinking, however, could be expressed only within a domestic context. Edgeworthian heroines demonstrated rational restraint and moral prepossession and thus secured a happy domestic life; antiheroines such as Mrs. Freke of *Belinda* led careless and destructive lives that disrupted households. The double message of independent thinking and its domestic limits promoted both courage and deference, sagacity and doubt. The teaching of the Edgeworthian method proved difficult, an art mastered only by those preceptors who themselves had readily balanced passion and reason.

At the age of twenty-seven Rachel Mordecai initiated her experiment with seven-year-old Eliza Mordecai; between them a generation gap widened as the elder intellectually enlightened yet culturally traditional sister enforced a strict moral discipline upon the engaging and impulsive child. Eliza's impulsiveness presented the Edgeworthian dilemma, how to manage a "good girl." Goodness, however, conveyed the Edgeworthian ambivalence: independent thinking, yet acceptance of the family hierarchy. Eliza rebelled against the double message: express critical thinking, yet submit unquestioningly to elders. Her silly, irrational, indifferent behavior exposed the contradiction, the false sense of self at the heart of the rational method. Self-incrimination, ostracism, strict accountability repressed her passionate nature. The sharp lessons only heightened her determination to obtain justice—a more consensual method of education that recognized her maturity and individuality. Her victory followed enlightened precept (the formation of a democratic family order), yet as a female she struggled to adjust to a domestic life that limited her agency. If holiness meant becoming what Divinity intended, Eliza released her passionate, literary nature, which abjured a self-absorbed rationality, and embraced the "rights" of a mature-thinking and emotionally expressive individual.

Rational method did not therefore necessarily dictate the direction and form enlightened lives would take. Eliza resisted enlightened goodness and remained an Orthodox Jew. Rachel adapted Edgeworthian pedagogy to Jewish precepts but converted to Evangelical Protestantism. The method clearly challenged both individuals and initiated a habit of critical thinking, but context imposed the more crucial interpretation of questioning. Jacob Mordecai's early immersion in enlightened and Revolutionary thinking and his religious reversal later in life provided two separate patterns for the generations within his family. Rachel matured in an open, almost directionless environment where her busy parents neglected all but the rudiments of her education. Her own curiosity and ambition spurred intense study, and her experience within the Warrenton Female Academy conditioned her for a more systematic teaching method. Eliza's disciplined education contributed to her identification with her parents' increasingly loyal devotion to Orthodox Judaism.

However, Eliza's rebellion against authoritarian discipline merged with a changing American literary context, expanding to include Continental Romanticism. Romantic themes of revolutionary consciousness and domestic harmony, translated into the vernacular by Eliza, suggested the maintenance of individual rights and women's moral importance within family and society. Her literary exercises and musical talent reinforced a sense of empowerment, although like a true Romantic heroine she suffered the consequences of a passionate attachment to an impoverished spouse. The precepts of childhood goodness gave way to holiness as she filled her domestic life with works of charity hallowed by her death, as she cared for the casualties of the Civil War.

After Rachel Mordecai Lazarus left her father's house and attached to a community of Evangelical women, systematic questioning remained a more salient factor in her life. She countered Maria Edgeworth's biased and sometimes mythical understanding of Judaism, ultimately questioned southern slavery in the aftermath of the Nat Turner revolt, and embraced Evangelicalism after a ten-year period of doubt. Yet questioning led to a nonrational course. In the end she held on to nothing but Providence; her contradiction of husband and father shattered the traditional image of goodness, the obedient wife, the good daughter.

Ellen Mordecai's "Past Days" offers an enigmatic interpretation of Rachel Mordecai Lazarus's life and a transformation of the enlightened method. Rachel Mordecai's experiment, permeated by Orthodox beliefs and prayers, attests to faith in Providence with open-ended possibility. "Past Days," written with proselytizing intent, assumes a more controlled method. Questioning fits a predetermined form, an ordained process of justification and sanctification. The result is an authentic testimony of Ellen's grief but a fictional account of Mordecai family history, especially the nature of Rachel Mordecai's religious crisis. Ellen's perceptual shift altered history in order to suggest a consistent movement of the Evangelical spirit. However, underlying the story is a mysterious turmoil, an anguish and guilt never expressed but contained within every spirit-directed response; such is the path to Evangelical holiness.

Ellen transposed the light of reason with "religion's rays";[2] religion, not reason, penetrated the heart. Ellen wrote of Mary/Rachel's heartbreak: "Like Diamonds shining when they're broke, / That ray will light them still."[3] The refractive power of holiness remained within but shattered the unity of the Orthodox Mordecai family. In contrast, goodness, the rational virtue practiced within the Edgeworth family, maintained an uneasy balance between the dominant though benevolent patriarch and the companionable, stabilizing network of domestic female relationships. Maria Edgeworth praised her family unity, yet few achieved independence in that household until after her father's death. Rachel and Eliza through their pedagogical dialogue contested enlightened virtue and hierarchical family relationships. The enlightened contest led not straight to assimilation but to the independent practice of holiness. Ellen's intimate yet uncontested relationship to Rachel favored a more didactic approach to teaching and a more emphatic approach to holiness. Her pedagogical dialogue acted as a medium of the message, the necessity of conversion.

Early Republican religio-ethnic family relationships invested rational method with Providential meaning. In the dialogic process change occurred, but as a deflection, not an absorption, of enlightened secular values. Assimilation proved a truly refractive process among the religio-ethnic family members who appropriated the enlightened method; they maintained the practice of holiness, variously defined in separate Jewish and Evangelical communities.

The Diary
of
Rachel
Mordecai
Lazarus

Sunday May 19th

It has long been my intention to commence writing juvenile, I should rather term them, "nursery anecdotes," of my little Eliza.[1] Since three years of age, this child has been a constant source of delight to her whole family. Her earliest observations full of mind, & of goodness, seemed worthy of memorial; but procrastination, alike the thief of time, and its events, has robbed me of all but a confused recollection of them. I will not however occasion myself future reproach by longer deferring, what in future years, should they be granted me, will be a source of gratification. I wish too to see if the tender bud which promises so fair, will bloom into a fragrant, lovely, and unfading flower. Should it seem good to the Most High to suffer *it,* and *me,* to continue on this great theatre of existence, I will watch over, and mark its daily progress, I will endeavor to destroy each canker that would enter its bosom to render it less sweet and lovely, And O! may I be rendered capable of forming the materials which nature has bountifully placed in my hands; may reason, combined with virtue, and nourished by education, form a character eminently fitted to discharge every duty of this life, and when called from this transitory state of being, worthy to repose eternally in the presence of its Creator.—

This day May 19th[2] Eliza's sister Caroline:[3] having received a present of a few strawberries (first we had seen this season), sent them to her parents & the rest of the family. There were so few, that no one would eat them, and some one proposed that half should be given to Eliza to make a feast, with one of her little companions, and the other half returned to Caroline. Eliza, who tho' in the room the whole time, had not asked for one, was now highly delighted, and began to skip about the floor. At this moment she was sent out on a message, and before she returned, a servant had taken them all away to Caroline. Eliza came back, and her sister Rachel[4] told her what had happened, adding that she did not wish to send for them again, as Caroline had kept none for herself. For *a moment* she looked a little disappointed, but her countenance afterwards resumed its accustomed serenity. Rachel then told her she might go and get 2 dozen filberts[5] to play with, she was now as much delighted as before, and thanked her sister many times. Just then the servant re-entered with half the strawberries saying that Caroline insisted upon Rachel's taking them. Rachel, ate a few, then called Eliza and gave her the rest, saying, "I give you these, my dear, with pleasure, because you were not discontented when you were deprived of them, you see goodness is always rewarded."

Eliza: "No sister Rachel not *always* you know."

Rachel: "Not always in this way my dear, but always by the pleasure of feeling that it has done right."

Eliza: "O yes, sister Rachel it always has that reward. Sister Rachel if you please to eat some more of these strawberries."

Eliza has never been taught any thing in play, neither have her studies ever been made *tasks,* tho' forming regularly a part of each day's occupation. To learn something new has been made the reward for becoming perfect in any little study in which she might be engaged. To this arrangement may probably be attributed her being attached to all her employments. Sitting one day with her mama,[6] she said "mama I have a great many pleasures, I will count them & see how many I have." She then began her enumeration, and reckoned eighteen. Among these were saying her different lessons, reading for her own amusement, taking her music lesson, watering her garden, doing little regular offices of *assistance* to her brother Solomon,[7] being a good girl &c.—Some time after having met with the word catalogue, she was desirous of having it explained, her sister Rachel told her that she would write her a catalogue of her *pleasures,* if she would tell her what they were: when it was finished her sister said, "But Eliza which do you like best of all your pleasures?" She hesitated a moment as if reflecting then said, "Oh! I like 'being a good girl' the best." Her sister did not wish her to think that she had said any thing extraordinary, she therefore did not praise her, but merely said, "I thought my dear that would be your choice."

July 10th

Eliza picked up a note from a young lady of the place,[8] inviting several little girls to spend the day with her.

Eliza: "Don't you think sister Rachel, that this shews that Miss C. R. is very fond of company?"

Rachel: "Perhaps it does my dear."

Eliza: "Do you think it is right for people to be so fond of company sister Rachel?"

Rachel: "Not too fond Eliza."

Eliza: "Well Sister Rachel, I think so too, and if I was Miss C. R. and had so much time, I would read a great many books, because that would do more good than having so much company."

On the same day, her sister had mislaid a letter which had been given her to read, but hearing it had been picked up, and restored to its owner, she sent to her apologizing for her carelessness, and begging to see the letter (as she had not before read it) again. Eliza who heard the message given, said to her sister, "Don't you think Sister Rachel it would be a good way, for you to punish yourself for being careless, by not sending for the letter again, that you want to read?"

July 14th

Eliza had heard, some time since, the game of four corners described, the rules of which are, that when bidden to hold the handkerchief you are to let it fall, but when told to let it go, it is to be held. She proposed playing it with her sister, after having tried it two or three times her sister said to her, "Eliza I do not think this is a very good play."

Eliza: "Why?"

Rachel: "I want you to think & tell me the reason, yourself." After considering a little she replied, "Oh I believe it is because it might teach me, not to mind what was said to me."

"This is Saturday," Eliza said this evening, "I think Saturday is a very bad day for me, I always get so tired, because I do not have any employment." [9]

August 20th

Eliza conjugating the verb "to clothe" asked how "clad" would be used.

Rachel: "You might say of a soldier, 'He was clad in armour.'"

Eliza: "Oh yes! & you could say of the moon 'She was clad in silver'—or of the Sun 'He was clad in gold.'"

Rachel asked her if she recollected why "he" was applied to the Sun & "she" to the moon. She answered, "O yes" & explained it with simple accuracy. It had been told to her some time in the preceding winter. Rachel asked if she knew how "durst" the imperfect of the verb to dare, would be used.

Eliza: "Yes I believe so, I say in *Ellen the Teacher* (a little book which she had been reading) [10] 'She durst not ask for a candle.'"

On the next day conjugating the verb "to write," in the passive voice, she said, "being written; yes, you could say, the letter being written, was put into the post office, I wish brother Samuel [11] would say so." She had written a little letter to him some time before, and promised that she would try to break herself of a trick of lolling about on the sopha, [12] of which he had often told her. It was to a reply to this *letter* that she now alluded, and she almost immediately added, "I think *it* was a very good way to break myself of a *bad habit*"—"What was [that] Eliza?" asked her sister.

Eliza: "Why to make that promise in my letter, you know you told me Sister

Rachel that you were afraid for me to make that promise for fear I should not be able to keep it, but I have, for I have never been on the sopha since."

Rachel: "But did you think of what I said of breaking your word?"

Eliza: "Yes, sometimes, but not so often as I did about my letter; I thought of *that,* whenever I was going to get on the sopha. Suppose sister Rachel, I try now to break myself of another bad habit, of speaking in a wrong tone of voice, maybe I could *do* that too."

September 1st

Eliza has been accustomed almost ever since she *could* speak, to tell of her own accord, of any fault she had committed. She has been also constantly sent by her other sisters to her sister Rachel with messages indicating the manner in which her different employments had been executed. From having sometimes to say the mortifying & unpleasant words, "I have been very inattentive" or "Sister Ellen [13] says I am too impatient" or "Sister Caroline, I am rather idle about my French," she has acquired a habit of hesitating & speaking when she delivers a message in a tone different from her natural one. Of this her sisters had frequently told her and she now thought of trying to correct it. Her sister Rachel wrote on the first page of her spelling book: "On Wednesday the 21st of August, Eliza began to break herself of a bad habit, of speaking in an unnatural tone of voice." Today is the 1st September and she has already in part succeeded, when she shall have entirely divested herself of this fault, it shall be noted in this faithful record, with the reward which it is in her sister's mind to bestow on her. That any is intended, she has, however, no idea. It will be far more beneficial to her to do well, for the sake of knowing that she does so, and to trust to her own approbation, and that of her friends for her reward, than that her mind should turn to any extrinsic advantage that might accrue to her. Still, as a memorial of the pleasure arising from successful exertion, a pleasure which she will deserve to have recalled to her mind, she shall have an *extrinsic* reward.

On Friday August 30th Eliza reading in *Sandford & Merton* [14] some account of the Spartans, her sister told her where they lived.

Eliza: "Yes, Mrs. Affable (the governess in "Misses Magazine") [15] says something about Greece, she says that the Greeks were bad people."

Rachel: "Not all the Greeks Eliza."

Eliza did not seem to recollect perfectly the circumstances to which she alluded, but continued: "I do not think Mrs. Affable taught *her children* well, she told them too many fairy tales: I think it would have been better if she had told them stories than tales; [16] true stories about sensible people, and then if they could not understand it, *as it was,* Mrs. Affable would know how *to say it,* so that they could understand it."

Rachel: "Don't you like to read the tales?"

Eliza: "Yes I like them very well, but I think true stories would be a great deal better."

I daily perceive the good effects of proper early instruction. Since Eliza was 3 years of age, I have frequently amused and instructed her with such little narratives as she could perfectly understand, a story on Friday night has been for two years her reward, for being a good girl during the week, a reward which she has seldom forfeited. Before that time, she generally had a little story at *night* after being good during the *day.* She was too young to look forward for a whole week. This has been by no means a hard task, for such simple incidents as were calculated to interest her, would readily present themselves to the mind, and when company or business interfered, it was but to represent to her how circumstances were, & she readily acquiesced in the necessity, & made herself happy in some other way. Thus she exercised reflection, & patient resignation, to an unavoidable evil. The same degree of self command, ennobled by disinterestedness, & considerate affection, she has often shewn when I appeared fatigued or at all indisposed. At such times she has repeatedly said to me, "If you please sister Rachel, not to tell me my story tonight, I would rather not hear it when you are tired." I have sometimes yielded to her with a kiss of approbation, but oftener said, "No, my dear, we should always endeavour to perform our promises, and I will now exert myself to give you pleasure, as you have been good, and deserved it. At some other time when *you* do not feel altogether inclined to do something which I wish, *you* will think of this, and exert yourself to give pleasure to *me.*" Other more obvious advantages I have found to arise from this mode of early instruction; the story of the evening might be adapted to the correction of some error observed during the day, it conveyed instructive hints capable of being improved as occasion offered, gave birth to new ideas, and by affording subject for frequent allusions, strengthened the impression intended to be made upon her, by subsequent advice or admonition, more than without such auxiliaries could have been hoped or expected. Trifles, in the abstract, may be readily comprehended by children at a very early age, but unless enforced and illustrated by familiar examples, the impression will not probably be of long continuance. Eliza when told of the charms of good humour, or of an obliging disposition, of the necessity of attention, or the good effects of perseverance, has been so much accustomed to connect with them, the character of some of her young imaginary friends, that it is not unusual with her to say, "That was like Rosamund," "Then I shall be like Frank," or "Delphine or Eugenia did so." [17]

It has always appeared to me, important to mark very plainly the distinction between what was true, & that which was only imaginary; and Eliza has always been particularly pleased & attentive, when I have said, "this is a true story." I have seldom ventured on those flights of fancy in which imaginary beings, fairies, genie, &c are introduced; when I have, it has been always with the precaution of prefacing it: "I am going to tell you rather a foolish story now, for it is about things which could never have happened, and I only tell it to amuse you." By this means, I now find the value of this kind of writing, is considerably lessened in her estimation, and in her remark on Mrs. Affable's mode of instruction, I could not but perceive that a plant had grown up, from the seed long since sown. I think the last story of this kind that I told her, was "Aladdin or the Wonderful Lamp"[18]—at least 17 or 18 months ago. Eliza, as may be supposed, looked upon me at first, as the *end,* of all the fund of instruction & entertainment which I conveyed to her: she often expressed surprise when I shewed her a book, & said, "It was in this, that I read such a story, which you liked so much." She became anxious to learn to read, and had no sooner conquered the first difficulties, & learned to read fluently, than she became quite as fond of it as I could wish her to be. On the 17th of August[19] she was seven years old, and I am well pleased to reflect on the improvement she has made during the past twelve month[s]. I must again regret that this record was not begun sooner, I might then have precisely ascertained what her progress has been. I will mark what is her present state of improvement with respect to her different occupations, that I may be better prepared for a similar examination, should we both be allowed life & health through another revolving year.

Eliza has read,

Mary & Her Cat[20]
Early Lessons, Miss Edgeworth[21]
Part of the *Parent's Assistant,* d[itt]o[22]
Elements of Morality translated from the German by M. Wolstonecraft[23]
Little Jack, Tho's Day[24]
Part of *The Looking Glass*[25]
Children in the Wood[26]
Blind Child[27]
Parts of *Evenings at Home*[28]
d[itt]o of *Robinson Crusoe*[29]
d[itt]o of *Children's Miscellany*[30]
Ellen the Teacher, Mrs. Hofland[31]
Early Lessons—in Continuation[32]
Tales for Children by M. J. Crabbe[33]
Part of *Tales of the Castle*[34]
Poems for Young Persons[35]
Part of *Sandford & Merton*[36]

ထော့ထော့ထော့

Several juvenile poems she has committed to memory, learning a few lines on one day in each week—Saturday.

ထော့ထော့ထော့

Writes—a very good large hand & reads writing without difficulty.

⋆⋆⋆⋆⋆⋆

Of French she knows several pages of nouns, which she pronounces & translates.

In arithmetic, she adds any numbers with facility & knows the multiplication Table well—She enumerates with little difficulty.

⋆⋆⋆⋆⋆⋆

In Geography, commenced in June, she knows the first principles, can find the latitude & longitude of places, & knows the boundaries, & chief cities, & rivers in Europe, these she has learned entirely from the map.

In Grammar, she understands the principles well, can tell with readiness any of the declinable parts of speech, comprehends the moods & tenses, & conjugates with facility, verbs either regular or irregular. This is the only part of grammar in which she has employed a book; the rest has been taught her by verbal instruction.

⋆⋆⋆⋆⋆⋆

In Music, for which she has always shewn great fondness, and in which she commenced taking lessons in January, having learned the notes last year; she plays:
"Little Bo Peep" [37]
"Mal Brook" [38]
2 Allegros
3 Waltzes
"Irish washerwoman" [39]
"Soldier's Joy"
"Minuet of St. Domingo"
"Dance of the Naiads"
Song in the "Spoiled child"
"Washington's March" [40]
"Allegro" by Pleyel [41]
Nicolai's "1st Sonata" & "Rondo Cotillion" [42]
Edelman's minuet. [43]

She sews plain work tolerably well, and has marked the large & small alphabet on a sampler.

The author of *Sandford & Merton* [44] is frequently rather incorrect, in the use of the relative pronoun "who," as, "the Lion who," "the Wolf who," "these two dogs who" &c. The first time Eliza met with one of these expressions, she stopped suddenly: "Well! the lion *who!* do pray sister R. rub out that *who,* and write *which.*" Her sister did so: but this happened to be an unfortunate page;

three times did the very same error occur, and each time was the aid of the pencil called in to rectify it, at last Eliza, laughed & exclaimed, "Why, Mr. Thomas Day, I do believe, that you never *did learn* grammar."

Harry Sandford one day walking in the fields is unmercifully beaten by Squire Chace, for refusing to tell which way a hare had run, which he had seen, and of which this gentleman was in pursuit. A few minutes after the Squire is thrown from his horse, and dragged along with his foot still entangled in the stirrup. Harry succeeds in an attempt to stop the horse, and thus saves the life of the person who had just before treated him with so much cruelty. Eliza paused at this passage, and said, "I think this was a very good punishment for Squire Chace, he must have felt so ashamed when he found that it was Harry, who had helped him, and that such a little boy, was so much better than he was." [45]

Eliza saw one day at the well, two old Negro women, a black boy (Robin), who was drawing water for them, and several dogs. "Look sister Julia," [46] said she, "there is *Jacob* drawing water for the *maidens;* and the dogs, you see, are *for* the sheep." [47]

Six or eight months since, Eliza read a story of Miss Edgeworth's, "Tarlton." [48] Loveit, one of the most conspicuous characters, is described as a very good natured boy, but of so yielding a temper, that to use Miss Edgeworth's expressive phrase, "he could never have the courage to say — no." A few evenings since, reading in the "Visit for a Week," [49] "the Excursion a moral tale," aloud for Eliza, her sister found a similar character delineated. The language of this book, tho' very good, is not adapted to the capacity of young children; Rachel, therefore, began to explain, in more simple terms, the account of Charles, which she had just read, and she was quickly convinced of Eliza's having imbibed a correct idea of the character portrayed, for, after listening attentively, she said, "Yes, Charles was just like Loveit."

Friday September 13th

Eliza came as usual in the middle of the day to say her grammar lesson &c, but was rather heedless, and her sister after trying several times to fix her attention, without success, said, "Eliza, you let your thoughts wander so much, that I cannot hear you your lesson; I am very sorry to find you so heedless today, but it is not worth while for me to ask you any thing more, now, because until you can *think* of what I say to you, my questions will only confuse, instead of instructing you. Go, and I will try this evening, if you can attend, and say a good lesson." Eliza looked very much mortified and went down stairs; as she entered her mamma's room, her mamma met her, and said, "here Eliza is a cake I have made for you." "Thank you mamma, but I *expect* I do not deserve it now, if you please mamma, to put it away till I do," [said Eliza].

All the afternoon Eliza mentioned not a word of the cake to her sister; in the evening she came again to say her lesson, seemed to exert herself to attend, & said a part well, the rest less correctly than usual. When it was finished, her sister said, "you know Eliza this is Friday night, and I always read to you, or tell you a story, on that night, when you are a good attentive little girl; what is to be done tonight?"

"Why, Sister Rachel, I believe I must go without the story."

Rachel: "But that would not be exactly fair, you have said your lessons well, all the week until today, and you have been a good girl; so if I do not read for you, the punishment will not be in proportion to the fault. You know what I mean by 'in proportion'?"

Eliza: "You mean, one will not be like the other, one will be *more* than the other."

Rachel: "Yes, the punishment will be greater than the fault deserves. So how shall we manage to make them equal?"

Eliza: "I don't know."

Rachel: "Suppose papa employed a man to work for him, and promised to pay him 5 dollars at the end of the week if he worked industriously for 5 days. The man worked very diligently four days, but not so well on the fifth, ought he not to be paid any thing?"

Eliza: "Yes I think he ought to be paid four dollars for the four days that he worked, and not any for the fifth. O yes, and sister Rachel it would be right, would it not, for you to read a *part* of a story for me instead of a whole one, that would be in proportion?"

Rachel: "Yes, Eliza, that would be *right* and as I read 25 pages for you last Friday night, I will just take out as many pages, as one night's reward would come to. You know how many fives are in twenty five?" (after a moment's consideration)

Eliza: "Yes, five times five, are twenty five."

Rachel: "Then I will just take five pages away, and you know how many will be left?"

Eliza: "Yes, twenty."

Eliza then told her sister of the cake which her mamma had made her, and asked if she might have it then. Her sister told her, yes, that she deserved to have it, because she had been a good girl, in not taking it after being heedless, at the time her mamma first gave it to her: and that besides the cake she had earned a kiss, which her sister gave her.

It happened that the conclusion of the twenty pages to be read this night, occurred in the most interesting part of the story.

Eliza: "O sister Rachel—if you please to read only *one* page more."

Rachel: "You know Eliza that I do not read the other five pages, because I want you to remember *another time,* if you are inclined to be heedless, that your having been so *now,* deprived you of a part of your pleasure; and thinking of that, may make you more attentive. But I will leave it to yourself; if you now wish it, I will read a page more?"

Eliza: "No. Maybe I had better do without it; so, good night sister Rachel."

Mr. LaTaste[50] has for some time had a dancing school here, and as Eliza, tho' not a scholar, is allowed to caper about, and amuse herself in the dancing room on Saturday afternoon, she no longer thinks that "Saturday is a very bad day for her."

Sunday, September 22

Yesterday, Saturday, September 21, Rachel had occasion to go down town[51] & call at several places in the afternoon. While she was dressing, she said, "Eliza will you go down with me this afternoon, or go into the dancing room?"

Eliza: "I like to walk down town very much, but then, when I think how all the young ladies, are dancing in the school room, I want to be with *them*. If it was this morning I would rather go down town, because then, I could go there and dance too."

Rachel: "Yes, but it is not this morning, and you cannot do both, so you must decide which you would rather do."

Eliza: "Then sister Rachel, I will stay."

Rachel: "But there is one thing we have not thought of; if you stay, I shall have to go down alone."

Eliza: "O! sister Rachel, I did not think of that, I would rather go."

Rachel: "No, my dear, I do not wish you to go, on that account, I only wanted to remind you, of all that was to be considered."

Eliza: "But Sister Rachel, I would a great deal rather go, *for the pleasure of your company and the pleasure of obliging you, will be a* great deal greater pleasure, than to go into the dancing room."

This was said with an artless earnestness which shewed that it came from the heart, and proved, (if proof were wanting,) that it is *there,* that *true* politeness holds her seat. A child who had been taught to make polite, set speeches, might have used the same *words,* but how different would have been the expression! Eliza accompanied her sister, enjoyed her walk, and returned in time to hold her sister Ellen's hand while she danced her favorite cotillion.[52]

September 25th

On the 25th of September I had the pleasure of receiving a reply to a letter written some time since to Miss Edgeworth.[53] My parents, brothers & sisters, participated in my gratification, and the animation of every countenance, as well as the expressions of pleasure which flowed from every tongue, shewed Eliza who was present, that something extraordinary, & very agreeable had occurred. For several reasons I did not wish this little event, agreeable as it was in itself, to be generally known, and had cautioned my brothers & sisters against mentioning it. Eliza looked at me, but did not ask a question. I called her to me & took her in my lap. "Eliza, you see we are all very much pleased, do you know why?"

Eliza: "No, only I believe it is about something that was in that letter."

Rachel: "Yes, but it is a secret: I will tell it to you tho', if you think you can keep it; but I must first explain to you what is *meant* by *keeping a secret.* A secret means something which is not to be told to any body without permission from the person who tells it to you. If it comes into your mind ever so often, you are still to remember that you are not to speak of it, and that if you do, you break the promise that you have made to *keep* the *secret;* and you do not deserve to be trusted again. Now if you think that you will be able to keep from mentioning it to any of your companions when you are playing with them, or speaking of it at all, I will tell you *my secret."*

Eliza: "Sister Rachel, I would not tell it on purpose, but maybe you had better not tell me, because maybe, I might forget."

Her sister gave her a kiss and told her she was a very prudent little girl. To think of this sometimes when she was playing with her little companions, and that when she thought she could *keep from forgetting,* she should hear the secret. About a fortnight after Eliza said to Rachel, "Sister Rachel, will you tell me that secret now, I have thought of it very often, and I think I shall remember not to tell it." Her sister complied with her request, & was much amused by Eliza's expressions of wonder that the very same Miss Edgeworth who wrote *Practical Education*[54] which lay on the drawers, and *The Parent's Assistant,*[55] should have written a letter to sister Rachel & that it should come so far, all the way from Ireland! That this was her very name, that she wrote her-self! "Why sister Rachel, I can hardly think of it!"

October 9th

In page 10[56] is mentioned my intention of bestowing a reward on Eliza should she again persevere in endeavouring to overcome a bad habit. She has ever since taken great pains to correct the fault I then told her of, which was speaking sometimes in a disagreeable, and not natural tone. Her other sisters have observed her & they agree with me in thinking that she has almost entirely succeeded. On Wednesday October 9th I said to her, "Eliza I am very glad to see that you have taken pains to cure yourself of that silly tone, when you deliver a message & I am going to reward you for it. I thought, at the time I told you to try to break yourself of it, that I would reward you, if you persevered, tho' I did not tell you so then."

Eliza: "I know the reason I believe, sister Rachel, why you did not tell me of it then: it would have seemed as if I had tried to do what you told me only get the reward, and I am glad you did not *promise* it to me."

Eliza was much pleased to find that her reward was a little terrestrial Globe, inclosed in a case, the lining of which represented the Celestial. Her papa, had a few days before, given her a little atlas, and she said they would both be very useful to her. I think they will, for she is very attentive to her lessons in Geography, and remembers well all that her brother[57] is so good as to tell her.

October 10th

Eliza met with the word "variegated," and asked the meaning; her sister told her it meant, of more than one colour.

Eliza: "Are not roses sometimes called variegated roses? I believe I heard some body call one so last summer."

Rachel: "Yes, it was a rose with leaves striped with white & red."

Eliza: "I have often thought if some rose was not called '*a blushing rose,*' if it did not grow deeper & deeper when any thing touched it."

Eliza said one day to her sister Julia, "Sister Julia, the Sun is not a person."

Julia: "No, why do you say that?"

Eliza: "Well then can the sun *know* any thing, you know I say every morning in my prayers, 'My God who makes the Sun to *know.*'"[58]

Friday, October 25th

Eliza came to her sister Rachel looking very melancholy, and taking her hand begged she would go in the other room, for she had something to tell her. Rachel went. Eliza began, "Sister Rachel, Augustus[59] is angry with me," & burst into tears.

Rachel: "What is he angry with you about Eliza?"

Eliza: "I did not do any thing to make him angry, but when I was going to say my repetition in Geography, he was standing by me & I asked brother Solomon[60] to let him say with me, and brother Solomon asked him where the Philippine Islands were & he answered wrong, & brother Solomon told him he had better look in the map and he would see he was mistaken. And then I shewed him in the map that he was thinking of the *Molucca* Islands, instead of the *Philippine,* when he said they lay east of Borneo; and then, (crying again,) he said I was proud, and was so angry with me. But I did not say so because I was proud, for I know it was not any thing to proud of, just to know my lesson, and I told Augustus so, and so did brother Solomon. But Augustus would not stay with me any more, and he went and stood by the window. And as soon as I had finished my lesson I went to him, and asked him if he pleased not to be angry with me any longer, but he told me to go away, and I have been so uneasy ever since."

Rachel: "My dear, Augustus is too hasty, and he was wrong, but when I tell him how unhappy he has made you, & that his unkindness made you cry, I know he will feel sorry, & he will know he was wrong & will not be angry with you any longer."

Eliza: "But sister Rachel if you please not to be angry with Augustus, I did not tell you, to tell tales on him, or for you to be angry with him."

Rachel: "I know my dear you did not, you only told me because you always tell me all your little pleasures, & little troubles. I am going now to speak to Augustus and make you good friends again."

Eliza: "You can't make *me* good friends, because I have not been angry with Augustus, and I have been friends with him all the time."

Rachel: "Then I will make him *friends* with you."

Rachel spoke to Augustus, and he looked sorry when she told him how much he had distressed Eliza, but he could not be persuaded to go & tell her so. Just then she came in & when her sister told her that Augustus was sorry for his fault, she went up to him, & took his hand, which Augustus gave, tho' with a little reluctance, & he told her that he was not angry with her. Augustus has a good heart, & after his passion is over he is sorry for having done wrong, but he is not easily convinced that the shame lies in committing & not in repairing an error; his expressions of regret, were not therefore on this occasion, quite so open & cordial, as they ought to have been. As soon as this affair was settled Rachel took the book in which she had promised to read on that evening for Eliza, and accompanied by her, went into their mother's room. Scarcely had she read a sentence before Eliza said, "if you please Sister Rachel let me call Augustus, he will like to hear this story."

Rachel: "I did not intend to let Augustus hear the story tonight, but as you are a very good girl, I will indulge you by letting you call him." Eliza ran from Augustus, who was more sorry when he saw how kind she was to him, and they passed the evening very pleasantly together.

Some time ago Eliza read in *Sandford & Merton,* of Tommy's seeing a poor ragged boy, who told him that he could not sometimes get bread enough to eat. Tommy ran to Mr. Barlow's and got a suit of his own clothes, & a loaf of bread, and gave to him.[61] Eliza stopped here, & said, "was it right sister Rachel for him to take the loaf of bread without asking Mr. Barlow?"

October 27th

Last evening October 26, she read that a Robin having flown into Tommy's room in winter, he ran to Mr. Barlow, and asked if he might go & get some crumbs of bread and feed it. "Ah!" said she, "Tommy has learned better, since he took the loaf of bread without asking." This little bird became quite sociable with Tommy, & both he & Eliza were much attached to it, when it unfortunately fell into the power of a merciless cat, which destroyed it without pity. Rachel asked Eliza what ought to be done to the cat.

Eliza: "Not any thing, but let it go."

Rachel: "But why ought it not to be punished for eating the poor little Robin?"

Eliza hesitated a moment, and then said, "because the cat did not know any better."

The same argument is made use of, in both instances, a little below in the book; but the question was put to her in the latter, & the observation made, in the former instance immediately after the circumstance was read which gave rise to them.

December [no date]

Eliza's memory is very good as to retaining, but she has often shewn herself deficient in that useful talent styled "recollective memory." When circumstances were recalled to her mind she knew them well, but when it depended upon herself to think of something at a particular time, it was generally forgotten or neglected. Her sister desirous to conquer this defect resolved to give her motives for recollection which might occasionally rouse her dormant powers. Rachel happened to be reading the life of Peter the Great,[62] & was one afternoon speaking to her brother Solomon of his uncommon character, & singular marriage. Eliza became interested, and begged to be told something about Peter the Great. "If you will remind me of it tonight, just before you go to bed, I will tell you what you want to know." Eliza ate her supper, talked & played: bed time came—Peter was not thought of. Her sister went into the room where she was undressing, thinking thus to remind her of him, but recollection did not come. When Eliza had been in bed about half an hour, she called to beg her sister (who was in the next room) [if she] would tell her about "Peter's marriage."

Rachel: "No Eliza, you know I promised to tell you, if you reminded me of it, *before* you went to bed. Now, you must wait till tomorrow evening, if you recollect at the right time *then,* I will tell you, but not else."

Eliza was mortified at having forgotten, and disappointed at not hearing *the story.* These two causes combined had a greater effect upon her *temper,* than had ever shewn itself before. She fretted and said that "if every thing must depend upon her remembering, she never should have any pleasure." "That she *had* thought of it in the *evening,* if she did not, just at the very moment." Her sister endeavored to reason with her on the necessity there was, of learning to think of things in proper time; and to convince her, that when *she* had not fulfilled *her* part of the engagement, it was quite unreasonable to wish or expect another to do *even more,* than was promised. Eliza for the first time, would not *listen to reason;* she continued to murmur, and her sister who had left her employment to go & talk to her, now returned to the next room. A door which communicated from one room to the other stood open, & Eliza's complaints were plainly heard. Rachel shut the door telling Eliza that it must remain closed, for that no one liked to be disturbed by murmuring & ill humour. For some time the door remained closed, at length Eliza called and begged it might be opened, she was now still & her request was granted. A little while after, her sister Ellen happened to go into the chamber; she found Eliza crying softly, with her face turned to the pillow. She asked, "why do you cry Eliza?"

Eliza: "Because I know I have behaved wrong, & I want to tell sister Rachel so."

Ellen returned with a petition that Rachel would go, & set Eliza's heart at rest. Rachel did so, & Eliza then told her, that when the door was shut, she left off fretting, & prayed to God to make her a better girl. Rachel told her that she must remember *this night,* and as she found she did not feel happy, when she was not good, that she must exert herself to be good, & then if she prayed to God, he would assist her. Eliza then received a kiss for good night, and was asleep in a few minutes. The next day she was good, and as she remembered to ask at the appointed hour, in the evening, she was gratified by hearing some account of Peter the Great.

This was not an unsuccessful experiment, but a *single* experiment will not purchase recollective memory.

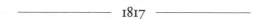

1817

February 9th

Two months have passed since the occurrence just related took place, and now I cannot begin a new page with pleasure, for the observations I have since made on Eliza's habits, and conduct, have too frequently been sources of uneasiness. It is said that after 7, the age of infancy ceases, and the character & propensities of children begin gradually to unfold themselves. It is this reflection that has increased my anxiety, on viewing the errors which in the last few months have shewn themselves. May Heaven grant to this beloved child a continuance of those amiable dispositions, which blessed her infancy, and promised so fair a progression.

Eliza has never been an active child, but what used to seem steadiness, now seems to shew a want of animation. When her sisters go to walk, she begs to stay behind, and if not permitted to do so, walks slowly at their side. In order to induce her to run & play in the open air, one or two of her little companions generally accompanied her, but even then, tho' she would run with them when bid to do so, it was evident that she obeyed rather from duty than inclination. Looking mean time pale, and thin, and frequently complaining, her sister thought it would be good exercise, to jump the rope for some time, regularly every day. In a few minutes she would complain of being tired, & her sister determined to give her a certain number of times to jump, hoping both to give her an idea of regularity, and to oblige her by indirect means, to take more exercise. She had learned to jump with some degree of ease & dexterity, so that she could accomplish her 600 turns of the rope in about a quarter of an hour. One morning her sister was above stairs when she heard Eliza counting & jumping in the passage below. "Forty nine, *fifty, sixty* one," Rachel listened, thinking it had been a mistake, or that she had not heard rightly—"sixty nine, *seventy, eighty* one"—it could not be doubted. She called, "Eliza how are you counting?"

Eliza: "Right, was not I sister Rachel?"

Rachel: "Right Eliza! what when you passed from seventy to eighty one?"

Eliza: "Did I sister Rachel?"

Rachel: "Yes Eliza, you must *know* you did, for it was done more than once, I could not believe at first, that I heard rightly."

When Rachel went down stairs she told Eliza how very sorry she was to find her capable of trying to impose, and how wicked it is to say we *have* done any thing, when in truth we have not. Eliza said, she did not know it was wrong to pass over the tens in counting, and her sister willing rather to believe that the child had not a clear idea of the power of numbers, than that she had deliberately formed a plan to deceive, contented herself with telling her never to count in that manner again, reminding her also that exercise was necessary for her health, & that by thus depriving herself of it, she was doing herself harm in another way, as well as acting wrong. Finding *after* this, that she was still done jumping in a very short space of time, when she declared that she had counted through the whole hundred her sister thought that she possibly forgot the number of hundreds. She therefore stuck six pins in Eliza's needle case, & told her whenever she went to jump, to take this with her, & to take out one pin at every hundred, & lay it on the chair, then when all the pins were out she might be sure she had jumped 600. Eliza *says* she has done so since, and her sister hopes she may believe, tho' it has not been in her power to observe her. Yes, I fain would hope so, but more than once since has my heart been pained by similar appearances of duplicity. Eliza has told her sister Ellen that she had practiced *all* her lessons when she had not, she has told me *falsely,* that she had studied her multiplication table, which she knows, but is required to look over once forwards, & once backwards every day. Each time she has been spoken to, & each time we hoped would be the last, that she would be censured for such a mean, and wicked propensity; but last night, I was again shocked and afflicted by discovering a repetition of the same offense. Some time since I mentioned, that on one day in the week, Eliza learned by rote a few lines of poetry. In order to occupy a part of Saturday morning, as well as to keep her from forgetting, I bade Eliza read over the little poems she had before learned, after she knew her two new verses. Yesterday February 8th when I entered the room to breakfast Eliza said, "Sister Rachel, I have been over my verses & learned my new ones too." Rachel: "Have you!—why you have been very industrious indeed." In the evening when Rachel was at leisure she called Eliza, "Now come & let me hear your verses." The 8 new lines she knew pretty well; her sister then desired her to repeat one that she had learned some time before. She began but stammered and did not repeat with confidence, as if she knew it to be fresh in her memory.

Rachel: "How do you go over your verses Eliza, that you do not remember them better?"

Eliza: "Why, I go over one verse a great many times, and—"

Rachel: "No Eliza that is impossible, but do you go over them once?"

Eliza: "Yes, Sister Rachel."

Rachel: "Have you been over every one today?"

Eliza looked down & made no answer.

Rachel: "You have *not,* tell me then which of them, you *have* been over."

Eliza stretched out her hand to take the book.

Rachel: "No, you can tell me without looking."

Eliza hesitated.

Rachel: "Have you been over the Bird's nest?" [63]

Eliza: "No."

Rachel: "My Mother?" [64]

Eliza: "No."

Rachel: "Employment?" [65]

Eliza: "No."

Rachel: "Have you been over *any* but your new lines?"

Eliza hung her head and did not speak.

Rachel: "Get up out of my lap, Eliza; so, the very first words you said to me, when I came *in* this morning was to tell me a falsehood." Eliza looked very pale, her countenance was almost agonized. Her sister's heart was so too, but with a calm & resolute tone, she bade two little girls who had been waiting to play with Eliza, to go, that they must not play with Eliza that afternoon. "When you are bad I do not let Eliza play with you, & now she is bad, you must not play with her." Soon after this her sister left the room, on entering not long after, Eliza was seated with the volume of poems in hand, reading them. This child has no sullenness in her disposition. I have sometimes feared that she was deficient in sensibility, but I am perhaps deceived by my anxieties and wishes. After Eliza & Emma[66] had been put to bed their sister went again into the room; she went to their bed, kissed Emma & bade her good night, but took no notice of Eliza, who always when good, receives the first kiss. She lay quite still, but soon after when Emma began to talk & play with her, she answered, & seemed willing to play, but her sister said: "No Emma, you must not play with sister Eliza tonight, she is not a good girl." Both then were quiet.

In the morning when Eliza came into the breakfast room, she seemed not to know whether she might speak to her sister, who looking seriously at her said, "Good morning Eliza." "Good morning, sister Rachel." After breakfast Rachel called Eliza to bring her slate, and do two sums, which indisposition had prevented her doing on Thursday & Friday. She took particular pains to do them both—they were right the first time. Eliza then said, "Sister Rachel, if you please to let me say my verses now."

Rachel: "Why, Eliza?"

Eliza: "Because I did not say them yesterday."

Rachel: "No Eliza, I like you to repeat your verses, & to say them *well,* but it is not, for not saying your verses that I am displeased with you, but for telling me an untruth about them. Did you see what I wrote last night in your list book?" (This is a little book in which Eliza's daily lessons & her conduct are written, and I had put down what Eliza's fault was, adding "God does not love people who tell *lies,* nor will any one have confidence in them." I said *people,* lest she should imbibe the idea that this license was forbidden to children only, and I used the term *Lies,* because I wished the *term* to represent the *vice* & be as abhorrent as possible.)

"Yes," said Eliza, "I saw it."

Rachel: "Well you see then the inconvenience you have brought on yourself; that no one can now put confidence in what you say. I *saw* you reading your poems yesterday, but I do not know whether you went over all."

Eliza: "No, I did not."

Rachel: "Give me the book, I will divide them, so that you may not have so many to read at one time as to tire you, & induce you to tell me a falsehood. If you found you had too much to do, you should have told me so, & I would have given you less. I shall request mamma to be so good as to hear you read what I have marked for you, each Saturday morning, and when *she* tells me you have learned them, I shall know it is so. Is mamma in here when you look over the multiplication table every day?"

Eliza: "Sometimes mamma, & sometimes sister Julia."

Rachel: "I must then in future apply to them, to know when you have studied that too, I do not wish to give you an opportunity of deceiving me, and it will now be a long time before any of us can believe what *you* say, unless some one who *always* tells [the] *truth,* assures us that *they know* what you say, to be so. But now I think of it, you were playing with P. & R. when I came in, why did you play with them, till you had been told you *might* do so?"

Eliza: "We had just begun, & I *thought* I would ask you, before I played with them."

Rachel: "Perhaps so, Eliza."

Eliza: "Yes, Sister, I *did think* so."

Rachel: "Well, Eliza, as I said before, *perhaps* you *did* but as I told you, I cannot be *certain* that you speak the truth. But you may go now & play with the children, I do not want you to *promise* me that you will *never* tell me another falsehood—because you cannot promise *certainly* whether you will or not. I *hope* you will not, & as you see the great disadvantage it is, not to speak truth; as well as know it to be a crime, that you will not commit the same fault again."

Tho' it has given me much pain to write this account, yet I have been particular in narrating it, for I wish as I continue to observe the effect produced, to be enabled to recur to the cause which produced it, I shall then be the better able to decide on the course which it will be best to adopt, for checking this, as well as other errors, which may hereafter appear.

What must the cares & anxieties of a mother be, when those of a sister are so very sensibly felt! Should this child of my hopes & wishes, ever read these pages, may she shrink from this early trait of deliberate falsehood, and congratulate herself that the pain she today felt, shall have rendered yesterdays untruth the very last.

February 16

Nothing of importance has occurred this week—except on Tuesday, two little instances of equivocation. I threatened to punish a repetition of the fault, but advised a careful attention to what she said, lest Eliza should unguardedly be guilty of saying what was not *exactly* the truth.

Shewed Eliza this morning, some little experiments with a magnet, which she understood very well, & was much pleased with the discovery, that only contrary poles attract each other.

Tuesday, February 18th

Eliza as part of her grammar lesson was examining the different substantives in Mr. Murray's[67] first table of Etymological parsing. She met with "An Alexander." "An Alexander!" she repeated, "why how does that mean? that there *is* more than one?" Her sister explained the term, & Eliza said without difficulty, that used in that manner it must be a common, instead of a proper substantive. Repeated explanations have often been found necessary, to give other children a clear idea of the effect of the article in such expressions, it was therefore the more pleasing to see that she readily conceived it correctly.

"And only see sister Rachel; Mr. Murray has placed 'A Conqueror' next to 'an Alexander,' and here next to 'the Sun,' is, 'the Planets.'" (She had inquired what was meant by the planets a few days before.) She then busied herself in discovering the resemblances & oppositions which occur throughout the table.

February 20th

Eliza asked the meaning of the word *serene;* her sister explained it, & asked her if she did not think it was a pretty word; she said it was. "And don't you think sister Rachel, that any word with *S* in it always looks smiling? No, not *sour,* sour don't look smiling, but when you see *smile* written, how smiling it looks!"

February 23rd

Eliza had a little dew plant given her at the beginning of the winter, which began to sprout very prettily and had two or three new leaves on it. Eliza was charged with the care of this plant and required to attend to having it set out every morning when the weather was not too cold, & taken in at night. It too often happened that when evening came, Eliza had to be reminded of her plant, or that her brother George[68] took it in for her, when he would ask the next morning at breakfast, "Eliza, who took care of my plant last night?" at last one day[69] her sister went to look at it & found it quite withered, and dead.

Rachel: "Oh, Eliza! see, your dew plant is quite dead!"

Eliza: "Is it, sister Rachel?"

"Why," said brother Solomon, "has not Eliza told you that it was left out the night before last?"

Rachel: "No, I have not heard any thing of it."

Solomon: "I am sorry for that, for I spoke to Eliza about it early yesterday morning, and told her how careless it was, especially as you had so often reminded her to take care of it."

Rachel: "Why did you not tell me of it Eliza, when I came in, to breakfast."

She hesitated and then said, with her head hanging down, "Because I thought you would be angry with me."

Rachel: "But did not you know I should be more displeased with you for concealing it? Tell me, which is the greatest fault, heedlessness or deceit?"

"Heedlessness," answered the child.

Rachel: "Why surely you do not know the meaning of the words; heedlessness, means want of thought or of care, deceit, is trying to make people believe that we are better than we are, it is false, like lying."

Eliza, without raising her eyes: "I think deceit is the worst."

Rachel: "You have been guilty of *both* these faults instead of one; had you told me immediately of your plant having been left out, I should have blamed & perhaps punished you for carelessness, but I should have thought well of you & been pleased at your telling me *the truth* at once. But what can I say to you now, or how can I put any confidence in you? When I asked you last night too, whether you had been quite a good girl, you told me, yes, you had. You must surely have recollected this, at that very time, & could you bear for me to kiss you and call you a good girl, when *you knew* you did not deserve it?" Her sister said no more. Eliza seemed rather ashamed than sorry and a few minutes afterwards she seated herself & took a book to read. Such an appearance of indifference or something so nearly resembling it pierced me to the heart, I hardly had spirits to pursue my ordinary avocations. I could not trust myself to speak to her immediately again, but I begged her sister Ellen to converse with her the next morning, and question her about it in an unrestrained manner; she did so, & Eliza then told her she had thought of it several times, but the fear of my anger prevented her telling me. Ellen used much the same arguments that I had before done, and when Eliza appeared to understand & be convinced of their truth, told her how unhappy I had been made, by her bad conduct, and advised her if she really was sorry for it, to tell me so.

Eliza: "Had I not better tell sister Rachel at the same time, that you reminded me to do it?"

Ellen: "Think of that for yourself Eliza, & when you have told me *your* opinion, I will tell you mine." Eliza after a little reflection, said she thought *that* would be the right way, & her sister Ellen concurred with her in opinion.

April 10th

Eliza after hearing the first rule of Syntax, was told to try to correct the exercise under it. "50 pounds of wheat contains 40 pounds of flour." She found no difficulty in discovering & rectifying the error, & without any allusion to the word wheat which stood next the verb, said the reason it was wrong was that *pounds* was plural & *contains,* singular. In the sentence, "What avails the best sentiments &c," I supposed the interrogative form might perplex her, but she discovered & pointed out the impropriety immediately. The next sentence, "Thou should love thy neighbour &c" which I thought would be more evident, she found less easy: she did not perceive the form of the auxiliary to be wrong, & had to conjugate the verb, before she could discover the impropriety. On the same day reading "Instructive Rambles,"[70] she smiled on finding it observed of "Mary," that she found study irksome: on being asked why she smiled, she said, "Because Mary was so different from me."

April 13th

Since the occurrence on the 23d of February, I have but once had occasion to remark, any tendency to prevaricate and that, not in a serious degree. She seems even impatient to acquaint me with any fault she may have committed lest it should slip her memory, & I have again hopes of fixing firmly in her little, but expanding mind, the principles of truth & candour. I have found the plan of dividing Eliza's poems into separate parts, a very good one; she continues learning new ones, and by reviewing in regular succession each week a *small* part of those she had learned before, she continues to retain, & is amused, instead of being fatigued, by the employment. I frequently call for the exertion of her recollective faculties, and sometimes with success. She has a little blank book in which her daily lessons & conduct are set down. On the 28th of March no lines being ruled for the next week, I told Eliza, that if she thought of reminding me the next day, I would rule them, but if she forget it, no lessons would be set down for her, the next week. We were near a window when I spoke. Eliza thought a moment, & then said, "Oh, I'll be sure to remember it."

Rachel: "How do you *know* that Eliza, when you so often forget?"

Eliza: "I can't tell you now, but I know, I've got a good way to remember." The next day came & tho' Eliza was at play with some of her little companions, the list was punctually remembered.

Rachel: "Well Eliza, what was your good way?"

Eliza: "Why my wall flower was standing on the shelf by the window, and when I looked, I knew I had to think of watering that, & I thought every time *that* came into my head, I would think of my list, and I have thought of it a good many times today."

I was pleased with the invention of this little instance of *artificial memory*. The *fall of the dew* plant too, has had a good effect, for it has made Eliza very careful of her wall flower, and tho' the season does not now require it, she constantly asks, when there is any change of weather, to have it taken in at night.

I gave Eliza some time since one of her little poems to learn, addressed to a little girl who has told an untruth. It begins "And has my darling told a lie?"[71] "Sister Rachel," said Eliza, "do you think her mother ought to have said *darling* then!" In another part it says,

> "Tell me you're sorry, and will try
> To act the better by & bye, &c"

Eliza observed this, and said, "but maybe she might *say* she was sorry, when she was not, could not that line be altered sister Rachel?" Rachel thought it might with advantage, and accordingly made it:

> "Be *truly sorry,* and then try."

Thursday, April 17th

When I was setting down Eliza's day's lessons &c I asked about her work.

Eliza: "I must tell you about that *myself* today, sister Rachel, for nobody was with me when I was at my work, mamma & sister Julia were both out, but I think sister Rachel I was not quite diligent enough I know I was not so diligent as I am every day."

Rachel: "Well I shall put down your work not very diligent; but you are a candid little girl, & for that I must give you a kiss."

Eliza had for some months been learning a little of French, but about 6 weeks ago she shewed some impatience while learning her lessons, and was unwilling to go over a verb often enough to know the conjugation. Her sister Caroline spoke to her of her conduct, & receiving an answer which she thought improper, would not hear her the lesson, & wrote a note to Rachel mentioning the reason of it. Rachel blamed Eliza, then fastening the note into the book containing her list of lessons, told her that she should request her sister Caroline not to let her say any more French lessons till she had more good sense & more patience, for that till then her lessons could be of no use to her. She said she would rather go on with them, but Rachel told her no, that it was not worth while then; but that when she thought she should take pleasure in being attentive to her lessons, perhaps sister Caroline would be so good as to begin to instruct her again. No more said on the subject, till in the course of the last week Eliza came to her sister & told her she had finished all her morning's employments, then asked her to give her a little piece of paper & a pen. She wrote the little note which is inserted here,[72] and after folding it up, asked her sister to read it when she was not busy. It contains a request to begin French again. Her sister Rachel told her she must give the note to sister Caroline, & see if she would be so kind as to teach her; reminding her at the same time, that she would have a great many hard lessons to learn before she could be able to read French books, or write French letters, & that she could not learn to conjugate verbs without patience. She said she knew all that, but that she would be very patient & attentive. Her sister Caroline said she would again begin to instruct her, and the day after tomorrow she will say a French lesson.

April 20th

Yesterday April the 19th some one used the expression an opaque body. I asked Eliza if she knew the meaning of opaque, which I had told her some time before. She replied "any thing that you can see through."

Rachel: "Is what you can see through, opaque?"

Eliza: "No, sister Rachel, any thing thick."

Her sister now imagined that her meaning was right tho' improperly expressed, till Eliza said immediately after, "I do not know the meaning of opaque, I only said *thick* because I saw every body laugh when I said it meant what you could see through, & then I said the other way." Her sister was pleased with her candour, & every body thought it better, than even remembering the meaning of opaque.

A few minutes after this Eliza & Emma were told to go to bed, & tho' it was earlier than Eliza's usual bed time, & she looked as if she wished to sit up a little longer, she bade every one good night, and went immediately. A gentleman in company had at this moment prepared the petal of a large purple flag to examine with his microscope. It had a most brilliant & beautiful appearance, & little Emma hearing from the adjoining room, many exclamations of wonder & delight, ran in the parlour again, & begged to look at the beautiful thing. After some time when every one had examined it, Rachel went in the next room & asked Eliza, why she had not come when Emma did?

Eliza: "I thought you would not be pleased sister Rachel, if I came out after you had told me to come to bed."

Rachel told her, she had hoped that was the reason, & was pleased to find it to be so, but that as she had been so good a girl she should not be denied the pleasure of seeing the beautiful flower. After looking at & admiring it, she again kissed her sister & retired to rest.

Thursday April 24th

Eliza was asked by her brother at dinner if she would be helped to some chicken, there was but a small dish of it on the table, as it is a season when fowls are scarce, and that had been cooked on his account because he was not well.[73] Eliza thanked him, but said she did not want any. He smiled and asked her if she refused because she saw sister Rachel do so? She said, no, that was not the reason. "I am glad," said Rachel, "to see that Eliza is so considerate, I think she acts very properly." After dinner Eliza came to her sister, & said, "What was that you said about me just now sister Rachel, what made you say I was considerate?"

Rachel: "Because you did not take any chicken when you saw there was not plenty for every body & knew that brother Solomon was not well, & could not eat other things."

Eliza: "No, sister Rachel, I did not think of that, I only did not take it because I did not want any."

Rachel stroked her head & said, "you are right my dear, not to take praise which you do not deserve, and now you get some that you *do* deserve, for being a good candid little girl."

Saturday, April 26th

Eliza in repeating her verses met with the words *join,* & recline, as terminating words which she disapproved, she said she did not know how they could be *put* for a rhyme. In another part "But hark from the lowlands what sounds do I hear?

> The voices of pleasure so gay;
> The merry young haymakers cheerfully bear,
> The heat of the hot summer's day." [74]

She said she thought there ought to be some more words, that after it asked the question it just went on to tell what the hay-makers did without answering it. Her sister explained to her that it meant, "It is the merry young hay-makers who &c."

In the evening her sister was reading for her part of the story of Aladdin in the *Arabian [N]ights Entertainments.* It amused her very much, but after hearing the extravagant description of the procession of slaves, she said, "How in the world sister Rachel, could anybody think of writing so much *stuff.*"

When her sister left off reading, Julia asked Eliza how she liked the story? She said, "very much indeed."

Julia: "Which do you like best, that or Miss Edgeworth's tales?"

Eliza: "I don't know *which* you mean."

Rachel: "'The Little Merchants' for instance." [75]

Eliza: "Oh, I like 'The Little Merchants' best."

Rachel: "Why?"

Eliza: "Because that is the prettiest."

Rachel: "That is not a good reason, what do you mean, by *the prettiest,* you said you like Aladdin, *very much indeed.*"

Eliza: "Yes, but I like 'The Little Merchants' better because I think that has more *sense* in it."

Rachel: "That is a very good reason; it *has* more sense in it, & more truth too, therefore it deserves to be preferred."

April 30th

Eliza passing the pronoun "*I*" said, "I don't think it ought to be the *first* person to speak of *ourselves,* because we ought not to think of ourselves, before we do of any body else; ought we?"

Saturday, May 3

Eliza again put on her criticizing cap. Learning in verse the fable of "The Fox & the Crow"[76] some weeks since she observed the expression "flew up in the *trees,*" and said she thought it ought to be *tree,* "because, sister Rachel, you know a tree is so large that to be sure *one* tree would be enough for a *Crow* to fly on." Rachel explained to her that in poetry such liberties were allowed, as the word *trees* was there used to rhyme with *cheese.* Today however another incongruity presented itself, as she repeated the same fable. "You told me the other day sister Rachel, about 'flew up in the *trees,*' but here in the next verse it says,

> 'A Fox who lived nigh,
> To the *tree* saw her fly—'

if it said *trees* before, why does it not say so again?"

Rachel: "I think my dear, it probably means by, '*in* the trees,' *among* the trees, that is, where there is a grove, or a number of trees together; & when it says afterwards '*to* the tree saw her fly,' that the fox observed the particular tree on which she rested. This is I think the way in which the *author* would probably explain it." With this decision of the matter the young critic was *tolerably* well satisfied.

On the same day Eliza came to her sister looking sad & unhappy.

Rachel: "What is the matter Eliza, have you been doing something wrong?"

She said, "yes," and hesitated.

Rachel: "Tell me Eliza what it is that you have done, you have not told an untruth, have you?"

Eliza: "No, sister Rachel, but I was playing with Emma & Miss Louisa,[77] & there were a good many boards a little way off, and we took them up, & were carrying them to our house, to make it, and I did not remember it was Saturday, (here she began to cry) till I had been moving them some time, and then when I thought of it, I left off, & told them, I would go up stairs then, that I could not play any more."

Rachel: "Well my dear, as you did not do it after you recollected that it was wrong, God will not be angry with you, for he loves those who try not to offend him. Only be cautious in future not to do any thing like work on the Sabbath, because it is that day which God has appointed to us for a day of rest. You are a good child for being so thoughtful of what is right & wrong."[78]

The account here given by Eliza was confirmed by her sister Ellen to whom I afterwards mentioned the circumstance. She had seen Eliza's employment without thinking to forbid it, & was surprised when she observed her suddenly stop & leave her companions, saying only that she "must go up stairs *then.*"

A few days since reading in "Instructive Rambles"[79] the epitaph of the Tradescants,[80] at Lambeth palace—she met with the lines of "The first died in his spring, the other two, lived till they had travell'd art and Nature through."

Rachel: "What does it mean Eliza by 'the first died in his *spring*?'" After considering a moment she said, "it means, he fell into some *water,* does not it? and died there, was drowned." Rachel advised her to read it again & think a little, she read it, & then said, "does it mean, in the spring of the year?"

Rachel: "Think again Eliza."

Eliza (after a pause): "Oh! I see what it *means now!* That he died while he was young, and so it says *his spring,* because then every thing begins to grow."

Rachel: "Yes, Eliza, that is the meaning & in the same way you may observe that the different periods or *times* of life may be represented by the different seasons." This she traced and readily understood. The discovery being made by herself seemed to give her real pleasure. And the remainder of the epitaph in which there are several figurative expressions she understood readily and explained the allusions after a little reflection with much animation & pleasure.

May 9th

When Eliza rose from her knees after saying her prayers before she went to bed, her sister blamed her for saying them too quickly, as if she did not think of what she said. She replied, "Sister Rachel it is so hard to keep *my thoughts from wandering.* I read in the 'Misses Magazine,'[81] (a twelvemonth ago) where Lady Witty said that she would always try to think of God when she was praying to him. But thinking of that very thing makes my thoughts wander, for then I begin to think of the 'Misses Magazine.'"

These were the very words used by the child. I was surprised both by the observation & the terms in which it was conveyed. It is very gratifying to see a child endeavour thus to trace the operations of her own mind, especially when directed to subjects of such abstract but superior importance.

May 15th

I had been explaining to Eliza the distinction between the words, knowledge & understanding.

"I think," she said, "it is very pretty to use figurative language sometimes."

Rachel: "But what makes you observe that now Eliza?"

Eliza: "Because you said just now, something about a *cultivated* mind, and I thought it was pretty, because that *seemed like* the mind was a garden that seeds could be planted in."

I had before been *unconscious of having* used the term.

May 16th

Eliza while saying her French lesson miscalled the article "*les*" for the article "*des.*" "How Eliza?" asked her sister Caroline. "*Des,*" replied Eliza, in a voice of confirmation as if she had said so at first. Caroline blamed her for speaking in this tone, but she persisted that she had said the same at first, tho' Caroline who had been *attentively* listening, was *certain* she had not. As soon as Eliza saw her sister Rachel, she told her: "When I was saying my French lesson sister Caroline asked me the plural of 'Da,' & I said '*L'des*' & sister Caroline asked me over again, and I said '*des*,' & Sister Caroline told me that I said it in a wrong tone of voice, as if I had said it right at first, when I did not."

Rachel: "Well I suppose you did not say right at first, therefore the tone was wrong, because it was intended to seem, as if you only repeated what you had said before."

Eliza: "Well sister Rachel, I am sure I did say it right at first, only sister Caroline *thought* I did not."

Rachel believed the child & thought Caroline might have been mistaken but on asking her a few minutes afterwards in Eliza's presence, she said that she had not been mistaken, that sister Eliza had heard & remarked the same thing at the same time, and that Eliza was wrong in persisting to the contrary. Eliza had not mentioned that her sister Ellen also was present, and now when the circumstance was thus clearly related, and her sister Rachel told her that she had shewn a want of candour, & a wish to deceive, she cried and seemed much distressed, but no longer denied her fault. Rachel told her how much she was distressed at her conduct, that until she could have candour & resolution to acknowledge her faults, no one could have confidence in her. That had she acknowledged the first fault which might have proceeded from want of thought, she would have done rightly, & no one would have been displeased with her, but that after persisting in denying that, she had, to confirm it, told a second falsehood. Eliza appeared at this time *really* to feel, and shed tears abundantly. Her sister left her, and in the course of the afternoon while her sister was busy Eliza came, & stood near her & when she saw that she had finished what she was doing, gave her a paper and asked her if she pleased to read it. It was a note which she had written.[82] Rachel told her after reading it, that she hoped she would let the unhappiness she had felt prevent her doing wrong in the same way in future, & asked if any one had told her to write the note, and how she knew how to spell all the words? She said that no one had told her to write & that she asked sister E how to spell *equivocate,* that she knew all the rest. Ellen afterwards confirmed this, she had seen her take the paper and write the whole, without any one's speaking to her, after Rachel left her. Eliza seemed still so unhappy at having done wrong, that her sister hoping that the pain she had already felt would deter her from a similar fault in future, told her that she would forgive her. This was Friday night & when Rachel told Eliza as the candles were lighted, that she must leave Aladdin in Africa a whole week longer, Eliza said, sighing, that she knew it, & went quietly to bed.

May 18th

As Rachel was writing a letter, Eliza came to her & said in a sorrowful tone, "Sister Rachel just now I was at the office & sister Ellen gave me a ball of soap to carry to sister Caroline & I let it fall & break, and Miss Louisa (a little girl she was playing with) took it up, & presently brother Solomon came by, and said, why have you broken the soap, & I did not say any thing, & Miss Louisa said, 'yes,' and then sister Ellen told me it was wrong in me not to say any thing."

Rachel: "And why Eliza did you not say that you had broken it, is it possible you are afraid to confess *any* little fault you may commit? And have you so soon forgotten what you suffered on Friday? I am afraid Eliza that if no one had seen you break the soap, you would not have confessed that you had done it."

Eliza: "Sister Ellen said *she* thought I would not, and I am afraid so too."

Rachel: "Well you are right in telling me so, if you think so, but you must try to have more resolution, and determine when you have done something wrong, that you *will* tell it directly."

Eliza: "I am afraid to determine for fear I should not be able to do it."

Rachel: "You mean, to *promise;* but I want you to determine within yourself, you know when you were a year younger you *determined* not to sit on the sofa, when brother Samuel told you not & you have never done it since."

Eliza: "Yes I know that."

Rachel: "Then if you would determine to tell immediately of a fault you have committed you can do that too." Eliza said she would try to determine, & her sister Ellen just then entering was pleased to find that she had come to tell of her fault. In speaking of it, Ellen mentioned, that Louisa had the soap in her hand, that Solomon had addressed his question to *her* & she answered, yes, Ellen hearing this, had blamed Eliza for not saying that it was herself instead of Louisa who had broken it. Rachel told Eliza that she had understood it differently from her, that she did not know she had suffered Louisa to bear the blame instead of herself. Eliza said she thought that her sister Rachel had understood her so, that she meant to tell it in that manner, for that it was just so in her mind. Rachel thought it not improbable that she had unintentionally placed the circumstance of her silence, before Louisa's speaking; which prevented her account from being rightly understood. She therefore only told Eliza how much the circumstance of suffering another to be blamed instead of herself, increased her fault, & that mamma & sister Caroline, to both of whom she had related the affair, probably misunderstood it also. That if they knew exactly how it was, they would think her fault greater, but that they would approve of her candour. She said directly "I will go & tell them." She ran lightly away, & soon returned as lightly, saying that mamma had understood her, but sister Caroline had not, but now they both knew it. Rachel told her she had now done rightly this time, and that she was sure she felt pleased with herself. Louisa was now in the room & Rachel told her, that if she understood the question about the soap as addressed to her alone, she should not have said, "yes," that if she did not wish to accuse Eliza she ought to have remained silent, & that tho' generosity was praiseworthy *truth* ought on all occasions to be the first consideration.

"But sister Rachel," said Eliza, "it was not half as great fault in Miss Louisa to say yes, as it was in me not to say any thing, was it?"

Rachel: "No Eliza it was not, there was something *like right* in Louisa's saying, 'yes' and nothing but what was wrong in your being silent, now if both had told the simple truth, *all* would have been *right,* and I hope you will both think of that & do so the next time."

Monday, June 2d

Eliza has of late been scrupulously exact in giving voluntarily, each day, an account of her little errors. Monday June 2 while she was reading to her sister Rachel her sister Ellen entered the room & said, "When Eliza had finished her music lesson today, I told her to tell you that she had played it very well indeed. She afterwards came to me & reminded me that in one part she had played a bar wrong, several times; and I was pleased with her for doing so, as I thought it shewed she did not wish her lesson to be put down 'Very Well Indeed,' unless she entirely deserved it." Rachel praised Eliza for this proper, and honorable conduct, & told her she hoped she would always be as careful not to accept of praise, which she did not feel that she merited.

Eliza: "But sister Rachel I did not think of my *'very well indeed,'* when I reminded sister Ellen of my playing that bar wrong; I only told her because I thought she did not remember it, or else she would have told me to tell you something about *that,* when you put down my lesson."

Rachel: "Well my dear you are very right to explain this exactly as you meant it, and if you had not deserved the praise we gave you before, you would deserve it for the very same kind of good conduct now, and I am sure such praises must give you greater pleasure than all that you could receive without deserving them."

Eliza's list on the 2d of June says "A very good, candid little girl, who will be rewarded with *two kisses* tonight."

July 27th

It has been some time since I last wrote anecdotes of my little Eliza, indeed nothing particular has occurred to induce me to do so. I have observed with much satisfaction that she is scrupulously exact in acknowledging or rather acquainting me with every little fault she commits, and is even precisely particular in informing me of any thing which she thinks may be wrong. Sometimes in saying her lessons after answering a question readily & correctly, she will say, "but I believe sister Rachel I guessed at that," or "I knew that by something you said just now." She has of late frequently obtained praise by declaring she did not deserve that which was given to her & shewing why she did not. This amendment is truly satisfactory, I have only to hope that it may continue and be confirmed into a habit of candour & probity.

Eliza's greatest fault lately has been heedlessness, she sometimes appears to listen without hearing & will afterwards ask what one has been saying to her, if sent on a message will forget to bring the answer, and appear quite abstracted from what ought to occupy her attention. I have thought that this may perhaps arise from her mind's being exercised beyond its strength, for it does not appear to proceed at all from volatility, and I have determined to try if by giving her fewer employments her mind may not become more capable of steady attention during the short time its attention is claimed. I mentioned that at her own desire she had recommended French. I have now decided to let her decline it for a year or so, till she can attend to it without fatigue. I mentioned my intention to her today and asked her how she liked it. She said that if I thought it was better she would rather leave it off, for that she did not like it much. I was pleased with her answer for it could not be expected that a child of her age could find pleasure in learning to conjugate French verbs, & her having continued to learn her lessons well for some time before, shewed that she had made the exertion because she thought it was right to do so, & because she knew her attention would give her friends[83] pleasure.

August 17th[84]

This day completed Eliza's 8th year. While she is making herself happy with some of her little companions, who are sharing with her some fruit and cakes given her by mamma, I will mark the day and take a glance at her progress during the past year.

Has read principally:
Sandford & Merton[85]
Father's Tales[86]
Instructive Rambles by Mrs. Helme,[87] with which she was much pleased.
Parts of *Paul & Virginia*[88]
Part of Mrs. Wakefield's *Instinct Displayed*,[89] which not being well understood
    is for the present laid aside.
Delia's Birth-day[90]
part of *Rose & Emily*[91]
Young Traveller,[92] just commenced.

Continues to recite a few lines of poetry once a week—now learning the "Shepherd & the Philosopher." Gay.[93]

She understands all the little poem she had learned, and sometimes repeats them with a good deal of expression.

Improvement in writing not considerable.

French as before mentioned discontinued.

Arithmetic, does sums in the four first simple rules with facility, and understands their principles tolerably well.

In Geography she has progressed well, has a good knowledge of all the European maps in addition to the different clusters of Islands in the map of the world; and has begun to study Asia.

In Grammar her progress has also been good, she has been through Syntax & understands the rules very well, she also corrects without difficulty the exercises in syntax, given at the end of the smaller grammar, and explains their improprieties. Begins to parse easy sentences without difficulty and as her lessons are very short finds them agreeable.

In Music

Plays correctly & with distinctness; has learned a number of lessons among them the Variations to "The Little Sailor,"[94] "Up & War them A' Willie"[95] & is now learning the "Overture of Henry IV."

She works but little & rather slowly but generally very well.

With Eliza's attainments then I have no reason to be dissatisfied, and I hope by a regular course of short lessons that her mind without being overburdened will be gradually improved.

1818

January 15th

Many anecdotes & incidents have occurred since my last date, some from having unavoidably been suffered to pass unremarked, have escaped my memory, others I will endeavour to recall as correctly as possible. It was mentioned that Eliza was committing to memory the fable of the "Shepherd & the Philosopher." She could not prevail on herself to approve entirely of the Shepherd's mode of acquiring knowledge, or rather of the general censure cast on literature in the line "Books as deceiful are, as men," when the Shepherd says,

> "For man is practiced in disguise,
> He cheats the most discerning eyes," &c

she said she did not think that the *language* was very proper for a man who was just a *shepherd,* for that as he had no education, she did not think he would be able to use such words. Some weeks after she had learn'd this fable, her sister Rachel began to read to her the story of "Alphonso & Dalinda,"[96] when the character & pursuits of Thelismar are described, she laid her hand on her sisters arm, & with an intelligent look repeated:

> "Hast thou through many cities stray'd
> Their customs, laws & manners weighd?"

Eliza had long been promised that when her sister Rachel went to visit their friends in Richmond,[97] she should be her companion. In November last 1817, such a trip was hastily & unexpectedly decided on, and Eliza anxiously enquired if she might go. Her sister unwilling to disappoint her, & still more so to deviate from her promise, obtained her parents' consent and all things were arranged for the journey, when as all were waiting, completely equipped with bonnets, pellices,[98] gloves, ready for a summons to the carriage, a servant entered with the unwelcome tidings that one of the horses refused to draw, & was so restive as to render travelling with him dangerous, if not impossible. What was to be done? No other horse was at that moment to be had, & it was doubtful if one could be obtained at all, so the bonnets & pellices must be taken off, & laid aside for today, & probably, the journey relinquished altogether. This was a great disappointment, but Eliza did not disgrace the example of patience and *philosophy* set by her brother and sister. After the first expressions of regret her brother Solomon took his book, her sister, her work, & Eliza began her usual lessons. In the course of the day, a servant was sent to various places to endeavour to procure a horse. Every time his returning footsteps were heard at the door, Eliza's countenance brightened with hope & shew'd by its animated anxiety, how much she wished for favourable accounts, but when repeatedly the unwelcome sound met her ear, "I could not get a horse there, master," she only looked sorry without any expression of discontent, & continued her employment. Her father and brother were pleased with her sensible conduct, and wished more than ever to gratify her. One neighbour remained to be tried, and an application to him proved successful. He readily lent his horse, in exchange for the unaccommodating animal which had so nearly deprived us of our anticipated pleasure, but to which Eliza is indebted for her first occasion of exercising cheerfulness & resignation under an unavoidable evil. She retired to bed very happy, and arose in high spirits next morning to commence her journey. During the first day's ride, Eliza constantly mistook little creeks & branches, for rivers, until arriving at the Roanoak, she saw & comprehended what a river really is. She also learned at the expense of no inconsiderable number of jolts, what is meant by a causeway.[99] Early the next morning we had to cross the Meherin, (a name which it is probable Eliza will long remember,) the bridge had been carried away by a late freshet, & only way of crossing, was by means of a little boat, in which the ferryman could carry over but one person at a time.

At a short distance above the ferry, stood a mill, the noise of whose wheels, with the foam & dashing of the waters which fell over the dam, was not a little calculated to alarm a young traveller. Eliza did not however express great fear, but she held fast her brother's knees, till both were safely landed on the other side. She looked pale & told her sister, she had been so frightened that it had made her feel sick. The remainder of the journey was to be performed in the stage, a most uneasy vehicle, at every turn of which from side to side, Eliza's squeezed her sister's hand, & asked if it would not turn over, this was repeated so often that it at least became troublesome. It happened that before we had travelled many miles, an old man who was standing at a house door waiting for the stage to pass, took a seat with us. To him too, it seems, this was a new mode of conveyance, and he expressed his apprehensions, almost as freely as Eliza had done. Some of the passengers diverted themselves at the expense of his timidity, endeavouring to increase his fears, the driver too joined in the plot, & whenever the road would at all justify it, drove as fast as possible, telling him, he wanted to shew what good driving was. In the mean time, poor Mr. Kid, that we found to be the name of our fellow passenger was not the only sufferer, by these theoretick & practical jokes. Every fearful prediction occasioned Eliza new alarm, till her sister bade her observe, that the silly timidity of the old man made him ridiculous, & that people thought he deserved to be frightened & laughed at. She told her, she hoped there was no real danger, but that if there were, constant complaints & expressions of fear could not prevent it, & that perhaps if she shewed so much cowardice, people would amuse themselves by plaguing her as they had Mr Kid. After this Eliza shewed more resolution, and just after dark were arrived safely in Petersburg.[100]

The next morning she was somewhat surprised to see *so many* houses, all made of brick, & standing *so close together*. But as we drove through the streets, her wonder & admiration were still more strongly excited by the signs over many of the doors. She had never seen, until now, any sign but that of the bell tavern in Warrenton. Her head was first popped out at one side of the stage, than at the other, "Why," said she, "they have all sorts of taverns here! Horse taverns, & shoe & boot taverns, & saddle taverns, & every sort!" During the ride to Richmond, more questions were asked than in a stage crowded with strangers it was convenient to answer. Mayo's[101] bridge excited fresh wonder & admiration: it was such a long one! & the horses could go over it as fast as if they were in the street! They had not to walk along as they did over the other bridges. But now, we entered the city, & in a few minutes more were welcomed at Mr. Myers'[102] elegant mansion[103] by a large group of affectionate friends. Sister Ellen who had gone there some time before in quest of health was of the number. Eliza was delighted to see her sister & aunt & cousins,[104] but her joy did not make her forget that she had a pair of coarse worsted stockings drawn over her shoes and no sooner had she entered the elegant parlour, than making herself at once quite at home, she seated herself on the carpet in the middle of the floor, & began to disencumber herself of this clumsy and unbecoming part of her equipment.

This spacious & delightful house, with its appropriate furniture, & neat tasteful garden, was quite fairy land to Eliza, & then two of her cousins were excellent play mates for her, every thing wore the additional charm of novelty, & she was as happy as happy could be.

The books from which she usually studied we had brought with us, & Eliza learned every day nearly the same lessons that would have been given her at home. And it was very satisfactory to see that even here, where so many temptations presented themselves to withdraw the mind from its ordinary course, Eliza could command her attention when necessary, learn her lessons with her usual accuracy, & without a shadow of reluctance. When they were finished however she was very joyful, & ran to seek her cousins, to play with, or to examine the contents of their library. A good friend of ours Miss H[o]ch who perfectly understands French, & has taught it with great ease to some of her nieces told Eliza one day that she would give her a lesson. She taught her to read & pronounce & then to translate a page in a little French book. This did not fatigue & perplex Eliza & she liked it very well. Miss H. advised that this plan should be pursued with her for some time, in order to form her pronunciation, & accustom her a little to the words of the language, and that a grammar should not again be put into her hands, until it could be learned with ease. Eliza said she wished I would let her learn that way, & I have since upon her return complied with her desire. It is yet to be seen whether this attempt will prove more successful than the two which preceded it.

Among other pleasures which Eliza enjoyed in this visit was that of renewing her acquaintance with Margaret Brown, a little girl who she had seen in Warrenton & whom she had been very fond. On the morning, however, succeeding a day which she had passed with this child, she said: "Sister Rachel, I don't think Margaret is as good a little girl as she used to be, for when her mamma told her to do some thing yesterday, she said, so that Mrs. Brown could not hear her, 'I won't, I won't.' And she did some other things too which I did not think were right."

Margaret has been brought up by an excellent & sensible mother, & was formerly remarkable for docility & obedience. I was sorry to hear of these improper traits, but I could not forbear attributing them to the mixed society, & improper associates too commonly incident to public schools. Margaret had been placed at one not long before, & I too, without seeing much of her, thought I perceived a change for the worse in her manners & conduct. I rejoiced afresh at having constantly prevented Eliza's intercourse with children whose disposition & manners I did not approve.

Eliza's good conduct & obedience were observed with pleasure & commendation by all her friends & the good sense & simplicity of many of her observations, at once surprised and amused them. Her brother & sisters were one day going to visit the Museum, it had been lately established & does not contain a great number of articles, so they were less fearful of fatiguing or perplexing her attention. She had often heard a whale & an Elephant described, and a large rib of the former & a hoof of the latter probably attracted as much of her attention as any thing that she saw. In the painting room some fruit pieces particularly struck her fancy, an ingeniously contrived painting also, which viewed from the door of entrance, presented the stern countenance of the old military commander, but on advancing to the center of the room his years & ferocity diminished with your steps, till you discovered in a different uniform a young & handsome officer, who on your arrival at an opposite door, was again found to be transformed into a gay & fashionable lady. Her brother Samuel was so good as to explain to her, the simple means by which this deception was produced, and which at the moment she appeared to understand. On the whole Eliza's visit to the Museum was not greatly enjoyed, the variety of objects, was sufficient to distract her ideas, & prevent her having a clear conception of more than a very few, & on being asked soon after leaving the house, what she had seen there, she mentioned in a confused way some few articles, knitting her brows as she endeavoured to recall the recollection, and appearing to be fatigued with thinking on the subject.

But now ten days, the limited term of our visit had nearly elapsed. Her sister asked Eliza one morning if she should like to set out for home . . . She quickly answered, "no," for that she should be so sorry to leave Richmond; but as quickly added "yes I shall too, for I want to see mamma & Emma, but if they and papa, & all my brothers & sisters were here, I should want to stay in Richmond always." The morning came, and after taking an affectionate leave of our friends, we again set out on our journey. As we had come from Petersburg, Eliza . . . expressed a wish that she *had a book* "for it was so *tedious,* just riding along, & doing nothing." She now had one, which her brother Samuel had given her called, "London," [105] which contained an account of the first visit of some young folks to that great city. With this she was quite delighted, for she said, it was just like herself, that *Richmond,* was London to her. No sooner had we passed through Manchester [106] & entered on the public road, than Eliza asked for her book, saying, that "now we had passed all the rattling pavements, & besides there was nothing amusing to look at." She read with much earnestness & abstraction, only stopping occasionally, to utter an exclamation, & wishing she could only read *that* to me. I told her she might do so, but she said, "I am afraid the lady who sits before us will hear me, I will read it for you, when we are by ourselves in the carriage tomorrow, if Brother Solomon & Sister Ellen please."

Soon after this, Eliza became very hungry & the bag of gingerbread & apples was not to be readily come at. The lady just mentioned, kindly presented her with some crackers. A little while after, finding a way to the contents of our bag, one of her sisters, desired her to offer the lady an apple, but she replied in a whisper, "If you please sister Ellen don't let me do that, it will seem like paying her for the crackers." Her sister smiled and endeavoured as well as circumstances would admit, to explain the case, & remove her delicate scruples. The remainder of our journey home was, sufficiently fatiguing & unpleasant, but afforded little incident. Eliza thinks she never shall forget what part of a carriage the swingletree [107] is, because ours broke, when we were in the middle of a miry road, after dark, and we found much difficulty in getting it fastened together. She was rejoiced to see again one of our landladys on the road, who as we went on had the goodness to fill her bag with biscuit. We had occasion now & then to remind her of old *Mr. Kid,* but on the whole she gave as little trouble as could be expected in a little traveller who had cold weather, bad roads & and uneasy carriage to contend with. And now we are again at home, let us see whether Eliza will recompense her friends for the indulgence they have granted her.

For some days after their return home Eliza's sisters were particularly engaged, & unable to bestow on her their usual degree of attention, and when matters began to proceed once more in a regular train, they found her so prone to her old fault heedlessness, that it was almost impossible to confine her attention to any thing. In the course of a lesson she would some times forget she was saying it, would apparently *listen* to an explanation, but scarcely *hear* a word of it; & if sent to carry a message, or perform some little commission, would almost invariably forget the one, or blunder in executing the other. Besides this, some little part of every day's business was sure to be *forgotten,* and her sister sometimes reminded her of the account she had read of "Menaleas, the absent man,"[108] adding, "I am afraid some of these days, when I call *Eliza* Mordecai you will not know who it is, & will run to look for her!"

This fault tho' greatly increased by her late unusual recreation, & less regular habits, had been for some months observed, and tho' an errour so incident to childhood, might by some be overlooked as trivial & capable of being entirely self-corrected, her sister found so much daily inconvenience arising from it, that she was unwilling to trust its correction to the gradual influence of time & experience. Her plans were readily coincided in, and assisted by every member of the family. No one would send Eliza on an errand, declaring that they feared she would forget by the way, even her good and kind father, who seldom blamed her, said, he could not trust her to do any thing for him. Every day she had the trouble of looking for some thing which had been left out of place & the time passed in looking for it was not particularly agreeabl[e], especially as it often interfered with that which would otherwise have been given to amusement. The *List* was brought every evening, & every evening for many days, was "Heedless girl," "Heedless child," or "Eliza forgot to put away her books" or "forgot to say her notes" or *forgot* a dozen other things, repeated again & again, till her sister was tired of writing, & Eliza ashamed of seeing it written. Friday night too, came, but it came unattended by its usual pleasant companion, an entertaining story; neither could Eliza be indulged in sitting up half an hour later than usual. Her kind brother Solomon had written some very pretty & affectionate lines in poetry which he gave her . . . These she had committed to memory but their good effects were not immediately perceptible.

She did however begin seriously to think of trying to cure herself of a fault, which proved so troublesome to herself, & prevented her from enjoying the approbation of her friends. The next week's diary wears a more pleasing aspect, Eliza exerted herself & not in vain, to get the better of her provoking enemy: It is true he took advantage of her once, or twice, but she so much oftener succeeded in escaping or repelling his attacks, that at the end of the week she was acknowledged victor, and received smiles and a *story,* as her well earned prize. Early in the next week Eliza happened to mention before her sister Ellen that her bandbox[109] was so old and torn that she could scarcely keep any thing in it. Sister Ellen told her that if she would keep from being heedless or forgetful a whole fortnight she should have a large new band box. A fortnight seemed a very long time, but Eliza determined *to try.* The fortnight has now just passed, and, joyful to relate! Eliza deserves the bandbox. Sister Ellen is not now at home but, as soon as a deep snow, which now covers the ground shall have disappeared, Eliza shall take a walk down town with sister Julia & choose it for herself.

"Evenings at Home"[110] has never been put into Eliza's hands as a regular *reading book,* but she has been occasionally allowed to use it. It had happened however that from sometimes opening it at parts which she could not understand, she contracted a prejudice against the book, & never heard it mentioned in terms of approbation, that she did not express her wonder how any body *could* like it. Her sister did not attempt to control her opinion or to eradicate her prejudice, but simply told her that she would probably be better pleased with this book at some future day, & that for the present she wished her to lay it completely aside and never even to open it. To this interdict Eliza gladly promised obedience. Some months have passed since this circumstance February 4th occurred, but a few days ago, while standing beside her sister in the school room, Eliza heard a little girl read something that interested her, she looked into the book, it was *Evenings at Home.* She begged to be allowed to read *that* story.

Rachel: "On condition Eliza that you do not read or look into any thing else which the book contains without asking me."

She promised, and I can *rely* on her *promises.* It was the drama of "Alfred" that she had wished to read, but having finished that she looked over the index, & begged to read some other parts. Permission was granted for all that she could well understand.

Eliza: "Sister Rachel, I should like *Evenings at Home* very much if it was not for 'Tutor, George, & Harry.'"

Rachel: "Some time ago Eliza you did not like many other parts which you now find very agreeable, so it may at some future time be, with 'Tutor, George, & Harry.' In the mean time you must never look into those dialogues."

Eliza: "I will not, only you know, I can't help *seeing* them as I turn over the leaves of the book."

On the preceding page I mentioned that I could rely on *Eliza's promises.* I repeat with pleasure that for many months, she has paid strict regard to them, and paid in every instance the strictest regard to truth. She regularly in the evening tells of any fault she may have committed during the day, and they are frequently those which would otherwise remain concealed, such as "I got a little angry today when I was playing with Emma, & thought I would not play with her any more, but I soon got over it, & that's the way sister Rachel, I do very often."

On the 11th of Jan[uar]y as Eliza & her sister Rachel sat by themselves in a room Eliza expressed a strong desire to be allowed to go to school & learn her lessons in classes as other children did. That she should love her studies so much better, because maybe she could get to the head of the class, & have the *medal.*

Rachel: "I dare say my dear, it might be more agreeable & more interesting to you to do so, but there are several objections to your request. In the first place the lessons learned by any class that you could join are much longer than you are accustomed to, & I could not teach you as well when saying with many others, because I could not stop every moment to explain what you did not understand. Besides these there is another objection which I have often mentioned to you, the necessity there would then be for your staying a good deal with the girls from whose manners & conversation you could reap no improvement."

Eliza (sighing): "I thought you would say so, but if I had only *one* companion to learn, & to play with me, I should be satisfied."

Rachel: "Well my dear that is quite a reasonable wish, but have patience, & perhaps when papa leaves off keeping school, one of your little cousins will come and study, & play with you."

Eliza: "But that will be so *long,* I am afraid papa never will leave off."

Rachel: "Do you think Eliza if I tell you a secret that you can keep it? It is of great consequence, & if I tell you, you must not mention it to *any one* till I give you leave. Can I trust you?"

Eliza: "Yes, sister Rachel, I think you can because when I did not know whether I could keep a secret before [111] I told you so, & since you told me that one, I have never mentioned it, so you need not be afraid to tell me this."

Rachel: "Then Eliza my secret is, that papa is not going to keep school any longer than this year!"

Eliza started from her seat. "Oh! *Sister Rachel* is it possible! I can hardly believe it! It seems as if it cannot be true!"

Rachel: "It is quite true I assure you that such is his intention, but tell me Eliza why are you so much rejoiced at it?"

Eliza: "Oh! because I want him to leave off so much."

Rachel: "But that is no *reason.*"

Eliza: "But the reason is, that then we could live in a house by ourselves, and we should not have such a large family, and there would not be so much noise sometimes, & every body would not have so much to do, I mean papa, & brother Solly [112] & you & sister Caroline & all the family."

Rachel: "I think your reasons are very good Eliza, so now you may make yourself happy in *thinking* of all this, but remember, it is not to be mentioned to any one."

About a week after this conversation, Eliza said, "sister Rachel, may I ask you a question? Why were you so particular in saying that I must not mention what you told me to *any one,* what harm would there be in speaking of it to papa and mamma?"

Rachel: "There would be no harm in it, if you had not promised me not to do so, but now it would be breaking your word. And I forbade you mentioning it to any one because I wish you to learn, to *know* things without feeling an inclination to speak of, or tell them, then you may safely be trusted with secrets."

Eliza: "But why does papa want this to be a secret?"

Rachel: "I cannot tell you all the reasons, but one is, that he thinks it might be a disadvantage to his business if it were known now, in June he will let it be publickly known."

Eliza: "Well then when June comes, I may tell it."

Rachel: "Not till I have given you leave."

Eliza: "I *wish* that time would come I feel so impatient, as if I could hardly keep from speaking of it so long."

Rachel looked very grave: "I should be very sorry Eliza, if you could not, both because telling it might do harm, & because you would then have forfeited your word, & would be unworthy to be trusted again. Besides when you are a great deal older you will think of your conduct in this affair, with pride & pleasure, or with pain & shame, according as you may or may not adhere to your promise. I hope therefore that you will never again allow the *possibility* of telling the secret to enter your mind."

Eliza: "Sister Rachel, I *know* I shall not tell it."

Rachel: "You now see Eliza that we are not always made happier by knowing *secrets,* and we should never be willing to hear any that do not concern us. I told you this because I thought it would give you pleasure, but I now think I was wrong, & that I have more probably given you some trouble & pain."

This is indeed true & I blame myself not only for putting the child's *honor* to so severe a test, but for disclosing to her a secret which is not as in the former instance *exclusively mine* & which therefore I was not completely at liberty to hazard. In giving lessons, I not unfrequently receive them. A week or two have passed since the preceding conversation, & Eliza has never alluded to the subject except one day when she said in a hesitating whisper: "Sister Rachel, will you tell me whether papa is going to live in *Richmond* when you know?"

Rachel: "He is not yet determined as to any thing of that kind."

Eliza: "I shall be very glad if he does, but I shall be sorry to leave my little garden."

Rachel: "I don't recollect any thing in your little garden to be sorry for."

Eliza: "What not my rose bush, & my Turkey violets, & my Flowering Almond! Oh! I would not lose my [F]lowering Almond for the world!"

Rachel (laughing): "You speak as extravagantly Eliza, as an Arabian Night princess."

Eliza: "Why do they speak extravagantly? Oh yes, I know, in the story of Aladdin; but I need not have said for *the world,* for if I had it, I am sure I don't know what I should do with it."

January 23d

Rachel was reading aloud to Eliza that chapter in Exodus which contains the Commandments. When she came to the "Thou shalt not take the name of the Lord thy God in vain"[113] Eliza said, "What is the reason *sister* Rachel, that so many good people *do that?* There's Mr. ———. He does it *very* often, I observed it; and in *books* I see *that word* put when it is not speaking of any thing *good,* but just in a little story, or any thing of that kind. It is right to use it so?"

Rachel: "No, my dear it is not, I have frequently observed the same thing, & I think it very improper. Sometimes too, in plays which are performed on the stage, prayers are introduced, but it is very wrong that they should be. No address should ever be made to God, but what is serious, & with all our hearts."

Eliza: "Yes sister Rachel & when I meet with *that word* in books, I would rather leave it out, or say some other instead of it."[114]

February 3d

Eliza was reading "Frank," in the continuation of *Early Lessons,*[115] her sister was drawing a pattern, but on cutting her pencil, it proved to have no more lead in it, & she was at a loss how to proceed.

Eliza started up. "I know where to get one of sister Ellen's that she gave me to keep for her, a long time ago," and she ran & brought it. "Now I am useful as well as Frank, ain't I sister Rachel?"

The lesson happened to conclude with a passage in which Frank regrets that there are so many things, which he cannot *yet* understand.

Eliza: "I think Frank was a very sensible little boy; he was very desirous of gaining knowledge."

A day or two ago mamma desired that Eliza's being very dilatory in dressing every morning, should be mentioned on her list. This was accordingly done, her sister observing at the same time, that she hoped Eliza would avoid such censure in future. She said, she would try, and she has kept her word, rising early and dressing so quickly as to be able to learn & say a part of her lessons before breakfast. It is very pleasing to her friends to see her thus careful to correct her faults, and she herself finds the pleasures & advantages resulting from such exertion. She now has plenty of time to read or amuse herself in any way that is most agreeable; & she feels cheerful, active, & lively. She said this evening: "Sometimes I feel, sister Rachel as if I could not help being good, as if I could not do any thing wrong. What is the reason of it?"

Rachel: "Perhaps, my dear, you have that agreeable feeling when you know that you *have been good;* when we do everything well, that we have to do, it makes us feel light & cheerful, and then it seems easy for us to continue to do right."

Eliza: "I dare say that is the reason, for I feel so now that I have got up early."

Rachel: "But tell me Eliza do you ever feel as if you could not help doing wrong?"

Eliza: "No, that I do not."

February 9th

On Friday night the 6th [of February] Eliza was rewarded for her good conduct during the week by her sister's reading for her half an hour longer than usual. The story of Cogia Hassan in the *Arabian Nights* amused and interested her very much. This afternoon in an exercise on syntax the sentence occurred, "Tho' the fact be extraordinary, it certainly did happen." After correcting the inaccuracy, she said, "I was thinking as I went over my lesson, that Hassan when he was telling his misfortune to Saadi, about the kite's flying away with his turban, might have said this sentence, 'tho' the fact *is* extraordinary *it certainly did* happen.'"

I have chosen this period, to give Eliza at intervals some insight into these marvelous tales because it seems to me that her time, when a little older will be too precious to be thus bestowed, and yet I wish her to know, & remember something of them. They are said to convey correct ideas of the manners & customs of the Eastern nations, they leave many playful & agreeable impressions on the mind and they are in fact so frequently alluded to in various works both of fancy & instruction that it is necessary to have formed some acquaintance with them. I also prefer reading them to her occasionally, [rather than] . . . putting the book into her own hands. I do not wish her to be led away by the charms of novelty, or so deeply fascinated by the brilliancy of invention which they constantly display, as to devour their contents, as I once did, without pausing to reflect on the morality of some parts, the absurdity of others, or to consider why a taste for this kind of reading, so very agreeable & entertaining, may not be indulged to the extent of our wishes. Observations tending to introduce all these ideas, & fix them in the mind, naturally occur, in the course of our evening's amusement, and being induced to make them herself, it requires no argument to convince Eliza of their justness.

February 11th

Robinson Crusoe Eliza is now reading for her own amusement. [T]his morning February 11th she said, "I think it is a wonder that a cannibal like Friday, should be so grateful."

Rachel: "His being so shewed that he had naturally a good disposition, but perhaps we ought not to think it wonderful that a cannibal should feel grateful, tho' it would be, if he shewed compassion or humanity."

Eliza: "I think some parts of *Robinson Crusoe* are very affecting, you know when Robinson tells Friday to go away & leave him, Friday brings a hatchet, & says, 'Here, you kill Friday, you no care for Friday, you tell him go leave you.'"[116]

Sunday February 15th

Eliza came to her sister in the evening and said, "I have got a little history to give you; this morning before we were up, some fire snapped out upon the floor. I got out of bed and began to brush it up with Emma's shoe, but papa told me to get the wing.[117] I began to look, but could not find it directly, & papa called me stupid & told me to look in the washstand drawer, I looked there & found it, & after I had brushed up the coal from the floor, I got into bed. But—I—felt a little angry, because I did not think I was stupid; & Emma asked me what was the matter?"

Rachel: "But why did Emma ask you what was the matter?"

Eliza: "Because I *looked* angry, I believe, & I told her that papa called me stupid. Papa was getting up then & he said 'what?' & then he seemed to recollect & just said, 'Oh' & went out of the room. And when he was gone, I asked mamma what made papa call me stupid, & she said, because I was awkward & took so long to find the wing. After that I got into a good humour, but I do not think I *was* stupid."

Rachel: "My dear, it is the duty of a child to submit, without complaining, to the blame or punishment which a parent thinks proper to inflict. We should feel sorry for having displeased our parents, but never allow ourselves to feel *angry,* at any thing they say or do to us. They are very seldom unjust, & when they are so, they are sorry for it, & shew by their kindness that they wish to make us amends. But even if they do not, we *must be wrong* in blaming them, & we ought to submit with as much gentleness as possible."

(Timidly) *Eliza:* "Well sister Rachel, I do not deserve to sit up tonight, do I?"

Rachel: "Yes my dear I think you do, it would not be just in me to punish you for a fault which was committed only in your thoughts, & which you have so candidly acknowledged. I think without being punished you will remember what I have said and as you know you have been wrong will take care to avoid the fault another time. Now take a kiss and then go & read or do what you please till tea time."

February 24th

Several times within a few days, Eliza in giving her daily account of herself, has said, "I was going to say something cross to Emma or, I was beginning to get a little out of humour, but I thought how bad I should feel to tell you of it this evening, & then I got over it directly."

Tuesday, March 10th

Reading in *Early Lessons* of Ellen a very good girl employed in a manufactory, who was particularly kind to some little children, employed in the same way, Rosamund says, "Laura would have done just so mamma." [118]

Eliza: "Yes sister Rachel and so would I, if I had been in Ellen's place, there are not *any* poor people about here," added she in a sorrowful tone, "that any body can do any good to."

Thursday, March 12th

Sister Ellen being absent Eliza entreated to be permitted to sleep up stairs with sister Rachel & was indulged. After lying quite still in bed for some time she said to her sister who sat reading at the fire, "Sister Rachel, if you want to say or do any thing that you don't want me to know, don't do it now because I am not asleep."

Rachel: "I do not want to say or do any thing that I don't want you to know, why do you tell me this?"

Eliza: "Because I was afraid you thought I was asleep as I laid so still, & I had rather tell you that I was not."

Sunday March 15th

Rachel said to one of the servants who had been particularly attentive on some occasion, "you are a good soul, Lucy." When Lucy had left the room, Eliza said,

"Sister Rachel when any of the servants do any thing for me I never say, you are a good *servant* or any thing like that, because it seems as if it would make them feel bad, to put them in mind that they were our servants, would not it."

Rachel: "No, my dear, I believe not, they have always been servants, and do not feel their situation a disgrace as they might do if they had ever been in different circumstances. But why do you say this?"

Eliza: "Because you called Lucy a good servant, just now & then I thought of it."

Rachel: "You are mistaken, I said *good soul.*"

Eliza: "But are you sure she understood you so?"

Rachel: "I am not sure, but I think it probable she did; still your observation was correct, only you must remember that it *is praise* to call a servant, a good servant, as well as it is, to call you a good girl."

March 25th

Eliza met with the example in her grammar lesson, "this is true charity, that is only its image." [A]fter receiving some little explanation of the sense, she said, "The way that Lady Augusta & Helen Temple behaved, is like true charity and its image, you know, in the story of 'Mad[emoiselle] Panache,' . . . when the poor old woman had been hurt by lady D[iana]'s horse running over her, Helen went to see her, & did every thing she could to relieve her, without telling every body of it; but lady Augusta just gave her little grand daughter some money, when every body saw her, & wrote her name down upon a paper, so I think *that* was true charity, *this* was only its image; but I don't know what she wrote her name for?" [119]

The intention of a subscription paper, was of course explained. [120]

April 5th

Eliza: "Sister Rachel, my wall flower is full of buds, & I was thinking as I looked at it today why it was called *wall* flower. I thought may be it was first brought from the banks of the [W]aal in the Netherlands."

April 7th

Brother Solomon observed the traces of tears on Eliza's countenance, & on enquiry found they had been occasioned by her having heard orders given to have a pigeon killed. He mentioned it to Rachel who enquired of Eliza why she had been particularly affected at this time, when she often before heard the same order given without emotion?

Eliza: "Because sister Rachel, aunt Tabby (a servant) said she could not catch a pigeon, & when they came into the room down stairs, she scattered some crumbs on the floor, & said when they came to eat the crumbs, she would catch one & kill it, and then I could not help crying . . ."

July 20th

[While] Eliza was admiring the appearance of the clouds at sunset after a shower she said, "Sister Rachel, I was walking in the garden the other evening and when I looked at the cloud[s] I felt *afraid*, they looked so beautiful." Was this or was it not, a first impression of Sublimity? I should incline to answer in the affirmative.

Tuesday, July 21st

In saying her parsing lesson, she met with the line "Whose days are dwindled &c," & remarked, "are dwindled cannot be a *passive* verb for it never could have been *active*; O, I see! it is a neuter verb with just the passive form." I was pleased with the observation as it had escaped my notice & shewed attention, & that she perfectly understood the *nature* of the three kinds of verbs.

In the next line, "And Heaven will bless &c," she said "Heaven *is* a proper substantive, and yet we say *Heavens*, & that is not an *individual*, but stop, don't tell me, I know now—When we say *The Heavens*, we mean the same as the sky, or the clouds, but when we say *Heaven*, we mean that particular place."

Those who feel interested in the education of children, may often receive from those children useful hints on the subject, & be taught the best means of correcting errors & of training both the mind & the morals. I have before mentioned Eliza's wish to attend in the school room. Tho' I could not consent to indulge her entirely, I have done so, so far, as allowing her to work in the afternoon with the other children & she is employed on a sampler in the same frame with another little girl, a very good child, who is also working one. When Eliza began she was so awkward & progressed so slowly that I more than once said to her: "Eliza I am afraid I shall be obliged to let you leave off working on your sampler until you grow larger & handle your needle better." At last one day when we were alone she said, "Sister Rachel, if you would only *think* I could go on with my sampler, I know I could do it better, but when you say, I shall have to let it alone, it discourages me, & I cannot try so well."

Rachel: "If that is the case my dear, I will *think* that you can do it as well as any body, & I hope you will *convince* me I am not mistaken."

I did not "discourage" Eliza any more and she immediately began to improve.

On *Tuesday* the 21st [of July] Caroline,[121] with whom [Eliza] is working, received a good deal of praise for the neatness of her work; Eliza had been industrious but merited no such particular commendation.

After leaving the working room, she said to one of her sisters, "Caroline got so much good praise this afternoon, & I did not get any." This was mentioned to her sister Rachel who said to her the next day: "Eliza you mentioned Caroline's having been praised, & not yourself, did you feel sorry that she was praised?"

Eliza: "N—o, but I wish you had praised me too."

Rachel: "But she deserved it my dear, & you did not, must not I tell her that she does well when she does so? You know I did not find *fault* with you. Suppose you had done remarkably well, would not you wish to be praised, even if Caroline did not deserve it?"

Eliza: "Yes."

Rachel: "Well then my dear, you see it is not by *wishing,* but by doing well that you can obtain commendation, when you do *very well,* I shall take pleasure in telling you so."

Eliza took pains that very afternoon, was successful, and obtained the *good praise* she had so much desired. A day or two afterwards, it happened that Caroline did herself less credit, and her work was censured. When alone with Eliza, Rachel said, "Well Eliza did you like to hear Caroline blamed this evening?"

Eliza: "No, I did not want her to be *blamed."* The emphasis seemed to say, *but I don't want her to be praised.*

Rachel: "But tell me, my dear, did you like better to hear her praised, the other day, or found fault with now?"

Eliza half looked up & with a countenance abashed but full of ingenuousness said, "I *believe*—I—liked to hear her found fault with—a *little* the best."

Rachel: "You are right my dear to be so candid, & I love you for it; besides when you tell me truly what you feel, I can tell you better how to correct your faults. You recollect the story of 'Envy & Emulation' in *Evenings at Home,* which I read to you some time ago, I wish you now to read it to yourself, and remember my dear, that *Envy* or the sorrow we feel at another's pleasure or praise, is not amiable & will make us very uncomfortable & unhappy; so we must try as much as we can to check it."

Eliza: "But I don't know how I *can* check it sister Rachel."

Rachel: "The best way I believe my dear, is, to keep in our minds that it is *wrong,* & when we feel it coming on, try to see for *ourselves* the good things for which any one is praised, and endeavour to praise them too; after *trying* once or twice the task will become easier because you will feel pleased with yourself for having made the exertion, and at last you will find only the pleasant feeling of being just & generous & none of the painful feeling of *Envy*. Now give me a kiss & we will go on with your lessons."

Sunday July 26th

This Evening Eliza begged me to come into the room where she was undressing to go to bed.

"Sister Rachel," said she blushing, "I have not been as good a girl yesterday & today as I was in the week."

Rachel: "How so my dear?"

Eliza: "Oh, I have been out of humour with Emma a good many times, & I did not feel right when you kissed me last night, because I had not told you."

Rachel: "Well my dear you may have your kiss now, but you must try & be as good on Saturday & Sunday when you are not employed, & when I do not generally set down your conduct, as you are on the other days in the week, when you are busy with your studies & when I do."

August 8th

Eliza was repeating a poem in which a little worm complains of those, who among other cruelties practiced on his species, use them as baits for fish.

Eliza: "Fishing must be a very cruel amusement, you know it is cruel because it hurts the fish, & the worms too that are used to catch them."

This remark introduced a conversation of some length on the propriety of man's destroying animals for his own security and use. Eliza recollected one of her sister's having told her, at the time she cried about the pigeon's being killed a story (contained in one of Goldsmith's Essays) of the situation in which the world would probably [end] if all animals were suffered to live.[122] At last recurring to the first subject which her sister had forgotten, "think," said she, "how far the poor little worm has led us!"

August 9th

Tomorrow will begin Eliza's 10th year.[123] Within the last [year] her improvements have in most respects equalled my wishes. Not once in the whole year has an instance of the want of candour occurred, indeed in the account which she gives me every evening of her conduct through the day I not infrequently find her "of herself, a judge severe." She is much less heedless than she was some months since, and exerts herself to remember what she is told or requested to do.

She is too averse to early rising, too apt to be dilatory in dressing, has a habit of laughing frequently which sometimes makes her too silly, is acquiring a *stoop* of which I must endeavour to break her—and, here I believe ends the catalogue of her faults—I mean, of course, habitual ones. In her different employments she has generally made good progress.

Of Grammar she has a remarkably correct idea for a child of her age, has reviewed the small grammar several times & will begin to study the notes in the larger grammar (Murray's)[124] this week. She parses very well and can generally supply with little difficulty any ellipses that may occur in parsing sentences in poetry.

In Geography, to which she is seldom otherwise than attentive, she has a good knowledge of the maps of all the countries in Europe, Asia, & Africa, & has studied the general maps of S[outh] & N[orth] America, with part of the United states with which she is now occupied. In the maps of the separate states commencing North, she has proceeded as far as Virginia.

Arithmetic, she is now reviewing, having proceeded as far as the rule of three. She prefers the compound rules to the simple ones, finding them equally easy & more amusing. She does but few sums, sometimes (if difficult) not more than one a day, but she is not allowed to proceed one step without understanding— *Why;* nor indeed does she ever wish it.

In writing her progress has been tolerable.

In French her sister Caroline is well pleased with her late attention & improvement. She reads it tolerably well & begins to translate a little.

Music [is] not entirely equal to what the last year promised. She is apt to forget former lessons and does not always play with animation or correctness.

Of work as I have before remarked, she is not sufficiently fond.[125] She is now much pleased with her sampler, and will I trust, by degrees acquire the knowledge requisite of useful plain work, about which when I have more time to devote to her, I shall be more particular.

Dancing she has been learning this year, but tho' she is very fond of it, she must be acknowledged to shew more of agility than of grace.

The books she has read have been principally:

London.

Early Lessons in Continuation,[126] much pleased with the "Wager" & some other
    parts not liked, because not understood on a previous reading, some
    months before.

The conversation on poetry[127] not understood and passed over.

Pictures of English & *Grecian History,*[128] merely read once.

Parts of *Evenings at Home.*[129]

Robinson Crusoe.

Rural Walks (Charlotte Smith) [130] not much liked, observations made on it just and correct.

Moral Tales (Edgeworth) [131] in part—some not understood.

Admired the "Elegy in a Country Church yard," [132] but could not understand it all.

Prince Lee Boo [133]

William Tell [134] translated from the [F]rench of Florian, [135] [a]dmired exceedingly.

Gustavus or the Macaw [136]

Anecdotes of the Horse, [137] a great favourite.

Adventures of a Donkey [138] not liked because not written naturally, opinion very correct.

Abridgement of *Gulliver.* [139]

Tales of the Castle [140] begun to be read regularly as lessons.

August 10th

Eliza has commenced her 10th year very well, she endeavours to avoid the faults that have been pointed out to her, & exerts herself to be good. From her docility, candour, & good sense, I form sanguine hopes of future excellence. I seek to train her in such a manner, that she may be prepared to meet, & to support herself under those vicissitudes, from which the most fortunate life is not exempt. That she may be sensible, well informed, mild, sincere, is my ardent wish & I would have her beloved for being amiable, rather than admired for being brilliant.

August 14th

Reading the story of "Alvarez" in *Alphonso and Dalinda,* she met with the expression, "of all the blessings allotted to man, *Hope* surely is the greatest." She stopped & said: "Sister Rachel: I don't think so, I do not feel happy when I *hope,* for I always *fear* too, and my being afraid that what I *hope* will not happen keeps me from being happy."

October 18th

Yesterday Eliza came to me with a sorrowful countenance & told me that Sister Caroline had blamed her for some thing & that she had replied to her in a petulant manner, that Sister Caroline said she should tell me how Eliza had behaved, but she begged her not, that she would come & do it herself.

Rachel: "Well Eliza I suppose you feel much happier & better pleased with yourself since you have acted in that manner."

Eliza: "Sister Rachel, why do you say so? You know I don't feel happy at all."

Rachel: "Indeed! why do you act so then? You know such conduct must displease your friends, and you say it does not make you feel at all happy."

Eliza: "But it seems I can't help doing wrong sometimes."

Rachel: "Perhaps not, but then when you do wrong, you must be punished, & as you do not like punishment, you will be more careful to avoid it by not doing wrong."

Eliza: "But what must my punishment be now?"

Rachel: "Not to play tomorrow (Sunday) as usual, with your little companions."

Eliza: "All day Sister Rachel?"

Rachel: "Yes, all day, unless the punishment was severe enough to be felt, it would not be worth while to inflict it, & I hope you will shew that you are a good, and a sensible child, by bearing it cheerfully."

Eliza: "I will try to bear it as well as I can. But Sister Caroline is angry with me, I begged her not to be, but she said she did not feel pleased with me. May I write her a note tomorrow and ask her not to stay angry with me any longer?"

Rachel: "Yes my dear you may, & you must try to amuse yourself tomorrow with reading and not waste the day in useless wishes that you could go to play with Caroline & Mary."

The note to sister Caroline was written, & . . . no one saw it 'till it was sent. The day was passed without a wish being once uttered, and as Eliza tried to amuse herself with her books, her sister when she saw her a little tired of reading, entertained her by reading for her a wonderful account of the Hydra, Polypes, an animal which being cut in various directions or even turned inside out, continues to live and thrive as before.[141] She wondered that Madame de Elemire[142] had not said any thing about them in the story of *Alphonso & Dalinda*. In reading this story Eliza had been much struck with the phenomenon of the intermittent spring. Rachel asked if she would like to know the reason of its flowing only at intervals. Yes, she replied, but rather in a hesitating manner which shewed that she feared the exertion probably necessary to understand it.

Rachel: "*Yes,* I believe means, no, and you are afraid of the trouble, tell me truly, would you rather hear it explained or not?"

Eliza: "I believe I would rather not."

Rachel: "Well Eliza you are right for telling the truth, so I will not explain it to you till by & by, when you have more good sense and a greater desire to improve."

Eliza: "But I don't know what the use is sister Rachel of knowing the reason of things."

Rachel: "I assure you, my dear, that there is use in it, & a great deal of pleasure too, when you find out the reasons of some things you will think as I do."

Some weeks after this conversation Rachel shewed Eliza the action of a small syphon, she soon understood the cause pretty well, & was amused with the effect. Rachel then shewed her a figure representing the course of a continual spring, and another thus:

explaining at the same time that water is capable of rising to a level with its source.

She readily perceived that the syphon being larger than the first channel, would discharge the water faster than the other could supply it.

Rachel: "Well what must happen then, when the Syphon can convey no more water?"

Eliza: "The spring must stop."

Rachel: "Till when?"

Eliza considered a little & then said, "till there is enough water carried into that place (reservoir) below the little stream, for the syphon to be filled again."

Rachel: "And what will happen then?"

Eliza: "It would flow again, Oh! now I see, it is that very kind of spring that I was reading about, that Alphonso saw."

Rachel: "Well do you like to know the reason now?"

Eliza: "Yes, I did not know you were going to shew me any thing about that, I like it very much, thank you Sister Rachel."

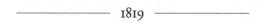

———————— 1819 ————————

August 19th

Time has fled rapidly tho' its flight has not been invariably marked by pleasing events during the long period which has elapsed since I merely commenced & closed this little volume, not imagining that a twelve-month would elapse ere it should again be opened.[143] But tho' my pen has failed to remark the daily progress of my little charge, my eye has never lost sight of her, my mind has constantly busied itself in endeavours to improve her, and my prayers are daily offered up to the Giver of All Good, to enable me to overcome the difficulties which now and then obstruct my way.

Eliza had been entrusted with the secret of our father's intention to give up the institution over which he had for ten years presided. Her self-command has been previously tried, and it proved adequate to this more important trial. She was rejoiced at the idea of a change which promised to all the friends around her a release from the numerous cares by which she had long seen them almost overpowered; in the contemplated removal to the vicinity of Richmond, near her little cousins, her young fancy anticipated a thousand pleasures, & she longed to converse about them with her dear little companion Louisa, but she had been told that till permission was given not a word must escape her, and she told her sister that she tried not to think of it, that she might never *forget,* and say something or other about it. The time at last arrived, her lips were at liberty to unclose themselves, and she enjoyed the double pleasure of recounting her anticipated joys & of knowing that she had acted prudently, and might be trusted another time.

I have before mentioned my fear that Eliza tho' blessed with a humane & excellent disposition, did not possess that kind of soft & tender sensibility which when properly directed & judiciously curbed, evinces the kind, affectionate heart, & gives a charm of the female character. Still I have been cautious in my endeavours to teach her to *feel.* Pretended sensibility has nothing to recommend it. I have not said you ought to feel sorry, when you see me so; you ought to weep when your companions are in distress. I have wished, it is true to see a greater appearance of sympathy, but I have resolved to trust its culture to example, education, and to that, which above all, I trust this child possesses—a good heart. It was not then without pleasure that in February last, I observed her seated alone reading very attentively while the tears ran down her cheeks. I asked her what was the matter. "Oh! Sister Rachel, it is so mournful!" It was the death of Abel, & the expression of Eve's feelings had excited hers.[144] She was very sorry to leave Warrenton tho' it was to come to Richmond & has since often lamented her separation from Louisa to whom she occasionally writes.

Reading not long since a passage from Cowper's Task,[145] on cruelty to animals, commencing, "I would not enter on my list of friends" &c, not being accustomed to blank verse, I was doubtful whether she would understand well enough to admire the beauty & excellence of the passage; but on concluding she exclaimed with an unusual degree of enthusiasm; how beautiful this is!—On both these occasions I have sought to shew rather by my manner than by words that I approved of her feelings & sentiments.

Eliza has borne with perfect good humour several disappointments in visiting

Richmond (our residence is five miles distant) [146] and knowing thus early to bear little ills without repining she will hereafter be able I trust to submit patiently to great ones, should such be her portion. At present it is but fair to remember that "Little things are great to little—girls."

This morning August 19th while reading her lesson Eliza met with the line "Learn to contemn all praise betimes." [147] I stopped her to remark: "I do not think Eliza that the author means, to contemn *all* praise—In haste to continue she interrupted me—"Well but sister Rachel, he says *betimes.*"

Rachel: "What is that to the purpose, what does *betimes* mean?"

Eliza: "Betimes, means *all times.*"

Rachel: "You are mistaken. I thought you did not know the meaning of the word, and you should not have interrupted me; look for it." Eliza went with a slow & heavy step up stairs for the dictionary. Just as she reached the top, Rachel called, "come down again, Eliza, & try to run up briskly & cheerfully." She obeyed, went up more lightly, but did not look the picture of good-humour when she returned with the book. When the word was looked for & its bearing on the sense ascertained, Rachel said: "You see you were wrong to interrupt me, for as I supposed, the line without explanation would either have been misunderstood, or have made a wrong impression; besides it has an appearance of conceit to interrupt one who is making observations to you, to suggest your own opinions, if when I had finished you had something to say, you know I should listen to you with pleasure." Eliza took up her reading book, but as she seated herself, Rachel saw her lips move, and the expression of her countenance was too much that of resentment. She said in a mild but firm tone, "You are saying something to yourself Eliza, tell me what it is." Eliza blushed & was silent. "It was something wrong, was it not Eliza?"

Eliza (blushing but without hesitation): "Yes, sister Rachel, it *was.*"

Rachel: "Well to punish yourself, you had better tell me, besides it is necessary for me to know what passes in your mind, that I may be the better able to advise and direct you; tell me."

Eliza (weeping): "I cannot tell you it is so bad."

Rachel: "Write it then on your slate, you know you should not be [more] afraid to acknowledge a fault than to commit it."

Eliza: "But you will be so angry with me."

Rachel: "No I shall not, I am, & shall be very *sorry,* but I shall have more reason to be satisfied with you, when you shall have exerted yourself to do right after doing wrong. Besides it is only cowards who are afraid to own their faults because they dread punishment; you are not afraid that I should whip, or shut you up in a closet, but you are afraid of my anger. Shew more good sense & as you have done wrong, be willing to bear the punishment."

Eliza still crying, wrote with some hesitation: "I said, I thought you were conceited yourself."

Rachel read & smiled, "No, Eliza I believe I am not conceited, for I am very sensible that I have many faults & I am very glad when any one is so good as to point them out to me. You know, when I am doubtful about any thing, or do not know it, I tell you so. Therefore when I tell you that something is wrong you ought to believe that I know it to be so. Think that I am older & must have more knowledge & experience than you, & you will be willing to submit. Now go on with your lesson."

Eliza: "But are you not angry with me, sister Rachel?"

Rachel: "No, I assure you I am only very sorry."

Eliza looked sorry too, but went on reading & took pains with the remainder of her lesson. In the evening she brought her list to have her lessons put down; Rachel did so, but left "*Conduct*" blank saying, "*that* you must put down to-day Eliza, yourself." Eliza took the pen & wrote "One *great* fault, *otherwise* a good girl."

Eliza's improvement during the past year is not on the whole to be complained of, yet is not completely satisfactory. In her studies with the exception of French she has progressed well, in that she has done almost nothing. Her sister Caroline had given her short reading lessons to translate but tho' she translated them without difficulty, she acquired a habit of stammering & repeating words, reading too in a monotonous tone, which was very disagreeable. After trying unsuccessfully several plans to correct this fault, Rachel on whom (Caroline being absent) the business of teaching devolved, thought it best to adopt a different plan & made her lay aside for the present reading and translating, & commence learning short lessons in a familiar & well written introduction to French grammar, (Ouiseau's) [148] which she is perfectly capable of understanding. By this means she acquires by little & little that knowledge which must be acquired sooner or later, & as she will not read again til she is better acquainted with French words & with the construction of French sentences, it is reasonable to suppose that she will proceed with more ease & satisfaction & that the bad habits above mentioned will thus correct themselves.

Of her needle she is still not sufficiently fond, nor does she use it with that ease & dexterity which seem intuitive in most females; her unhandy manner sometimes provokes the exclamation, that she must have been intended for a boy! A deficiency in this necessary art, is productive of so much inconvenience, that no pains are spared to instruct and give her a taste for it. Still to do her justice she is very neat in her person, repairs immediately and of her own accord a rent, or broken string in her frock or other apparel.

To walking, running or other active exercise she is too apt to object, probably because she has no companion of her own age to engage in her sports, for when with children of her own age she is as lively and playful as any of them. Her sister Emma, a busy, bustling, industrious little thing cannot enter sufficiently into her pursuits to be altogether a companion for her. When they play together, Eliza generally yields to her with much good nature, only checking and advising her when she is about to do wrong.

Studies for the past year from August 1818, to August 1819 [included] Murray's larger grammar[149] as far as Syntax, learned with considerable ease, and well understood, having each lesson carefully explained, before beginning to study it. Parsing in poetry, attended with no difficulty.

In Geography has completed the American maps, and is acquiring a more particular & perfect knowledge of the whole studying alternately a lesson in America & in one of the other three quarters. After fixing the maps well in her mind she will proceed in the course of the ensuing year to read Guthrie,[150] and acquire some idea of the manners customs, & history of countries with whose situation alone she is as yet acquainted.

In Arithmetic she has been through the single & double rule of three, & nearly completed the examples in practice. She understands the manner of calculating the latter very well, but many of the sums are too complicated to be improving to her at present. After finishing the rule she will turn back & review from Compound Addition.

Writes pretty well—improvement might be greater.

In French, (as above,) not much progress.

In History, has studied a *tiny,* but useful little volume of the History of England, & one of Greece.[151] Is about to commence Abridged history of America.[152]

Music—makes some improvement not very considerable.

Her reading has been principally confined to books before perused. In reading again Miss Edgeworth's *Moral Tales, San[d]ford & Merton,* &c, she has been pleased to find passages very amusing, which had before seemed tedious & been passed over, because they were not *then* understood.

The Death of Abel,[153] a few of Mrs. Hofland's tales,[154] some stories in the *Arabian Nights,* which had previously formed her Friday evening's recreation, being read aloud to her by her sister Rachel; & some pieces in prose & poetry contained in a part of "Elegant Extracts"[155] (a set of which has been presented to her by her good brother Samuel) comprises her reading for the past year. She readily acceded to a hint given her, that she should in future keep an account of all the books she read. Such attentions contribute to form in the mind a love of order & exactness, & should therefore be encouraged.

Tuesday, September [no date]

Eliza was sitting with her sisters when the conversation happened to turn on the subject of religion. Eliza asked what could be the reason that *Jews* were always spoken so ill of in books. That she had often observed it & that in Captain Riley's narrative,[156] of which she had just read a part, every thing bad was said of them. Rachel told her that in most countries in Europe they were sadly persecuted, not allowed the same privileges as other men; & that they had no character to support, nor any encouragement to endeavour to obtain one. That besides few had the benefit of a liberal education, consequently their society could not be sought for, nor their manners improved by intercourse with polite and well bred people; that in America the case was different, there were no religious distinctions & that the Jews knowing their respectability, & their standing in society, to depend like that of other men, upon their own merit & improvement, were found to equal in talents & acquirements the general society by which they were surrounded. In this country therefore it might be observed that the prejudice was in a great measure removed. Eliza listened very attentively and after pausing a moment said: "there are two things sister Rachel that I love better than any thing else in the world."

Rachel: "What are they, Eliza?"

Eliza: "My *religion* & my *country*."

October 26th

I hope my little Eliza does not want feeling and yet she often pains me by neglecting those little common but affectionate attentions, which soothe & please & which to me it appears difficult to withhold. Yesterday sister Ellen was unwell—little Emma ran up, as soon as she heard her stirring to inquire how she was. Eliza met her at breakfast table but made no enquiry, nor seemed to remember that any was necessary. This was mentioned in the course of the day & Eliza reminded that when her good & kind brother Solomon was very unwell some weeks before, she had not once asked him how he was, nor shewn any solicitude to be of service to him. This he had mentioned at the time to one of his sisters, (he is now in Philadelphia,)[157] but it was the first time that Eliza had been told of its being observed. The feelings that induce affectionate manners, should be the spontaneous impulse of the heart; wherever they appear, they should be cherished and cultivated, but they should not be planted, & forced to grow, lest they degenerate into affected sensibility, perhaps into deceit. Eliza said that she had thought every day of asking brother Solomon how he felt, but that she heard every body else, ask him so many questions about it, that she did not think it was worth while for her to. She was reminded that if she had felt as much interested as others she would not have waited till they had all made their enquiries, & that there were besides many little services that even a little girl like her might render to a sick person if she wished & sought occasion to do so. No more was said on the subject. Eliza was much affected & shed tears on bidding her brother farewell. I remark this because I so much dread a coldness of character that it is a comfort to me to remark every gleam of amiable & natural feeling.

It has been justly observed in favour of public education that it affords the stimulant of emulation, which when properly regulated, accelerates the attainment of knowledge inspiring an eagerness to excel which almost involuntarily surmounts obstacles, scarcely taking time to reflect that they exist. This is an advantage of which the private pupil and domestic instructor experience the want. Without some frequently renewed stimulus to exertion the human mind whether juvenile or adult becomes at times sensible of fatigue, is inert, & listless. Fully sensible that to combine pleasure with improvement is a great point gained in the arduous progress of regular daily instruction, I have always sought for rewards which might give a zest to the *words* of praise for successful application.

A friend of mind who is much interested in the success of a Charity school, mentioned not long since, that tickets for good behaviour, attention &c were given to the children, that *seven* good tickets entitled them to [one] *red* one, which procured them a reward of books, or something useful or agreeable. I determined to pursue a similar plan with my little sisters,[158] & made them tickets on which are written, Early rising, study & work, bad habits overcome, &c &c they also have tickets on which are written the faults to which they are most liable, as, Carelessness, heedlessness &c & when these penalties are incurred two *good* tickets are to be forfeited. 7 good tickets obtain a red one on which is written—Reward—and the reward is then selected by themselves & if not unreasonable, is readily granted. The plan I find a very good one, exertions are made with greater alacrity and spirit than formerly because the recompense is immediately in view; and the happy sound of "I've got a ticket, I've got a ticket," obtains a smile of approbation for the little student from others besides her preceptress.

October 30th

On Thursday, October 28th Eliza being entitled to a reward, chose that her sister should read a story for her the next evening. But on Friday it happened that Eliza did not behave as well as usual while saying one of her lessons, &

Rachel told her she should on that account delay her reward, (already due,) till the next night. On Saturday Eliza learns & repeats a few lines of prose or po-etry—she came but was imperfect, & Rachel contrary to her usual practice, gave her more to learn, apparently as a punishment for inattention. Eliza came a moment afterwards with a countenance not expressive of her usual good-humour & asked "must I learn *all* this."

Rachel: "No, Eliza you need not learn any of it. I gave it to you to study not as a punishment, but that you might entitle yourself to receive the reward I was obliged to withhold yesterday. As you are dissatisfied & impatient I shall not give you this opportunity of retrieving what you have forfeited, & you must wait some days longer." Eliza tried to excuse herself but her pleas were not accepted & she left the room not in anger but in sorrow. In the course of the day Rachel reflected on her decision & not being altogether satisfied with it she called Eliza & said: "I want you to tell me Eliza, exactly what you think of my not giving you your reward, do not be afraid to say just what you think."

Eliza: "Why, sister Rachel, I will tell you, I thought it was not quite *just* for you to deny me my reward, for what I did today, because you know I had *earned* it three days ago, & if I had chosen something else, I should have had it then, so it does not seem right that I should lose it for not being attentive today."

Rachel: "I think Eliza, your reasoning is very good, I asked you because I had been considering the matter in the very same way myself; so you will have your story tonight, & I hope you will next Saturday learn your verses so well, as to deserve praise instead of censure."

A company of performers is at this time in Richmond & Eliza frequently hears the theatre spoken of: Rachel took *The School for Scandal* [159] as the enter-tainment of the evening, warning Eliza if she did not understand it to say so, & something else should be substituted. She had never heard or read a play before except Miss Edgeworth's *Comic Dramas.* [160] In the course of the first act she remarked "that she wondered all these people were not afraid that as soon as one of them went out, the others would begin to say something bad of him, like they did of every body else." Sir Peter Teazle [161] soon afterwards evinced similar apprehensions. She was highly diverted with the *action* of this admirable com-edy, the wit she was not capable of relishing & asked frequent explanations of the most brilliant & lively turns. These were given soberly & patiently, & she was told that a few years hence she would read this play with much greater satisfaction, because she would understand it all. Joseph Surface [162] & his *senti-ment* put her completely out of patience, & she rejoiced in his complete discom-fiture. Never was evening more happily spent, & when thanking her sister for the amusement she had afforded her, Eliza said that she was glad she knew now all about "little *Premium,*" [163] that she had wanted to be acquainted with him ever since she read "Baring Out"—a story in the *Parent's Assistant*,[164] in which he is mentioned.

Thursday, November 11th

This morning papa read in the North Carolina paper, an account of a melancholy accident which had happened to a stage passenger near Warrenton. In the course of the recital the names of a number of our old acquaintances occurred. Some minutes after Rachel met Eliza & saw the traces of tears on her cheek. Rachel did not at the moment inquire the cause, but in the evening asked Eliza what had made her cry that morning? She hesitated an instant, blushed, and said "because she was sorry for the gentleman papa read about, & because all of it put her so much in mind of Warrenton that she could not help crying." A child who is capable of so strong an attachment to her native village, will surely at a future day evince in an equal degree tenderness & gratitude towards the protectors of her infancy, the guides of her childhood, the instructers of her opening youth. On good feelings, strengthened by principle, & controlled by reason, I rely, as the surest basis of worth & virtue. May the Giver of all Good, bestow the one, it shall be my constant endeavour to implant and foster the other.

December [no date]

Eliza reads every morning a chapter in an excellent little work, entitled, "Elements of the Jewish [F]aith."[165] The commandment "Thou shalt not bear false witness against thy neighbour," is explained to embrace defamation & evil speaking of all kinds. After reading it Eliza asked whether we ought not then to consider it a *sin,* "to talk scandal as they call it, or to take notice of what others do wrong, & like to talk about it."

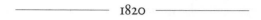

1820

January 4th

This morning Eliza said to me, blushing, "Sister Rachel, if I tell you something will you be angry with me?"

Rachel: "I do not know, but you had better tell me at any rate."

Eliza: "Well, this morning I was sitting by Emma & she pushed me, but she did not go to do it, and I was angry, & shooed her away with my foot."

Rachel: "I am very sorry, both that you have suffered yourself to get angry at a trifle, & that you set your little sister a bad example; but you were right to tell me of your fault, & even if I punished you, I should love you better for your candour."

Eliza: "But sister Rachel I am not sure that I should have told you but sister Julia saw me, & told me I must."

Rachel: "Well, Eliza, you are right *now,* then, not to take praise which does not belong to you, tell Emma if you have not already done so, that it was wrong in you, to set her a bad example, that she must not do as you did, & that you will try not to do so any more."

Eliza: "Yes, I will, but may not I tell her that you told me to tell her so?"

Rachel: "Yes, if you would rather."

Sunday, January 16th

Last evening brother Samuel sent Eliza a book as a New Year's gift, it was *Instructive Rambles* [166] which she has read several times. She was gone to bed, & her sister carried it to her & said, "here Eliza is a pleasure & a disappointment for you." She looked at the title page and exclaimed, "O, sister Rachel!"

Rachel: "Well, Eliza, what will you say to brother Samuel when you see him?"

Eliza, repressing her disappointment, and in an animated tone, replied, "I will tell him that I am *very* much obliged to him, but I will not tell him that I have read it before."

Rachel: "Why not?"

Eliza: "Because you know it would make him feel bad to think that his present did not give me as much pleasure as he wished it should."

Rachel: "That is very right my dear, you are a good girl, give me a kiss, and good night."

March 2d

The pleasure is frequently allowed me of remarking the expanding intelligence & goodness of heart and disposition with which my little Eliza is blest. In her observations on what she reads, in her mode of expression in speaking, and in her style of writing her improvement is adequate to my most sanguine wishes. I was pleased with a neat little turn of thought in a letter she lately addressed to her little friend Louisa: "I have just finished learning two songs, 'Come live with me & be my love' [167] & the 'Mermaid's Song.' [168] I think the former would apply very well as an invitation to my dear Louisa."

This morning she said, "I want to tell you something, Sister Rachel, but if you please not to be angry with me."

Rachel: "What is it my dear?"

Eliza: "This morning I was drest as soon as Emma & when Rosina[169] came in, I begged her to tie my clothes first, because you know I had a great deal more to do than Emma before breakfast; but Rosina said she *would* tie Emma's first & would keep me waiting every day. And then I was very angry & I told her, I would slap her if I could."

Rachel: "Well, Eliza I need not tell you that you were wrong, because you know it; but you should be careful to check yourself whenever you feel any thing like ill temper, or when you are older it will get the better of you. You may easily see that the same feelings which made you *wish* to slap Rosina, might have tempted you to do it, if you had been older & her mistress. She was wrong, but you know she is a poor, ignorant servant, & does not know right from wrong as well as we do. I shall tell her to dress you first, whenever you are ready first, and then there need be no more said about it."

This evening Eliza was eating her supper rather later than usual just as the rest of the family were assembled to tea.

Her sister said playfully, "I do not know what such little folks as you want with supper every night, I think it might be left for us."

"Don't you know," replied Eliza very quickly, "that the road to the blissful regions is as open to the peasant as to the prince?"

Rachel, laughing, "then your road to the blissful regions is strewed, I suppose, with bread and butter."

Eliza: "No, no, but I thought the peasant & the prince *seemed something like* you all, and me."

Caroline: "You mean to say, Eliza, that the *allusion seemed applicable* to us & to you; but where did you get your quotation?"

Eliza: "O, I had it yesterday in my exercise."

She has just commenced Murray's Grammatical exercises and Prosody in the larger grammar; with both . . . studies she is much pleased.

March 28th

The holy days[170] were approaching; Rachel told Eliza she need not say any lesson during those days. She replied in a sorrowful tone, "Not *any* lessons sister Rachel! You know how long the days seemed when my eyes were sore & I could not do any thing: please let me learn *some* lessons."

Rachel: "Well then you may learn such as you prefer, & that give you least trouble, and as your eyes are now well you will be able to read you know."

Thus was the affair adjusted.

A short time since, as one of Eliza's *rewards,* I read for her the poem of "Blanch," by Miss Mitford;[171] her observations on it were generally good & she said she liked it "very much." The next week, I read to her, Campbell's "Gertrude of Wyoming,"[172] which is in every respect far superior to "Blanch." She said she liked it "very well," but that she liked "Blanch," better. I confess I was a little disappointed at this want of judgment, in a case which to me appeared self-evident; but a moment's reflection shewed me that the measure in which Blanch is written would best please an unpracticed ear, & the story tho' very faulty, possesses much to touch & interest the feelings. I did not therefore tell her that her judgment was erroneous, but simply said that I greatly preferred Gertrude; that she should read both poems two or three years hence, & tell me if *her* opinion continued the same. I immediately perceived the good effect of not having alarmed the dawning sensibility of taste, by direct censure, for she continued her liliputian criticism by observing, that the *style* ("as you say sister Rachel") of "Blanch," seemed to her a great deal easier than that of "Gertrude," that the former was something like parts that she had heard of Scott's poems. The last observation was just; the author is one of the many humble imitators of Scott's[173] inimitable poetry. And it was quite natural that the dignified stanza of Campbell, with its unfrequently recurring rhymes, should with all its sweetness, appear to the ear of a child deficient in ease.

Reading the story of "Order & Disorder" in *Evenings at Home*[174] she said "she did not think Juliet was right to shew the old lady the flower as if she had done it all herself, that she ought to have told that *order* helped her." Like one of the children mentioned in *Practical Education*[175] she also remarked that Order ought not to have come, because Juliet cried for her. The remark respecting Juliet's candour, was conformable to her own practice. Emma the other day had been chattering to one of the servants, about some family matters. Eliza called her away, & afterwards very properly & in quite a gentle manner, mentioned the affair to one of her older sisters, that Emma might be told its impropriety. In the evening, however, when her conduct was about to be marked on her list, as "a good girl," she held her sister's hand & said, "About Emma this morning, I told what she had done, partly because I knew it was right for you to know it, and a little too, because I felt angry with her for being so foolish, and I *wanted* to tell about it, but I knew that was wrong afterwards, and felt sorry for it."

This confession did not change the verdict of *good girl,* which she had arrested in its progress.

To her sister Caroline she observed, that she dreaded the time when she should be grown up, for that she did not think she should ever be as happy as she was now. It is a great blessing to be sensible of, & to acknowledge happiness, at the moment when we enjoy it; too often is it known only by a comparison of the *past,* with the less favoured present.

June 30th

I have been pleased with a new instance of my little Eliza's discretion and strict regard to keeping her word. Seated at work with her sisters, the conversation turned on the power of keeping a secret. "Well," said Eliza with great simplicity, "I know *something* that nobody knows but Miss Helen Wilson & another young lady. I said I would not tell till a long time after, but this *is* a long time, & I believe I can tell now."

Rachel: "Do not do so, Eliza, unless you are quite sure that you are right."

Eliza: "Yes, I am sure I may tell it now. You know when Miss H[elen] was sick & used to ride every day, I went with her sometimes. [O]ne day we were riding & one of the other young ladies with us, and Miss H[elen] asked George to let her take the reins, & try to drive the Phaeton a little way. He gave them to her & she let one of the wheels run over a stump, & the jolt threw me out, into the middle of the road. I don't know whether I got up myself or whether George (the servant) lifted me up, but when he put me in the Phaeton, Miss H[elen] was crying very much, and I begged her not to cry, & told her I was not hurt & that I would not tell any body. So *at last* Miss H[elen] left off crying but she told me I must not tell in a very long time, and I never told till now."

Rachel: "But were you not very much frightened Eliza?"

Eliza: "Oh *yes,* I trembled all over, but I got over it, before I got home."

Eliza is naturally very timid, she therefore deserved the more credit for concealing her alarm. This little affair happened three years ago, in 1817; she was then but eight years old.

August [no date]

Eliza was reading that beautiful hymn of Cotton's [176] in which these lines occur:

> "In the dark watches of the night
> I'll count thy mercies o'er,
> I'll praise thee for ten thousand past,
> And humbly sue for more."

She said, "I do not think that is right sister Rachel."

Rachel: "What Eliza?"

Eliza: "Why, to say, I'll praise thee for *ten thousand* past mercies, and yet ask *for more.* It seems if we were never contented."

Her sister smiled at her scrupulous delicacy and represented to her that human beings are feeble, and can do nothing without the favour & assistance of the Almighty in whom it is our duty to confide, as in a kind parent, to whom we are allowed to pray for those good gifts of which we feel ourselves in need, and who only requires in return the exercise of gratitude and sincere adoration. This she understood, and considering the phrase under this point of view, withdrew her objection.

August 10th

Closed Eliza's eleventh year; I have much reason to be thankful for the continued improvement which has marked the course of the last twelve month[s]. At her present age the expansion of the mind becomes more rapid, & is constantly rendering itself perceptible; it may aptly be compared to a bud, which gradually increasing from the germ, bursts at length the envelope which surrounded it and expands itself in new born loveliness to the view.

Her remarks on what she reads & hears, generally shew good sense & reflection; and I congratulate myself on the course I have invariably pursued of not prematurely urging her progress. Thus, books which two years ago were laid aside as uninteresting are now read with avidity & pleasure, because she can now understand them; & the habit of considering whether she does understand what she reads, is so well formed, that she never passes over a passage which is not clear to her, without reviewing, and endeavouring to comprehend it. Her disposition is all that I could wish it, and tho' not free from faults, she has none which time and her own good sense will not enable her to correct. Heedlessness, and the want of *recollective memory,* are the chief. She sometimes incurs censure for neglect of those little attentions which are so pleasing from children to grown persons, but as she listens to blame with docility, and endeavours, *as long as she thinks of it,* to correct her faults, I may venture to hope that she will at length entirely succeed. Of her candour I have frequent proofs; she will not accept praise to which she is not entitled. For instance, I commended her the other day for having fulfilled some little office which she had been lately blamed for omitting. She answered, "Sister Ellen put me in mind of it, or I am afraid I should not have thought of it now."

The Studies in which she has been employed during the past year are:

English Grammar—Syntax & part of Prosody.

Ouiseau's French grammar [177]—In this branch I am glad to say she improves. She now reads easy books with pleasure, & translates with little difficulty.

History. Snowden's *America* [178]—reviewing miniature History of Greece & England [179]—a lesson every Friday.

Geography—reviewing the maps, & reading Guthrie. [180]

Arithmetick—reviewed Practice & has been over the preceding rules, as far as Reduction.

Parsing—in verse promiscuous.

Reading lessons, *Elegant Extracts,*[181] prose & verse alternately.

A chapter in the Bible every day.

Murray's grammatical Exercises.[182]

With the volume of Exercises I gave Eliza the "key" with a charge never to open it unless by my direction. Emma had since asked me if I would let sister Eliza open that book, that she had asked her just to raise the cover & she would not.

Progress in Musick satisfactory.

And to the needle, rather less dislike than heretofore, but still great room for improvement.

In reading the Bible I have found it necessary to look over many chapters previously, & direct her to omit them, telling her at the same time that tho' the Bible was all excellent, yet owing to the difference of time, and the change of manners since it was written, there were some passages which it was not now, necessary or agreeable to read.

The books read during this year are as follows:

Son of a Genius—Mrs. Hofland[183]

Barbadoes Girl d[itt]o[184]

Officer's Widow d[itt]o

Merchant's Widow d[itt]o

Clergyman's Widow d[itt]o[185]

Parts of *Arabian Nights*

d[itt]o of Edinburgh reviews[186]

Biography of Carteret[187]

d[itt]o of Rittenhouse[188]

Life of Pythagorus[189]

Part of Riley's *Narrative*[190]

Telemachus[191]

2 Vols. *Elegant Extracts*

Sketch Book—6 numbers[192]

Search after Happiness—H. More[193]

Holiday Reward—Edwin & Jessy[194]

Gulliver's Travels

Lady Montague's letters[195]

Percival's *Tales*[196]

The good Godmother—Mrs. Hofland[197]

Life of Baron Frenck[198]

Popular Tales—Miss Edgeworth[199]

Kotzebue's life[200]

Letters of a Hindoo Rajah—Mrs. Hamilton[201]

Scott's "Lay of the Last Minstrel"[202]

Pelew Islands[203]

Castle Rackrent—Miss Edgeworth[204] together with some few books read before & not necessary to be here noticed.

In the course of the summer Eliza was indulged with a visit to the Theatre;
the play was "The Lady of the Lake." I soon after read to her Scott's beautiful
poem, with which tho' not capable of entering into all its beauties, she was
much delighted.[205] It is only within a few months that she has acquired a relish
for poetry except of the simplest kind, I have not sought to form her taste prematurely, and now as she becomes more capable of comprehending, she begins
to admire it. With "The Lay of the Last Minstrel" she was highly pleased; a
twelve month since she had taken it up, but laid it aside again as uninteresting,
because as she said she could not understand it.

December 9th

Eliza's 12th year will probably be marked by a considerable change in *her* situation, in consequence of that which is about to take place in her sister's. In
deciding on this change, I could not for a moment think of separating myself
from this child of my care, at least until her education should be nearer it[s]
completion, and her habits of mind more matured. The kind partner of my
future years,[206] cheerfully acceded to my wish, and our dear parents have with
equal kindness consented to let her continue my charge. Previous trials have
given ample proof of her discretion. I did not hesitate to entrust her with the
secret, informing her also that when I left home, she would accompany me. She
shewed such feelings as the intelligence ought to have inspired—[she] blushed
& wept. I asked her why? If she was sorry to have a new brother, or if she did
not wish to go with me? She replied, "I don't know how I feel sister Rachel. I
am glad & sorry. I do want to go with you, but I cannot help crying to think of
leaving all at home."

Notes

1. Eliza Kennon Mordecai (1809–61) was the second daughter and the fifth child
of Jacob Mordecai's second marriage to Rebecca Myers.

2. Rachel's marginal note: "Eliza will be 7 years old in August."

3. Caroline (1794–1862) was the third daughter and sixth (and last) child of Jacob
Mordecai (1762–1838) and his first wife, Judith Myers (1762–96). At this time Caro-

line was twenty-one years old and teaching in her father's school, the Warrenton (North Carolina) Female Academy.

4. Rachel (1789–1838), the author of the diary, was the third child and oldest daughter of Jacob and Judith Mordecai. Throughout the diary Rachel refers to herself in this detached way, rarely in the first person.

5. Commonly known as hazelnuts.

6. Rebecca Myers (1776–1863) married Jacob Mordecai c. 1798. Rebecca was the younger half-sister of Jacob's first wife, Judith.

7. Solomon (1792–1869), the third son and fifth child of Jacob and Judith Mordecai, was only sixteen years old when he began teaching in his father's school, besides managing the institution's accounts and other administrative duties.

8. A student in the Mordecais' school.

9. Because the Mordecais were Jewish, Saturday, the Sabbath, was observed as a day of rest, and thus no schoolwork was done by the family members. The boarding school they ran was nonsectarian, however, and each student was allowed to attend the church of her parents' choice.

10. *Ellen, the Teacher: A Tale for Youth* (1814) was written by Barbara (Wreaks) Hoole Hofland (1770–1844), a prolific British author of children's books. She began writing children's stories to support herself and her small son after the death of her first husband, but she continued her literary career even after her marriage to the artist Thomas Christopher Hofland. She also conducted a school at Harrowgate (*Osborne Collection*, 1:260, 2:896).

11. Samuel (1786–1865), second son and second child of Jacob and Judith Mordecai, was a commission merchant who lived in Richmond. He never taught in the family-run school, but he did occasionally offer financial advice and procure necessities for the Mordecai enterprise.

12. Sofa.

13. Ellen (1790–1884), the fourth child and second daughter of Jacob and Judith Mordecai, taught in the family school and later educated her half-sister Emma.

14. *The History of Sandford and Merton* is a famous children's book written by Thomas Day (1748–89) and published in three volumes between 1783 and 1789. Day, an eccentric moral reformer and disciple of Rousseau, was a good friend of Richard Lovell Edgeworth, father of Maria Edgeworth, who was also a noted children's author (*Osborne Collection*, 1:243).

15. *The Misses Magazine* was not a periodical but a two-volume book published in 1757 by Jeanne Marie Le Prince de Beaumont (1711–80). Its full title is indicative of its contents: *The Young Misses Magazine, Containing Dialogues Between a Governess and Several Young Ladies of Quality Her Scholars: In Which Each Lady is Made to Speak According to Her Particular Genius, Temper and Inclination; Their Several Faults are Pointed Out, and the Easy Way to Mend Them, as Well as to Think, and Speak, and Act Properly: No Less Care Being Taken to Form Their Hearts to Goodness, Than to Enlighten Their Understandings With Useful Knowledge. A Short and Clear Abridgement is Also Given of Sacred and Profane History, and Some Lessons in Geography. The Useful*

is Blended Throughout With the Agreeable the Whole Being Interspersed With Proper Reflections and Moral Tales. There were five young ladies, ages five, seven, ten, twelve, and thirteen, taught by Mrs. Affable. Volume 1 contained more tales, while volume 2 emphasized instruction. The story of "Beauty and the Beast" first appeared in this work (ibid., 1:128).

16. Rachel writes in a footnote, "Mrs. Affable explains to her pupils the distinction between a story & a tale, that the one is a true account of something that has happened, the other merely an amusing fiction; Eliza appears to have remarked this."

17. Rosamund and Frank are characters in Maria Edgeworth's *Early Lessons* (1801). Madame Anne Louise Germaine de Staël wrote *Delphine,* published in 1802. See *Delphine,* trans. Auriel H. Goldberger (DeKalb: Northern Illinois University Press, 1995). It has not been possible to determine what stories featured Eugenia.

18. "Aladdin or the Wonderful Lamp" is one of the stories in the *Arabian Nights Entertainment.*

19. In 1816 and 1817 Rachel and the rest of the family celebrated it a week later than the actual date, 10 August. The family celebrated her birthday on the correct date in 1818.

20. *Mary and Her Cat* probably appeared in various editions. One version, later than that which Eliza read since it was published in 1821, was written *In Words Not Exceeding Two Syllables.* Mrs. Trimmer commented on it in the *Guardian of Education:* "We rank it with interesting and innocent books, which is all an author can aim at in publications for infants" (*Osborne Collection,* 1:282).

21. *Early Lessons,* by Maria Edgeworth (1767–1849), was first published in 1801. It contains little stories featuring Rosamund, Frank, and the siblings Harry and Lucy. The children discover natural wonders and learn natural science as well as improve their behavior and morals through reasoning.

22. *The Parent's Assistant* (1796) was the first of Maria Edgeworth's books of moral stories for children.

23. Mary Wollstonecraft (Godwin) (1759–97) emerged as an early feminist writer, best known for her book *A Vindication of the Rights of Woman* (1792), which stressed education for women. Wollstonecraft's English translation of *Elements of Morality* was published in two volumes in 1790. The German original was *Das moralische Elementarbuch* by Christian Gotthilf Salzmann (1744–1811), a German Protestant minister, educator, and author. It was published in Leipzig in 1785. Wollstonecraft changed the story to an English setting so that child readers would not be distracted by foreign manners and customs that would keep them from focusing on morality (*Osborne Collection,* 1:295).

24. *The History of Little Jack* (1787) was written by Thomas Day, the author of *The History of Sandford and Merton.* It was first published in *The Children's Miscellany* (ibid., 1:243, 409). See notes 14 and 30.

25. The reference may be to either of the following two works. *The Looking Glass: A True History of the Early Years of an Artist* (1805) by Theophilus Marcliffe was actually written by William Godwin (1756–1836), the husband of Mary Wollstonecraft. The subject of this biography was William Mulready (1786–1863), an Englishman

who painted scenes of rural life. Perhaps it is more likely that Eliza read *The Looking-Glass for the Mind,* a collection of moral tales translated by Richard Johnson from Arnaud Berquin's French *L'Ami des enfants.* It was first published in 1787 and was extremely popular, with editions appearing until the mid–nineteenth century (ibid., 1:164). See also Carpenter, *The Oxford Companion to Children's Literature,* 325.

26. *The Children in the Wood* was also later known as *The Babes in the Wood.* A version of this story was in print as early as 1593, and numerous editions have appeared since that time, both in the original ballad form and in prose (*Osborne Collection,* 1:23).

27. Mrs. Pinchard, the author of *The Blind Child, or Anecdotes of the Wyndham Family* (1791), was the wife of an attorney. Her goal for this book was "to repress that excessive softness of heart which too frequently involves its possessor in a train of evils and which is by no means true sensibility, that exquisite gift of heaven" (ibid., 1:289).

28. *Evenings at Home; or the Juvenile Budget Opened* contained a collection of stories written by John Aikin (1747–1822) and his sister Anna Laetitia (Aikin) Barbauld (1743–1825). The work appeared in several volumes from 1792 to 1796 (ibid., 1:229).

29. Daniel Defoe (c. 1660–1731) first published the famous novel of the shipwrecked Robinson Crusoe in 1719.

30. *The Children's Miscellany* (1787), published as a collection of eleven stories, contained Thomas Day's *The History of Little Jack* (*Osborne Collection,* 1:409).

31. See note 10.

32. *Early Lessons—In Continuation,* more stories by Maria Edgeworth about the children featured in *Early Lessons,* was published in two volumes in 1814.

33. *Tales for Children* by Maria Joseph Crabb appeared in a fourth edition in 1816 (*National Union Catalog*).

34. *Tales of the Castle* by Stéphanie Félicité Ducrest de Saint-Aubin, comtesse de Genlis (1746–1830) was published in French in 1784 and in a five-volume English translation by Thomas Holeroft in 1785. The work consisted of a series of "moral tales based on the author's recollections of her childhood and of her experiences as a governess" (*Osborne Collection,* 1:255).

35. Author and source unknown.

36. See note 14.

37. "Little Bo Peep" was probably a piece based on the Mother Goose nursery rhyme, to which there are apparently several tunes (Cushing, comp., *Children's Song Index,* 401).

38. Possibly Eliza was playing the French nursery song "Malbrough s'en va-t-en guerre" (Marlbrouk goes forth to war), a piece with sixteenth-century words and an eighteenth-century tune. The name was spelled various ways, including Malbrouk (ibid., 422).

39. "The Irish Washerwoman" is a sprightly folk tune still known by that name.

40. Composer unknown.

41. Ignaz Josef Pleyel (1757–1831) was a composer, music publisher, and piano manufacturer active in France. As a young man he studied with Franz Joseph Haydn.

He wrote a variety of works, including some small keyboard pieces, that were extremely popular in the United States as well as in Europe (Sadie, ed., *The New Grove Dictionary*, 15:6–10).

42. Valentino Nicolai (fl. 1775–98), a composer and pianist who performed in London and Paris. Little biographical information is known about him. Some of his sonatas were popular enough in the United States as well as in Europe to be reprinted during the nineteenth century. Sonata op. 3, no. 1 in C was among his most celebrated works; the piece was taught at many schools in Britain (ibid., 13:215).

43. Jean-Frédéric (or Johann Friedrich) Edelmann was born in Strasbourg on 5 May 1749. He moved to Paris, where he played and taught harpsichord and piano and also composed works that were popular and even praised by Wolfgang Amadeus Mozart. He suffered as a victim of the Reign of Terror during the French Revolution and was guillotined in Paris on 17 July 1794 (ibid., 5:835).

44. Thomas Day.

45. Harry Sandford, the son of a farmer, is a very kind, moral, and obliging little boy who is being educated by Mr. Barlow, the village minister, in *The History of Sandford and Merton*. Squire Chace is a cruel and much-disliked gentleman of the neighborhood.

46. Julia Judith (1799–1852) was the oldest child of Jacob and Rebecca Mordecai. At times she helped teach in the school as well as assist with school and home management. She was later responsible for the education of the youngest sister, Laura, who, although born in 1818, is never mentioned in this diary.

47. Eliza refers to the biblical story in Genesis 29:1–12, where Jacob, arriving near the home of his uncle Laban, draws water for the flocks of his cousin Rachel.

48. The story "Tarlton" is found in *The Parent's Assistant*. Loveit is unable to say "no" because he wants always to be thought the best-natured boy in the school. Tarlton, the "bad" boy of the piece, continually tempts Loveit and persuades him to do what he knows he should not do.

49. *The Visit for a Week: or, Hints on the Improvement of Time* (1794) by Lucy Peacock contained various natural and moral tales focused on Clara and her brother's visit to their aunt. During the course of the visit Clara learned to correct her faults (*Osborne Collection*, 1:287).

50. Mr. LaTaste, the dancing teacher, may have been a refugee from the revolt in Santo Domingo (Cohen memoirs, 29).

51. "Down town" is Warrenton, North Carolina, county seat of Warren County. Both the town and the county were founded in 1779 and named for Gen. Joseph Warren, who died at the Battle of Bunker Hill. The town was not large (even in the twentieth century it had less than fifteen hundred inhabitants), but besides a courthouse on the square, a tavern, at least one store, and a number of houses, Warrenton had considerable culture and several other private schools and academies with which the Mordecais managed to compete successfully. The other schools were the Warrenton Male Academy, where Jacob Mordecai served two years of successful stewardship before he opened his own school in 1809, and the Nicholson Grammar School, founded in 1811. Mordecai founded his school for girls to rival the splendid Falkner

School, which that same year boasted five teachers and eighty students and was praised throughout the entire South. From the very beginning, the Mordecai school diverted attention from the Falkner School, which was forced to remain closed in 1810 (Wellman, *The County of Warren, North Carolina,* 82–83, 86; Federal Writers Project, *North Carolina,* 476).

52. A ballroom dance that took its name from the eighteenth-century French dance the *cotillon.* The cotillion consisted of a series of intricate figures danced by four couples who formed a square. During the nineteenth century, cotillion patterns became more varied, and the word finally came to denote ballroom dancing for debutantes (*The Encyclopedia Americana,* international ed. [1992]).

53. In 1815 Rachel Mordecai wrote a letter to Maria Edgeworth protesting Edgeworth's stereotypical treatment of the Jewish villain, a coachmaker named Mordecai, in her novel *The Absentee* (1812). The letter referred to in the diary was Maria's reply and also included a note from her father, Richard Lovell Edgeworth (1744–1817), an engineer and educator who co-authored the book *Practical Education* (1798) with his daughter. These letters began a correspondence between the two women that lasted until Rachel's death in 1838. A succession of women in the two families continued the correspondence until 1942.

54. *Practical Education* (1798), written by Maria Edgeworth and her father, utilized the method and experience developed by Richard Lovell Edgeworth and his second wife, Honora Sneyd Edgeworth.

55. See note 22.

56. See the entry beginning 20 August 1816.

57. Solomon, Eliza's brother, taught her geography.

58. The prayer is from the poem "A Morning Song" by Isaac Watts (1674–1748) (Brewton and Brewton, *Index to Poetry,* 545).

59. Augustus (1806–47), the fourth child and third and last son of Jacob and Rebecca Mordecai, was the brother closest to Eliza in age. This episode is the only time he is mentioned in the diary.

60. Solomon.

61. Tommy Merton, the spoiled son of a gentleman, is sent to live with and be taught by Mr. Barlow the clergyman after his parents observe the good example set by Harry Sandford, whom Mr. Barlow has trained.

62. Peter the Great, or Peter I of Russia (1672–1725), married twice. Peter's first marriage, to Eudoxia in 1689 when Peter was only seventeen, arranged for political purposes, demonstrated that Peter was sufficiently adult to rule without a regent. Peter soon ignored this wife and sent her to a convent in 1698. Catherine, his second wife, was of lowly birth, but he loved her and had several children by her before he married her in 1712. Upon his death she succeeded him on the throne as Catherine I.

63. There are several poems with this title. Mary Elliott (1794–1870) wrote such a poem in *Simple Truths in Verse* (1812). Later she authored some prose moral tales. Perhaps Elizabeth Turner (d. 1846), author of *The Daisy, or Cautionary Tales in Verse—Adapted to the Ideas of Children from Four to Eight Years Old* (1807), wrote the poem alluded to in the text. These little poems deal with good and bad behavior and

rewards, providing simple, didactic method. They were so popular that Turner produced three more books of verse: *The Cowslip* (1811), *The Pink* (1835), and *The Crocus* (1844) (Carpenter, *The Oxford Companion to Children's Literature*, 139–40, 165).

64. "My Mother" is probably Ann Taylor's (1782–1866) best-known piece of children's poetry. Although there are other poems with this title, it is most likely Taylor's. Ann and her sister Jane (see note 65) wrote several books of children's poetry, including *Original Poems for Infant Minds* (c. 1804), *Rhymes for the Nursery* (1806), and *Hymns for Infant Minds* (1810) (ibid., 516–17).

65. "Employment" is by Jane Taylor (1783–1824), sister of Ann (see note 64). Jane is best known for her poem "The Star" ("Twinkle, twinkle little star") (ibid., 516–17).

66. Emma (1812–1906), the sixth child and third daughter of Jacob and Rebecca Mordecai, was Eliza's closest sister in age. Apparently these two sisters shared a bed in their parents' room.

67. Parsing is identifying and analyzing the parts of speech in a sentence. Lindley Murray (1745–1826) was born in Philadelphia and worked as a lawyer in New York until failing health prompted him to move to England in 1784. His *English Grammar* (1795) was written to help some friends who were teaching at a girls' school in York. His *English Exercises,* sold with or without a key, had gone through thirty-four editions of ten thousand copies each by 1826. Murray's grammar books remained popular and in print at least until 1867 (*Osborne Collection*, 2:723).

68. George Washington (1801–70), second child and oldest son of Jacob and Rebecca Mordecai, assisted with the school in 1817 and after. This is the only time he is mentioned in the diary.

69. Rachel's marginal note reads "February 23, [1817]."

70. *Instructive Rambles in London and the Adjacent Villages. Designed to Amuse the Mind, and Improve the Understanding of Youth,* 2 vols. (1798) by Mrs. Elizabeth Helme (d. 1816) was followed in 1800 by a two-volume sequel, *Instructive Rambles Extended in London and the Adjacent Villages* (*Osborne Collection*, 1:183).

71. The poem is "To a Little Girl Who Has Told a Lie" by Ann Taylor (see note 63).

72. The note to Caroline is not included.

73. Solomon became ill from overwork at the school and sometime in 1817 had to leave for an extended vacation. At this time his younger half-siblings Julia and George took his place.

74. Author and source unknown.

75. "The Little Merchants," a story in *The Parent's Assistant,* is set in Naples, Italy, where honesty brings the young gardener Francisco success, and deception lands the young Piedro in jail.

76. In Aesop's fable of the fox and the crow, a crow is sitting in a tree with a piece of meat in its mouth, which the fox wants. The fox begins to flatter the crow, telling it that it is such a fine bird that it could be king of the birds if only it had a voice. To prove that it has a voice, the crow begins to caw as loudly as possible and, of course, drops the meat. As the fox picks up the meat he remarks that the crow would be a great king if only he also had brains (Aesop, *Fables*, 12).

77. Miss Louisa, perhaps a student at the school or a neighbor child, was one of Eliza's favorite playmates.

78. Eliza, sensitive to the Jewish prohibition against work on the Sabbath, regretted her actions even though her "work" was merely play.

79. See note 70.

80. Nothing has been discovered about the Tradescants.

81. See note 15.

82. Eliza's note is not included.

83. Rachel often uses the phrase "her friends" to mean Eliza's relatives.

84. Again, Rachel miscalculates Eliza's birthday; it is actually a week later.

85. See note 14.

86. Possibly *A Father's Tales to His Daughter* (translated into English from French in 1811) by Jean Nicholas Bouilly (1763–1842), who also wrote *A Father's Advice to His Daughter* (1813).

87. See note 70.

88. *Paul and Virginia* by Jacques Henri Bernardin de Saint Pierre (1737–1814), a friend and follower of Rousseau, was first published in French in 1788 as volume 4 of *Etudes de la nature* and then published separately in 1789. Helen Maria Williams translated the story into English. The story apparently has no moral and ends unhappily when the hero dies a victim of disappointed love. Williams suffered imprisonment by Robespierre during the Reign of Terror. The English version appeared in 1795 (*Osborne Collection,* 2:931).

89. *Instinct Displayed. In a Collection Exemplifying the Extraordinary Sagacity of Various Species of the Animal Creation* (1811) by Priscilla Bell Wakefield (1751–1832). Scientific information is presented as a series of letters between two girls (ibid., 1:215).

90. A version of Mary Sterndale's *Delia's Birth-Day and Other Interesting Stories for Youth* was published in London in 1821.

91. *Rose and Emily; or, Sketches of Youth* (1812) by Mrs. Roberts is a moral tale set in Derbyshire (*Osborne Collection,* 1:294).

92. Possibly a reference to *The Young Northern Traveller* (1813) by Barbara Hofland, a series of letters ostensibly written by Frederic to Charles during a trip through northern Europe in 1806 (ibid., 1:184).

93. See John Gay, introduction to *Fables* entitled "The Shepherd and the Philosopher" (1727, 1738; reprint ed., Los Angeles: William Andrews Clark Memorial Library, University of California, 1967).

94. Perhaps these are variations on a Dutch nursery song called "The Little Sailor" (Cushing, comp., *Children's Song Index,* 406).

95. The author is probably referring to the Scottish song "Up & Warn a' Willie" (Havlice, *Popular Song Index,* 737).

96. Author and source unknown.

97. Richmond, the capital of Virginia, was about 108 miles north of Warrenton, North Carolina, where the Mordecais lived. Located just below the falls of the James River, Richmond throve as a commercial and manufacturing town. Its growing popu-

lation—9,735 in 1810, increasing to 14,338 in 1817—supported two market houses, three banks, two insurance companies, four tobacco warehouses, six churches and a synagogue, a museum and academy of fine arts, and a female orphan asylum. It was also the location of the statehouse and governor's mansion, as well as a jail, almshouse, courthouse, state prison, and armory. The manufacturing of glass was carried on as well as nail making. Richmond also boasted an iron foundry and a rolling and slitting mill. Of the fourteen hundred houses in the city, eight hundred were brick and six hundred wood (Morse and Morse, *A New Universal Gazetteer*).

98. A pelisse is a type of loose cloak with a wide collar and fur trimming.

99. A causeway is a portion of road raised over wet ground or water.

100. Petersburg in Dinwiddie County, Virginia, is located just below the falls of the Appomattox River, 83 miles north of Warrenton, North Carolina, and 25 miles south of Richmond. It was a commercial and shipping center. Petersburg claimed a courthouse, jail, Masonic Hall, two banks, tobacco warehouses, flour mills, an insurance office, and five churches. In 1810 the population was 5,663 and had grown to 6,328 by 1820 (Morse and Morse, *A New Universal Gazetteer*).

101. John Mayo Jr. built Mayo's bridge in 1788. Preparations had been made by his father, who died before carrying them out. Although the bridge was wrecked that winter by ice, the first of many such disasters due to ice and floods, it was quickly rebuilt and earned considerable money in tolls for its owner (Dabney, *Richmond,* 45).

102. Samuel Myers (1755–1836) was the older brother of both of Jacob Mordecai's wives. After the death of Judith Mordecai in 1796, Rachel and Ellen lived in Richmond with the Myerses for several years until their father remarried (Cohen memoirs, 26–27).

103. Samuel Myers's home in Richmond, located on the corner of Broad and Governor Streets, was made of brick with high ceilings and wide halls. A large drawing room and dining room were separated by folding doors. The drawing room fireplace was particularly elegant, with a gray marble mantelpiece and carved woodwork painted white and nearly reaching the ceiling. Recessed bookshelves flanked the fireplace, and a pair of old-fashioned steel mirrors, called "girondolles," hung on the walls. The house had piazzas at the back and stood in a large garden of fruit trees, shrubs, flowers, and grapevines. There was also an arbor and an "office," a separate building where the young men slept (ibid., 15).

104. Judith Hays Myers (1767–1844) married Samuel Myers as his second wife. She bore all seven of his children. Samuel's first wife, Sarah Judah, whom he married in 1794, died soon after their marriage. Samuel and Judith were married 27 September 1796. The oldest of the cousins, Samuel Hays Myers (1799–1849) was then eighteen. He eventually married Eliza on 21 November 1827.

1827. Eliza most probably played with her twin cousins, Ella C. (1808–92) and Rachel Hays (1808–62), who were only a year older than Eliza.

105. Author and source unknown.

106. Manchester, Virginia, is located on the south side of the James River opposite to Richmond, with which it was connected in the early 1800s by two bridges, one of them Mayo's bridge.

107. A swingletree, also known as a singletree or whippletree, is the movable bar upon which the traces of the horses' harnesses are attached.

108. Author and source unknown.

109. A bandbox is a pasteboard or thin wooden box used for holding light articles of clothing.

110. See note 28.

111. Entry of 25 September 1816.

112. Solomon.

113. Exodus 20:7.

114. Orthodox Jews consider JHWH too sacred to utter. The word may be translated as God or Lord.

115. See note 21.

116. This incident occurs in the chapter "We Make Another Canoe" when Crusoe attempts to send Friday back to Friday's own country.

117. Nineteenth-century families used turkey wings to fan flames or extinguish sparks in their fireplaces and on their hearths.

118. In "The Silver Cup" Ellen earns extra money by working overtime to help the smaller children in the factory make their contribution to the purchase of a silver cup for their much-loved minister, who is leaving. Laura is Rosamund's kind and sensible older sister.

119. Mademoiselle Panache was Lady Augusta's worthless French governess. Part I of her story is found in *The Parent's Assistant. Moral Tales* (1801) is intended for older children.

120. The subscription paper is a pledge to donate money to help the injured woman.

121. This Caroline is the schoolgirl with whom Eliza worked her sampler, not Eliza's sister who taught her French.

122. This probably refers to Oliver Goldsmith's introduction to volume I of R. Brooks's *A New and Accurate System of Natural History* (1793), entitled "Introduction, of Quadrupedes in general, and their way of living." In the essay, Goldsmith wrote: "Though nature has provided that every species of animals should be . . . kept distinct, yet we have many reasons to believe, as has been observed before, that she has not been so solicitous for the preservation of them all." He then quotes the example of the mahout, "which is computed to have been at least five times as big as the Elephant." So huge a body, he points out, would "require the produce of an immense tract for its subsistence."

123. The family celebrates Eliza's birthday on the correct date.

124. See note 67.

125. "Work" refers to needlework.

126. In "The Wager" Rosamund and her brother Godfrey bet that she will not make one excuse a day for a week. This turns out to be impossible, because Rosamund continually makes excuses, but the experience does lead to Rosamund's breaking her habit of excuse making (Edgeworth, *Early Lessons—In Continuation*).

127. Probably *Conversations Introducing Poetry: Chiefly on Subjects of Natural His-*

tory, 2 vols. (1804) by Charlotte (Turner) Smith (1749–1806) (*Osborne Collection,* 1:212).

128. Alfred Mills (1776–1833) wrote *Pictures of English History, in Miniature,* 2 vols. (1809) and *Pictures of Grecian History, in Miniature* (1812) (ibid., 1:169).

129. See note 28.

130. *Rural Walks: In Dialogues,* 2 vols. (1795) by Charlotte (Turner) Smith (1749–1806) included twelve dialogues, each concluding with some poetry. The book aims to combine novel and schoolbook in order "to repress discontent; to check the flippancy of remark so frequently disgusting in girls of twelve or thirteen." Eliza also rejected Smith's other book, *Conversations Introducing Poetry.* See note 127. Smith separated from her husband, Benjamin, and wrote children's books to support their eight children.

131. See note 119.

132. "Elegy Written in a Country Churchyard" by the British poet Thomas R. Gray (1716–71).

133. *The Interesting and Affecting History of Prince Lee Boo, a Native of the Pelew Islands, Brought to England by Capt. Wilson. To Which is Prefixed a Short Account of Those Islands. With a Sketch of the Manners and Customs of the Inhabitants* (1789). Lee Boo was brought to England after the wreck of the *Antelope* in 1783 and died of smallpox in 1784. This is a children's version based on *An Account of the Pelew Islands* (1788) by George Keate (*Osborne Collection,* 1:166).

134. Jean Pierre Claris de Florian (1775–94) may have translated Johann Christoph Friedrich von Schiller's five-act play *Wilhelm Tell,* first acted in Weimar in 1804 (Schiller, *William Tell,* trans. Maj. Gen. Patrick Maxwell [London: Walter Scott, Ltd., n.d.]).

135. Jean Pierre Claris de Florian.

136. *Gustavus; or The Macaw, A Story to Teach Children the Proper Value of Things* was translated from German and published in London in 1814. Neither author nor translator is known (*National Union Catalog*).

137. Author and source unknown.

138. *The Adventures of a Donkey* (1814) by Arabella Argus (pseud.) depicts the supposed autobiography of Jemmy, an eighteenth-century patriotic donkey. A sequel, *The Further Adventures of Jemmy Donkey,* appeared in 1821 (*Osborne Collection,* 1:231).

139. *Gulliver's Travels* (1726) by Jonathan Swift (1667–1745).

140. See note 34.

141. The Hydra in Greek mythology was a gigantic monster with nine or more heads. If one head was cut off, two more grew in its place. Hercules killed the Hydra by burning the roots of the heads, thus accomplishing one of his twelve labors.

142. Author and source unknown.

143. Only ten months had elapsed since Rachel's last entry on 18 October 1818.

144. Pelatiah Chapin, "The Death of Abel," in *Evangelic Poetry for the Purposes of Devotion, Excited by Spiritual Songs and Conviction Urged by Gospel . . .* (Concord: Printed by G. Hough for the author, 1794).

145. William Cowper's (1731–1800) poem *The Task* (1785) was composed in six

books. This particular section is from book 6, "The Winter Walk at Noon," beginning with line 560:

> I would not enter on my list of friends
> (Though graced with polished manners and fine sense,
> Yet wanting sensibility) the man
> Who needlessly sets foot upon a worm.

Cowper continues to argue that it is justifiable to kill venemous creatures that have intruded into the house but wrong to destroy those found in nature.

146. The Mordecais' new residence, Spring Farm, located 5 miles from Richmond, was a two-story residence. Caroline Myers Cohen (1844–1928), Eliza's daughter, described the family home as a high, simple farmhouse painted white, with honeysuckle-covered porches and a separate "office" where the young men slept (Cohen memoirs, 45).

147. Author and source unknown.

148. J. Ouiseau edited a number of editions of Thomas Nugent's French-English dictionary in the early 1800s. He also wrote *The Manual of Youth Containing I. Sixty Fables French and English II. Remarks on Rhetoric III. A Large Collection of Extracts, in Prose and Verse, Selected from the Most Approved Authors, English and French* (1807).

149. See note 67.

150. William Guthrie (1708–70) first published *A New Geographical, Historical, and Commercial Grammar; and Present State of the Several Kingdoms of the World* in 1770. The work went through numerous editions, some of which were titled *A New System of Modern Geography; or, A Geographical Historical . . .* An atlas also accompanied the book (*National Union Catalog*).

151. This may be *Dr. Goldsmith's History of Greece, Abridged, for the Use of Schools* by Oliver Goldsmith (1730–74). The history was first published in two volumes in 1774 and in an abridged edition in 1787. The Mordecai school adopted both Goldsmith's "England" and "Greece." Alternatively, these may refer to works by Alfred Mills (*Osborne Collection*, 1:164; Cohen memoirs, 31). See note 128.

152. Probably *The History of North and South America. From Its Discovery, to the Death of General Washington* (1805), although no evidence of an abridged version exists (*National Union Catalog*).

153. See note 144.

154. See note 10.

155. *Elegant Extracts: or, Useful and Entertaining Passages in Prose, Selected for the Improvement of Scholars at Classical and Other Schools, in the Art of Speaking, in Reading, Thinking, Composing; and in the Conduct of Life* was edited by the Reverend Vicesimus Knox (1752–1821) and first published in 1783. A collection of poetry with the same title, but substituting the word "poetry" for "prose," appeared in the early 1790s. Knox also edited a twelve-volume compendium entitled *Elegant Extracts, a Copious Selection of Instructive, Moral, and Entertaining Passages, from the Most Eminent Poets* (1801–7) (*National Union Catalog*).

156. James Riley (1777–1840), *An Authentic Narrative of the Loss of the American*

Brig Commerce, *Wrecked on the Western Coast of Africa, in the Month of August 1815, with an Account of the Sufferings of the Surviving Officers and Crew, Who were Enslaved by the Wandering Arabs on the Great African Desert, or Zaharah; and Observations Historical, Geographical. &c., Made During the Travels of the Author, While a Slave to the Arabs, and in the Empire of Morocco,* published in Hartford and New York in 1817.

157. Solomon left home to attend the University of Pennsylvania Medical School in October 1819. After graduation in 1822, he opened a medical practice in Mobile, Alabama, in 1823.

158. Rachel has begun to instruct Emma as well as Eliza.

159. *The School for Scandal* (1777) by Irish-born playwright, impresario, orator, and Whig politician Richard Brinsley Sheridan (1751–1816), is often considered the greatest comedy of manners in English.

160. Maria Edgeworth's *Comic Dramas* (1817) consisted of three plays: *Love and the Law, The Two Guardians,* and *The Rose, the Thistle, and the Shamrock.*

161. Sir Peter Teazle, guardian of Joseph and Charles Surface as well as Maria, the object of both of the brothers' affections, is an older man who has recently married a young wife. She is a part of the scandalmongering group that appalls Sir Peter.

162. Joseph Surface speaks only moralisms and platitudes and yet is accepted as an upstanding person, but finally these characteristics are exposed as superficial.

163. Little Premium is actually the rich uncle Sir Oliver Surface in disguise, who, posing as a broker, purchases the family portraits from his spendthrift nephew Charles. This situation leads to the reformation of Charles and the downfall of Joseph, demonstrating that none of the three characters was actually who he seemed to be on the surface.

164. "The Baring Out" is a tale of schoolboys in rebellion. Early in the story, as the boys head down to their new theater to act out *The School for Scandal,* one boy says he will be Charles while his companion should be Little Premium.

165. Solomon Jacob Cohen, *Elements of Jewish Faith* (London, n.d.).

166. See note 70.

167. "Come Live with Me and Be My Love" is an old English ballad of uncertain authorship dating from the time of William Shakespeare (Chappell, *The Ballad Literature,* 213–15).

168. "The Mermaid's Song" may refer to a piece with words by F. H. Martens and music by Carl Maria von Weber (1786–1826), noted German composer, conductor, pianist, and critic (Cushing, comp., *Children's Song Index,* 444).

169. Rosina is a Mordecai family slave.

170. Passover is a festival that commemorates both the start of the barley harvest and the liberation of the Israelites from slavery in Egypt. The word "Passover" recalls how the angel of death "passed over" the houses of the Jews when he slew the first-born of the Egyptians. The Israelites were set free but left Egypt in such a hurry that they could not wait for the bread to rise, so they baked wafers of unleavened bread, or matzoth, to carry with them. The festival lasts for eight days in the Dispersion and seven in Israel. It begins with a special dinner called a seder, which means order.

The order is found in the haggadah, or "telling." The food served includes matzoth, unseasoned horseradish, a dish of chopped apples mixed with nuts, cinnamon, and wine, a shankbone of lamb, a roasted egg, vegetables such as parsley or radish, and saltwater, all of which have special symbolic meanings (Klein, *A Guide to Jewish Religious Practice*, 104–30; Belford, *Introduction to Judaism*, 111–14; Cohon, *Introduction to Judaism*, 118–24, 173–74).

171. "Blanch," a poem by Mary Russell Mitford (1786–1853), appeared in *Narrative Poems on the Female Character in the Various Relations of Human Life*, vol. 1 (1813) (*National Union Catalog*).

172. "Gertrude of Wyoming" by T. Campbell is from part 3 of *The Oneyda's Death Song* and is also known as "The Lament of Outalissi."

173. Sir Walter Scott (1771–1832), Scottish novelist, historian, poet, and biographer, is often considered the inventor of the historical novel. At this time he was only known for his poetry, however, because his first novel, *Waverley*, was published anonymously in 1814, and its authorship was not revealed until 1827.

174. See note 28.

175. See note 53.

176. Author and source unknown.

177. See note 48.

178. See note 152.

179. See note 128.

180. See note 150.

181. See note 155.

182. See note 67.

183. *The Son of a Genius: A Tale for the Use of Youth* (1812) is the best known of Barbara Hofland's children's books and was translated into many European languages. The story is based on the life of the author's second husband, Christopher Hofland, who was a good artist "but not a great practical economist" (*Osborne Collection*, 1:262). See also note 10.

184. *Matilda; or The Barbadoes Girl* (1816) concerns a wealthy, spoiled girl who converts to good morals and manners after a year with an English family (ibid., 1:261, 2:896).

185. *The History of an Officer's Widow and Her Young Family* (1809), *The History of a Merchant's Widow and Her Young Family* (1814), and *The History of a Clergyman's Widow and Her Young Family* (2nd ed., 1814) are all books by Barbara Hofland. Mrs. Hofland's own widowhood and single parenthood inspired this series (*National Union Catalog; Osborne Collection*, 1:260, 2:896).

186. The *Edinburgh Review, or Critical Journal* (nos. 1–510) published quarterly periodicals, sometimes irregularly, between October 1802 and October 1929. The periodicals appeared in an American as well as a British edition. The contributions in at least the first one hundred numbers were published anonymously (*National Union Catalog*).

187. Sir George Carteret (c. 1610–80) was one of the eight original proprietors of

the Carolinas and the holder of property rights to half of New Jersey, which his heirs sold to William Penn in 1682.

188. David Rittenhouse (1732–96) demonstrated varied talents as an astronomer, inventor, and builder of mathematical instruments. He observed the atmosphere of Venus and also surveyed the boundaries between Pennsylvania and neighboring states. In addition, he served as state treasurer of Pennsylvania (1777–89), first director of the United States Mint in Philadelphia (1792–95), and president of the American Philosophical Society (1791–96).

189. Pythagoras (c. 580–500 B.C.) was a Greek philosopher, mathematician, and founder of the mystical/religious Pythagorean brotherhood, whose ideas of astrology and number harmony influenced the development of classical Greek philosophy and medieval European thought.

190. See note 156.

191. Telemachus, the son of Odysseus and Penelope in Homer's *Odyssey,* helped his father slay the faithful Penelope's undesirable suitors. He later married Circe (Calypso).

192. Perhaps *The Sketch Book of Geoffrey Crayon, Gent.* (1819–20) by the American author Washington Irving (1783–1859). The more than thirty pieces in *The Sketch Book* included "The Legend of Sleepy Hollow" and "Rip van Winkle."

193. The *Search After Happiness; A Pastoral Drama, In Three Dialogues* (c. 1766) was authored by Hannah More (1745–1833), who also wrote "Cheap Repository Tracts," beginning in 1792, in which she admonished the poor to live soberly and industriously (*National Union Catalog*).

194. Authors and source unknown.

195. *Letters of the Right Honorable Lady M——y W——y M——e; Written, During Her Travels in Europe, Asia and Africa, to Persons of Distinction, Men of Letters, &c. in Different Parts of Europe, Which contain, Among Other Curious Relations, Accounts of the Policy and Manners of the Turks; Drawn from Sources that Have Been Inaccessible to Other Travellers* (1763) by Lady Mary Wortley Montague (1689–1762) (*National Union Catalog*).

196. Thomas Percival (1740–1804), a medical doctor, wrote *A Father's Instructions, Consisting of Moral Tales, Fables, and Reflections; Designed to Promote the Love of Virtue, a Taste for Knowledge, and an Early Acquaintance With the Works of Nature* (1778 or earlier), also known as *A Father's Instructions to His Children.* Percival designed *Moral and Literary Dissertations* (1784) as a sequel to his previous work (*Osborne Collection,* 1:287–88; *National Union Catalog*).

197. Rachel probably means Barbara Hofland's *The Good Grandmother, and Her Offspring; A Tale* (1817) (*Osborne Collection,* 1:261).

198. Author and source unknown.

199. Maria Edgeworth published *Popular Tales* in 1804.

200. August Friedrich Ferdinand von Kotzebue (1761–1819) established himself as a prolific German playwright; he wrote comedies of manners. His plays include *The Good Citizens of Piffleheim, The Two Brothers, False Shame, Thirty Years,* and *Lovers Vows.*

201. *Translation of the Letters of a Hindoo Rajah; Written Previous to and During the Period of His Residence in England, To Which is Prefixed, a Preliminary Dissertation on the History, Religion, and Manners, of the Hindoos* by Elizabeth Hamilton (1758–1816). Elizabeth Hamilton wrote a fictional account of the customs and manners of England, supposedly narrated by an Indian (*National Union Catalog*).

202. Sir Walter Scott wrote the poem *The Lay of the Last Minstrel* in 1805. See note 173.

203. *An Account of the Pelew Islands* (1788) by George Keate was the original from which the story of Prince Lee Boo was drawn (*Osborne Collection*, 1:166). See note 132.

204. *Castle Rackrent* (1800), the first of Maria Edgeworth's Irish novels, is generally regarded as her best. It is a witty depiction of the decline of a dissolute English aristocrat and the rise of a new Irish middle-class landowning and managerial family.

205. Sir Walter Scott published *The Lady of the Lake* in 1810.

206. Rachel married Aaron Lazarus (1777–1841) of Wilmington, North Carolina, a widower with seven children, on 21 March 1821. Phila, one of Aaron's daughters, had been a student at the Mordecai school. Aaron and Rachel had three daughters and a son, Marx Edgeworth (1822–95), whose middle name resulted from Rachel's admiration for Maria Edgeworth.

Bibliography

Aesop. *Fables of Aesop*. Trans. S. A. Handford. Baltimore: Penguin, 1954.

Belford, Lee. *Introduction to Judaism*. New York: Association Press, 1961.

Brewton, J. E., and S. W. Brewton. *Index to Poetry in Collections for Children and Youth*. New York: H. W. Wilson, 1942.

Carpenter, Humphrey. *The Oxford Companion to Children's Literature*. New York: Oxford University Press, 1984.

Chappell, William. *The Ballad Literature of Popular Music of the Olden Time*. 1859. Reprint New York: Dover, 1965.

Cohen, Caroline. Memoirs. Myers Family Papers, 1763–1923. Virginia Historical Society, Richmond.

Cohon, Beryl S. *Introduction to Judaism: A Book for Jewish Youth*. Rev. ed. New York: Bolch Publishing Co., 1946.

Cowper, William. *The Poetical Works of William Cowper*. Vol. 2. London: Bell and Daldy York Street, 1866.

Cushing, Helen Grace, comp. *Children's Song Index*. New York: H. W. Wilson, 1936.

Dabney, Virginius. *Richmond: The Story of a City*. Garden City, N.Y.: Doubleday & Co., 1976.

Federal Writers Project of the Works Progress Administration. *North Carolina, a Guide to the Old North State*. Chapel Hill: University of North Carolina Press, 1939.

Grainger, Edith. *An Index to Poetry and Recitations.* Rev. ed. Chicago: A. C. McClurg & Co., 1918.

Grant, Michael, and John Hazel. *Gods and Mortals in Classical Mythology.* Springfield, Mass.: G. & C. Merriam, 1973.

Havlice, Patricia P. *Popular Song Index.* Metuchen, N.J.: Scarecrow Press, 1975.

Klein, Isaac. *A Guide to Jewish Religious Practice.* New York: Jewish Theological Seminary of America, 1979.

MacDonald, Edgar E., ed. *The Education of the Heart: The Correspondence of Rachel Mordecai Lazarus and Maria Edgeworth.* Chapel Hill: University of North Carolina Press, 1977.

Morse, Jedidiah, and Richard C. Morse. *A New Universal Gazetteer or Geographical Dictionary . . .* 3rd ed. New Haven, Conn.: Sherman Converse, 1821.

The National Union Catalog Pre-1956 Imprints. 754 vols. London: Mansell, 1968–81.

Nuremburger, Ruth K. "Some Notes on the Mordecai Family." *Virginia Magazine of History and Biography* 49 (October 1941): 364–73.

The Osborne Collection of Early Children's Books: A Catalogue 1476–1910. Prepared by Judith St. John. 2 vols. Toronto: Toronto Public Library, 1975.

Sadie, Stanley, ed. *The New Grove Dictionary of Music and Musicians.* 20 vols. London: Macmillan, 1980.

Stern, Malcolm H., comp. *Americans of Jewish Descent: A Compendium of Genealogy.* New York: Ktav Publishing House, 1971.

Wellman, Manly Wade. *The County of Warren, North Carolina, 1586–1917.* Chapel Hill: University of North Carolina Press, 1959.

APPENDIX

Short Biographies of the Mordecai
and Edgeworth Families

The Mordecai Family

Jacob Mordecai was born in 1762 in Philadelphia to Moses Mordecai of Bonn, Germany, and Esther Whitlock of England and was raised in a mercantile family of patriots during the American Revolution.[1] Jacob married Judith Myers of New York in 1784 and migrated south in search of business opportunities, settling in Warrenton, North Carolina. The couple had six children: Moses, Samuel, Rachel, Ellen, Solomon, and Caroline. Judith Mordecai died in 1796. Jacob then married Rebecca Myers, Judith's half-sister, in 1798. This marriage produced seven children: Julia, George Washington, Alfred, Augustus, Eliza Kennon, Emma, and Laura.

Business failure drove Jacob Mordecai to an alternative venture, the founding of the Warrenton Female Academy in 1808. The academy proved to be a successful enterprise for a decade. The family then retired to Spring Farm outside of Richmond, Virginia. Unfortunately, the farm remained unprofitable, and the family sold it in 1832 and moved to Richmond. After a lengthy illness Jacob Mordecai died on 4 September 1838.

Moses Mordecai, the eldest child of Judith and Jacob Mordecai, was born in April 1785. Educated in Warrenton, he pursued legal studies, was licensed to practice in 1808, and thereafter rode circuit. His marriage in 1817 to Margaret Lane of Raleigh, a wealthy Christian woman, caused consternation in the Mordecai family. Margaret Lane died in 1821. Two years later Moses married her sister, Anne Willis Lane. Moses' health worsened in 1824, and despite attempts at rest cures, he died 1 September 1824.

Samuel Mordecai, born 24 July 1786, operated as a well-known tobacco and cotton merchant in Richmond and Petersburg, Virginia. His investments and financial advice supported the Mordecai family school but also led to straitened circumstances during business recessions. He never married, but his home in Petersburg became a refuge for various family members, including Eliza, Rachel, and Ellen. His health declined in 1860, and although he managed to survive during the Civil War years in Richmond, he died in Raleigh on 9 April 1865.

Rachel Mordecai Lazarus, the eldest daughter of Jacob and Judith Mordecai, was born 1 July 1788. She demonstrated her academic talents as the principal teacher at the Warrenton Female Academy and as mentor to her half sister Eliza. Rachel married Aaron Lazarus, a widower with seven children, in 1821. The couple had four children of their own: Marx Edgeworth, born on 6 February 1822; Ellen, born on 13 July 1825; Mary Catherine, born on 12 September 1828; and Julia Judith, born on 9 October 1830. Rachel converted to Christianity on her deathbed in June 1838.

Ellen Mordecai, born 10 November 1790, remained Rachel's confidante. Raised together in Richmond after their mother's death, Rachel and Ellen then shared the hardships of maintaining the academy. Ellen did the housekeeping and also taught at the school. Thereafter she taught her nieces and nephews. In demand within the family, she helped Caroline, Samuel, and Solomon with housekeeping. In 1848 she took a job as a governess with the family of Denning Duer in New York and earned an independent living. She then returned to her family to nurse her invalid stepmother. She spent her time writing Evangelical tracts and memoirs and lived until October 1884. She never married.

Solomon Mordecai, the third son of Jacob and Judith Mordecai, born 10 October 1792, displayed his talents early. He attended St. George's Academy but was soon recruited to teach at the Warrenton Female Academy. His duties included management of the family enterprise. Since he had always been in delicate health, Jacob decided to spare him the rigors of daily teaching and allow him to prepare for medical school. Solomon attended the University of Pennsylvania Medical School in Philadelphia in 1819. He graduated and took up his practice in Mobile, Alabama, in 1822. He married Caroline Waller, a Christian planter's daughter, in 1824. They raised nine children. His practice and pharmacy prospered; however, blindness and paralysis afflicted him in later life and necessitated his sisters, Caroline and Ellen, to assist in his care. He died an invalid in 1869.

Caroline Mordecai Plunkett, the youngest child of Jacob's first marriage, was born in August 1794. She taught in her father's school and in 1814 became romantically attached to an eccentric teacher on the faculty, Achilles Plunkett, former Santo Domingo planter and dance instructor. Despite family objections the couple married on 19 December 1820. The Plunketts eventually purchased the Warrenton Female Academy. Tragedy stalked the family, however, as all three of Caroline's children died in infancy. Achilles Plunkett himself died in

1824. Caroline sold the school in 1825 and then opened a succession of schools in places near her family: Warrenton, Raleigh, and Wilmington. She died in Raleigh in 1862.

Julia Judith Mordecai, born in May 1799 to Jacob and Rebecca Mordecai, taught in the Warrenton Female Academy and took over Solomon's management after his retirement from teaching. Overwhelmed by housekeeping and the teaching of younger children, Julia developed health problems. She never married and died in March 1852.

George Washington Mordecai, the eldest son of Jacob Mordecai's second marriage, born 27 April 1801, achieved a prosperous status as businessman and lawyer. He apprenticed with Samuel in Richmond in 1817, then returned briefly to relieve Solomon of his teaching responsibilities. George tried tobacco trading in Kentucky, but lack of success directed him toward his brother Moses in Raleigh in order to read law. Admitted to the bar in 1821, he commenced a successful legal practice. His business ventures included president of the Raleigh and Gaston Railroad from 1836 to 1852 and thereafter a director until 1871. Elected president of the North Carolina State Bank in 1849, he also served as president of Forest Mill, a paper mill, in 1860. Family members such as Eliza Mordecai and Marx Lazarus received generous donations from George in times of economic distress. He visited the Edgeworth family in Edgeworthstown in 1839. He died in 1871.

Alfred Mordecai, born in 1804 and educated at Warrenton Male Academy and by his siblings, entered West Point in 1819. He graduated first in his class and then taught at the Point. He received major appointments in Virginia, Washington, D.C., and Philadelphia as an engineer and ordnance officer. In 1833 he visited Edgeworthstown, and Maria and her family received him warmly. In 1855 he was sent to study military operations in the Crimea. During secession he resigned from the army as head of the Watervliet Arsenal in Albany, New York. He did not wish to fight against his family in the South, nor did he wish to join the Confederacy. After a period of poverty he taught mathematics in Philadelphia and became assistant engineer of the Mexico and Pacific Railroad from 1863 to 1866; he was later connected with the Pennsylvania Railroad. He died in 1887.

Augustus Mordecai, born in 1806, never entered a profession but tended his father's farm. Restless, he ventured into gold mining, but nothing came of it. In 1835 he married Rosina Ursula Young of Westbrook, a farm adjoining Spring Farm. After a sojourn in Raleigh the couple settled at Rosewood, another farm adjoining Spring Farm. Augustus began a successful ice storage business. The business prospered, but unfortunately, Augustus died in 1847.

Eliza Kennon Mordecai Myers, born 10 August 1809 and educated in Warrenton, benefited from the home schooling of her half sisters Rachel and, later, Ellen. She lived briefly with Rachel in Wilmington and was introduced to society there. She was known chiefly among the family as a talented musician. Eliza married her cousin Samuel Hays Myers in 1827; the couple went to live with Samuel Mordecai in Petersburg. Samuel Myers, in partnership with Samuel Mordecai, struck out on his own in tobacco trading in 1832. Afflicted by limited business success and gout, Samuel Myers never provided a comfortable home for Eliza and their two children, Edmund Trowbridge Dana, born 13 July 1830, and Caroline, born 5 December 1844. Eliza died tending to her nephew, injured in the Civil War.

Emma Mordecai, born in October 1812, was educated by Ellen and later at Caroline Plunkett's school in Warrenton. Emma taught school between 1841 and 1849 chiefly in her own school in Richmond; later she acted as governess for nearby families. After 1849 she stayed at home to care for her invalid mother. After her mother died in 1863, Emma taught in various schools and was employed as a governess. She is also remembered as the author of a harrowing account of the siege of Richmond. She remained single and died in 1906.

Laura Mordecai, born in 1818, was perhaps the family's most tragic figure. Beautiful and talented, engaged to be married to John Brook Young of Westbrook, the brother of Rosina Ursula Young Mordecai, Laura died suddenly of unknown causes on July 4, 1839.

The Edgeworth Family

Richard Lovell Edgeworth, born at Bath on 31 May 1744, was the son of Jane Lovell and Richard Edgeworth of Edgeworthstown (Mostrim), county Longford, Ireland. As heir to a country estate, Richard Lovell Edgeworth applied himself to its management but also busied himself with varied interests, namely, science and education. A member of the Lunar Society of Birmingham, he concerned himself with the application of scientific principles to industry. As an engineer he designed bridges, roads, and vehicles. His passion for educational theory led to his appointment to the Irish Committee on Education. He co-authored with his daughter Maria *Practical Education* and *Professional Education.* He married four times and fathered twenty-two children. He died in 1817.

Richard Lovell Edgeworth married Anna Maria Elers of Black Burton, Oxfordshire, in 1783. The couple had five children: Richard, Lovell, Maria, Emmeline, and Anna Maria.

Richard Edgeworth, born in May 1764 and the subject of his father's educational experiment based upon Jean Jacques Rousseau's *Emile,* became an unruly, undisciplined son. When private schooling did not remedy his character, Richard immigrated to America and began a new life. He married Elizabeth Knight in 1788 and had three sons. He died in 1796.

Lovell Edgeworth died as an infant in 1766.

Maria Edgeworth, born 1 January 1768, the co-author of *Practical Education* and *Professional Education,* became a celebrated English novelist at the turn of the century. Her novel *Castle Rackrent,* published in 1800, established her reputation as a comic writer who had given voice to the Irish. Apprenticed to her father in the management of the estate and the teaching of her younger siblings, Maria imbibed her father's educational theory. Together their projects on education, including children's fiction, brought them Continental fame. Thereafter, Maria Edgeworth's novels of character and morality confirmed her reputation as one of the most widely read of English novelists. The intellectual seriousness of *The Absentee, Ennui,* and *Ormond,* which fully developed Irish character, contrasted with her earlier comedic pieces. Maria never married, and she died at Edgeworthstown in May 1849.[2]

Emmeline Edgeworth King, born in 1770, married John King, or Konig, of Clifton, a surgeon who assisted Dr. Thomas Beddoes of the Pneumatic Institution. They had two daughters. She died in 1847.

Anna Maria Edgeworth Beddoes, born in 1773 in London, married the distinguished physician Thomas Beddoes in 1794. After Dr. Beddoes's death in 1808, Anna Maria and her four children frequently visited Edgeworthstown. She died in Florence in 1824. Her two daughters then lived at Edgeworthstown.

Richard Lovell Edgeworth was married a second time, in 1773, to Honora Sneyd of Lichfield, England. The couple had two children, Honora and Lovell. Honora Edgeworth was born in 1774 and died in 1790. Lovell Edgeworth, born in 1775, managed the estate after his father's death. Known for his school based upon egalitarianism and liberal principles of ethnic and religious toleration, Lovell nonetheless failed at his enterprises due to alcohol addiction. Maria Edgeworth took over the management of Edgeworthstown and acted as his agent in order to effect a family reconciliation. He lived in England on a small pension until his death in 1842.

Richard Lovell Edgeworth was married a third time in 1780 to Elizabeth Sneyd, sister of his second wife, and by her had nine children: Elizabeth, Henry, Charlotte, Sophia, Charles Sneyd, William, Thomas Day, Honora, and William.

Elizabeth Edgeworth was born in 1781 and died in 1800.

Henry Edgeworth, born in 1782, became a physician but died of tuberculosis in 1813.

Charlotte Edgeworth was born in 1783 and died in 1807.

Sophia Edgeworth died as an infant in 1784.

Charles Sneyd Edgeworth, born in 1786, practiced law in Dublin and married Henrica Broadhurst in 1813. Charles Sneyd supported Maria in the management of Edgeworthstown and of Edgeworth financial affairs. He wrote a biography of an Edgeworth ancestor, Abbé Edgeworth, the final confessor of Louis XVI and Marie Antoinette, entitled *Edgeworth's Memories.* It was published in London in 1815. He died in 1864.

William Edgeworth, born in 1788, died in 1790.

Thomas Day Edgeworth, born in 1789, was named for the eccentric writer and educator Thomas Day, a close friend of Richard Lovell Edgeworth. Thomas Day Edgeworth died in 1792.

Honora Edgeworth Beaumont, born in 1791, married Admiral Sir Francis Beaumont in 1838. She acted as one of Maria Edgeworth's trusted editors of her children's fiction. Honora remained in Maria's inner circle of copyists and proofreaders. She died in 1858.

William Edgeworth, born in 1794, was a rail and road engineer who laid out the road from Killarney to Glengariff. At Edgeworthstown his father trusted him to mentor young Francis Edgeworth. He died an early death in 1829.

Richard Lovell Edgeworth was married a fourth time on 31 May 1798 to Frances Anne Beaufort, a beautiful and talented woman younger than Maria Edgeworth. The couple had six children: Frances Maria, Harriet, Sophia, Lucy Jane, Francis, and Michael.

Frances Maria Edgeworth Wilson, born in 1799, remained Maria Edgeworth's favorite companion and trusted editor. Against the wishes of Maria Edgeworth, Frances married Lestock Peach Wilson in 1829. She died in 1848.

Harriet Edgeworth Butler, born in 1801, traveled extensively with Maria Edgeworth on the Continent and in the British Isles. She married the Very Reverend Richard Butler, dean of Clonmacnoise, and lived at Trim. Trim, a day's journey from Edgeworthstown, supported the literary circle of Edgeworth women who traveled between the estates. Harriet acted as editor and consultant on Maria's literary works. She died in 1889.

Sophia Edgeworth Fox, born in 1803, married her cousin Maj. Barry Fox of Annagmore, King's County, and left four children after her death in 1834. Her sister Harriet Butler raised the children.

Lucy Jane Edgeworth Robinson, born in 1805, married in 1843 the Reverend Thomas Romney Robinson, D.D., and resided in the Observatory at Armagh. She was always an invalid, yet she outlived all her brothers and sisters and died at the age of ninety-two in 1897.

Francis Beaufort Edgeworth, born in 1809, was the prototype for the character Frank, one of Maria Edgeworth's most popular creations in children's fiction. Educated at Charter House and Cambridge, he proved a disappointment to the family. Romantic intrigues led to an unsettled life and an early marriage in December 1831 to Rosa Florentina Eroles, a sixteen-year-old Spanish exile. He supported his family by tutoring students. In 1841 he took over the management of Edgeworthstown until his death in 1846.

Michael Edgeworth, born in 1812, achieved a distinguished record at Haileybury in Oriental languages and botany. He joined the civil service and went to India. He married Christina Macpherson of Aberdeen, and they returned to India. He published works in botany and also published a grammar of Kashmiri. He died in 1881.

NOTES

Abbreviations

AJA   American Jewish Archives, Hebrew Union College, Jewish Institute of Religion, Cincinnati

AMP   Alfred Mordecai Papers, Library of Congress, Washington, D.C.

DRFP   DeRosset Family Papers, Southern Historical Collection, Wilson Library, University of North Carolina, Chapel Hill

EBP   Edgeworth-Beaufort Papers, National Library of Ireland, Dublin

EFP   Edgeworth Family Papers, Bodleian Library, Oxford University, Oxford

EMP   Ellen Mordecai Papers, Southern Historical Collection, Wilson Library, University of North Carolina, Chapel Hill

JMP   Jacob Mordecai Papers, Rare Book, Manuscript, and Special Collections Library, Duke University, Durham

LMP   Little-Mordecai Papers, North Carolina Department of Cultural Resources, Division of Archives and History, Raleigh

MFP   Mordecai Family Papers, Southern Historical Collection, Wilson Library, University of North Carolina, Chapel Hill

MYFP   Myers Family Papers, 1763–1923, Virginia Historical Society, Richmond

PMP   Pattie Mordecai Papers, North Carolina Department of Cultural Resources, Division of Archives and History, Raleigh

Introduction

1. Richard Lovell Edgeworth and Maria Edgeworth, *Practical Education,* 2 vols. (Boston: T. B. Wait & Sons), 1:iv.

2. See Ruth Bloch, "Religion and Ideological Change in the American Revolution," in Mark A. Noll, ed., *Religion and American Politics from the Colonial Period to the 1980s* (New York: Oxford University Press, 1990); Ruth Bloch, *Visionary Republic: Millennial Themes in American Thought, 1756–1800* (New York: Cambridge University Press, 1985); James T. Kloppenberg, "The Virtues of Liberalism: Christianity, Republicanism, and Ethics in Early American Political Discourse," *Journal of Ameri-*

can History 74 (1987): 9–33; Mary Beth Norton, *Liberty's Daughters: The Revolutionary Experience of American Women, 1750–1800* (Boston: Scott, Foresman and Co., 1980), 126–32.

3. Definitions and historical and theological considerations of religious wisdom may be found in Ephraim Urbach, *The Sages: Their Concepts and Beliefs* (Cambridge, Mass.: Harvard University Press, 1979), 40, 65, 94; *Tanakh: The Holy Scriptures* (New York: Jewish Publication Society, 1988), 1244; Bruce J. Malina and Jerome H. Neyrey, "First Century Personality: Dyadic Not Individualistic," in Jerome H. Neyrey, ed., *The Social World of Luke–Acts* (Peabody, Mass.: Hendrickson Publishers, 1991), 67–96; Roland E. Murphy, *Wisdom Literature and Psalms* (Nashville: Abington Press, 1983), 34–45; Gerhard Von Rad, *Wisdom in Israel* (Nashville: Abington Press, 1972), 308. For a discussion of the transliteration of terms in German tradition, see A. G. Roeber, *Palatines, Liberty, and Property: German Lutherans in Colonial British America* (Baltimore, Md.: Johns Hopkins University Press, 1993).

4. James T. Kloppenberg, *The Virtues of Liberalism* (New York: Oxford University Press, 1998), 9, 22–23, 61–62; Daniel T. Rodgers, "Republicanism: The Career of a Concept," *Journal of American History* (June 1992): 11–38.

5. Kloppenberg, *The Virtues of Liberalism,* 24; Anya Jabour, *Marriage in the Early Republic: Elizabeth and William Wirt and the Companionate Ideal* (Baltimore, Md.: Johns Hopkins University Press, 1998); Norton, *Liberty's Daughters;* Linda K. Kerber, *Women of the Republic: Intellect & Ideology in Revolutionary America* (New York: W. W. Norton & Co., 1980); Ruth Bloch, "The Gendered Meanings of Virtue in Revolutionary America," *Signs* 13 (1987): 37–58; Jan Lewis, "The Republican Wife: Virtue and Seduction in the Early Republic," *William and Mary Quarterly* 44 (October 1987): 689–721; Catherine Clinton, "Equally Their Due: The Education of the Planter Daughter in the Early Republic," *Journal of the Early Republic* 2 (April 1982): 39–60.

6. Samuel Harrison Smith, "Remarks on Education; Illustrating the Close Connection between Virtue and Wisdom . . ." in Frederick Rudolph, ed., *Essays on Education in the Early Republic* (Cambridge, Mass.: Belknap Press of Harvard University Press, 1965), 170–76; Walter B. Kolesnik, *Mental Discipline in Modern Education* (Madison: University of Wisconsin Press, 1958).

7. See Von Rad, *Wisdom in Israel,* 128, 167.

8. For a discussion of the forms of wisdom literature, see James L. Crenshaw, *Old Testament Wisdom: An Introduction* (Atlanta: John Knox Press, 1981), 15, 22–25, 52, 62.

9. See Norbert Elias, *The Court Society,* trans. Edmund Jephcott (New York: Pantheon, 1983), 18, 20, 26.

10. Lenore Davidoff and Catherine Hall, *Family Fortunes: Men and Women of the English Middle Class, 1780–1850* (Chicago: University of Chicago Press, 1987), 198; Teresa Michals, "Commerce and Character in Maria Edgeworth," *Nineteenth Century Literature* 49, no. 1 (June 1994): 1.

11. Brian Stock, *The Implications of Literacy: Written Language and Models of Interpretation in the Eleventh and Twelfth Centuries* (Princeton, N.J.: Princeton University Press, 1983), 90.

12. Ibid., 86.

13. See Psalms 19:8, in *Tanakh,* 1126.

1. Mordecai Family Wisdom

1. Handbill, 18 August 1808, MFP.

2. Norton, *Liberty's Daughters,* 265–69; Kerber, *Women of the Republic,* 210–13; Joel Spring, *The American School, 1642–1996* (New York: McGraw-Hill, 1997), 52–53; Wayne Urban and Jennings Wagoner Jr., *American Education: A History* (New York: McGraw-Hill, 1996), 78; Barbara Beatty, *Preschool Education in America: The Culture of Young Children from the Colonial Era to the Present* (New Haven, Conn.: Yale University Press, 1995), 20.

3. Cynthia A. Kierner, *Beyond the Household: Women's Place in the Early South, 1700–1835* (Ithaca, N.Y.: Cornell University Press, 1998), 7.

4. Spring, *The American School,* 56.

5. Urban and Wagoner Jr., *American Education,* 78.

6. Harvey J. Graff, *The Legacies of Literacy: Continuities and Contradictions in Western Culture and Society* (Bloomington: Indiana University Press, 1991), 173.

7. Louis B. Wright, "Thomas Jefferson and the Classics," in Merrill D. Peterson, ed., *Thomas Jefferson: A Profile* (New York: Hill and Wang, 1967), 195, 203.

8. Donald H. Meyer, *The Democratic Enlightenment* (New York: Capricorn Books, 1976), ix; Peter Gay, *The Enlightenment, an Interpretation: The Rise of Modern Paganism* (New York: Alfred A. Knopf, 1966), 8, 130.

9. James L. Crenshaw, *Studies in Ancient Israelite Wisdom* (Atlanta: John Knox Press, 1973), 22–24; Von Rad, *Wisdom in Israel,* 109, 129; Leo G. Perdue, *Wisdom in Revolt: Metaphorical Theology in the Book of Job* (Sheffield: Almond Press, 1991), 13, 16.

10. Job 38:4, in *Tanakh.*

11. Edward Wilkinson, "Wisdom—a Poem" (Philadelphia, 1801), 10, Early American Imprints, American Antiquarian Society, 2nd series (microprints).

12. Ibid.; David Barnes, *The Wisdom of God in Appointing Men, Teachers of Men* (Boston, 1801), Samuel Worcester, *The Wisdom of God* (Boston, 1809), James Dana, *The Wisdom of Observing the Footsteps of Providence* (Hartford, 1805), William Morrison, *The Wisdom of Winning Souls* (Concord, N.H., 1812), Joseph Lathrop, *The Wisdom and Importance of Winning Souls* (Springfield, Mass., 1816), Ely Zebulon, *The Wisdom and Duty of Magistrates* (Hartford, 1804), and Samuel Ware, *Wisdom and Knowledge, the Main Pillars of a Republican Government* (Springfield, Mass., 1814), all from Early American Imprints, American Antiquarian Society, 2nd series (microprints); Burton L. Mack, *Wisdom and the Hebrew Epic: Ben Sira's Hymn in Praise of the Fathers* (Chicago: University of Chicago Press, 1985), 146–47; J. G. A. Pocock, *Virtue, Commerce and History: Essays in Political Thought and History, Chiefly in the Eighteenth Century* (New York: Cambridge University Press, 1985), 37; Gay, *The Enlightenment,* 11, 87, 108, 188–94.

13. In Rudolph, ed., *Essays on Education,* 170.

14. Gay, *The Enlightenment,* 194; Jane Turner Censer, *North Carolina Planters and*

Their Children (Baton Rouge: Louisiana State University Press, 1984), 42, 48–49; Jan Lewis, *The Pursuit of Happiness: Family and Values in Jefferson's Virginia* (New York: Cambridge University Press, 1983), 22, 30.

15. Emmanuel Levinas, *Time and the Other,* trans. Richard A. Cohen (Pittsburgh: Duquesne University Press, 1987), 7, 59.

16. Edgeworth and Edgeworth, *Practical Education,* 1:iv.

17. Mark E. Kann, *A Republic of Men: The American Founders, Gendered Language, and Patriarchal Politics* (New York: New York University Press, 1998), 1–7.

18. Ibid., 8–28.

19. See Jabour, *Marriage in the Early Republic,* 10.

20. Jay Fliegelman, *Prodigals and Pilgrims: The American Revolution against Patriarchal Authority, 1750–1800* (New York: Cambridge University Press, 1982), 1, 33, 107, 174; Edwin G. Burrows and Michael Wallace, "The American Revolution: The Ideology and Psychology of National Liberation," *Perspectives in American History* 6 (1972): 168–74, 187, 256, 277, 288; Benjamin Rush, "Benjamin Rush on Women's Education," in Wilson Smith, ed., *Theories of Education in Early America, 1655–1819* (Indianapolis: Bobbs-Merrill Co., 1973), 257–65; David Hackett Fischer, *Albion's Seed* (New York: Oxford University Press, 1989).

21. Alexander Altmann, *Moses Mendelssohn: A Biographical Study* (University: University of Alabama Press, 1973), 16–22, 28, 87; Eva Jospe, ed. and trans., *Moses Mendelssohn: Selections from His Writings* (New York: Viking Press, 1975), 4, 7–8, 10–11, 15, 24–27; Norman Linzer, *The Jewish Family: Authority and Tradition in Modern Perspective* (New York: Human Sciences Press, 1984), 9; Max I. Dimont, *The Jews in America: The Roots, History, and Destiny of American Jews* (New York: Simon and Schuster, 1978), 65–70.

22. Todd M. Endelman, *The Jews of Georgian England, 1714–1830: Tradition and Change in a Liberal Society* (Philadelphia: Jewish Publication Society of America, 1979), 24–25, 120–21, 145–46. For a contrast to Jewish immigration from Georgian England that demonstrates few resources and limited cooperative ventures, see the discussion of English Roman Catholic migration to America as a well-funded and organized enterprise underwritten by British patronage and Jesuit support in Joseph Moss Ives, *The Ark and the Dove: The Beginning of Civil and Religious Liberties in America* (New York: Cooper Square Publishers, 1969).

23. Myron Berman, *Richmond's Jewry, 1769–1976: Shabbat in Shockoe* (Charlottesville: University of Virginia Press, 1979), 14; Sheldon Hanft, "Mordecai's Female Academy," *American Jewish History* 79 (Autumn 1989): 72–93, 74; Edgar E. MacDonald, ed., *The Education of the Heart: The Correspondence of Rachel Mordecai Lazarus and Maria Edgeworth* (Chapel Hill: University of North Carolina Press, 1977), 325–26; "Non-Transportation Agreement," 25 October 1765, Pennsylvania Historical Society, Philadelphia (copy in AJA).

24. Jacob Mordecai to Marx Lazarus, 26 August 1828, MFP.

25. Gratz Mordecai, *Notice of Jacob Mordecai, Founder, and Proprietor from 1809 to 1818, of the Warrenton (N.C.) Female Seminary* (Philadelphia: American Jewish Historical Society, 1897), 41, in AMP.

26. Julia Mordecai, "Family Register for Alfred Mordecai," vol. 7, p. 1, AMP; Mordecai, *Notice of Jacob Mordecai,* 40; Hanft, "Mordecai's Female Academy," 74; Lance J. Sussman, "Our Little World: The Early Years at Warrenton," unpublished paper, 1979, biographies file, 2–4, AJA.

27. Berman, *Richmond's Jewry,* 14; Sussman, "Our Little World," 3; Jacob Mordecai to Moses, Samuel, Rachel, Ellen, Solomon, and Caroline Mordecai, 20 July 1796, MFP.

28. Jacob Mordecai to Moses, Samuel, Rachel, Ellen, Solomon, and Caroline Mordecai, 20 July 1796, MFP.

29. Judith Mordecai to Jacob Mordecai, 11 February 1793, MFP.

30. Berman, *Richmond's Jewry,* 14–15.

31. Ibid., 2.

32. Judith Mordecai to Myer Myers, 19 November 1791, MFP.

33. Jacob Mordecai to Moses, Samuel, Rachel, Ellen, Solomon, and Caroline Mordecai, 20 July 1796, MFP.

34. Ibid.

35. Carole R. Fontaine, "The Sage in Family and Tribe," in John G. Gammie and Leo G. Perdue, eds., *The Sage in Israel and the Ancient Near East* (Winona Lake: Eisenbrauns, 1990), 160–62.

36. Jacob Mordecai to Moses, Samuel, Rachel, Ellen, Solomon, and Caroline Mordecai, 20 July 1796, 27 September 1796, MFP.

37. Jacob Mordecai to the Wardens and Brethren of Johnston Caswell Lodge, 27 January 1796, PMP.

38. Jacob Mordecai to Moses, Samuel, Rachel, Ellen, Solomon, and Caroline Mordecai, 20 July 1796, MFP.

39. Ibid.

40. Ibid.

41. Ibid.

42. Judith Mordecai, "List of Rules," 29 June 1780, MFP.

43. Jacob Mordecai to Moses, Samuel, Rachel, Ellen, Solomon, and Caroline Mordecai, 20 July 1796, MFP.

44. Ibid.; addendum, 27 September 1796, MFP.

45. Sussman, "Our Little World," 6.

46. Jacob Mordecai to Rachel and Ellen Mordecai, 13 August 1797, JMP.

47. Jacob Mordecai to Rachel Mordecai, 18 March 1799, 14 May 1799, MFP.

48. Ibid.; see also Jacob Mordecai to Rachel and Ellen Mordecai, 4 September 1797, 31 July 1798, JMP.

49. Linzer, *The Jewish Family,* 68.

50. Bloch, "The Gendered Meanings of Virtue," 50; Emmanuel Levinas, *Difficult Freedom: Essays on Judaism,* trans. Sean Hand (Baltimore, Md.: Johns Hopkins University Press, 1990), 6.

51. Jacob Mordecai to Rachel Mordecai, 3 July 1798, MFP.

52. Jacob Mordecai to Rachel and Ellen Mordecai, 13 August 1797, 4 September 1797, JMP.

53. Jacob Mordecai to Rachel Mordecai, 3 July 1798, MFP.

54. Rachel Mordecai to Samuel Mordecai, 26 April 1818, MFP.

55. As quoted in Sussman, "Our Little World," 11.

56. Rachel Mordecai to Samuel Mordecai, 25 February 1816, MFP.

57. Ibid.

58. Hanft, "Mordecai's Female Academy," 79.

59. Rachel Mordecai to Samuel Mordecai, 1 March 1808, JMP.

60. Berman, *Richmond's Jewry,* 22; Urbach, *The Sages,* 571–72; Linzer, *The Jewish Family,* 9.

61. For a discussion of the wise man's creation of order and propriety, see Crenshaw, *Studies,* 23.

62. Handbill, 18 August 1808, MFP.

63. Ellen Mordecai to Samuel Mordecai, 25 January 1809, MFP; Mordecai, *Notice of Jacob Mordecai,* AMP.

64. Christie Anne Farnham, *The Education of the Southern Belle: Higher Education and Student Socialization in the Antebellum South* (New York: New York University Press, 1994), 2–3, 51.

65. Ibid., 36–41, 46–51; Kierner, *Beyond the Household,* 59–61, 67, 71, 106–8, 149, 157.

66. Isidore Epstein, *Judaism* (New York: Penguin, 1973), 23.

67. Ibid., 24–25.

68. Linzer, *The Jewish Family,* 20, 48, 123; David Kraemer, "Images of Childhood and Adolescence in Talmudic Literature," in David Kraemer, ed., *The Jewish Family: Metaphor and Memory* (New York: Oxford University Press, 1989), 65–76.

69. Nathan Tarcov, *Locke's Education for Liberty* (Chicago: University of Chicago Press, 1984), 184.

70. Ibid., 44–45.

71. Rachel Mordecai to Samuel Mordecai, 1 January 1809, MFP.

72. Ibid.

73. Hanft, "Mordecai's Female Academy," 81.

74. "Benjamin Rush on Women's Education," in Smith, ed., *Theories of Education,* 260.

75. Ellen Mordecai to Samuel Mordecai, 4 February 1810, MFP.

76. See figure 2, MFP.

77. Handbill, 18 August 1808, MFP.

78. Samuel Mordecai to the "girls," undated, MFP.

79. Ellen Mordecai to Samuel Mordecai, 25 January 1809, MFP.

80. Rachel Mordecai to Samuel Mordecai, 5 July 1809, MFP; Kemp Battle, "Sketches of Some of the Old or Extinct Schools in the Counties of North Carolina," in *Biennial Report of the Superintendent of Public Instruction of North Carolina for the Scholastic Years 1896–1897 and 1897–1898* (Raleigh, N.C.: Guy V. Barnes, 1898), 713, suggests Moses taught at the academy.

81. Ellen Mordecai to Samuel Mordecai, 25 January 1809, MFP; Battle, "Sketches," 713; Rachel Mordecai to Samuel Mordecai, 28 May 1809, 5 July 1809, MFP; Mordecai, *Notice of Jacob Mordecai,* 43; MacDonald, ed., *The Education of the Heart,* 11, 327.

82. "Recollections of Rachel (Mordecai) Lazarus, 1817–1821," 20, MYFP.

83. Rachel Mordecai to Samuel Mordecai, 27 February 1814, PMP.

84. Hanft, "Mordecai's Female Academy," 80.

85. "Recollections of Rachel (Mordecai) Lazarus, 1817–1821," 21, MYFP.

86. Urbach, *The Sages*, 408–9, 415; Linzer, *The Jewish Family*, 78.

87. Lewis, "The Republican Wife," 695; Bloch, "The Gendered Meanings of Virtue," 41, 47.

88. Rachel Mordecai to Samuel Mordecai, 12 February 1809, PMP.

89. Ibid.

90. 11 February 1810, PMP.

91. Rachel Mordecai to Samuel Mordecai, 16 December 1810, PMP. See also discussion of the hiring of Mr. Baker in Rachel Mordecai to Samuel Mordecai, 9 July 1811, MFP (microfilm).

92. 16 December 1810, PMP.

93. 27 February 1814, PMP.

94. Ibid.

95. Rachel Mordecai to Samuel Mordecai, 21 April 1816, MFP.

96. Ibid.

97. Rachel to Samuel Mordecai, 14 July 1816, MFP.

98. Ibid.

99. Urbach, *The Sages*, 217.

100. Rachel Mordecai to Ellen Mordecai, 30 January 1814, MFP.

101. Rachel Mordecai to Samuel Mordecai, 28 May 1809; Rachel Mordecai to Ellen Mordecai, 12 December 1813, MFP.

102. Rachel Mordecai to Samuel Mordecai, 28 May 1809, MFP; Charles Coon, *North Carolina Schools and Academies, 1790–1840: A Documentary History* (Raleigh, N.C.: Edwards and Broughton Printing Co., 1915), 597.

103. Samuel Mordecai to Rachel Mordecai, 4 May 1809, MFP.

104. Rachel Mordecai to Samuel Mordecai, 5 July 1809, MFP. The review of the examination signed by parents and judges lauds the teachers: "Through the course of a long and very strict examination, the young Ladies acquitted themselves in a manner, which, while it reflects honors on their own diligence, evinces the abilities and unremitted attention of their several Preceptors: and we should be wanting in justice to their merits, and to our own feelings, did we not assure them of our unqualified approbation" (undated, PMP).

105. Kerber, *Women of the Republic*, 243–45.

106. Editorial, 15 March 1810, quoted in Coon, *North Carolina Schools*, 597.

107. Ibid., 598–99.

108. Rachel Mordecai to Samuel Mordecai, 16 December 1810, PMP.

109. James L. Axtell, *The Educational Writings of John Locke* (New York: Cambridge University Press, 1968), 43.

110. Ibid., 43, 155–56, 170, 313.

111. Hanft, "Mordecai's Female Academy," 82.

112. Coon, *North Carolina Schools*, 600; *Raleigh Star*, 3 May 1811; Jacob Mordecai, draft for a newspaper article, MFP; Mordecai, *Notice of Jacob Mordecai*, 44.

113. Wilmington newspaper clipping, 7 May 1811, MFP.

114. Ellen Mordecai journal, vol. 4, 14 July 1816, LMP.

115. Ibid., 3 March 1816; Rachel Mordecai to Samuel Mordecai, 4 March 1816, PMP.

116. Rachel Mordecai to Sam Mordecai, 18 January 1817, JMP.

117. Ellen Mordecai journal, vol. 4, 14 July 1816, LMP.

118. Rachel Mordecai to Samuel Mordecai, 9 February 1817, JMP.

119. Ellen Mordecai journal, vol. 4, 22 June 1817, LMP.

120. Ibid., 5 January 1818.

121. Rachel Mordecai to Samuel Mordecai, 27 September 1818, JMP.

122. Ellen Mordecai to Samuel Mordecai, 1811, MFP.

123. Ellen Mordecai, *Fading Scenes Recalled or the Bygone Days of Hastings* (New York, 1847), EMP (microfilm).

124. Rachel Mordecai to Samuel Mordecai, 20 March 1814, PMP.

125. Rachel Mordecai to Samuel Mordecai, September 1814, PMP.

126. MacDonald, ed., *The Education of the Heart,* 11.

127. Berman, *Richmond's Jewry,* 92.

128. "A Discourse Delivered at the Synagogue in the City of Richmond on Wednesday the First of January 1812 in Consequence of the Loss of Life Occasioned by the Burning of the Theatre on the 26th of December 1811," MFP.

129. Jacob Mordecai, "Remarks on Harby's Discourse," 6 January 1826, unpublished paper, MYFP.

130. Stanley F. Chyet, "The Political Rights of Jews in the United States: 1776–1840," *American Jewish Archives* 10 (April 1958): 14–42.

131. Ibid., 26.

132. See Marcus, "Colonial American Jews," in Jonathan D. Sarna, ed., *American Jewish Experience* (New York: Holmes and Meier, 1986), 11–15.

133. Rachel Mordecai to Samuel Mordecai, 24 September 1810, PMP.

134. Jacob Mordecai to Samuel Mordecai, 29 November 1810, MFP (microfilm).

135. See, especially, David Levi, *Letters to Dr. Priestly* (London, 1793); David Levi, *Dissertations on the Prophecies of the Old Testament,* 2 vols. (London, 1796).

136. Rachel Mordecai diary, December 1819. See Berman, *Richmond's Jewry,* 52, for a discussion of the widespread use of the catechism.

137. AJA.

138. Ellen, Solomon, and Caroline Mordecai to Samuel Mordecai, 12 June 1816, MFP.

139. Rachel Mordecai diary, 3 May 1817, 183.

140. Rachel Mordecai to Ellen Mordecai, 30 January 1814; Rachel Mordecai to Samuel Mordecai, 30 January 1814, MFP.

141. Lance J. Sussman, "Jewish Intellectual Activity and Educational Practice in the United States: 1776–1840," unpublished paper, 1978, Small Collections, 8–9, 22–23, AJA; Martin E. Marty, *Pilgrims in Their Own Land: 500 Years of Religion in America* (New York: Penguin, 1985), 169–87; Samuel Mordecai to Rachel Mordecai, 18 November 1805, JMP; Rachel Mordecai diary (Eliza uses *Elements of Jewish Faith*); Samuel Mordecai to Rachel Mordecai, 27 July 1819, MFP.

142. Rachel Mordecai to Ellen Mordecai, 30 January 1814, MFP.

143. Samuel Mordecai to Rachel Mordecai, 16 February 1817, MFP.

144. Samuel Mordecai to Rachel Mordecai, 22 February 1818, MFP.

145. Ellen Mordecai journal, vol. 4, 21 July 1817, LMP.

146. Samuel Mordecai to Rachel Mordecai, 22 February 1818, MFP.

147. Levinas, *Time and the Other,* 6–7, 14, 58, 67.

148. Urbach, *The Sages,* 217; Malina and Neyrey, "First Century Personality," 67–96; Linzer, *The Jewish Family,* 9, 19, 31.

149. See Robert Kegan, *The Evolving Self: Problem and Process in Human Development* (New York: Cambridge University Press, 1982), 31.

150. Mordecai, *Fading Scenes Recalled,* 5–6, n. p. 5.

151. Ellen Mordecai journal, vol. 4, 11 August 1817, LMP.

152. Rachel to Solomon, 2 August 1817, JMP; Ellen Mordecai journal, vol. 5, 22 October 1819, MFP.

153. Rachel Mordecai to Solomon Mordecai, 24 February 1820, JMP.

154. Rachel Mordecai to Samuel Mordecai, 25 January 1816, MFP.

155. Ibid.

156. Ibid.

157. 10 November 1816, MFP.

158. Matthew Frye Jacobson, *Whiteness of a Different Color: European Immigrants and the Alchemy of Race* (Cambridge, Mass.: Harvard University Press, 1998), 171–72. For a discussion of "positionality," defined by Joe Kincheloe and Shirley R. Steinberg as the inability of individuals to "separate where they stand in the web of reality from what they perceive," see "Addressing the Crisis of Whiteness: Reconfiguring White Identity in a Pedagogy of Whiteness," in Joe Kincheloe, Shirley R. Steinberg, Nelson M. Rodriguez, and Ronald E. Chennault, eds., *White Reign: Deploying Whiteness in America* (New York: St. Martin's Press, 1998), 3; see also Valerie Babb, *Whiteness Visible: The Meaning of Whiteness in American Literature and Culture* (New York: New York University Press, 1998), 8; Ruth Frankenberg, *White Women, Race Matters: The Social Construction of Whiteness* (Minneapolis: University of Minnesota Press, 1993), 162; Ruth Frankenberg, ed., *Displacing Whiteness: Essays in Social and Cultural Criticism* (Durham: Duke University Press, 1997), 1–34.

159. David Roediger, *Towards the Abolition of Whiteness: Essays on Race, Politics, and Working Class History* (New York: Verso, 1994), 184.

160. Samuel Mordecai to Rachel Mordecai, 11 October 1816, 6 April 1817; Julia Mordecai to Samuel Mordecai, August 1816; Rachel Mordecai to Caroline Mordecai, 3 October 1819, MFP; Sussman, "Our Little World," 10.

161. Rachel Mordecai diary, 15 February 1818, 200.

162. MacDonald, ed., *The Education of the Heart,* 27.

163. Ibid., 327.

164. Solomon Mordecai to Samuel Mordecai, December 1815, MFP.

165. MacDonald, ed., *The Education of the Heart,* 327.

166. MFP.

167. Ellen Mordecai journal, vol. 4, 22 October 1817, MFP.

168. Rachel Mordecai to Moses Mordecai, 4 October 1817, MFP.

169. Ibid.

170. Solomon Mordecai to Ellen Mordecai, 4 October 1817, MFP.

171. Ellen Mordecai journal, vol. 4, 22 October 1817, MFP.

172. Ibid., 9 December 1817.

173. Ibid., 11 December 1817.

174. Samuel Mordecai to Solomon Mordecai, 16 December 1821; Moses Mordecai to Ellen Mordecai, 26 September 1823; Ellen Mordecai to Solomon Mordecai, 2 October 1823; Moses Mordecai to Ellen Mordecai, 19 August 1823; Julia Mordecai to Ellen Mordecai, 11 January 1824; Ellen Mordecai to Solomon Mordecai, 13 July 1824; Julia Mordecai to Ellen Mordecai, 6 August 1824; Samuel Mordecai to J. D. Plunkett, 1 September 1824, MFP; MacDonald, ed., *The Education of the Heart,* 327.

175. Samuel Mordecai to Solomon Mordecai, 9 November 1811, MFP.

176. Rachel Mordecai to Samuel Mordecai, 5 July 1809; Solomon Mordecai to Samuel Mordecai, 2 December 1812, MFP.

177. Rachel Mordecai to Samuel Mordecai, 27 July 1817, MFP.

178. Ellen Mordecai journal, vol. 6, 10 June 1823, LMP.

179. Ibid., vol. 5, 15 January 1820, MFP.

180. Ibid., vol. 5, 10 May 1820.

181. Ibid.

182. Jacob Mordecai to Achilles Plunkett, 26 September 1820, MFP.

183. Ellen Mordecai journal, vol. 6, 28 October 1820, LMP.

184. Ibid.

185. Ibid.

186. Rebecca Mordecai to Jacob Mordecai, 22 December 1820, MFP.

187. Urbach, *The Sages,* 326–27, 330, 333–34, 337.

188. Rachel Mordecai to Samuel Mordecai, 27 September 1818, JMP.

189. Samuel Mordecai to Rachel Mordecai, 8 November 1818, MFP.

190. Rachel Mordecai to Caroline Mordecai, 8 April 1819; Ellen Mordecai to Solomon Mordecai, 3 February 1820, MFP.

191. Rachel Mordecai to Samuel Mordecai, 4 October 1818, MFP.

192. Rachel Mordecai to Samuel Mordecai, 15 November 1818, MFP.

2. Enlightened Wisdom

1. MacDonald, ed., *The Education of the Heart,* 6.

2. Ibid., 7–9.

3. Edgeworth and Edgeworth, *Practical Education,* 1: iv.

4. MacDonald, ed., *The Education of the Heart,* 4, 12, 21, 25, 291.

5. Maria Edgeworth to Frances Edgeworth, 26 April 1825, Eng. lett. c. 699, fol. 8, EFP.

6. Maria Edgeworth to Harriet Edgeworth, 21 June 1818, Eng. lett. c. 704, fol. 1; Maria Edgeworth to Frances B. Edgeworth, 21 October 1831, Eng. lett. c. 700, fol. 119; Maria Edgeworth to Frances B. Edgeworth, 25 August 1839, Eng. lett. c. 701, fol. 144, EFP.

7. Honora Edgeworth, "Edgeworthstown Weekly Register," 1 May 1811, 22, 471 #3, EBP.

8. Ibid.

9. Roger Chartier, *Cultural History: Between Practices and Representations,* trans. Lydia G. Cochrane (Ithaca, N.Y.: Cornell University Press, 1988), 78.

10. I am indebted to Laura Mason, who contributed this point to my chapter.

11. Michals, "Commerce and Character," 1; Marilyn Butler, *Romantics, Rebels and Reactionaries* (New York: Oxford University Press, 1983), 96; Julie Schaffer, "Not Subordinate: Empowering Women in the Marriage-Plot—The Novels of Frances Burney, Maria Edgeworth and Jane Austen," *Criticism* 34, no. 1 (Winter 1992): 53; Elizabeth Kowalski-Wallace, *Their Fathers' Daughters: Hannah More, Maria Edgeworth, and Patriarchal Complicity* (New York: Oxford University Press, 1991), 12, 110.

12. Davidoff and Hall, *Family Fortunes,* 198.

13. Michals, "Commerce and Character," 1–2.

14. Davidoff and Hall, *Family Fortunes,* 8–30, 51.

15. Ibid., 234–40, 283.

16. "Draft of Irish Education Bill" (1799), 22471 #1; "Regulations Proposed for Irish Provincial Schools," 22471 #7, EBP.

17. Harriet Edgeworth Butler to Charles Sneyd Edgeworth, 10 December 1827, Eng. lett. c. 741, fol. 24; D. A. Beaufort Jr. to Frances B. Edgeworth, 16 August 1826, Eng. lett. c. 738, fol. 215, EFP.

18. Richard Lovell Edgeworth, *Memoirs of Richard Lovell Edgeworth,* ed. Maria Edgeworth, 2 vols. (Shannon: Irish University Press, 1969), 1:20, 26–27, 30.

19. Ibid., 1:29.

20. Ibid., 1:29–30.

21. Marilyn Butler, *Maria Edgeworth: A Literary Biography* (Oxford: Clarendon Press, 1972), 19–23; Elizabeth Harden, *Maria Edgeworth* (Boston: Twayne Publishers, 1984), 7.

22. Edgeworth, *Memoirs,* 1:276, 363.

23. Jean Jacques Rousseau, *Emile, or On Education,* trans. Allan Bloom (New York: Basic Books, 1979), 97.

24. Ibid., 84.

25. Ibid., 82–84, 252.

26. Ibid., 42, 250.

27. Ibid., 80, 157, 342, 445.

28. As quoted in Butler, *Maria Edgeworth,* 432.

29. Harden, *Maria Edgeworth,* 8.

30. Honora Edgeworth to Maria Edgeworth, 5 February 1778, 10166 #2, EBP.

31. 10 October 1779, 10166 #14, EBP.

32. Richard Lovell Edgeworth to Maria Edgeworth, 6 April 1780, 10166 #27, EBP.

33. Richard Lovell Edgeworth to Maria Edgeworth, 4 November 1780, 10166 #35, EBP.

34. Harden, *Maria Edgeworth,* 10–11.

35. Maria Edgeworth to Charlotte Sneyd, 3 October 1787, 10166 #58, EBP.

36. Richard Lovell Edgeworth to Maria Edgeworth, 3 December 1782, 10166 #50; Richard Lovell Edgeworth to Maria Edgeworth, 12 February 1782, 10166 #51, EBP.

37. Richard Lovell Edgeworth to Maria Edgeworth, 12 February 1782, 10166 #51, EBP.

38. "Note by Maria Edgeworth on Richard Lovell Edgeworth's Habit of Over-Praising," 22471, EBP.

39. Harden, *Maria Edgeworth*, 19.

40. Butler, *Maria Edgeworth*, 61–62.

41. Richard Lovell Edgeworth to Dugald Stewart, 17 June 1803; Dugald Stewart to Richard Lovell Edgeworth, 17 July 1803, 22471 #2, EBP.

42. Edgeworth Family Papers, Eng. lett. c. 860, EFP.

43. Butler, *Maria Edgeworth*, 62–67.

44. "Notes on Practical Education," 22471 #7, EBP.

45. Unknown to Richard Lovell Edgeworth, 24 July 1772, 22471 #1, EBP.

46. Richard Lovell Edgeworth to unknown, c. 1798, 22471 #1, EBP.

47. *The Life and Letters of Maria Edgeworth,* ed. Augustus J. C. Hare, 2 vols. (New York: Houghton Mifflin Co., 1895), 1:12.

48. Ibid., 1:165.

49. Maria Edgeworth to Mrs. Frances B. Edgeworth, 2 August 1804, 10166 #419, EBP.

50. 22471 #3, EBP.

51. F. V. Barry, ed., *Maria Edgeworth: Chosen Letters* (New York: Houghton Mifflin Co., 1932), 62.

52. Hare, *Maria Edgeworth,* 1:12–13.

53. John Locke, *Some Thoughts Concerning Education,* ed. John W. and Jean S. Yolton (Oxford: Clarendon Press, 1989), 116–18, 126, 138–40, 145, 153, 255.

54. Thomas J. Scheff and Suzanne M. Retzinger, *Emotions and Violence: Shame and Rage in Destructive Conflicts* (Lexington, Mass.: Lexington Books, 1991), 115; Gershen Kaufman and Lev Raphael, *Dynamics of Power: Fighting Shame and Building Self-Esteem* (Rochester, Vt.: Schenkman Books, 1991), xiv, 77.

55. Edgeworth and Edgeworth, *Practical Education,* 1:209.

56. Maria Edgeworth to Mrs. Ruxton, 11 March 1792, 10166 #89, EBP.

57. Edgeworth and Edgeworth, *Practical Education,* 1:214.

58. Ibid., 1:218, 222.

59. Ibid., 1:238.

60. Ibid., 1:251.

61. Terry Castle, "The Female Thermometer," in *The Female Thermometer: Eighteenth Century Culture and the Invention of the Uncanny* (New York: Oxford University Press, 1995), 23–25.

62. Frances B. Edgeworth to Harriet Beaufort, 24 February 1808, 13176 #17; Charles Sneyd Edgeworth to Honora Edgeworth, 4 October 1809, 13176 #20, EBP.

63. Maria Edgeworth to Pakenham Edgeworth, 14 February 1834, Eng. lett. c. 715, fol. 59, EFP.

64. "Untitled Story Composed by Honora Edgeworth in 1787," Eng. lett. c. 898, fol. 1, EFP.

65. Eng. lett. c. 896, fols. 7–13, EFP.

66. Ibid.

67. Castle, "The Female Thermometer," 34; Terry Eagleton, *The Rape of Clarissa* (Oxford: Basil Blackwell, 1982), 13ff.; Anne Douglas, *The Feminization of American Culture* (New York: Knopf, 1977); Janet Todd, *Sensibility: An Introduction* (London: Methuen, 1986); John Mullen, *Sentiment and Sociability: The Language of Feeling in the Eighteenth Century* (Oxford: Clarendon Press, 1988); G. J. Barker-Benfield, *The Culture of Sensibility: Sex and Society in Eighteenth Century Britain* (Chicago: University of Chicago Press, 1992); Ann Jessie Van Sant, *Eighteenth Century Sensibility and the Novel* (New York: Cambridge University Press, 1993).

68. Butler, *Maria Edgeworth,* 66–67.

69. Ibid., 254–59.

70. Edgeworth and Edgeworth, *Practical Education,* 2:127, 137, 148, 195, 212, 239, 260.

71. Ibid., 2:132, 256.

72. Ibid., 2:148.

73. Ibid., 2:30; see also Sylvia Tomaselli, "The Enlightenment Debate on Women," *History Journal Workshop* 19 (1985): 101–24.

74. Maria Edgeworth, "Harry and Lucy," in *Early Lessons* (London: George Routledge and Sons, 1856), 309–427; "Forester," in *Moral Tales for Young People,* 3 vols. (London: J. Johnson, 1802; reprint New York: Garland Publishing, 1974), 1:1–194; "Rosamund," in *Rosamund: With Other Stories* (New York: Harper & Brothers, 1854), 8–316; "Angelina or L'Amie Inconnue," in *Moral Tales for Young People,* 2:147–255.

75. Edgeworth, "Harry and Lucy," 310.

76. Edgeworth, "Angelina," 152.

77. Maria Edgeworth, "The Good French Governess," in *Moral Tales for Young People,* 3:11–13, 18, 41–45, 64.

78. Ibid., 3:147–236.

79. Maria Edgeworth, *Ormond,* in *The Longford Edition of Tales and Novels by Maria Edgeworth,* 10 vols. (New York: AMS Press, 1967), 9:287.

80. Ibid., 9:354.

81. Ibid., 9:494.

82. Ibid., 9:418.

83. Maria Edgeworth, *The Absentee,* in *The Longford Edition of Tales and Novels,* 6:43.

84. Ibid., 6:38.

85. Maria Edgeworth, *Patronage,* in *The Longford Edition of Tales and Novels,* 7:14.

86. Maria Edgeworth, "The Modern Griselda," in *The Longford Edition of Tales and Novels,* 6:410.

87. Ibid., 6:427.

88. Ibid., 6:438.

89. Maria Edgeworth, *Belinda,* in *The Longford Edition of Tales and Novels,* 3:42.

90. Ibid., 3:221–22.

91. Christina Colvin, ed., *Maria Edgeworth: Letters from England, 1813–1844* (Oxford: Clarendon Press, 1971), 205.

92. Richard Lovell Edgeworth to William Edgeworth, February 1817, 22471 #6, EBP.

93. 12 October 1828, Eng. lett. c. 746, fol. 91, EFP.

94. Ibid.; Francis Edgeworth to Frances Edgeworth, undated, Eng. lett. c. 737, fol. 49, EFP.

95. Maria Edgeworth to Fanny Edgeworth, 15 December 1831, Eng. lett. c. 707, fol. 122; Francis Edgeworth to Frances B. Edgeworth, 19 December 1831, Eng. lett. c. 735, fol. 257; Maria Edgeworth to Sophy Ruxton, 27 December 1831, Eng. lett. c. 719, fol. 121; Francis Edgeworth to Frances B. Edgeworth, 31 December 1831, Eng. lett. c. 737, fol. 139, EFP.

96. Maria Edgeworth to Fanny Edgeworth, 15 December 1831, Eng. lett. c. 707, EFP.

97. Maria Edgeworth to Fanny Edgeworth, 22 April 1838, Eng. lett. c. 709, fol. 27, EFP.

98. Maria Edgeworth to Rosa Edgeworth, 4 September 1846, Eng. lett. c. 714, fol. 236, EFP.

99. 17 March 1814, 22471 #5, EBP.

100. Bishop of Armagh to Richard Lovell Edgeworth, 24 March 1814; Richard Lovell Edgeworth to Trustees of Erasmus Smith, March 1814, EBP.

101. Lovell Edgeworth to Frances Beaufort Edgeworth, 7 April 1815, 10166 #1093, EBP.

102. Lovell Edgeworth to Richard Lovell Edgeworth, 10 September 1815, 22471 #5, EBP.

103. Lovell Edgeworth to Richard Lovell Edgeworth, 13 November 1815, 10166 #1140, EBP.

104. Lovell Edgeworth to Frances Beaufort Edgeworth, 10 March 1816, 10166 #1175, EBP; Maria Edgeworth to Frances B. Edgeworth, 1 May 1818, Eng. lett. c. 696, fol. 8, EFP.

105. Maria Edgeworth to Aunt Ruxton, 5 September 1819, 717 #57, EBP; Maria Edgeworth to Sophy Ruxton, 9 August 1824, Eng. lett. c. 719, fol. 17, EFP.

106. Maria Edgeworth to Frances B. Edgeworth, February 1821, Eng. lett. c. 697, fol. 84; Lovell to J. Moilliet, 25 June 1822, Eng. lett. c. 747, fol. 7, EFP.

107. Maria Edgeworth to Pakenham Edgeworth, 10 September 1833, Eng. lett. c. 715, fol. 53, EFP.

108. Butler, *Maria Edgeworth,* 420–23, 426–27.

109. Maria Edgeworth to Frances Edgeworth Wilson, 29 May 1836, Eng. lett. c. 139, EFP.

110. Ibid.

111. Maria Edgeworth to Frances B. Edgeworth, 1 January 1831, Eng. lett. c. 700, fol. 58; see also Harriet Butler to Frances B. Edgeworth, 1 October 1829, Eng. lett. c. 736, fol. 51, EFP.

112. 30 November 1839, Eng. lett. c. 709, fol. 134, EFP.

113. Harriet Edgeworth to Fanny Edgeworth, 10 November 1812 or 1813, 10166 #844; Maria Edgeworth to Sophy Ruxton, 26 December 1814, 10166 #1053, EBP; Maria Edgeworth to Frances B. Edgeworth(?), 1822, Eng. lett. c. 698, fol. 105; Maria Edgeworth to Lucy Edgeworth, 2 June 1824, Eng. lett. c. 714, fol. 36; Maria Edgeworth to Fanny Edgeworth, 19 February 1830, Eng. lett. c. 707, fol. 10; Maria Edgeworth to Fanny Edgeworth, 12 April 1830, Eng. lett. c. 707, fol. 29; Maria Edgeworth to Fanny Edgeworth, 5 June 1832, Eng. lett. c. 707, fol. 157; Maria Edgeworth to Fanny Edgeworth, 22 April 1838, Eng. lett. c. 709, fol. 23, EFP.

114. Maria Edgeworth to Frances B. Edgeworth, 15 May 1818, Eng. lett. c. 696, fol. 5, EFP.

115. Maria Edgeworth to Harriet Butler, 21 May 1824, Eng. lett. c. 712, fol. 18, EFP.

116. Maria Edgeworth to Harriet Butler, 21 May 1824, Eng. lett. c. 712, fol. 18; Maria Edgeworth to Frances Edgeworth Wilson, 16 April 1832, Eng. lett. c. 707, fol. 146; Maria Edgeworth to Frances Beaufort Edgeworth, April 1833, Eng. lett. c. 700, fol. 135; Maria Edgeworth to Harriet Butler, 1845, Eng. lett. c. 713, fol. 164; Maria Edgeworth to Harriet Butler, 13 November 1847, Eng. lett. c. 713, fol. 37, EFP.

117. Maria Edgeworth to Honora Edgeworth, 23 April 1827, Eng. lett. c. 704, fols. 150–51, EFP.

118. Maria Edgeworth to Honora Edgeworth, 22 November 1820, 13 August 1824, Eng. lett. c. 704, fols. 65, 116, EFP.

119. Maria Edgeworth to Frances B. Edgeworth, 29 June 1824, Eng. lett. c. 706, fol. 79, EFP.

120. Maria Edgeworth to Frances Edgeworth, 26 July 1824, Maria Edgeworth to Frances Edgeworth, 18 October 1824, Maria Edgeworth to Honora Edgeworth, 15 October 1824, Maria Edgeworth to Fanny Edgeworth, 1 April 1820, Eng. lett. c. 706, fols. 86, 103, 107, 28; Maria Edgeworth to Frances Beaufort Edgeworth, 14 February 1829, 6 May 1838, Eng. lett. c. 709, fol. 33, EFP.

121. Maria Edgeworth to Mrs. Ruxton, 2 August 1822, Eng. lett. c. 717, fol. 124, EFP.

122. Maria Edgeworth to Frances Edgeworth, 18 November 1833, 12 December 1833, Eng. lett. c. 707, fol. 250, EFP.

123. Maria Edgeworth to Frances Edgeworth, 19 February 1830, 12 April 1830, 5 June 1832, Eng. lett. c. 707, fols. 10, 29, 157; 22 April 1838, Eng. lett. c. 709, fol. 23, EFP.

124. 3 March 1821, EFP.

125. 30 August 1825, Eng. lett. c. 699, fol. 20, EFP.

126. Ibid.

127. Maria Edgeworth to Mrs. Ruxton, 2 August 1822, Eng. lett. c. 717, fol. 124, EFP.

128. Maria Edgeworth to Mrs. Ruxton, 3 March 1821, Eng. lett. c. 717, fol. 82, EFP.

129. Richard Lovell Edgeworth to Dr. Rees, 18 August 1812, 22471 #4, EBP.

130. Maria Edgeworth to Frances Edgeworth Wilson, 29 May 1836, Eng. lett. c. 139, EFP.

131. Maria Edgeworth to Honora Edgeworth, 31 October 1824, Eng. lett. c. 704, fol. 136, EFP.

132. Ibid.

133. Harden, *Maria Edgeworth*, 8.

134. Maria Edgeworth to Emmeline King, 7 January 1842 (1843), Eng. lett. c. 703, fol. 16, EFP.

135. 25 September 1825, Eng. lett. c. 699, fol. 36, EFP.

136. Maria Edgeworth to Frances Edgeworth Wilson, 30 November 1839, Eng. lett. c. 709, fols. 134–35, EFP.

137. 15 May 1823, Eng. lett. c. 698, fol. 137, EFP.

138. Maria Edgeworth to Frances E. Wilson, 23 April 1836, Eng. lett. c. 708, fol. 137, EFP.

139. 12 April 1828, Eng. lett. c. 703, fol. 169, EFP.

140. Ibid.

3. Wisdom Tested

1. Rachel Mordecai diary, 19 August 1819, 212.

2. Rosemarie Zagarri, "Morals, Manners, and the Republican Mother," *American Quarterly* 44, no. 2 (June 1991): 192–215; Lewis, "The Republican Wife," 689–721; Bloch, "The Gendered Meanings of Virtue," 37–58.

3. For a further discussion of republican motherhood and the education of Eliza Mordecai, see Jean E. Friedman, "The Politics of Pedagogy and Judaism in the Early Republican South: The Case of Rachel and Eliza Mordecai," in Christie Farnham Pope, ed., *Women of the American South: A Multicultural Reader* (New York: New York University Press, 1997).

4. For a discussion of the emergence of praxis as central to the understanding of theory, see Anthony Giddens, *Central Problems in Social History* (Berkeley: University of California Press, 1979), 1–8; Sherry B. Ortner, "Theory in Anthropology since the Sixties," *Comparative Studies in Society and History* 26, no. 1 (January 1984): 126–32. The importance of both religious and secular character training in the new republic is discussed by Lewis, "The Republican Wife," 689–92; Censer, *North Carolina Planters,* 44–45. The breakdown of pre-Revolutionary patriarchalism may be traced in Norton, *Liberty's Daughters,* 229–38; Fliegelman, *Prodigals and Pilgrims;* Kierner, *Beyond the Household,* 140, 147–49, 209.

5. Eugene B. Borowitz, *Exploring Jewish Ethics: Papers on Covenant Responsibility* (Detroit: Wayne State University Press, 1990), 17–22.

6. Locke, *Some Thoughts,* 23–28.

7. Norton, *Liberty's Daughters,* 5, 125; Kerber, *Women of the Republic,* 27; Carole Pateman, *The Disorder of Women* (Stanford, Calif.: Stanford University Press, 1989), 71–84.

8. Rachel Mordecai to Ellen Mordecai, 30 January 1814, MFP.

9. Censer, *North Carolina Planters,* 56.

10. Rachel Mordecai to Samuel Mordecai, 25 February 1816, MFP.

11. Ibid.

12. Ellen Mordecai to Samuel Mordecai, 21 April 1816, MFP.

13. MacDonald, ed., *The Education of the Heart,* 11–12. Copyright © 1977 by the University of North Carolina Press. Used by permission of the publisher.

14. Rachel Mordecai diary, 19 May 1816, 157.

15. Urbach, *The Sages,* 326.

16. Rachel Mordecai diary, 23 January 1818, 198.

17. Urbach, *The Sages,* 124.

18. Rachel Mordecai diary, August 1820, 221.

19. Ibid., 9 May 1817,183.

20. Ibid., 25 March 1818, 202.

21. Ibid., 20 July 1818, 203.

22. Ibid., 19 May 1816, 158.

23. Ibid., 3 February 1818, 199.

24. Ibid., 15 March 1818, 202.

25. Nineteenth-century families used a turkey wing to extinguish sparks or to fan the flames in their fireplaces.

26. Rachel Mordecai diary, 15 February 1818, 200.

27. Ibid.

28. Zagarri, "Morals, Manners," 199–203.

29. Rachel Mordecai diary, 25 October 1816, 169.

30. Ibid.

31. Michel Foucault, *Discipline and Punish: The Birth of the Prison,* trans. Allan Sheridan (New York: Vintage Books, 1979), 23.

32. Rachel Mordecai diary, 13 September 1816, 25 September 1816, December 1816, 165, 167, 171.

33. Foucault, *Discipline and Punish,* 103.

34. Rachel Mordecai diary, 26 July 1818, 205.

35. Foucault, *Discipline and Punish,* 104.

36. Rachel Mordecai diary, 9 February 1817, 174.

37. Ibid., 23 February 1817, 177.

38. Locke, *Some Thoughts,* 118.

39. Edgeworth and Edgeworth, *Practical Education,* 1:208–9.

40. Ibid., 1:208.

41. Tarcov, *Locke's Education,* 188.

42. Ronald Duska and Mariellen Whelan, *Moral Development: A Guide to Piaget and Kohlberg* (New York: Paulist Press, 1975), 20.

43. Rachel Mordecai diary, 1 September 1816, 160.

44. Ibid.

45. Kegan, *The Evolving Self,* 88.

46. Rachel Mordecai diary, December 1816, 171.

47. Ibid.

48. Ibid.

49. I am indebted to Grace Elizabeth Hale for this point.

50. Edgeworth and Edgeworth, *Practical Education,* 1:185–87.

51. See Ross D. Parke, "Some Effects of Punishment on Children's Behavior," in Urie Bronfenbrenner and Maureen Mahoney, eds., *Influences on Human Development,* 2nd ed. (Hinsdale, Ill.: Dryden Press, 1975), 257–59.

52. Edgeworth and Edgeworth, *Practical Education,* 1:187.

53. Rachel Mordecai diary, 28 March 1820, 10 April 1817, 3 May 1817, 178, 182, 220.

54. *Identities* (Chicago: University of Chicago Press, 1995), 3; *Black Literature and Literary Theory* (New York: Methuen, 1984), 24.

55. Rachel Mordecai diary, 15 January 1818, 193.

56. Ibid.

57. Ellen Mordecai journal, 9 October 1817, MFP.

58. Rachel Mordecai diary, 15 January 1818, 194.

59. Edgeworth and Edgeworth, *Practical Education,* 1:151, 239.

60. Kegan, *The Evolving Self,* 145.

61. Rachel Mordecai diary, 24 February 1818, 201.

62. Ibid., 10 March 1818, 201.

63. Ibid., 25 March 1818, 202.

64. Ibid., 19 August 1819, 211.

65. Ibid.

66. Ibid.

67. Ibid., 30 April 1817, 182.

68. Ibid., December 1819, September 1819, 217, 214.

69. Maria Edgeworth, "Frank," in *Early Lessons,* 213.

70. Rachel Mordecai diary, 30 August 1816, 161.

71. Ibid.

72. Robert Alter, *The Art of Biblical Narrative* (New York: Basic Books, 1981), 47–52.

73. Rachel Mordecai diary, 30 August 1816, 164.

74. Frankenberg, *White Women, Race Matters,* 198.

75. Rachel Mordecai diary, 15 March 1818, 202.

76. Roediger, *Towards the Abolition of Whiteness,* 187.

77. Lewis, *The Pursuit of Happiness,* xiv, 11, 15, 21–22, 30.

78. Rachel Mordecai diary, 2 March 1820, 219.

79. Ibid.

80. Farnham, *The Education of the Southern Belle,* 2–3.

81. Rachel Mordecai diary, 26 October 1819, 215.

82. Ibid., 30 October 1819, 216.

83. Ibid., 11 November 1819, 217.

84. Ibid., 16 January 1820, 218.

85. Ibid., 30 June 1820, 221.

86. Ibid., 10 August 1818, 207.

4. Ways of Wisdom

1. Jacob Mordecai, "Remarks on Miss Martineau's Pamphlet," in "Apologetics," 2:52, AJA.

2. Urbach, *The Sages,* 266.

3. Levinas, *Difficult Freedom,* 17, 27.

4. Ibid., 6; Ben Zion Bokser and Baruch M. Bokser, eds., *The Talmud: Selected Writings,* trans. Ben Zion Bokser (New York: Paulist Press, 1989), 5.

5. See Mordecai, "Remarks on Miss Martineau's Pamphlet" and "New Testament," in "Apologetics," 2:1–55, AJA; Berman, *Richmond's Jewry,* 120–24.

6. Mordecai, "Preface," in "Apologetics," 2:n.p.

7. Urbach, *The Sages,* 472, 482.

8. See Kathleen Neils Conzen, David A. Gerber, Ewa Morawska, George E. Pozzetta, and Rudolph J. Vecoli, "The Invention of Ethnicity: A Perspective from the U.S.A.," *Journal of Ethnic History* (Fall 1992): 3–41; Lawrence H. Fuchs, "Comment: 'The Invention of Ethnicity': The Amen Corner," *Journal of Ethnic History* (Fall 1992): 53–58.

9. As quoted in Mordecai, "Remarks on Miss Martineau's Pamphlet," in "Apologetics," 2:22, AJA.

10. Ibid., 2:1, 14.

11. Ibid., 2:n.p.

12. Matthew 2:15.

13. Jacob Mordecai, "Introduction to the New Testament," in "Apologetics," 2:13, AJA.

14. Michael A. Meyer, *Jewish Identity in the Modern World* (Seattle: University of Washington Press, 1990), 12, 16; Malina and Neyrey, "First Century Personality," 72; Jonathan Bloom-Feshbach, "Historical Perspectives on the Father's Role," in Michael E. Lamb, ed., *The Role of the Father in Child Development* (New York: John Wiley and Sons, 1981), 82.

15. Mordecai, "Remarks on Miss Martineau's Pamphlet," in "Apologetics," 2:14, 17, 19, 22, 55.

16. Mordecai, "Remarks on Harby's Discourse," 2.

17. Ibid.

18. Ibid., 9.

19. Ibid., 10.

20. See Malina and Neyrey, "First Century Personality," 83; Bokser and Bokser, *The Talmud,* 5–9.

21. Levinas, *Difficult Freedom,* 7, 17.

22. See V. N. Volosinov, "Marxism and the Philosophy of Language," trans. L. Matejka and I. R. Titunik, in Pam Morris, ed., *The Bakhtin Reader* (New York: Edward Arnold, 1994), 48–61.

23. MacDonald, ed., *The Education of the Heart,* 24.

24. Ibid., 83.

25. Ibid., 62–63.

26. Ibid., 25.

27. Ibid., 167.

28. Ibid., 208.

29. Edgar E. MacDonald notes that the friendship between Maria Edgeworth and Rachel Mordecai was "based on their mutual respect for the father image" (ibid., xii).

30. Ibid., 14.

31. See ibid., x, 16, for a discussion of Rachel's deftness in the discussion of Harrington.

32. Ibid., 26, 28.

33. Ibid., 206.

34. Ibid., 21.

35. Ibid., 30.

36. Kowalski-Wallace, *Their Fathers' Daughters,* 12–22.

37. Edgeworth, *Patronage,* 7:38.

38. Ibid., 7:157.

39. Edgeworth, *The Absentee,* 6:14, 38.

40. Ibid., 6:43.

41. MacDonald, ed., *The Education of the Heart,* 72.

42. Ibid., 256.

43. Maria Edgeworth, *Helen,* in *The Longford Edition of Tales and Novels,* 10:28.

44. Ibid., 10:31.

45. Ibid., 10:70.

46. Ibid., 10:256.

47. Ibid., 10:324.

48. Ibid., 10:234.

49. Edgeworth, "The Modern Griselda," in *The Longford Edition of Tales and Novels,* 6:424.

50. Ibid., 6:438.

51. For an account of Rachel's dream, see chapter 1, 18.

52. Phila Lazarus Calder Nye and Margaret Atkinson Segal, "Records and Recollections of the Calders of Wilmington," 4, 7–11, AJA.

53. Rachel Mordecai Lazarus to Samuel Mordecai, 28 June 1821, PMP.

54. Ibid.

55. MacDonald, ed., *The Education of the Heart,* 27.

56. Rachel Mordecai Lazarus to Ellen Mordecai, June 1821, MFP.

57. Nye and Segal, "Records and Recollections," 12.

58. Rachel Mordecai Lazarus to Ellen Mordecai, 8 November 1821, MFP.

59. Rachel Mordecai to Ellen Mordecai, 14 October 1821, MFP.

60. Rachel Mordecai to Caroline Mordecai, 17 May 1821, MFP.

61. Nye and Segal, "Records and Recollections," 26.

62. Ellen Mordecai journal, vol. 6, 12 February 1821, MFP.

63. Rachel Mordecai to Caroline Plunkett, 17 May 1821, MFP.

64. See Rachel Mordecai diary, 224.

65. For a discussion of dislocation and its effect on an adolescent, see Kegan, *The Evolving Self,* 194.

66. Rachel Mordecai to Samuel Mordecai, 28 June 1821, PMP.

67. MacDonald, ed., *The Education of the Heart,* 148.

68. Rachel Mordecai to Solomon Mordecai, 10 February 1820, JMP.

69. Rachel Mordecai to Solomon Mordecai, 24 February 1820, JMP.

70. Rachel Mordecai to Ellen Mordecai, 12 April 1821, MFP.

71. MacDonald, ed., *The Education of the Heart,* 27.

72. For a discussion of the practical balance of affection within and outside of the disciplinary event, see Martin Hoffman, "The Role of the Father in Moral Internalization," in Lamb, ed., *The Role of the Father,* 309–78. On the question of separation and individuation, see Frances Fuchs Schachter, "Sibling Deidentification and Split-Parent Identification: A Family Tetrad," in Michael E. Lamb, ed., *Sibling Relationships: Their Nature and Significance across the Lifespan* (Hillsdale, N.J.: Lawrence Erlbaum Associates, 1982), 123–51; Peter Blos, *The Adolescent Passage: Developmental Issues* (New York: International Universities Press, 1979), 304.

73. Rachel Mordecai to Ellen Mordecai, 18 May 1821, addendum, MFP.

74. Eliza Mordecai to Ellen Mordecai, 10 June 1821, MFP.

75. For an understanding of adolescent development, see Brenda K. Bryant, "Sibling Relationships in Middle Childhood," in Lamb, ed., *Sibling Relationships,* 87–121.

76. Rachel Mordecai Lazarus to Ellen Mordecai, 1 August 1821, 14 October 1821; Eliza Mordecai to Augustus Mordecai, 21 October 1821, MFP.

77. Rachel Mordecai Lazarus to Caroline Plunkett, 17 May 1821, MFP.

78. Eliza Mordecai to Ellen Mordecai, 27 January 1822; Eliza Mordecai to Rebecca Mordecai, 28 July 1822; Rachel Lazarus to Eliza Mordecai, 18 August 1822; Rachel Mordecai Lazarus to Ellen Mordecai, 9 March 1823, MFP.

79. Rachel Mordecai to Ellen Mordecai, 14 January 1823, 3 January 1824, MFP.

80. I am indebted to Joseph R. Berrigan for his view on the translator's task.

81. Stéphanie Félicité de Genlis, *Queen of the Rose of Salency: A Comedy in Two Acts,* in *Theatre of Education,* 3 vols. (London: T. Cadell, Elmsly and T. Durham, 1783), 3:109–54, Smith College Library, Sophia Smith Collection, History of Women (microfilm). Eliza Mordecai Myers's translations may be found in MYFP. For a contemporary translation of Goethe's *Sorrows,* see Elizabeth Mayer and Louise Bogan, trans. (New York: Random House, 1971).

82. An account of the feminist possibilities of neoclassical allegory may be found in Doris Kadish, *Politicizing Gender: Narrative Strategies in the Aftermath of the French Revolution* (New Brunswick, N.J.: Rutgers University Press, 1991).

83. Ibid., 4. See also Nancy Armstrong, *Desire and Domestic Fiction* (New York: Oxford University Press, 1987), 5.

84. Genlis, *Queen of the Rose,* 110.

85. Lynn Hunt, *Politics, Culture and Class in the French Revolution* (Berkeley: University of California Press, 1984).

86. Genlis, *Queen of the Rose,* 111.

87. Ibid., 116–17.

88. Goethe, *Sorrows of Young Werther,* 25.

89. Ibid., 49.

90. Ibid., 97.

91. For a discussion of Romanticism and the relationship between the individual and society, see Michael O'Brien, "The Lineaments of Antebellum Southern Romanticism," in *Rethinking the South: Essays in Intellectual History* (Baltimore, Md.: Johns Hopkins University Press, 1988), 38–56; Morse Peckham, *Romanticism and Behavior: Collected Essays II* (Columbia: University of South Carolina Press, 1976), 21; Lillian R. Furst, *Romanticism in Perspective: A Comparative Study of Aspects of the Romantic Movements in England, France and Germany* (New York: St. Martin's Press, 1969).

92. Friedrich von Schiller, *Schiller's Works,* ed. J. G. Fischer, 4 vols. (Philadelphia: George Barrie, Publisher, 1883), 3:169.

93. For a discussion of Romantic notions of morality, see Lawrence S. Lockridge, *The Ethics of Romanticism* (New York: Cambridge University Press, 1989), 51.

94. Ibid., 74.

95. Ibid.

96. For a discussion of the battleground experienced in adolescent moral life, see Louise J. Kaplan, *Adolescence: The Farewell to Childhood* (New York: Simon and Schuster, 1984), 13–14, 110–15, 136–45; Blos, *The Adolescent Passage,* 74–75.

97. D. W. Winnicott, "From Dependence towards Independence in the Development of the Individual," in *The Maturational Processes and the Facilitating Environment: Studies in the Theory of Emotional Development* (New York: International Universities Press, 1965), 91.

98. Rachel Lazarus to Ellen Mordecai, 20 January 1822, MFP.

99. Rebecca Mordecai to Rachel Lazarus, 31 March 1822, MFP.

100. Schachter, "Sibling Deidentification," 124.

101. Rebecca Mordecai to Rachel Lazarus, 19 January 1823, MFP.

102. Rachel Mordecai Lazarus to Ellen Mordecai, 29 June 1823; Ellen Mordecai to Solomon Mordecai, 2 October 1823; Rachel Mordecai Lazarus to Ellen Mordecai, 26 October 1823, 29 February 1824, MFP.

103. Locke, *Some Thoughts,* 83. See also John Locke, *An Essay Concerning Human Understanding,* ed. Peter H. Nidditch (Oxford: Clarendon Press, 1975), 132–35.

104. Rachel Lazarus to Ellen Mordecai, 20 December 1823, MFP.

105. Rachel Lazarus to Ellen Mordecai, 29 February 1824, MFP.

106. Kaplan, *Adolescence,* 19. For an original discussion of adolescent maturation, see Nancy Felson, *Regarding Penelope: From Character to Poetics* (Princeton, N.J.: Princeton University Press, 1994), 67–91.

107. Alex Comfort, "The Ideology of Romanticism," in Robert F. Gleckner and Gerald E. Enscoe, eds., *Romanticism: Points of View* (Englewood Cliffs, N.J.: Prentice-

Hall, 1970), 165–80; Morse Peckham, "Toward a Theory of Romanticism," in ibid., 231–58.

108. Kaplan, *Adolescence,* 136, 145–46, 154.

109. MYFP.

110. Rachel Mordecai diary, 160–62.

111. MYFP.

112. For examples of Eliza Mordecai's fairy tales, see "Lines by the Little Kiowa" and "History of the Mason Family," MYFP.

113. See Lockridge, *The Ethics of Romanticism,* 44, 48.

114. Julia Mordecai to Ellen Mordecai, 18 December 1824; Ellen Mordecai to Solomon Mordecai, 30 March 1824, MFP.

115. 29 May 1825, MFP.

116. Ibid.

117. "To [Anonymous]," MYFP.

118. MYFP.

119. MYFP.

120. Winnicott, "From Dependence," 84; Kaplan, *Adolescence,* 14; Lockridge, *The Ethics of Romanticism,* 43–44.

121. Ellen Mordecai to Caroline Plunkett, 22 January 1827, MFP.

122. MacDonald, ed., *The Education of the Heart,* 333; Rachel Lazarus to Ellen Mordecai, 27 August 1827, MFP.

123. MacDonald, ed., *The Education of the Heart,* 148. Copyright © 1977 by the University of North Carolina Press. Used by permission of the publisher.

124. See Blos, *The Adolescent Passage,* 74–78, 88–89.

125. Eliza Kennon Mordecai Myers to Rachel Mordecai Lazarus, 4 December 1827, MYFP.

126. George Mordecai to Ellen Mordecai, 25 December 1827; Ellen Mordecai to Samuel Mordecai, 1 June 1828, MFP; MacDonald, ed., *The Education of the Heart,* 149.

127. Rachel Mordecai to Ellen Mordecai, 21 September 1828; Ellen Mordecai to Samuel Mordecai, 5 April 1829; Julia Mordecai to Ellen Mordecai, 2 September 1829; Ellen Mordecai to Samuel Mordecai, 8 October 1829; Ellen Mordecai to Rachel Lazarus, 12 September 1831, MFP.

128. MacDonald, ed., *The Education of the Heart,* 200.

129. Eliza Kennon Mordecai Myers to Rachel Mordecai Lazarus, 29 May 1831, MYFP.

130. Ibid.

131. Ibid.

132. Eliza K. Myers to Ellen Mordecai, 18 October 1831, MYFP.

133. "Parody of Stanzas of the Second Canto of 'Childe Harold': provoked from E[liza] K[ennon] [Myers] and L [unknown] by an uncommon press of disagreeable work, on a cloudy day, Petersburg, 1833," MYFP.

134. Rachel Mordecai to Samuel Mordecai, 27 July 1817, JMP; Rachel Mordecai to Ellen Mordecai, 8 February 1818; Rachel Mordecai to Samuel Mordecai, 8 March

1818, 29 March 1818, MFP.

135. Ellen Mordecai journal, vol. 4, 29 January 1818, MFP.

136. Diana Hochstedt Butler, *Standing Against the Whirlwind: Evangelical Episcopalians in Nineteenth-Century America* (New York: Oxford University Press, 1995), 31–33; Richard Rankin, *Ambivalent Churchmen and Evangelical Churchwomen: The Religion of the Episcopal Elite in North Carolina, 1800–1860* (Columbia: University of South Carolina Press, 1993), 37, 58; Robert Bruce Mullin, *Episcopal Vision/American Reality: High Church Theology and Social Thought in Evangelical America* (New Haven, Conn.: Yale University Press, 1986), 79.

137. Rankin, *Ambivalent Churchmen,* 9, 55–59, 128–29.

138. Ellen Mordecai journal, vol. 4, 29 January 1818, MFP.

139. Ellen Mordecai to Samuel Mordecai, 25 February 1818, JMP; Ellen Mordecai journal, vol. 4, 29 February 1818, MFP.

140. Ellen Mordecai journal, vol. 4, 5 January 1818, MFP.

141. Ibid., 29 January 1818, MFP.

142. Ibid.

143. Nye and Segal, "Records and Recollections," 27.

144. Ibid.

145. Ibid., 14.

146. MacDonald, ed., *The Education of the Heart,* 30.

147. Ibid., 30–31.

148. Rachel Lazarus to Ellen Mordecai, 21 April 1830, MFP.

149. Ibid. and 26 May 1830, MFP.

150. Rachel Lazarus to Ellen Mordecai, 20 April 1823, 8 July 1829, MFP.

151. Rachel Lazarus to Ellen Mordecai, undated (c. 1823), MFP.

152. Rachel Lazarus to Ellen Mordecai, 8 July 1829, 7 January 1830, 26 January 1830, MFP.

153. Rachel Lazarus to Ellen Mordecai, 15 February 1830, MFP.

154. Rachel Lazarus to Ellen Mordecai, 20 January 1822, MFP.

155. Rachel Mordecai Lazarus to Ellen Mordecai, Wilmington, undated; Rachel to Ellen, 9 April 1835; Aaron Lazarus to Ellen Mordecai, 22 June 1839; George Mordecai to Ellen Mordecai, 2 August 1842, MFP; Samuel Mordecai to Ellen Mordecai, 21 April 1848, JMP; Ellen Mordecai to Samuel Mordecai, 8 November 1848; George W. Mordecai to Ellen Mordecai, 27 November 1848; Ellen Mordecai to Ellen Lazarus, 2 May 1848, MFP; Mary Ellen Brown to Marx Lazarus, 13 April 1856, MYFP; MacDonald, ed., *The Education of the Heart,* 328.

156. Rachel Mordecai Lazarus to Ellen Mordecai, 9 May 1832, 21 July 1832, MFP.

157. MacDonald, ed., *The Education of the Heart,* 328.

158. September 1814, PMP.

159. 27 February 1814, PMP.

160. See Rachel Mordecai diary, 19 May 1816, 20 July 1818, 157, 203; Berman, *Richmond's Jewry,* 52.

161. See chapter 3 and Rachel Mordecai diary, 23 January 1818, 198.

162. MacDonald, ed., *The Education of the Heart,* 6.

163. Rachel Lazarus to Samuel Mordecai, 18 June 1817, JMP.

164. Rachel Lazarus to Ellen Mordecai, 14 September 1824, MFP.

165. See Rachel Mordecai diary, August 1820, 221.

166. Rachel to Ellen, 11 February (1822); Mrs. M. L. Orme to Ellen, 26 September 1828; Aaron Lazarus to Ellen, 10 October 1828; Rachel Lazarus to Ellen Mordecai, 11 September 1831, MFP; Ellen Mordecai journal, vol. 6, 10 June 1823, LMP.

167. 26 October 1828, MFP.

168. Rachel Mordecai Lazarus to Ellen Mordecai, 18 September 1836, MFP.

169. See Herbert Aptheker, *American Negro Slave Revolts* (New York: International Publishers, 1983).

170. Mary Jean Corbett, "Public Affections and Familial Politics," *English Literary History* 61, no. 4 (Winter 1994): 877–97.

171. MacDonald, ed., *The Education of the Heart,* 80. Copyright © 1977 by the University of North Carolina Press. Used by permission of the publisher.

172. George Lipsitz, *The Possessive Investment in Whiteness: How White People Profit* (Philadelphia: Temple University Press, 1998), vii–viii, 3; David R. Roediger, *The Wages of Whiteness: Race and the Making of the American Working Class* (New York: Verso, 1999), 12–13.

173. MacDonald, ed., *The Education of the Heart,* 69. Copyright © 1977 by the University of North Carolina Press. Used by permission of the publisher.

174. Roediger, *The Wages of Whiteness,* 7.

175. MacDonald, ed., *The Education of the Heart,* 154.

176. Rachel Lazarus to Ellen Mordecai, 11 September 1831, MFP.

177. MacDonald, ed., *The Education of the Heart,* 212.

178. Ibid.

179. Ibid.

180. Ibid., 223; Julia Mordecai to Ellen Mordecai, 16 October 1831, MFP.

181. MacDonald, ed., *The Education of the Heart,* 298–99, 304–7.

182. See George Fredrickson, *The Black Image in the White Mind: The Debate on Afro-American Character and Destiny, 1817–1914* (Middleton, Conn.: Wesleyan University Press, 1987), 1–10, 11, 16–17, 25.

183. Harry L. Watson, *Jacksonian Politics and Community Conflict: The Emergence of the Second American Party System in Cumberland County, North Carolina* (Baton Rouge: Louisiana State University Press, 1981); Marc Kruman, *Parties and Politics in North Carolina, 1836–1865* (Baton Rouge: Louisiana State University Press, 1983); Charles Sellers, *The Market Revolution: Jacksonian America, 1815–1846* (New York: Oxford University Press, 1991).

184. Mary Ryan, *Cradle of the Middle Class: The Family in Oneida County, New York, 1790–1865* (New York: Cambridge University Press, 1981), 11–12, 77.

185. For an understanding of the Second Great Awakening, see Bloch, *Visionary Republic;* Jon Butler, *Awash in a Sea of Faith: Christianizing the American People* (Cambridge, Mass.: Harvard University Press, 1990); Paul Conkin, *Cane Ridge: Amer-*

ica's Pentecost (Madison: University of Wisconsin Press, 1990); Nathan O. Hatch, *The Democratization of American Christianity* (New Haven, Conn.: Yale University Press, 1990).

186. Jean E. Friedman, *The Enclosed Garden: Women and Community in the Evangelical South, 1830–1900* (Chapel Hill: University of North Carolina Press, 1985).

187. Rankin, *Ambivalent Churchmen,* 37, 43–47, 78–97, 102.

188. See note 140, this chapter.

189. Berman, *Richmond's Jewry,* 111.

190. Rachel Mordecai Lazarus to Ellen Mordecai, 7 May 1828, 11 September 1831, MFP.

191. Emma Mordecai to Ellen Mordecai, 25 November 1832; Rachel Mordecai Lazarus to Ellen Mordecai, 26 June 1835, PMP; Aaron Lazarus to Ellen Mordecai, 8 May 1835; Jane Robertson to Ellen Mordecai, 13 May 1835; Julia Mordecai to Ellen Mordecai, 1 June 1835; Emma Mordecai to Ellen Mordecai, 5 June 1835; Rachel Mordecai to Ellen Mordecai, 22 July 1835, MFP.

192. 29 July 1835, MFP.

193. Ellen Mordecai, "History of a Heart" (1845), 3, microfilm #11–847, MFP.

194. Rachel Lazarus to Ellen Mordecai, 9 October 1831, MFP.

195. Butler, *Standing against the Whirlwind,* 33.

196. For a discussion of the Enlightenment's devastation of Jewish belief and ritual structure, see Meyer, *Jewish Identity,* 1–29.

197. Conzen et al., "The Invention of Ethnicity," 3–4.

198. Urbach, *The Sages,* 255–59.

199. Butler, *Standing against the Whirlwind,* 31.

200. Rachel Lazarus to Catherine DeRosset, 1 August 1835, DRFP.

201. Rachel Lazarus to Ellen Mordecai, 29 July 1835, MFP.

202. Ibid.

203. Rachel Mordecai Lazarus to Jacob Mordecai, 19 August 1835, MFP.

204. Rachel Lazarus to Jacob Mordecai, 19 August 1835, MFP.

205. Rachel Lazarus to Ellen Mordecai, 18 September 1836, MFP.

206. Rachel Lazarus to Ellen Mordecai, 6 September 1835, MFP.

207. Rachel Lazarus to Ellen Mordecai, 18 September 1836, MFP.

208. Rachel Mordecai Lazarus to Ellen Mordecai, 6 September 1835, MFP.

209. Rachel Mordecai Lazarus to Ellen Mordecai, 6 September 1835, MFP.

210. Rachel Lazarus to Ellen Mordecai, 24 September 1835, MFP.

211. 6 September 1835, MFP.

212. Rachel Lazarus to Ellen Mordecai, 21 August 1836, MFP.

213. Ibid.

214. Rachel Lazarus to Ellen Mordecai, 26 June 1836, MFP.

215. Ibid.

216. Ibid.

217. Rachel Mordecai Lazarus to Ellen Mordecai, 18 September 1836, MFP.

218. Ibid.

219. Rachel Lazarus to Ellen Mordecai, 21 August 1836, MFP.

220. 18 September 1836, MFP.

221. See Donald G. Mathews, *Religion in the Old South* (Chicago: University of Chicago Press, 1977), 59–61.

222. Ibid., 61.

223. Rachel Mordecai Lazarus to Ellen Mordecai, 21 August 1836, MFP.

224. Ibid.

225. Mathews, *Religion in the Old South,* 64.

226. Rachel Lazarus to Ellen Mordecai, 16 February 1837, MFP.

227. 23 October 1836, MFP.

228. Ibid.

229. Rachel Lazarus to Ellen Mordecai, 16 February 1837, MFP.

230. Rachel Lazarus to Ellen Mordecai, 16 April 1838, 29 April 1838; Laura Mordecai to Ellen Mordecai, 13 June 1838, MFP.

231. Rachel Lazarus to Emma Mordecai, 11 June 1838, MFP.

232. Emma Mordecai journal, vol. 6, 23 June 1838, MFP.

233. Reverend Barblett to Ellen Lazarus, 23 July 1838, MFP.

234. Ellen Mordecai journal, vol. 5, 23 June 1839, MFP.

235. See Urbach, *The Sages,* 272, 321.

236. Ibid., 327.

237. Mathews, *Religion in the Old South,* 61.

238. For a discussion of liminality, see Victor Turner and Edith Turner, *Image and Pilgrimage in Christian Culture: Anthropological Perspectives* (New York: Columbia University Press, 1978), 249–51; Arnold van Gennep, *The Rites of Passage* (Chicago: University of Chicago Press, 1960), 21, 105; Robert M. Torrance, *The Spiritual Quest: Transcendence in Myth, Religion, and Science* (Berkeley: University of California Press, 1994), 10–12; Maria C. Lugones, "Structure/Antistructure and Agency under Oppression," *Journal of Philosophy* 87, no. 10 (October 1990): 500–507; Anthony Appiah, "'But Would That Still Be Me?' Notes on Gender, 'Race,' Ethnicity, as Sources of 'Identity,'" in ibid., 497.

239. Reverend B[arblett] to Ellen Lazarus, 23 July 1838, MFP.

240. Eliza Kenon Mordecai Myers to Caroline Plunkett, 21 June 1839, PMP.

241. Emma Mordecai journal, vol. 6, 25 June 1838, MFP.

242. Eliza Kenon Mordecai Myers to Caroline Mordecai Plunkett, 21 June 1839, PMP.

243. Emma Mordecai journal, vol. 6, 11 July 1838, MFP.

244. Caroline Plunkett to Ellen Mordecai, 26 July 1846, MFP.

245. See Friedman, *The Enclosed Garden,* 3–20.

246. 21 June 1839, PMP.

247. 1 October 1839, PMP.

248. Laura Mordecai to Emma Mordecai, 6 May 1839; Eliza K. Myers to Caroline Plunkett, 20 April 1840, MFP; Eliza K. Myers to Caroline Plunkett, 12 January 1840; Emma Mordecai to Ellen Mordecai, 3 February 1842, PMP; Emma Mordecai to Caroline Myers Cohen, 22 January 1865, MYFP.

249. Eliza K. Myers to Caroline Plunkett, 12 January 1840, PMP.

250. Ibid.

251. Eliza K. Myers to Ellen Mordecai, 25 August 1839, MYFP.

252. Ibid.

253. Eliza K. Myers to Caroline Plunkett, 12 January 1840, PMP.

254. 2 April 1844, MFP.

255. Eliza K. Myers to Caroline Plunkett, 12 January 1845, 3 August 1845, PMP.

256. Ellen Mordecai to Mary Mordecai, 3 August 1847, MFP.

257. Eliza K. Myers to Julia Judith Mordecai, 1838(?), MYFP.

258. Emma Mordecai to Ellen Mordecai, 1 March 1850, JMP.

259. Eliza K. Myers to Edmund Myers, 4 August 1845, MYFP.

260. Eliza K. Myers to Emma Mordecai, May 1861, MYFP.

261. Ibid.

262. Urbach, *The Sages,* 667.

263. Ibid., 482.

264. Rachel Mordecai Lazarus to Ellen Lazarus, 24 June 1836, 16 February 1837, MFP.

5. Wisdom Transformed

1. L.N., "Past Days, a Simple Story for Children" (1840), 13, MYFP.

2. Ibid., 27.

3. Shlomith Rimmon-Kenan, *Narrative Fiction: Contemporary Poetics* (London: Methuen, 1983), 127–29.

4. Virginia Lieson Brereton, *From Sin to Salvation: Stories of Women's Conversions, 1800 to the Present* (Bloomington: Indiana University Press, 1991), 5, 10–13.

5. See Friedman, *The Enclosed Garden;* John B. Boles, *The Great Revival, 1787–1805* (Lexington: University Press of Kentucky, 1972); Mathews, *Religion in the Old South;* Anne C. Loveland, *Southern Evangelicals and the Social Order, 1800–1860* (Chicago: University of Chicago Press, 1977).

6. Mathews, *Religion in the Old South,* xvi, 59; Brereton, *From Sin to Salvation,* 25–26.

7. L.N., "Past Days," 8, 14.

8. MacDonald, ed., *The Education of the Heart,* 7.

9. Ibid., 10. Copyright © 1977 by the University of North Carolina Press. Used by permission of the publisher.

10. "Recollections of Rachel (Mordecai) Lazarus, 1817–1821," 19, MYFP.

11. Ibid., 21.

12. Bloch, "The Gendered Meanings of Virtue," 42, 47–52.

13. L.N., "Past Days," 16.

14. Ibid., 14.

15. Ibid., 98–99.

16. Microfilm #82, MFP.

17. Philadelphia, 1845, microfilm #591–91a, MFP.

18. Ellen Mordecai journal, vol. 4, 17 September 1815, LMP.

19. Ibid.

20. Ibid., 21 October 1815.

21. Ibid.

22. Ibid., 4 July 1815.

23. Ibid., 17 May 1817; vol. 5, 28 March 1819, 28 June 1820, MFP.

24. Ellen Mordecai to Solomon Mordecai, 6 January 1820, JMP.

25. Ellen Mordecai to Solomon Mordecai, 15 January 1814, JMP.

26. Solomon Mordecai to Ellen Mordecai, 4 May 1817, JMP.

27. Ibid.; Ellen Mordecai journal, vol. 4, 11 August 1817, LMP.

28. Ibid., 9 October 1817.

29. Ibid., 8 December 1817.

30. Rachel Mordecai to Ellen Mordecai, 28 November 1818, MFP.

31. As suggested by Von Rad, *Wisdom in Israel,* 178–85.

32. Rachel Mordecai Lazarus to Ellen Mordecai, 26 October 1829; Ellen Mordecai to Solomon Mordecai, 17 February 1828, MFP; MacDonald, ed., *The Education of the Heart,* 329.

33. Ellen Mordecai to George Mordecai, 10 January 1839; Ellen Mordecai to Solomon Mordecai, 31 December 1838, MFP.

34. Mr. Murray to Mary Revick Simpson, 8 March 1842; W. S. Simpson, Statement, November 1846, MFP.

35. Mathews, *Religion in the Old South,* 59; Rankin, *Ambivalent Churchmen,* 31.

36. L.N., "Past Days," 27.

37. Ibid., 22.

38. Ibid., 49.

39. Ibid., 51, 52.

40. Ibid., 64–66.

41. Ibid., 116.

42. Ibid., 18.

43. Ibid., 122.

44. Ibid., 123–24.

45. Ibid., 131.

46. Ibid., 133.

47. Ibid.

48. Ibid., 138.

49. Ibid., 139.

50. See Nancy F. Partner, "History without Empiricism / Truth without Facts," in Christine McDonald and Gary Wihl, eds., *Transformations in Personhood and Culture after Theory: The Language of History, Aesthetics, and Ethics* (University Park: University of Pennsylvania Press, 1994), 1–2; Peter Berek, *The Transformation of Allegory from Spenser to Hawthorne* (Amherst, Mass.: Amherst College Press, 1970), 5–7; Gay Clifford, *The Transformations of Allegory* (London: Routledge and Kegan Paul, 1974), 1–14.

51. See Liz Stanley, *The Auto/biographical I: The Theory and Practice of Feminist*

Auto/biography (Manchester: Manchester University Press, 1992), 59–61; Rimmon-Kenan, *Narrative Fiction,* 122–25.

52. See Paul Ricoeur, *History and Truth,* trans. Charles A. Kelbley (Evanston, Ill.: Northwestern University Press, 1965), 291–93.

53. Alfred Mordecai to Ellen Mordecai, 14 July 1838, AMP.

54. Rachel Mordecai Lazarus to Ellen Mordecai, 24 September 1835, 26 June 1836; Ellen Mordecai to Solomon Mordecai, 3 July 1838; George Mordecai to Ellen Mordecai, 8 September 1838; Rebecca Mordecai to Aaron Lazarus, 16 November 1838; Emma Mordecai journal, vol. 6, 23 June 1838, MFP.

55. See Ricoeur, *History and Truth,* 287, 301, 303. See also Paul Ricoeur, *Oneself as Another,* trans. Kathleen Blamey (Chicago: University of Chicago Press, 1992), 203–11, 240–48 for a discussion of the relationship between self, a moral norm, and a "practical wisdom."

56. As quoted in Stuart E. Rosenberg, *The New Jewish Identity in America* (New York: Hippocrene Books, 1985), ix.

57. Benjamin Kaplan, *The Eternal Stranger: A Study of Jewish Life in the Small Community* (New York: Bookman Associates, 1957), 16.

58. Levinas, *Difficult Freedom,* 5.

59. William Petersen, Michael Novak, and Philip Gleason, *Concepts of Ethnicity* (Cambridge, Mass.: Belknap Press of Harvard University Press, 1982), 58–59.

60. Meyer, *Jewish Identity,* 29.

61. Quoted in Rosenberg, *The New Jewish Identity,* xi.

62. L.N., "Past Days," 77.

63. Ibid., 109.

64. Ibid., 121.

65. Ibid., 147.

66. 23 October 1836, MFP.

67. See McDonald and Wihl, eds., *Transformations in Personhood,* vii.

68. Nina Auerbach, *Communities of Women: An Idea in Fiction* (Cambridge, Mass.: Harvard University Press, 1978), 8. For a discussion of the workings of divine Providence, see Thomas Vargish, *The Providential Aesthetic in Victorian Fiction* (Charlottesville: University Press of Virginia, 1985), 1, 3–11, 15–18, 21–26, 31–39; John Beer, *Providence and Love: Studies in Wordsworth, Channing, Myers, George Eliot, and Ruskin* (Oxford: Clarendon Press, 1998), 3–4, 99–100; Thomas F. Tracy, ed., *The God Who Acts: Philosophical and Theological Explorations* (University Park: Pennsylvania State University Press, 1994), 1; Maurice Wiles, "Divine Action: Some Moral Considerations," in ibid., 18–21.

69. L.N., "Past Days," 3.

70. Ibid., 29.

71. Rimmon-Kenan, *Narrative Fiction,* 33.

72. L.N., "Past Days," 49–50.

73. Ibid., 63.

74. Ibid., 120.

75. For an understanding of narrativity and the consequences for moral develop-

ment, see Jan Clayton, "The Narrative Turn in Minority Fiction," in Janice Carlisle and Daniel R. Schwarz, eds., *Narrative and Culture* (Athens: University of Georgia Press, 1994), 58–63, 72; Martin Cortazzi, *Narrative Analysis* (London: Palmer Press, 1993), 12; M. M. Bakhtin, *The Dialogic Imagination: Four Essays by M. M. Bakhtin,* ed. Michael Holquist, trans. Caryl Emerson and Michael Holquist (Austin: University of Texas Press, 1981); Mark Tappan and Martin Packer, *Narrative and Storytelling: Implications for Understanding Moral Development* (San Francisco: Jossey-Boss, 1991), 6–20; Paul Ricoeur, *Time and Narrative,* vol. 1, trans. Kathleen McLaughlin and David Pellauer (Chicago: University of Chicago Press, 1984), 3, 32.

76. L.N., "Past Days," 11–12.
77. Ibid., 12.
78. Ibid., 89.
79. Ibid., 81.
80. Ibid., 57.
81. Ibid., 22.
82. Ibid., 23.
83. Ibid., 25–26.
84. Ibid., 26.
85. Ibid., 31.
86. Ibid., 32.

Afterword

1. Edgeworth and Edgeworth, *Practical Education,* 1:iv.
2. L.N., "Past Days," 109.
3. Ibid.

Appendix

1. These short biographies are adaptations of the excellent genealogical descriptions in Appendices A and B of MacDonald, ed., *The Education of the Heart.* Copyright © 1977 by the University of North Carolina Press. Used by permission of the publisher.
2. Butler, *Maria Edgeworth,* 351.

INDEX

DATE DUE

GAYLORD   #3522PI   Printed in USA